W. McMORDIE

ENGLISH IDIOMS

AND HOW TO USE THEM

REVISED BY

R. C. GOFFIN, M.A.

OXFORD UNIVERSITY PRESS

Oxford University Press

OXFORD LONDON GLASGOW NEW YORK
TORONTO MELBOURNE WELLINGTON CAPE TOWN
IBADAN NAIROBI DAR ES SALAAM LUSAKA ADDIS ABABA
KUALA LUMPUR SINGAPORE JAKARTA HONG KONG TOKYO
DELHI BOMBAY CALCUTTA MADRAS KARACHI

First published 1909
This edition © Oxford University Press 1965
Reprinted in 1966 from the 3rd edition (1954)
Fourteenth impression 1976

ISBN 0 19 432766 3

Reprinted by Golden Crown Printing Co. Ltd., 3–5 Station Lane, Kowloon, Hong Kong
Published by Oxford University Press, News Building, North Point, Hong Kong

PREFACE TO THIRD EDITION

THE world-wide popularity gained by this book—written originally for students of the subcontinent now divided into India and Pakistan—and also the lapse of time since its first revision over forty years ago, render a further revision necessary.

The structure of the book in its present edition remains unchanged. The first chapter has been brought into line with contemporary scholarship, and the Appendix on the Bible has been made more comprehensive but less detailed. Further, wherever called for, the examples have been modernized in style and broadened in subject matter to suit a wider circle of readers.

R.C.G.

CONTENTS

CONTENTS

CHAPTER I

INTRODUCTORY

SOURCES OF THE ENGLISH LANGUAGE
ON THE STUDY OF ENGLISH IDIOMS GENERALLY

1. The English language belongs to the **Indo-European** group or family of languages. The ' Indo-European language ' consists of a collection or ' vocabulary ' of reconstructed and theoretical linguistic forms from which most of the present European languages —together with most of those of India and Persia—have been shown to have descended.

Many thousands of years B.C., starting perhaps from somewhere near the Hindu Kush mountains, this language began to spread both west and east, as the tribes that spoke it migrated in both directions. And, as it spread, it naturally acquired particular local characteristics, modifications of its original form. This differentiation and individual development were brought about by the various conditions and circumstances encountered—geographical, climatic, ethnical, and, particularly perhaps, linguistic, as it came into contact with other tongues.

2. Thus the language or dialects brought to Europe from the original home grew in the course of ages into a number of languages, distinct from one another in many ways, yet showing kinship even in their separation, and bearing traces of a common ancestry. Similarly, among the Aryans (i.e. the ' noble ' as they called themselves) who migrated to India, there also gradually rose up modifications of language; while the same thing occurred among those who remained nearer the original home, and who became the ancestors of the Persians.

When we remember the parts of the world over which these languages have spread, we understand why these tongues are called *Indo-European*.

We note in passing that a *Living Language* is one which is used in common speech; while a language which has ceased to be spoken but is found in writings of the past, is a *Dead Language*. Hindi and French are living languages, but Sanskrit and Latin are dead languages.

3. The Indo-European family of languages, then, is divided into two main groups, the Eastern and the Western. These may again be subdivided, as follows:

1

Eastern Group. 1. **Balto-Slavic**, including all the Slavonic tongues; 2. **Indo-Iranian**, including the Sanskrit-derived languages of India, and **Persian**; 3. **Armenian**; 4. **Albanian**.

Western Group. 1. **Hellenic**, including all the Greek dialects, ancient and modern; 2. **Italic**, Latin and all its associate tongues; 3. **Celtic**, derived from which are the surviving tongues Gaelic and Welsh; 4. **Germanic**: this includes Icelandic, Swedish, Norwegian and Danish, the Scandinavian branch; the languages of Germany and of Holland, Flemish, and finally, English.

4. As for the other languages of the civilized world, they are divided by philologists between the *Semitic* family and the *Turanian* family.

To the *Semitic* family belong Hebrew, Phoenician, Syriac, Arabic, Maltese, Ethiopic, etc. It is a characteristic feature of the Semitic languages that they have roots formed of three consonants which remain unchanged in all relations, and that modifications of the meaning are expressed by changes of vowels only.

Under the head of *Turanian* are put several groups of languages: the *Scythian* group, including Turkish, Hungarian, Finnish, Lappish, Mongolian; the *Dravidian* group, including Tamil, Telugu, Kannada, and the languages of North-Eastern Asia; the *Malaic* or *Malay-Polynesian* or *Oceanic* group, including the dialects of Malaya, Java, Sumatra, etc.; certain South African dialects; also Chinese, Siamese, Burmese, Tibetan; dialects of South America; and a dialect called Basque, spoken in parts of Spain and France.

5. We now turn back from our general survey to trace further the sources of the English language.

We have seen that the English tongue belongs to the Germanic branch of the great Indo-European family of languages. It is the language brought into Britain by bands of invading Teutons who came from the lowlands of north-western Germany. These Teutonic invaders began to come in A.D. 449, and for a hundred years afterwards they still kept coming. They found in Britain Celtic inhabitants, most of whom they drove to the mountainous parts of the island. Bede, the old English chronicler, says that these invaders were of three tribes—Jutes, Saxons, and Angles. Long before the Norman Conquest in 1066, these Teutonic tribes had become so welded together as a nationality that they called their adopted country *Ængla-land*, land of the Angles, or England, and their language *Ænglisc*, or English.

English then is the language brought into Britain by these Teutonic invaders. It became the predominant language in South Britain as early as the middle of the sixth century of the Christian era. From that time till now it has undergone many changes, occasioned by its growth as a living language. It has adopted many words from other tongues, and many of its modes of expression have considerably altered. The language in its old form was rich in inflections, but most of the inflections have been dropped, and their function is now performed by prepositions and auxiliary verbs. So that Modern English is in reality a developed form of the language brought into Britain by the Jutes, Saxons and Angles. At first sight there is no close similarity between Old English and the language as now used; but Old English has grown into Modern English by gradual changes, and the successive stages of development are easily traceable in English literature.

6. The English of the period before the Norman Conquest has often had the name ' Anglo-Saxon ' applied to it; but it is better called Old English, in order to indicate by the name the unbroken continuity of the language. English has been perhaps the most plastic of all the European tongues—and we use the word ' plastic ' in the sense of ' formative '—the most plastic, in that it has readily taken hold of and assimilated for its own purposes elements from other languages. The Angles and Saxons adopted from the Celts some words to be found in Modern English. At and after the Norman Conquest there was a great influx of French words into English speech, for the language of the Normans was a dialect of French; and for a time the influence of the Normans was so overpowering that French threatened to become the literary language of England, and to degrade English to the rank of a patois, i.e. a tongue spoken by the peasants only. But the Saxons in England far outnumbered the Norman invaders, so that English still lived on the lips of the common people. Through the working of political causes, Normans and Saxons were drawn more closely together; wars with France engendered a dislike to everything French; Chaucer's writings gave a mighty impulse in favour of English; and in course of time the so called ' Middle English ' dialects asserted their supremacy. But the English vocabulary had meantime been enriched by the addition of many French words. Norman French was itself a popular form of Latin; so that the Norman invasion led to the introduction of many new words of Latin origin into the English tongue. Most of the words relating to feudalism, to war, to law, and to hunting, came into English through Norman French.

When the study of the classical languages was revived in Europe in the sixteenth century—a revival of study which owed much to the invention of printing and to the Reformation—a great number of words from Latin and some from Greek were brought into English. Many of these new classical importations were in time discarded; nevertheless, a great many remained to enrich the English tongue. Modern scientific terms are mainly derived from Greek. Moreover, the extensive intercourse which the English people have carried on with all parts of the world for the last three hundred years, has led to the adoption of several foreign words of miscellaneous origin.

English, then, is essentially a Germanic language, which has been enriched in its growth by the addition of a very considerable Romance or Latin element, and by a small proportion of words from miscellaneous sources. The intermingling of Germanic and Romance elements has given to English a greater power of expressing delicate shades of meaning than could be found in a language altogether Romance or altogether Teutonic.

7. The extent to which English has spread is truly marvellous. No other language, ancient or modern, has ever been so widely spoken. English is now the general language of Great Britain and Ireland, the United States and British America, Australia, New Zealand, South Africa, the West Indies, and is used widely in India. The use of English continues to grow. As the eminent German linguist, Grimm, in his work *On the Origin of Language*, noted: ' English possesses a veritable power of expression such as perhaps never stood at the command of any other language of men. Its highly spiritual genius and wonderfully happy development and condition have resulted from a surprisingly intimate union of the two noblest languages in modern Europe, the Teutonic and the Romance. It is well known in what relation these two stand to one another in the English tongue; the former supplying in far larger proportion the material groundwork, the latter the spiritual conceptions. In truth, the English language, which by no mere accident has produced and upborne the greatest and most predominant poet of modern times as distinguished from the ancient classical poetry (I can, of course, only mean Shakespeare), may with all right be called a world-language ... In wealth, good sense, and closeness of structure, no other of the languages at this day spoken deserves to be compared with it.'

8. There is, then, nothing strange in the fact that so many foreign students should wish to learn English; for most books found to be generally useful are written in English, and if any valuable book is written in another language, an English translation of it is sure to be speedily published. The English-speaking people want no monopoly of knowledge; and anyone who masters the English tongue acquires a key which will open to him whatever is valuable in the literature of the world.

9. English has, as we have seen, drawn elements from many

sources: hence its copiousness of vocabulary and its great power of expressing distinctions of meaning. It is particularly rich in idiomatic expressions. Under ' Idiom ' we include peculiar uses of particular words, and also particular phrases or turns of expression which, from long usage, have become stereotyped in English. A few examples will make our meaning plain.

When we say of a woman that *she has a tongue*, we seem to say something that does not give much information. But then this expression according to its common usage in English means that the woman spoken of has a *scolding tongue*. The sentence, *she has a tongue*, is commonly equivalent to, *she is a scold*.

Again, *on* and *upon* are commonly equivalents, and are often interchangeable. Thus we correctly say, either *He acted on my advice*, or *He acted upon my advice*; either, *Madras is on the sea coast*, or *Madras is upon the sea coast*. But though we can idiomatically say, *Carry on business*, we cannot say, *Carry upon business*; this last expression is meaningless.

Further, many English verbs derived from Latin are compounded of a Latin prefix and a Latin verb. Some of these verbs in English take a preposition after them in composition, while others do not. For example, *abstain* is from *abs* and *teneo*; and *contain* is from *con* and *teneo*. But *abstain* is followed by the preposition *from*, corresponding to the prefix *abs*, while *contain* takes no preposition after it.

> Abstain from all appearance of evil.
> This book contains much valuable information.

Many similar instances might be given. English idiom established by usage requires that some of these verbs from Latin should be followed by a preposition and others not; but no rule can be given showing which usage should be followed in regard to any particular verb.

Again, it is not easy to explain why we can say *make a journey*, and not *make a walk*, but must say, *take a walk*; or why we can say of one statute that it is a *dead letter*, but cannot say of another statute that it is a *living letter*; or why we speak of a bird flying as a bird *on the wing*, and yet must speak of a man walking as *on foot* and not *on the foot*; or why we say *take in hand*, and not *take in hands* or *take into hands*; or why we must say *stare one in the face* and not *stare at one's face*, or *stare one in his face*; or why we can say *set free* and *set at liberty*, but not *set at freedom*; or why while we speak of a farmer's *implements*, we must speak of a surgeon's *instruments* and a carpenter's *tools*; or why we *call in* a doctor, while we *employ* a carpenter; or why we must say *lay a foundation*, and not *set* or *put* or *place a foundation*; or why we must say *live from hand to mouth*, and not *live from the hand to the mouth*, or why we say *upside down* and not *downside up*; or why when we can correctly say either *take hold of* or *lay hold of*, we can also say *take care of*, but not *lay care of*; or why it must be *take care of* and not *keep care of*; or why we must say that a tree *sheds* its leaves and a bird *casts* its feathers; or why to do one *a good turn* should mean to do him a *kindness*. But long usage has fixed the idiomatic expression in each case, and from the idiom we may not swerve.

10. Idiomatic turns of expression are usually forcible, terse, and vivid; the same meaning could be set forth in some other way, but not with equal force and brevity. It is the idiomatic part of a language that is the most difficult part for a foreigner to master. It adds to the difficulty that often no reason can now be given as to how or why a particular idiomatic phrase has assumed its present form. When the English turns of expression differ from those which set forth the same meaning in his own language, the foreign student is liable to go astray. As a general rule an idiomatic phrase cannot be altered; no other synonymous word can be substituted for any word in the phrase, and the arrangement of the words can rarely be modified; any attempted change in the wording or collocation will commonly destroy the idiom and perhaps render the expression meaningless. Frequently an idiomatic expression omits several words by ellipsis; but to fill in the words so omitted would destroy the idiom. Hence the foreign student must be careful to note the precise words that make up any idiom, and also the exact arrangement of those words.

11. Idiomatic expressions are to be found in the daily speech of English people rather than in elaborate, polished compositions. Likewise, on the radio, in novels, newspaper and magazine articles, and books of travel, idiomatic turns of expression abound. The same may be said of the works of Defoe, Swift, Lamb, and others, whose writings draw largely on the Anglo-Saxon element of the language and but little upon the Classical. There is a steady tendency in writing English to develop a simple, vigorous, idiomatic style, and to get rid of stilted, high-flown composition. In learning English idioms, therefore, the student should carefully study good modern authors. Periodicals and radio talks may also prove useful. We would say to the student who wishes to acquire the habit of using English idioms correctly, ' Read much; note idiomatic peculiarities; commit idiomatic expressions to memory; compare passages in which the same idiomatic phrase occurs, and endeavour by translation into your own language to find out the precise force and scope of the idiom. When opportunity occurs, listen to an educated Englishman speaking, and endeavour to catch the exact expressions he uses. And write much, getting your compositions corrected if possible by an Englishman, and attend carefully to the corrections.' Perseverance in this course will in time give the student power in using English fluently and idiomatically.

12. We add a word of caution. While a good dictionary or a reliable book explaining English idioms will be a valuable help, a professed help in the shape of an untrustworthy book is worse than useless. Very often the explanation given in such a book is of an idiom only in the particular application in which it was used in the college class text-book, and it is hardly possible that a teacher's full explanation could be taken down word for word by an ordinary student. In fact, students greatly need to be warned against books which profess to interpret English idioms, and which have been compiled by men whose mother tongue is not English. We gladly acknowledge that many have so learnt English as to be able to speak and write it well and fluently; yet it must be admitted that few such could write an ordinary letter or essay without betraying some ignorance of English idiom.

CHAPTER II

CONTRACTION OF WORDS. INTERROGATIVES

13. In English there are several **recognized contractions of words** which are used in conversation, and in compositions which reproduce conversational language. They usually abbreviate an expression by omitting a letter—usually a vowel and sometimes a consonant —or by joining two words together. The word *not* is often abbreviated, and joined to the end of a short word, in the form *n't*, the whole being regarded as one word, as *don't* for *do not*. And there are other contractions which also have become current through long usage. The most common of these will be found below. The apostrophe represents one or more letters omitted.

can't	for	cannot	shan't	for	shall not
couldn't	,,	could not	she's	,,	she is, *or* she has
daren't	,,	dare not	she'd	,,	she would, *or* she had
didn't	,,	did not	shouldn't	,,	should not
don't	,,	do not	that'll	,,	that will
e'en	,,	even	that's	,,	that is
e'er	,,	ever	there's	,,	there is, *or* there has
'em	,,	them	they'd	,,	they would, *or* they had
'gainst	,,	against			
hasn't	,,	has not	they'll	,,	they will
he'd	,,	he would, *or* he had	they're	,,	they are
he'll	,,	he will	they've	,,	they have
here's	,,	here is	'tis	,,	it is
he's	,,	he is, *or* he has	'twas	,,	it was
I'd	,,	I would, *or* I had	'twill	,,	it will
I'm	,,	I am	wasn't	,,	was not
isn't	,,	is not	we'd	,,	we would, *or* we had
it'll	,,	it will	we'll	,,	we will
it's	,,	it is, *or* it has	we're	,,	we are
I've	,,	I have	we've	,,	we have
let's	,,	let us	what's	,,	what is
mayn't	,,	may not	who'll	,,	who will
mightn't	,,	might not	who's	,,	who is, *or* who has
needn't	,,	need not	won't	,,	will not
ne'er	,,	never	you'd	,,	you would, *or* you had
o'clock	,,	of the clock	you'll	,,	you will
o'er	,,	over	you're	,,	you are
oughtn't	,,	ought not	you've	,,	you have

Of the foregoing *e'en, e'er, ne'er,* and *o'er* belong to poetry, the letter *v* being elided in each. *Ta'en* for *taken* and *'gainst, 'tis, 'twas, 'twill,* also belong to poetry. *D'you* and *'em* are colloquial.

Instead of *is* written in full, *'s* is often joined to the end of a singular noun: as, *The Lord's my shepherd*.

We give a few general examples.

Othello's occupation's gone. I'd rather be a dog and bay the moon than such a Roman. My intention's very good and you shouldn't despise it. I'm convinced you've done a thing that'll bring you credit. O here's Frank: we'd better tell him all about it, and he'll tell us what she'd like best. What's that you're saying? Who'll have the money when she's gone? Who'd have thought of all this happening! i.e. Who would have thought, etc. I've a great deal that I wish to say. What I'm to do, I don't know. I thought you'd like it. There's a man I wish to see. It wasn't my fault, and you needn't blame me. The gentlemen mayn't come, but if they do, they'll not like to see this. 'Tis greatly wise to talk with our past hours and ask them what account they've borne to heaven.

We have also in common use (the words in italics are Latin).

A.D.	for	*anno domini*	in loc.	for *in loco*, in its place
a.m.	„	*ante meridiem*, before noon	inst.	„ *instant*, present month
anon.	„	anonymous	p.m.	„ *post meridiem*, after noon
cf.	„	*confer*, compare	pp.	„ pages
do.	„	ditto	pro tem.	„ *pro tempore*, for the time being
D.V.	„	*Deo volente*, God willing	prox.	„ *proximo*, the coming month
ib. *or* ibid.	„	*ibidem*, in same place	U.K.	„ the United Kingdom
id.	„	*idem*, the same	ult.	„ *ultimo*, the last month
i.e.	„	*id est*, that is	viz.	„ *videlicet*, namely
incog.	„	*incognito*, unknown		

On 14th ult. the ship was 24° W. and 13° N., i.e. on the 14th of last month the ship was 24 degrees west longitude and 13 degrees north latitude.

The following are also recognized abbreviations.

B.A.(Oxon)	for	B.A. of Oxford University	M.D.	for Doctor of Medicine
Bart.	for	Baronet	Messrs.	„ *Messieurs* (gentlemen)
Capt.	„	Captain	M.P.	„ Member of Parliament
Col.	„	Colonel	Mr.	„ Mister
Dr.	„	Doctor	Mrs.	„ Mistress (pronounced Misses)
Esq.	„	Esquire	O.H.M.S.	„ On Her Majesty's Service
F.R.C.S.	„	Fellow of the Royal College of Surgeons	Ph.D.	„ Doctor of Philosophy
Gen.	„	General	Prof.	„ Professor
G.P.O.	„	General Post Office	Rev. } Revd. }	„ Reverend—applied to a clergyman
Hon. } Hon'ble }	„	Honourable	R.S.V.P.	„ *Répondez, s'il vous plait*, please reply
Kt.	„	Knight	Rt. Hon.	„ Right Honourable
Lieut.	„	Lieutenant	U.S.A.	„ United States of America
LL.D.	„	Doctor of Laws	V.C.	„ Victoria Cross
M.	„	Monsieur	Xmas	„ Christmas
M.A.(Cantab.)	„	M.A. of Cambridge University.		
Ma'am	for	Madam		

Many others will be found in any good dictionary.

14. INTERROGATIVE FORMS. In interrogative sentences in English, the nominative commonly occupies a position different from that which it ordinarily has in declarative sentences. The verb *do* is often brought in as an auxiliary into interrogative sentences when the principal verb has no other auxiliary; and the nominative commonly stands between the auxiliary and the principal verb. The verb following the auxiliary *do* is, of course, in the infinitive mood. *Do*, as an auxiliary, is not used in interrogative sentences where the principal verb is *be, can, have, may, must, ought, shall, will.*

There are also in English several interrogative words which mark questions: as, *who, which, what, when, where, why, how, whither, whence, whether, wherefore.*

A few examples of the different forms which interrogative sentences assume in English will help to guide the student to the correct idiom. Students frequently ask questions in a wrong way, because the idiom in their own language is different. It will be noted from the examples that even into a sentence which has an interrogative pronoun or interrogative adverb, the auxiliary *do* is sometimes introduced.

1. Examples of questions marked by auxiliary verbs and the position of the nominative.

> Must I take all this luggage?
> Will you have a cup of tea?
> Can a doctor cure every disease?
> Can you not stay till tomorrow?
> Did you receive the letter I sent you?
> Should we not attend to God's commands?
> Do they hope to find the missing documents?
> Does the water leak out of the canal, and if so, where?
> Could you identify the man that you met yesterday on the road?

2. Examples of interrogative sentences having the verb *be* either as a principal verb or as an auxiliary.

> Are you leaving town?
> Are the biscuits spoiled?
> Am I not taller than James?
> What sort of rulers were the Mughals?
> Have you been ill, and are you better?
> How are you, and how is your father?
> Why is this man here?   Is he a witness?
> Was William the Conqueror a Scandinavian?
> What is the matter with the child?   Is he ill?
> Is this man a native of London or of New York?
> Was there not a total eclipse of the sun last year?
> Is any man able perfectly to keep the commandments of God?
> Which of the two is the better student, John or Richard?
> What were the characteristics of the Tudor sovereigns of England?

3.   Examples of questions marked by interrogative words.

Who built your house?
What country is this?
Whose car did he ask for?
Where has he put my note book?
By whose authority was this done?
Which of the horses do you prefer?
When did the gardener prune the vine?
To whom will he give the appointment?
What kind of wood is this box made of?   *or, better,*
Of what kind of wood is this box made?
When was the Battle of Hastings fought?
What do the Scriptures principally teach?
How is the boy getting on with his studies?
At what hour does the evening train arrive?
Why are you afraid of meeting your father?
Where is the new canal to be made and when?
How large should a school-house for two hundred children be?
Why does oil not mix with water when both are put into one vessel?

Whence, whether, whither, and *wherefore,* are found as interrogative words in the English of a past period rather than in current English prose.   Poetry, which often uses archaic forms, still retains *whence* and *whither*; but in prose, instead of *whence,* its equivalent *where from* is now commonly used; and instead of *whither,* its equivalent *where to.*   But in such cases *where* and *from* usually stand apart in a sentence; so also do *where* and *to.*   We do not now in prose write—

Whence comes all this cavalcade?
Whence did this package of books come?
Whither did he go when he left Southampton?
Whither have the released slaves been taken?

Current idiomatic English would prefer the following.

Where does all this cavalcade come from?
Where did this package of books come from?
Where did he go to when he left Southampton?
Where have the released slaves been taken to?

Whence, however, sometimes points to *cause* or *source,* and is then scarcely synonymous with *where from.*   In such a case, instead of saying,

Whence are volcanic fires fed?
Whence arises the discontent of the people?

current idiomatic English, not rhetorical, would prefer,

From what source are volcanic fires fed?
From what cause does the discontent of the people arise?

4.   **Dependent Interrogative Sentences.**   Sometimes an interrogative expression is the dependent clause in a complex sentence.

When a sentence is changed from the direct interrogatory form into a dependent interrogatory clause, the nominative takes the same position as if the clause were a declarative sentence, and the auxiliary verb *do*, if brought into the direct form of the question, is omitted in the indirect or dependent question. A direct question takes the note of interrogation after it: a dependent interrogative clause does not. The following are examples.

> I cannot imagine how this trick is done.
> The lawyer is unable to say when this case may come on.
> I do not remember whether he came on Friday or Saturday.
> The boy went out an hour ago, but I do not know where he was going.

Some students, after having learnt the correct mode of putting direct questions in English, blunder over these indirect forms, and would write the above examples wrong, thus—

> I cannot imagine how is this trick done.
> The lawyer is unable to say when may this case come on.
> I do not remember whether did he come on Friday or Saturday.
> The boy went out an hour ago, but I do not know where was he going.

It must not be overlooked that a complex sentence which has a dependent interrogative clause may have a direct question as the principal clause. In such a case, the order of words in the dependent interrogation is the same as in a declarative sentence; but the note or mark of interrogation stands at the close of the whole sentence, because the direct question in the principal clause requires it.

> Have you made up your mind what you will do?
> Did the guard tell you why the train doesn't move on?
> How is it you cannot tell me where you put my dictionary?
> Did he give any reason why he did not keep his appointment?
> Can you describe what it was that made King John grant the demands of the barons at Runnymede?

5. In reply to a negative direct question, the answer ' No ' confirms the negative as correct; and the answer ' Yes ' reverses the negation in the question.

For example, in reply to the question, *Is India not a rich country?* the answer ' Yes ' means that India is a rich country; while the answer ' No ' confirms the negation of the question, and means that India is not a rich country.

So, in reply to *Are you not coming?* the answer ' No ' would mean *I am not coming*; while ' Yes ' would mean *I am coming*.

These examples will be sufficient to show the idiomatic force of a reply to a negative question.

In direct affirmative questions, there is no difficulty, and therefore no fear of blunders. In reply to such a question, ' Yes ' confirms the affirmation, and ' No ' negatives it.

CHAPTER III

PARTICULAR WORDS AND PECULIAR IDIOMATIC MEANINGS

15. An exhaustive list of words that might fairly be dealt with under the above heading, would be very long indeed; we can therefore do little more than call attention to those words and meanings which have been known to present special difficulty to students. We first take Auxiliary Verbs, and begin with two of them which require to be carefully distinguished in usage.

16. SHALL and WILL

These two auxiliary verbs occasion much perplexity. We shall first consider them separately, and then bring them into contrast.

I. Shall.

1. In regard to *shall* with the first person—*I shall, we shall*— the action expressed by the principal verb strictly arises through some influence beyond the speaker's will: as, *I shall suffer*; *we shall see*; *we shall be left to ourselves*; *I shall not be admitted*; *we shall not be disturbed here*. So that, as *shall* has originally the idea of obligation, *I shall go* ought strictly to mean that I am obliged to go, or that some external thing, independently of my will, influences me to go.

But *I shall, we shall*, have been softened down so as to express simple futurity, the idea of obligation having disappeared.

> We shall be glad to see your friend.
> I shall have much pleasure in coming to hear his lecture.

2. *Shall*, with the second and third persons, usually conveys a promise, or threat, or command. If in these persons emphasis is laid on *shall*, the command is more positive, or the promise or threat more certain.

Shall, therefore, with the second and third persons, is the word used in representing the highest form of authority or of general command.

Hence the form of the Divine commandments.

> Thou shalt not steal. Thou shalt not covet.
> Thou shalt not bear false witness against thy neighbour.
> He that knoweth his Master's will and doeth it not, shall be beaten with many stripes.

So Acts of Parliament and other authoritative declarations use *shall*.

> The Governor for the time being shall be Chancellor of the University.
> Whoever commits robbery shall be punished with rigorous imprisonment for a term which may extend to ten years, and shall also be liable to a fine.
> No student shall get credit for his attendance at lectures in the Faculty of Arts as a part of his College course, until he shall have matriculated.

In the language of adoration, addressed to God, we use *shall*. The reason, no doubt, is that all right conceptions of God's perfection of sovereignty exclude the idea that He is controlled or restrained by fate or any outside power.

> Thou shalt guide me with Thy counsel.
> Thou art the same, and Thy years shall not fail.

II. **Will.** *Will* originally expressed wish, intention, resolution on the part of the person speaking or acting.

1. In current English, *I will go* indicates that the choice to go or not to go rests with me, and that of my own free will I decide to go. And if emphasis is put upon *will* in *I will go*, determination or fixed purpose is thereby expressed.

> Expression of warning: ' Perhaps it is safer for you not to go into the town.'
> Reply expressing emphatic determination: ' I will go at all costs.'

Will with the first person—*I will, we will*—expresses the self-determination of the person acting.

> If I can do you a service, I will.
> On the fourth day from now I will be back.
> O Lord my God, I will give thanks unto Thee.—*Bible*
> Among traitors I will not dwell.—*Kingsley*
> I will keep the papers safe for him.
> We will not have this man to reign over us.—*Bible*

But inasmuch as *I will* obtrudes one's own volition, considerations of politeness have led to the softening down of *I will* into *I shall*; so that *I shall* has come to be the common form of simple futurity when there is no object in calling attention to one's own wish or choice.

2. In the ordinary usage of *will* with the second and third persons, the idea of wish, purpose, or determination vanishes; so that *will* in the second or third person indicates simple futurity.

> He will come at nightfall.
> You will easily find the book.
> They will not be able to do the work.
> The crops will be abundant this year.
> Complaints about taxation will never cease.

III. The following rime may be regarded as a useful summary of the rule about **shall** and **will**:

In the First person simply **Shall** foretells;
In **Will** a threat or else a promise dwells.
Shall in the Second and the Third does threat;
Will simply then foretells the future fate.

In the FIRST person,
Shall expresses a future event without regard to the wish or volition of the agent.
Will is used to express a promise, threat, or determination on the part of the agent.

In the SECOND and THIRD persons,
Shall is used to express a promise, threat, command, or resolve on the part of the agent.
Will is used to express the simple future without the agent's wish or volition.

The reader will note that the rule for the Second and Third persons is the reverse of the rule for the First person.

There are three kinds of future action: (*a*) The Simple Future; (*b*) The Future of Obligation or Necessity; and (*c*) The Future of Volition or Determination. And there are but two Auxiliaries to express these three Futures. Out of this defect arises all the difficulty and confusion in the use of *shall* and *will*.

From the foregoing it will be seen that there are two forms of the Future Tense: (1) That which expresses the Simple Future without reference to the will of the agent; (2) That which expresses the Future of Special Volition, as in promise, threat, command, or resolve. These have been aptly called the Simple Future and the Jussive (from the Latin=command) Future. The forms of these are,

I. THE SIMPLE FUTURE

Singular:	I shall come.	Thou wilt come.	He will come.
Plural:	We shall come.	You will come.	They will come.

II. THE JUSSIVE FUTURE

Singular:	I will come.	Thou shalt come.	He shall come.
Plural:	We will come.	You shall come.	They shall come.

A. Of these forms, the Simple Future should be used as follows:

1. To express future events which are doubtful.

Perhaps we shall call on you at four.
He will probably send his application tomorrow.

2. To express the feelings, since the feelings do not generally depend on an act of our will.

I shall be delighted if you come.
He will be greatly gratified by your letter.

3. To express necessary future events, which are not dependent on the will of the agent.

> I shall be thirty years old at Christmas and my brother will be twenty-five.

4. To express future free acts of the agent; though in regard to the First person, good writers vary, using sometimes the one form of the future and sometimes the other. In the Second and Third persons the Simple future is used.

> For this opinion we shall proceed to give our reasons.
> I shall do little more than indicate this.
> We will propose a very plain dilemma.
> I will not conclude this lecture without one further illustration.
> He will come tomorrow.
> You will reap your corn next week.
> I hope they will be able to assist me soon.

In the third and fourth of the preceding examples, *will* is probably intended to indicate slightly stronger volition than *shall* would do.

B. The Jussive form of the Future should be used as follows.

1. To express command, threat, or determinate purpose.

> Thou shalt not steal.
> He shall be charged with this offence before the magistrate.
> We will not let this matter rest, but must have it investigated.

2. To express promises which imply a special act of volition. This is the form used in prophecy.

> If I can see to this business tomorrow, I will.
> I tell you, Pyrrhus: you the Romans shall subdue.
> All kings shall fall down before Him: all nations shall serve Him.—*Bible*

But the forms *I will*, *he shall*, *you shall*, obtrude the speaker's volition; and so, when there is no particular reason for calling attention to the will of the speaker, the Jussive forms are often softened down into the Simple Future forms. An Inspector might correctly and politely write an order to a schoolmaster in this form,

> You will see that this roll is carefully kept.

IV. A few conclusions from the foregoing may here be set down:

1. From what has been stated, it follows that when the agent's will controls the action, he uses *will* when speaking of himself, and *shall* when speaking of others.

> I will take care that your interests do not suffer.
> We will propose a very plain dilemma.
> You shall leave the room, i.e. my determination is to make you leave the room.
> Not a penny shall you have: not one farthing more shall you get from me, i.e. I am determined not to give you any more money.
> They shall be dismissed, i.e. I am resolved to dismiss them, or to do my best to procure their dismissal.
> My house shall enable no one to defy the law, i.e. I am resolved that my house shall not be made a refuge by any one seeking to defy the law.

2.   It also follows that when a speaker wants to express simple futurity, he uses *shall* of himself and *will* of others: as in the following.

> I shall come to your office at four o'clock.
> We shall have an eclipse of the sun in September.
> Pursue that notion and you will be in the dark presently.
> Our rulers will best promote the improvement of the nation by strictly confining themselves to their own legitimate duties.—*Macaulay*

3.   *Shall* and not *will* should be used in such expressions as the following.

> I will be much obliged to you for your patronage.
> I will be under the necessity of prosecuting him.
> We will be compelled to shut our shop.
> We will be at a loss to know what to do.
> We will be reproved for what we have done.

It must be plain to the student that in all these examples *will* is wrong: it ought to be *shall*.

4.   It is also incorrect to say, *I will have much pleasure in going with you to the Exhibition*. This would mean that it requires an effort of my will to excite the pleasure, which obviously is not what is intended to be expressed. The expression should in all courtesy be, *I shall have much pleasure in going with you to the Exhibition*.

5.   It follows from the above that it is wrong to say, *I will be dismissed*. The dismissal depends on the will of another. The expression ought to be, *I shall be dismissed*.

6.   *Will I?* or *Will we?* is correct only when used as an exclamation, meaning, ' Do I wish it?   Certainly I do.'   ' Do we desire it?   Of course we do.'   But in ordinary interrogative sentences, *Will I? Will we?* are inadmissible: it ought to be *Shall I? Shall we?*

In questions with the Second person, if the latter is dependent on the volition of the person to whom the question is addressed, **will** should be used; but if the matter is independent of his volition, **shall** should be used, though some good writers here use **will**.

> Will you be good enough to tell me, etc.
> How old shall you be in July next?
> Will you be surprised to hear that, etc.

In questions with the Third person, **will** is commonly used; except that if the question be put to a person with whom the deciding of the question rests, **shall** must be used. Thus we may say to a doctor, *How often shall the patient take the medicine?*

V.   In the Dependent or Secondary clauses of complex sentences, *shall* is commonly used to express simple futurity in all the persons. If, on the other hand, will or determination is to be denoted, the verb *will* is used in all the persons. This is the general rule, but many apparent exceptions are to be found even in standard authors.

VI. Take now a few examples of *shall* and *will*.

What will a child learn sooner than a song?—*Pope*
You shall sit alone whenever you like.—*George Eliot*
I will undertake that you shall see her.—*Hichens*
He has promised that they shall not touch thee.—*Kingsley*
Can you undertake that I shall leave the house.—*Trollope*
We will drain our dearest veins, but they shall be free.—*Burns*
Of my own accord I will not go without the money I ask.—*Trollope*
If we stand by each other, we shall most likely beat them.—*Macaulay*
If she [the ship] will only bear her canvas, we shall go clear.—*Cooper*
We doubt greatly whether they will be read fifty years hence.—*Macaulay*
We will neither hang nor hurt thee if thou wilt take this letter safely.
—*Kingsley*
Will you let me know what intelligence you have of this poor child?
—*Dickens*
These poems will assuredly take high rank among the class to which they
belong.
The candidate who shall distinguish himself the most in English shall
receive an exhibition of thirty pounds per annum.
Where shall we find more complete unity of action than in an army?
—*Macaulay*
Our readers will probably infer . . . that the book has disappointed
us.—*Macaulay*
We will take this opportunity of making a few remarks on an error
which, etc.—*Macaulay*
How small will that distress appear when we think over the history of the
past forty years.—*Macaulay*
' I cannot tell her anything about you that will not vex her.' ' Well
then say what will vex her least.'—*Trollope*
' Let us ask this man,' said the Brahman, ' what the creature is, and I
will stand by what he shall say.'—*Macaulay*
We shall not, we hope, be suspected of a bigoted attachment to the
doctrines and practices of past generations.—*Macaulay*
One of those privileges we hold to be this, that such writers, when they
happen to fail, shall not be subjected to severe discipline . . . but shall
be gently reminded . . . that it is high time to wake.— *Macaulay*

17. SHOULD and WOULD

These auxiliaries follow the rules for *shall* and *will*, of which
they are the imperfect tense.

Should often conveys the idea of moral obligation, though
scarcely so strongly as *ought*. (See Section 20.)

Apart from grammatical distinction, there are certain idiomatic
usages of **shall**, **should**, and **would**.

I shall have to write an essay tomorrow, i.e. I must write, I am to write,
I am obliged to write.

Should is used to express a hypothetical meaning, as in

I should be glad if you would come.

Should the worst come to the worst, means, if the worst which can happen should happen.

> My means are nearly all spent, but if the worst should come to the worst, I can become a clerk and in that way earn a livelihood.

Should is also used with the appearance of a hypothetical meaning, to soften down an assertive expression of opinion.

> ' Will the servant be able to carry this box? '   ' I should think so,' or, ' I should say so,' i.e. ' My opinion distinctly is that he will be able.'

Would has an optative force very similar to *I wish*, except that no pronoun is expressed. When used with the past tense, it implies a strenuous desire which has not been and cannot now be fulfilled.

> Would that the doctor had arrived before my brother became unconscious.

Would is used as an auxiliary to express the past tense of continuous action.

> We would listen [=we used to listen] while he told us of his adventures.

18. MAY

I. **May** has *might* in the past tense, but has no infinitive and no participles. It is used only as an auxiliary, and is followed by a verb in the infinitive mood without *to*.

1. *May* indicates that there is no physical or moral obstacle to an action. It is used therefore to denote contingency or possibility, as in the conversational phrase, *may be*, which means *perhaps*

> May be he will come tonight.
> A man may be rich and yet not be happy.
> His statement may be true, though I can scarcely believe it.
> The General might have been seen this morning riding into the city.
> He may blunder without much chance of being detected.—*Macaulay*
> Some blemishes may undoubtedly be detected in his character.—*Macaulay*

2. From this first application comes a second, in which *may* expresses permission.

> You may use my pen if you like.
> He may bring his box into my house.
> ' May I have leave for tomorrow? '   ' You may.'

3. *May* is also used to express wish, whether of benediction, imprecation, or the like.

> May curses fall on his villainous head.
> May you have a prosperous voyage to England.

II. **May** and **Shall**. In asking questions, the difference between *may* and *shall* is to be noted. When I say to a person *May I read aloud?* I indicate that I wish to read aloud and that I ask his permission to do so.   But if I say to him, *Shall I read aloud?* I seek to know whether he wishes me to read aloud, so that I, without considering any desire of my own, may do as he wishes.   This distinction between *may* and *shall* in questions is often overlooked.

19.   Must

Must is a verb of incomplete predication, i.e. it cannot stand alone as a predicate in a sentence, but requires with it another verb expressed or understood to constitute a complete predicate.   It is therefore altogether an auxiliary verb.   It has no variations of form to mark tense, number, or person.   It takes after it a verb in the infinitive mood without *to*.

1.   *Must* is used to denote physical or moral necessity.

Must one not eat to live?   One must.
We must obey the laws of our country.
Every recruit must come up to a certain minimum height.

2.   *Must* is also used to denote fixed determination.

I must have my way in this matter.
Must you always be meddling with my affairs?

3.   *Must* is also used to express moral certainty, to convey the idea that a thing cannot but be as stated.   This application is akin to the first, but this use of *must* should have the attention of the student drawn to it.

The spirit within us must be immortal.
Most of those who fought at Alma must now be dead.
Life in a lighthouse on a barren rock must be very dreary.
I had no watch, but I judged from the height of the sun that it must have been nine o'clock when I crossed the river.

20.   Ought

This was formerly the regular past tense of *owe*.

This due obedience which they ought to the king.—*Tyndale*
He said you ought twice a thousand pounds.—*Shakespeare* in *Henry VI*

Hence what you *ought* to do is what is *owing* or due from you, what you should do, what it is your duty to do.   It is in the sense of moral obligation that the word *ought* is now used.   But it has become established in English as a present tense, and the past tense of *owe* is now the regular word *owed*.   In the above examples, *ought* is used in the sense of *owed*, but such use of *ought* is now quite obsolete.

Ought, as a present tense, has no form for the past tense, but past time is expressed by joining the perfect infinitive to *ought*.

You ought to help him, i.e. It *is* your duty to help him.
You ought to have helped him, i.e. It *was* your duty to help him.

Other examples of the use of *ought* are,

> You ought not to squander your money.
> He ought to have remembered.
> My brethren, these things ought not so to be.—*Bible*

Ought therefore is similar in meaning to *should* when *should* expresses obligation. There is, however, a slight distinction. Strictly speaking, *should* expresses obligation of expediency or fitness; and *ought* expresses obligation of duty. But this distinction is not closely adhered to; so that it is correct to say, either

> You should obey the laws; *or*
> You ought to obey the laws.
> You should always speak the truth; *or*
> You ought always to speak the truth
> He should, *or* ought to, write better than this if he wants the appointment.

The following direction also furnishes an example of what we are considering:

It should be noted, or ought to be noted, that *should* in current English takes the infinitive without *to*, while *ought* requires *to* before the infinitive.

21. WORTH

The ordinary meaning of *worth* is, *to be value for*.

> This article is worth three shillings.
> To reign is worth ambition.—*Milton*
> A merchant worth fifty thousand pounds.
> Is this worth while? i.e. worth the time spent on it.

When a man wants to disparage a thing and make it seem valueless, he says it is *not worth a straw*. Many other such phrases occur in conversational English: as, Not worth a pin, Not worth a farthing, Not worth a button, Not worth a row of pins, Not worth a fig.

Similarly, we have, Not to care a fig for, Not to care a pin for, Not to care a button for, i.e. not to regard as of more consequence than a fig, a pin.

> England need not care a pin for all the bluster of the newspapers.
> He will find that all his trickery is not worth a farthing.

22. DO

This common verb is used in current English in a great variety of idiomatic connexions. We consider it here as an auxiliary, and also as a substitutive verb. For *do* in other relations consult the Index.

I. As an auxiliary *do* is used in the present and past tenses, but has no compound tenses; and the verb following it is in the infinitive mood.

1. *Do* is used as an auxiliary in forming negative sentences. In poetic composition and in older English prose, a sentence is made negative by joining *not* to the verb: as, *My friend came not.* In modern prose this would be, *My friend did not come.* But *do* is not introduced into negative sentences when the principal verb is of a compound tense; nor is it joined in interrogative or negative sentences with the verbs *be, can, have, may, must, ought, shall, will.* For example, the negative form of *There were four men in the carriage,* is, *There were not four men in the carriage,* and not *There did not be four men in the carriage.* To make the usage clear by a corresponding example where *do* is brought in, we take this: The correct negative of *He went away at four o'clock* is *He did not go away at four o'clock.*

The following illustrate the use of *do* as an auxiliary in forming negative sentences.

> Do not look out of the window.
> This farmer does not till his fields well.
> It did not occur to me that the man was merely acting a part.

2. *Do* as an auxiliary is commonly used, as we have already seen, in forming interrogative sentences.

> What does he want?
> Why do you prefer Tennyson to Shakespeare?
> Did the soldier close the gate at the appointed hour?
> Does he not know that Delhi was the capital of the Mughals?

3. *Do* as an auxiliary is often used for emphasis. The following are common examples.

> Well, you do astonish me.
> Do be quiet. Do have patience.
> Now do go away. Do come and see me.
> This witness did say that he saw the robbery committed.

Sometimes *did* as an auxiliary emphasizes past time, and is intended to indicate that while a certain state of things existed in past time, it no longer exists.

> Why not try to solve the problem? I did try, but have given it up.
> I did respect him once, but I have ceased to regard him with any esteem.

II. *Do* is often substituted for a principal verb or a statement previously expressed in the sentence, to avoid repetition of the same words. The proper sequence of tenses has to be observed. This substitutive use of *do* gives a very useful and very common idiom in English. The following exemplify this idiomatic substitutive use of *do.*

He earns as much as you do.
You wrote a longer paper than I did.
I cannot write as quickly as he does.
>   Do they love their wives and work for them,
>   As husbands ought to do?—*English Song*

I love you more than you do me.—*Shakespeare*
' Shall I send you a few apples? '   ' Do, please.'
' Do you like apples? '   ' No, but my brother does.'
' Do you confess the bond? '   ' I do.'—*Shakespeare*
It was not the part of a real friend to say such cutting things as he continually did.—*Trollope*
I hear that you have extended your operations to the other kingdom. I hope I have not been the means of inducing you to do so.—*Trollope*

23. BECOME

The ordinary usage of this word is familiar; it implies transition into some other state.

The iron is fast becoming hot.
By steady attention to business he has become a rich man.

But *become* also has the meaning of the Latin *decet*, is becoming to, is suitable to, is proper for, is seemly for.

Modesty becomes a woman.
This hat becomes him, i.e. fits him and suits him.
It becomes children to be respectful and obedient to their parents.
I have known persons so anxious to have their dress become them, that, etc.—*Coleridge*

To become of means, to be the end of, to happen to.

What is to become of that young man?
We don't know what has become of John.
The child is lost and no one knows what has become of him.

24. CALL, CALLING, CALLS

To call has sometimes the meaning of, to pay a visit.

I came to call, i.e. I came to pay a visit, or make a call.
I called at your house, but you were not in.

A ship is said to *call at a port*, i.e. stop for a short time at the port and then proceed on her voyage.

To *call* (someone) *names* is to describe him by uncomplimentary names.

To *call a meeting* is to invite people to meet together for a specified business.

To *call to order*. When persons in a meeting or in a class-room become unruly, the chairman or teacher calls them to order.

The noun *calling* is often used in the sense of *vocation*, and the verb used with this is *follow*.

' What calling does this man follow? '   ' He is a carpenter.'

The noun *calls* often means claims or demands.

He has many calls on his time.
The calls of justice demanded his punishment.

25. CLEAR

This verb has some apt applications in idiomatic expressions.

To clear a hedge or fence, is to leap over it.
To clear ground, is to remove rubbish and weeds from it.
To clear the decks, is to remove obstructions on deck, to remove anything that is in the way.
To clear the course, is to prepare a racecourse for a race.
To clear the table, is to remove all articles from the table.
A judge gives orders to clear the court, i.e. to drive all the people out. (This would imply a forcible ejection, as by the police.)
Clear your mind of cant.—*Dr Johnson*
To clear one's reputation, is to free one's good name from reproach or unjust imputation.
This merchant cleared £5,000 on his cotton exports last season, i.e. he made profits of that amount.
The lecturer cleared his throat.
The Prime Minister's decision cleared the air.

26. DRAW

Draw has various meanings in several such idiomatic expressions as the following.

To draw the line, is to fix a limit.
To draw a tooth, is to extract a tooth.
To draw blood, is to cause blood to flow.
To draw or deduce a moral from a story.
To make a drawing, is to make a sketch with pen or pencil.
This lecture will draw a large audience, i.e. will attract, etc.
A rider draws rein, i.e. makes his horse stop by pulling the reins.
His pathetic story drew tears from the audience.
To draw a cheque, is to write the amount and name on a cheque and present it to the bank to get the money.
A drawing-board, a drawing-pen, a drawing-room, a drawn game, a drawn battle, are explained in Chapter IV.
To draw a person, or to draw a person out, is cleverly to elicit information from him which he might not wish to give. The first of these expressions is more colloquial than the second. As, In Parliament statements are often hazarded about the intentions of the Government in order to draw the responsible ministers, i.e. to get them to make a statement which will reveal their plans or intentions.
To draw a fox or a badger, is to force the creature to leave its cover or hiding-place that it may be hunted.
To draw the long bow, is grossly to exaggerate and even to lie. It is often used of one who describes himself as having encountered great difficulties or perilous adventures: as, This man is so prone to draw the long bow that I do not believe what he says till I get it corroborated.

'Draw it mild,' you say (colloquially) to a man who is exaggerating, when you wish him to make his statement without exaggeration.

A ship draws twenty feet of water, means that the ship requires a depth of more than twenty feet of water to float in.

The chimney does not draw, means that for some reason there is not a sufficient upward current of air in the chimney to carry the smoke up.

A man draws his salary.

27. DRIVE; RIDE

You *drive* in a conveyance of any kind. You *ride* on an animal, whether on horse-back, mule-back, donkey-back, camel-back, or elephant-back. Nowadays you may also *ride* a bicycle. It is not correct to say that you *rode* round the town in a car; you should say you *drove*.

Let the student explain the following.

Do you prefer a ride to a drive?
As I drove to the town, I met two men riding out to see me.

When there is no animal particularized, to *ride* is commonly understood to mean, to go on horse-back.

Both *drive* and *ride* are used in the present tense to express a thing habitually true.

He drives his own car, i.e. he owns a car and drives it.
He rides a good horse, i.e. he keeps and uses a horse for riding and it is always a good one.

28. FALL

It falls to you to divide the money, i.e. your part of the business is to divide the money.
Prices fall, i.e. become lower.
The wind falls, i.e. diminishes in force.
His countenance fell, i.e. he became abashed and ashamed.
He is riding for a fall, i.e. he is pushing on so recklessly that he will meet a catastrophe.
I hope to come to see you next fall, i.e. next autumn: so called because the leaves then fall from the trees. 'Fall' is generally used in North America for 'autumn'.

29. FEAR; HOPE

Besides being used as equivalent to 'dread', the verb *fear* is often used in the sense of, to expect something to arise or occur which is not desired; to feel anxiety about a thing. *To be afraid* is used in the same way.

Hope is the opposite of this and means, to expect a thing to arise or occur which you desire. To *hope against hope*, is to expect a desired thing when all reasonable ground for expectation is gone.

I fear the floods have done much damage in the city, i.e. I expect to hear that the floods have done much damage and I wish it were otherwise.

I am afraid his health is fast failing him, i.e. my belief is his health is fast failing, and I wish it were not so.

He hopes to see you at the fair next week, i.e. to see you is his expectation and desire.

My poor father will never be well, I fear.

I expected my brother here two hours ago: I hope he has not had an accident on the way.

The nouns *fear* and *hope* have idiomatic meanings corresponding to the foregoing.

30. GET

This verb has various idiomatic applications, and frequently takes a preposition or adverb after it, the two together forming a compound verb; of these we treat in Chapter IX. We here deal with some meanings of the simple verb.

1. *Get* means to procure, to obtain, to acquire by some means, to come into possession of.

You cannot get admission here.
He could get no employment in London.
Men get wealth by industry and economy.
He got a number of copper vessels at the auction.
How much better is it to get wisdom than gold.—*Bible*
This was he whose womanly care of me got him the name of a woman.
—*Lamb*, i.e. caused him to be called by a woman's name as a nickname.

2. *Get* means to receive, without implying effort on the part of the receiver.

Get a fever, get measles, get a fall, get one's discharge, etc.
I got a long letter from Charles yesterday.
They deserve the treatment they get.
Information which he had got in the city.
A wound which he got in a desperate attempt to defend his captain

3. *Get* means to prevail upon, to induce, to persuade.

They have got my father to contribute.
Can you not get him to prolong his visit?
Get him to say his prayers.

4. *Get* means to cause to be, to *have*, in the causative sense of that verb.

Get these books sent off.
He will get the work done as fast as possible.
He ordered me to get ready three fuses.—*Defoe*
You should get this book bound in Russia leather.
You never rested until you had got me married.
Find out some way to get my money sent me from London.

5. *Get by heart* means to learn, to commit to memory.

He has to get fifty lines of poetry by heart.

6. *Get* means to bring into a state or place.

> I got the chest down to my raft.
> We got all safe on shore.

7. *Get* is also used intransitively in the sense of, to bring oneself into a state or condition, to become or come to be.

> They have got safe to land.
> I got on board the ship.
> I wondered how I should get to shore with my goods.
> I got acquainted with the captain of the ship.
> The fence was so strong that nothing could get inside or over it.

8. *Get* sometimes has the meaning of *become*, and expresses the idea of gradually coming or growing into a condition.

> They got rich suddenly.—*Defoe*
> His chariot wheels got hot by driving fast.—*Coleridge*
> He gradually got accustomed to these impatient inquiries.—*Trollope*
> They already have got to love her as a sister.—*Thackeray*
> I am glad to know that your father has got well, i.e. has recovered from illness.

Get in idiomatic phrases is discussed in Chapter XII.

31. LEAVE and LEFT

A somewhat peculiar meaning of *leave* is to bequeath, to give by will, to give as a legacy.

> To leave a large legacy to a younger son.
> Has his wife had a fortune left her?
> A man is said to leave a good name behind him when he dies, i.e. his good name, his good reputation remains after death.
> One should leave well alone.
> His conduct leaves much to be desired, i.e. is unsatisfactory.

The following exemplify particular meanings of *left*.

> He has no strength left, i.e. his strength is quite exhausted, is quite gone.
> He bought articles till he had no money left.
> A parcel is left till called for, i.e. it is to remain till called for.

32. LET

Let has at least two meanings.

1. To allow. When used in this sense, it is usually followed by the infinitive mood without *to*.

> The jailor let the prisoners escape.
> Lady, kind lady, O let me go.—*Mrs Hemans*

2. Such phrases as *This house to let, This farm to let*, mean that the owner is willing to give the possession and use of the house or farm to a tenant for rent. These expressions are elliptical for *This house is to be let, This farm is to be let*.

> To let a farm for a year; to let a room to lodgers.

Certain phrases containing this verb may be explained.

To *let blood*, is to cause blood to flow, as from a vein. To *let drive* or *let fly*, is to discharge with violence, as an arrow or stone. To *let loose*, is to remove restraint from, to allow to wander at large. To *let* a thing *be*, is to leave it alone. To *let go*, is to permit to depart; to relinquish one's hold. To *let the cat out of the bag*, is to divulge a secret.

> He always lets his dog loose at night.
> Let me alone; I am finishing my essay.
> Let me go with this letter to the post, i.e. allow me to take it to the post.

33. LOOK

This verb has two peculiar meanings.

1. *Look* sometimes means, to seem, to appear.

> The sky looks rainy.   The sea looks very rough today.
> He looks every inch a king.   The patient looks much better.
> I thought she looked charming all the evening.
> I am afraid it would look more like vanity than gratitude.
> To look a gift-horse in the mouth, is to criticize a present.
> To look daggers at someone, is to look angrily at him.

2. *Look* also means to have a particular direction, to face.

> This house looks south, i.e. the front of the house faces toward the south.

34. MARK

The exact meaning of this verb as signifying to single out and indicate, is admirably exemplified in the following.

> An ordinary clever and sensible seaman will be able to make his way ashore at most ports; yet he has only to speak a sentence of any language to be known for an illiterate person; so also the accent, or turn of expression of a single sentence, will at once mark a scholar.—*Ruskin.*
> (' A scholar ' here means an educated scholarly man.)
> A marked man is one distinguished from his fellows.
> A marked tendency is one easily discerned.

35. PROPOSE

In certain collocations, the verb *propose*, when it stands without an accusative after it, means to propose marriage. It is the man only who *proposes*, not the woman. When a man has proposed to a woman and she has consented to become his wife, they both from that time to the time of their marriage are said to be *engaged*.

> The young barrister went to the judge's house intending to propose to his daughter. During the evening he found an opportunity of conversing with her alone and proposed and was accepted, so that now they are engaged.

36. RUN

Run as a verb has several peculiar meanings.

To run on wheels, like a train.

Ink runs [=spreads] on damp or porous paper; a drop of oil runs [=spreads over and through] on paper or calico.

Colours run in washing, i.e. the colours of a printed material like calico become mixed when the material is washed.

Fire will run along a street of wooden houses, i.e. one house takes fire and speedily the next and then the next and so on.   Fire runs along a hedge.

A speaker runs from one topic to another, i.e. passes hastily and confusingly from.

This street runs [=stretches] east and west.

This poem runs smoothly, i.e. it is so written that its rhythm is pleasing to the ear

The letter ran as follows, i.e. its contents were as follows.   The expression implies that the precise words used in the letter will now be quoted.

The sea ran high, i.e. swelled boisterously. So, the dispute ran high.

The mills are running full time, i.e. they are working full time.

The play ran [=was acted] for a hundred nights.

This bill has twenty days to run, i.e. it will be twenty days before payment of the bill can be claimed.

A coach runs [=plies back and forward] between these two towns.

To run an hotel, a business, a private school, is to own it and keep it up.

To run a blockade, is to pass through and evade ships which beleaguer a fortress.

To run a needle into one's finger accidentally as in sewing.

To run riot, is to act or move without restraint or control.

He (was an) also ran, means that he was not one of the leaders in the competition or race.

Run as a noun has noteworthy meanings.

A sheep run, is a place set apart for sheep to graze.

The ship has made a good run [=a quick voyage].

This book has had a good run [=has been bought rapidly]

A run of good luck: a run in cricket.

A run is often used colloquially for a trip, an excursion. I hope to take a run to Paris.

A run on a bank, means a rush of people to the bank to get cash for the bank's notes.

A run in music, is a succession of notes rapidly played or sung.

The common run of people, i.e. most of the people one meets, are averse to new things.

37. SINK

This verb is used in a variety of idiomatic expressions.

To sink a well, is to dig a well.

To sink a foundation, is to dig out the soil that the foundation may be laid.

The patient is sinking, means that the patient is getting worse, and is about to die.

One's spirits sink, i.e. become depressed.

The sun was sinking in the western sky.

He sank [=bent down] on one knee.

He sank into a gentle slumber.

A ship is said to be in a sinking condition when she is about to sink beneath the surface of the sea.

To sink money, is to invest it more or less permanently in an undertaking.

Sink or swim. A father pays off the debts of a spendthrift son and makes him a yearly allowance, telling him that with this sum he will leave him to sink or swim, i.e. to ruin himself by extravagance or to pay his way. The order of the words in this phrase must not be changed.

'I am sunk' is a modern colloquial expression for 'I am nonplussed' or 'at a loss'.

38. Take

Take has some peculiar meanings which are worth noting.

I take [=consider, regard, account] this to be right.

I took you for [=mistook you for] my cousin.

To take aim, is to aim as with a gun or bow.

To take the air, is to walk, drive, or ride in the open air.

To take alarm, is to become alarmed.

To take a thing amiss, or take a thing ill, is to be offended at it. He took it ill that you spoke of his poverty. How foolish to take sound advice amiss because it is unpalatable.

To take breath, is to pause and rest for a little. The waggoner let his horses take breath before going up the hill.

To take care, is to be careful. To take care of, is to keep safe, to attend to, to see to. You may say to a child using a knife, 'Take care and do not cut yourself.' This man has three horses to take care of.

To take a city, is to capture it.

To take effect, is to become effective. The medicine has taken effect. The firing soon took effect on the fortress.

To take fire, or catch fire, is to become ignited.

To take flight, is to flee.

To take heart, or courage, is to gain confidence or courage:

> Footsteps that . . . some forlorn and shipwrecked brother
> seeing, shall take heart again.—*Longfellow*

To take horse, is to mount a horse and ride him.

To take the lead, is to lead, to take the leading place.

To take leave, is to bid farewell; also, to take the liberty of doing something.

To take a house, is to acquire possession of a house.

To take offence, is to be offended, to feel slighted, to show annoyance.

To take oath, is to swear solemnly as in a court of justice.

To take pains, is to use diligent effort and if necessary undergo trouble in order to accomplish a thing. (A beginner sometimes wrongly says he will take much trouble to prepare his lessons. He should say he will *take great pains*, not, *much pains*.)

To take a newspaper, is to receive it regularly and pay for it.

To take a person prisoner, is to arrest him as a policeman might do.

Where does this river take its rise? i.e. where is its source?

To take root, is to begin to grow, to become established, said of plants or principles.

To take shelter, is to enter a sheltered place.

To take sides, is to join one of two opposing parties.

To take stock, is to make an inventory of goods on hand. (The phrase is also used colloquially for, to form an estimate of a person or a set of circumstances.) Some merchants take stock in the spring. He came to me with a letter of introduction, and in a brief conversation, I took stock of the man.

To take thought, is to consider.

To take a turn [= a walk] in the garden.

His affairs took an unexpected turn, i.e. became changed.

To be taken with a thing, is to be charmed with it, to be captivated by it.

We have further examples in the following.

I have taken a bad cold and he has taken fever.

I took him for a stiff-necked, pompous fool.

A horse is said to take a fence, i.e. to leap over it readily.

He who cannot take a joke, i.e. he who cannot bear a joke against himself, should not make one.

How much cloth will it take [= require] to make an overcoat?

Do you think this play will take? i.e. will please.

This work will take time, i.e. will require time; and the phrase *take time* used absolutely in this way means, require considerable time.

What took him to Madras? i.e. what object had he in going to Madras?

Did your vaccination take? i.e. did it take effect?

This verb *take* is used in many other idiomatic connexions. Consult the *Index* for other examples.

39. TOUCH

Apart from its ordinary sense this verb also means, to affect the feelings.

Touched with the feeling of our infirmities.—*Bible*

Serious evils of this kind touched the noblest part of his nature.

Further peculiar meanings are exemplified in

The food was nicely prepared, but the invalid would not touch [= eat] anything.

A ship is said to **touch bottom** when it gets into shallow water and its keel comes into contact with the ground. The phrase is also used metaphorically. When a man has been in adversity for some time and begins to prosper, he is said to have been in low water and to have touched bottom, i.e. he will not sink lower but will henceforth rise, his worst days of adversity are past and gone.

Touch has also the meaning of meddle or interfere with.

Don't touch my papers!

I have not touched your papers.

This touches, i.e. concerns you.

Touch also sometimes means to add a slight or delicate stroke with a brush or pencil, as to a picture.

40. Turn

The ordinary applications of this verb are well known, but it has some peculiar meanings, one of them being *to become, to change into* (used intransitively).

Water by freezing turns to ice.
This man has turned Moslem.
The milk will speedily turn sour.
His hair has quickly turned grey.
She turned pale at the sight of the tiger.
Wood when allowed to remain in certain water turns to stone.

Other meanings appear in the following.

In his difficulties he does not know where to turn [=to whom to have recourse].
To turn, in joinery, is to shape articles with a lathe.
He is turned fifty, means, He has passed his fiftieth year.
The success of the campaign turns on [=hinges on, depends on] the impending battle.

Turn as a noun occurs in phrases.

A turn [=a walk] in the park.
At every turn, means constantly, at every moment.
The pupils must answer in turn, i.e. one after another.
Turn and turn about, means the same as *in turn*.
To do one a good turn, is to do him a kindness at an opportune time.
    To do one an ill turn, is to do him an injury. As, if you withdraw your application in favour of mine, you will do me a good turn.

41. Used

Used=was accustomed to, was able to, followed by the infinitive, is the past tense of an obsolete verb. The *s* in the word with this meaning is pronounced as *c*, not as *z* as in the past tense of *use=* employ.

He used to show me all the tricks of the trade.
There was a great *Book of Martyrs* in which I used to read.—*Lamb*
You never used to speak of him except to praise him.

42. Some Neuter Verbs

Some verbs commonly transitive are also used with an intransitive or passive meaning.

The kettle boils.   This house is to let.
The chimney draws well.
Who is to blame for this mishap?
The stars are showing [=appear] tonight.
Your horse sold badly, i.e. was sold at a low price.
The old worn book showed it had been much read, i.e. bore marks of having been much used.

43. BRASS

This word is metaphorically used (colloquially) for impudence. *A brazen-faced fellow*, means an impudent fellow, one who can scarcely be put to shame.

> This young man's educational attainments are sufficient for the post, but he is too brazen-faced for me.
>
> (Money is sometimes vulgarly called *brass*.)

44. FELLOWS

Two separate articles making a pair, and matching each other are said to be *fellows*. The word in this sense is as a general rule applied only to boots, shoes, gloves, stockings.

> Two shoes that were not fellows.—*Defoe*

45. HABIT

Various verbs are idiomatically used with this noun.

> He has acquired the nasty habit of chewing tobacco.
> You should not indulge yourself in the habit of lying late in bed.
> You must get into the habit of looking intensely at words.
> My horse has a habit of kicking when a stranger comes near him.
> Walk erect, else the habit of holding your head down as you walk will grow upon you.
> It is not easy to break off a bad habit: most men when they get into a habit keep to it.
> An act often repeated, especially if it be agreeable, speedily grows into a habit.

A lady's habit, means her riding dress.

46. OPPORTUNITY

Several verbs are used with this word. An opportunity arises, happens, occurs, takes place. We give, afford, take, embrace, seize, or seize on, an opportunity; we watch an opportunity and avail ourselves of an opportunity.

> Give me an opportunity of showing what I can do.
> He afforded me an opportunity of stating my grievance.
> Being in town lately, I availed myself of the opportunity to visit the shops

47. THE WORLD

This term is often used in the sense of, people generally. So that the opinion of *the world* means the general or common opinion of men.

> His remarks were few and made only to his familiar friends; but they were such as the world might have heard with veneration.

The expression is also used in other idiomatic phrases.

> The medicine did me a world of good. (This is rather an exaggerated way of saying, a great deal of good.)
> If this story gets abroad, it will do a world of harm.
> What in the world am I to do? is a colloquial phrase expressing extreme perplexity and implies that I have no idea what I should do.
> His laugh is for all the world like Bezonji's, i.e. so much like Bezonji's as scarcely to be distinguishable from it.

To **rise in the world**, is to get into a higher or better position in life. The opposite is **come down**, or **go down, in the world**, which means, to sink in the social scale.

> By steadiness and diligence, any man may rise in the world.
> These people, to judge from their appearance and manners, have come down in the world.

48. Dead

This adjective has various idiomatic applications.

1. *Dead* means deprived of life, no longer living.

> Evidently these shrubs and trees are dead.
> He is dead to all sense of shame, i.e. no longer capable of feeling shame.
> The dead body of a man is called a corpse; the dead body of a beast is called a carcass.

The phrase *the dead* means those who have lived on the earth and have died. *A dead language* has *dead* in this sense of having been once living but not living now, as Sanskrit, Hebrew, Latin. A living language, being a spoken tongue, grows and is subject to change.

2. *Dead* means destitute of life, inanimate, never having had life: as, dead matter.

3. *Dead* also means, without motion, inert. A burden that has no springiness in it is sometimes spoken of as *a dead weight*. So *a dead lift*: that is, a thing lifted at the utmost disadvantage, as a corpse, a bag of sand. A dull heavy sound which does not reverberate is sometimes called *a dead sound*.

4. *Dead* also means unprofitable, bringing in no gain. Goods in a shop which lie on a shopkeeper's hands because no one will buy them, are sometimes described as *dead stock*. So a *dead heat* is applied to the result of a race where all are equally good and therefore no one wins.

> Once, years ago, the University boat race resulted in a dead heat.

5. *Dead* sometimes means blank, monotonous or unvaried, dull, without brightness. So in the phrases,

A dead colour, i.e. a dull colour, without any gloss.

Dead colouring is the first layer of colour that an artist puts on canvas in painting a picture.

A dead flat, or a dead level, i.e. a plain where there is no undulation to break the dull monotony of the view.

A dead wall, i.e. a wall unvaried by windows or anything else which would relieve the dull blankness.

6. *Dead* means wanting in spirit and vitality.

Faith without works is dead.—*Bible*

7. *Dead* in law means, no longer existing in the view of the law. An outlaw or banished person is said to be *dead* in the eye of the law, i.e. cut off from the rights of citizenship.

8. *Dead* in many phrases means complete, certain, having a special quality in a marked degree. We have examples of this and of other usages in the phrases below.

To be *dead against a thing* or *a person*, is to be altogether and determinedly opposed to that thing or that person.

My father is dead against my entering college.

A dead certainty, is said of a thing that is sure to take place, as in the following.

It is a dead certainty that this man will be adjudged guilty.

Dead beat, is completely beaten, utterly foiled, exhausted. Similarly in, I am *dead tired*.

A dead calm is a complete calm, unruffled calm.

At daybreak when I went on deck, it was a dead calm.

A dead sleep, is a deep, sound sleep.

Dead ahead or *dead in front*, is directly in front. The wind is dead ahead when it is blowing directly contrary to the course of a ship. A ship is said to be dead ahead of another when it is directly in front of that other.

Waiting for *dead man's shoes*, is waiting for an advantage expected to arise through the death of someone.

A dead halt, is a complete halt.

The cavalcade was brought to a dead halt by the foremost carriage breaking down.

A deadlock, is such an interlocking of things as produces entire stoppage, a complete stop caused by obstruction.

A dead loss, is a complete loss, a loss for which there is no compensation.

A dead shot. This phrase is applied to a man who certainly and usually hits the mark.

Dead silence, is complete, utter, unbroken silence.

A dead set, is a very determined onset or attack.

The dead of night; *the dead of winter*. These mean the middle of the night or the depth of winter, i.e. when night and winter may be expected to be most thorough.

> At the dead of the night a sweet vision I saw,
> And thrice ere the morning I dreamt it again.—*Campbell*

An invalid does not go visiting in the dead of winter.

A dead light is a shutter made to fit and cover a port-hole in a ship to keep out water in a storm.

Dead slow, is scarcely moving.

A dead letter does not at all mean a letter announcing someone's death. The phrase has two applications:

(1) A law which has fallen out of use and is no longer enforced, is often said to be a dead letter.

> Several enactments still on the statute book are now a dead letter.

(2) A letter which lies in the post office because the addressee cannot be found, is after a certain time called a *dead letter*, and is sent to a special department of the General Post Office to be opened and returned to the writer, or otherwise disposed of. The department of the General Post Office which deals with dead letters is called the *Dead Letter Office*.

A dead march is a well-known piece of mournful music usually played at the funeral of some distinguished person.

Dead-alive is really a compound word meaning half dead and half living.

> Go about your work vigorously and not in a dead-alive fashion.

Dead and gone. This phrase is applied to a person who died some time ago.

> The man you ask about has been dead and gone some years.

To leave a man *for dead*, is to believe that he is dead, and so believing, to leave him.

> The thieves beat him and left him for dead.
> He was left for dead on the battle-field, but he revived.

To strike a man dead, is to strike a living man and kill him with the blow.

49. GOOD

Good as an adjective has quite a variety of applications. Moreover, it is so frequently used that unless the student becomes familiar with its various shades of meaning, he will often, in using it, fall into mistakes of idiom.

1. The adjective *good* means excellent, proper, not bad: as

in the phrases, *the good old times*; *there is a good time coming*; *as good luck would have it.* Also,

> The book is printed on good paper.
> Do what seems good to you in the matter.

2.   *Good* also means kind, benevolent, friendly, favourable.

> They gave us a good reception.
> The men were very good to us.
> It was very good of you to recommend me for the post.
> Will the stationer be good enough to send me a packet of notepaper?

3.   *Good* means suitable, useful, wholesome, serviceable.

> Are all fruits good to eat?
> This man is good for a subscription of fifty pounds, i.e. you may count on his giving such a subscription.
> A good-for-nothing fellow is a useless, worthless fellow.

When one gets rid of a disagreeable person, or an unpleasant piece of business, he says it is a *good riddance*.

4.   *Good* means virtuous, pious, or tending to a virtuous or pious end.

> Be good, sweet maid, and let who will be clever.—*Kingsley*
> It is a good thing to give thanks unto the Lord.—*Bible*

5.   *Good* also means clever, dexterous, skilful.

> I am not good at making a speech.
> He is a good workman; a very good tailor.
> He is a good shot, i.e. he shoots cleverly and hits the mark.
> This fellow is a good hand at cricket and is besides a good horseman.

6.   *Good* sometimes means adequate, sufficient, valid.

> He had good cause to repent his bargain.
> I have a good mind to dismiss him, i.e. I have almost decided to do so.
> As good as dead, i.e. almost dead.
> He is good for heavy damages, i.e. he is quite able to pay a large amount as damages in a case of law.

7.   *Good* also means of considerable account, not few or small or insignificant. It has this meaning in such phrases as, *a good many*, *a good deal*, *a good way*. Also,

> I walked a good part of the way.
> He has got a good share of the property.
> There are a good many mosques in the city.

With a meaning akin to this one, *good* is in some phrases joined with another adjective intensifying its meaning. The force of *good* is then almost adverbial, and it becomes nearly equivalent to *very*, or *pretty* in the sense of *rather*. This idiomatic use of *good*, however, is limited in composition, though frequent in conversation. The following are a few examples of this usage.

A good long ride.	A good stiff breeze.
A good round sum.	A good hearty laugh.
A good sound sleep.	A good hot cup of tea.
A good sound scolding.	A good strong dose (of medicine).
A good warm cloak.	

8. *Good* also means fair, honourable, unblemished, or unimpeached. This is the meaning in such expressions as, *a good name*, *a good report*, *good repute*, *a good conscience*, i.e. one not conscious of any wrong-doing.

A good name is better than great riches.

9. *Good* also means full, complete, not deficient.

Good measure, pressed down, and running over.—*Bible*

10. *Good* in the phrase *in good earnest*, means real, serious, actual.

11. In certain idiomatic phrases, the word *good* occurs. It is used, for instance, in expressions of greeting and leave-taking, and indicates wishing well to the person addressed; as in the phrases *good morning*, *good day*, *good evening*, *good night*.

Good luck to your fishing.

For good means finally, permanently, as a fixed thing. Thackeray makes a girl home from a boarding school say, ' I've come home for good ', i.e. I have now left school and do not mean to return.

In the year 1882 she bade farewell to Indian shores for good.
He has either come home on furlough or for good.

For good and all is similar in meaning to *for good*, but is a shade more forcible as expressing greater finality. The word *all* in the phrase is equivalent to *altogether*.

He has left this town for good and all.
Say four pounds and you've got rid of him for good and all.

As good as means not less than, not falling short of; also, virtually, in effect, equally well.

I was as good as an almanac in those days.—*Lamb*
As good almost kill a man as kill a good book.—*Milton*
In the fens a mile is as good as four, i.e. it is as hard to walk one mile in the fens as to walk four miles on an ordinary road.

As good as done, means, almost accomplished or used up.

The work is as good as done.
The food in the besieged town is as good as done.

Note that while *as good as dead*, *as good as new*, mean *as good as if he were dead*, *as good as if it were new*, we must not fill up the ellipses by inserting *if he were*, *if it were*; if we fill up the ellipses we destroy the idiomatic character of the expressions. We must keep exactly to the words of the idioms.

As good as one's word is equivalent to, faithful to one's promise.

> I said I would make you a present at Christmas, and I'll be as good as my word.
> If the gentleman promised you an appointment, he will surely be as good as his word.
> If your employer said he would dismiss you, you may depend upon it he will be as good as his word.

To hold good or *stand good*, is to continue solid or fixed, to remain true after examination, to remain valid. A statement which was called in question or was supposed to be doubtful is said to *hold good* or *stand good* when it is proved to be correct. Evidence *holds good* when it is not shaken by cross-examination. A contract is said to *hold good* or *stand good* when it is legally made, i.e. in such circumstances it cannot be broken, it remains inviolable. An offer is said to *hold good* when it remains valid or continues in force.

> A corn rick has been maliciously burnt; a reward of twenty-five pounds has been offered for information that will lead to the arrest of the incendiary; and the offer will hold good (*or* stand good) for two months.

To make good is to accomplish, to establish, to supply defect, to compensate for. To make good a claim or an accusation, is to establish it beyond dispute.

> The police ran after the fellow, but he made good his escape.
> The loss is large, but the Insurance Company is bound to make it good.
> This creditor has made good his claim, and must get his money.
> My garden wall has been blown down, but the landlord will make it good, i.e. he will repair the injury or damage done.

To think good is to approve, to regard as proper or expedient.

> She thinks it good to defer her visit to us.
> He thought it good to open a school in his village.

To keep good. Fruit is said to keep good when it remains in a fresh or sound condition and does not spoil.

> Oranges if well packed should keep good during a long sea voyage.

50. HARD

Hard is used in some turns of expression in the sense of abundantly or severely.

> It froze hard last night.
> The wind blew harder than before.
> It rained so hard that I could not keep myself dry.

Hard of hearing, is rather deaf.

Hard to please, is difficult to please.

Hard times, are times of difficulty, seasons of adversity.

' He is having a hard time,' means, he is sore pressed with difficulties: he is in straits.

A hard bargain, is a bargain made rigorously and closely.

To be hard by, is to be near, to be at hand.

To follow hard upon, is to follow close behind.

To be hard up; *be hard put to*, mean, to be in extremities, to be sore pressed. These are colloquial expressions.

> I was never so hard up in my life, i.e. sore pressed for money.
> He was hard up for an excuse when he said that his aunt would not let him come.
> The men are hard put to for a living for themselves and their families.

To be hard upon, is to be severe upon.

> Do not be too hard upon your servants.

To run hard, is to run rapidly.

To try hard, is to make a strong effort.

51. HIGH

This adjective has considerable variety of application.

1. *High* means elevated, lofty, tall, raised up.

> The castle has two high towers.
> The sun is yet high, i.e. the sun is still a considerable distance from setting.
> The sun was high this morning when we started, i.e. had risen up a considerable way from the eastern horizon.

The Most High is a title applied to God, inasmuch as He is the supreme and absolute Sovereign.

2. *High* sometimes means very abstruse, difficult to comprehend.

> Wisdom is too high for a fool.—*Bible*
> Such knowledge is too wonderful for me; it is high, I cannot attain unto it.—*Bible*

3. *High* also means costly, of great price.

> You bought these articles at too high a price.
> A hundred and fifty pounds would be high for this horse.

4. *High* is used in the sense of arrogant, proud, boastful.

> He holds his head high, i.e. he has a proud look.

5. *High* also means great, distinguished, illustrious, remarkable. In this meaning it is applied to moral or intellectual eminence, or used regarding social standing or noble birth. Also, exceeding the common measure or degree, extreme.

> He is a man of high attainments.
> To get praise from this man is high honour.
> Here is a man who, though poor, claims to be of high descent.
> It is well to keep a high standard of moral excellence before men.
> The highest standard of moral excellence ever set before men is found in Jesus Christ.

A *high altar*, is the principal altar in a church.

High antiquity, is remote antiquity.

These manuscripts contain chronicles of high antiquity.

In the expressions, *high admiral*, *high bailiff*, *high steward*, *high priest*, the word *high* means principal or chief. It has the same meaning in *High Court*, *High School*.

High fare, is rich food, luxurious living.

High tea, is tea with meat or other extra dishes.

Solomon lived at ease and full of honour, wealth, high fare.—*Milton*

High living, is living on rich, luxurious food and drink

Gout is often brought on by high living.

High life, means aristocratic life, life among the upper classes.

A writer sprung from the humbler classes is almost sure to make bad blunders in attempting to depict high life.

The *high seas*, are the waters of the open ocean.

The fleet has often swept the high seas.

High pressure, is intense pressure, i.e. a pressure exceeding that of the atmosphere. A man is sometimes said to live or work at *high pressure* when he works under excitement produced by his having too much to attend to.

High tide or *high water*, is the greatest ordinary flow or elevation of the tide of the sea; also, the time at which such elevation takes place. We say *ordinary* flow, to exclude spring tides and to indicate that flow of the tide which occurs twice a day. The phrase is also used metaphorically.

What time is high water in Liverpool?

The agitation began to rise in the early part of the year and was at high tide in September last.

High water mark, is that line on the sea-shore to which the tide rises when at its highest; the limit of high water.

High noon, is full or complete noon, the time when the sun is on the meridian.

High treason, is treason committed against the sovereign or the highest authority in the state.

Yesterday I sent an officer to arrest some that were accused of high treason.

Game or venison is said to be *high* when it is strong-scented and tending to putrefaction (it is not necessarily, therefore, unfit for cooking).

Game should not be cooked before it is high.

High time. It is *high time* to do a thing, means the time for doing it is fully come.

It is high time to get up.

It is high time that class legislation should cease here and elsewhere.

It was high time that we had a readable memoir of this great statesman.

High words, are angry words used in a dispute or quarrel.

A high wind, is a boisterous wind.

A high colour. A person who has very red cheeks is said to have a high colour.

High and dry, used of a ship, means in a dry place, out of water, out of reach of the current or of the waves. So metaphorically, out of the current of events.

High and low. To search for a thing *high and low*, is to search everywhere for it. The news is interesting to *high and low*, means interesting to rich and poor.

To be high-handed, is to be arbitrary, tyrannical, overbearing, oppressive.

> Many a prince has brought himself to ruin by high-handed attempts to govern.

To be high-minded is to be of noble mind, to be magnanimous, and is opposed to *mean* or *base*.

> A high-minded man will bear adversity with patience.

High-principled and *high-toned* have this meaning of *high-minded*; and *high-spirited* is similar, with the added idea of courage.

6. *High* is used in other idiomatic phrases.

High day. The modern meaning of this is gala day, festival or holiday, as in the phrase ' high days and holidays '.

High latitudes are regions remote from the equator. Lord Dufferin yachting in the northern seas wrote a book which he called *Letters from High Latitudes*.

High Church is that section of the Church of England, in which much stress is laid on episcopal succession and the proper performance of ecclesiastical rites.

High Mass. This term belongs to the Roman Catholic Church and signifies a sung mass. It is distinguished from *Low Mass*, in which the prayers are recited without singing.

52. IDLE

1. *Idle* means unemployed, not occupied, doing nothing, not in use, not called into active service.

> I will never more endure
> To sit with idle hands at home.—*Tennyson*

Idle spear and shield.—*Milton*

Many an idle hour has he spent in my house.

2. *Idle* also means useless, unprofitable, vain, trifling.

> This custom is at best idle and may be prejudicial.
> Regrets for what might have been, are proverbially idle.
> After an idle descent on Cadiz, the Spanish expedition returned.

An idle fellow, is a lazy man, averse to employment.

53. LAME

The simple meaning of this adjective is crippled or disabled in a limb. Hence we speak of a lame arm, a lame leg, a person lame in one leg, or lame of one leg. .

> Helping, when you meet them, lame dogs over styles.—*Kingsley*

Lame, metaphorically, means imperfect, unsatisfactory. Hence Shakespeare speaks of a ' lame and impotent conclusion '. When a man gives an unsatisfactory reason for some questionable thing he has done, it is sometimes said he has given but a *lame excuse* for his conduct.

A lame duck, is a colloquial expression for a disabled or inefficient person, also a defaulter on the stock exchange.

54. POOR

This adjective is used in some peculiar ways. A *poor soil* is a sterile soil. A *poor essay* is an essay weak in thought and style, and therefore inferior. A *poor excuse* is a very insufficient, paltry, flimsy excuse. A horse or ox is said to be *poor* when lean or emaciated. When a man is sickly, he is said to be in *poor health*. *Poor* is also used as a word of pity and sympathy, or endearment.

> Poor fellow! I pitied him when I saw his wounds.
> My poor father is very ill, and I fear he will not recover.
> I have a poor opinion of this book, i.e. I think it an inferior book.
> The patient has passed a poor night, i.e. has not rested during the night.

The phrase, *the poor*, means poor people generally.

Poor spirited means cowardly. *Poor in spirit*, a Biblical phrase, means humble.

55. SORRY

Sorry is a word that has some peculiar applications. When it stands after the substantive it means *grieved* and expresses a feeling of the mind. *The fellow is sorry.* When it stands before the substantive, *sorry* means mean, worthless, contemptible. Thus a *sorry fellow*, is a worthless, good-for-nothing fellow. This latter seems to be a causative application of the word, and indicates something, the right contemplation of which is calculated to excite a feeling of sorrow. One can speak, for instance, of good fruit growing on *a sorry tree*. *A sorry excuse* is a poor, unworthy, unsatisfactory excuse; a *sorry bargain* is an unsatisfactory bargain, a bargain to be regretted. And other examples are,

> It is a sorry excuse to say that you are late because you slept so long.
> He made a sorry bargain when he agreed to give five hundred pounds for this house.
> Many a sorry marriage is made in countries where the young couple are not allowed to meet each other till the wedding day.

56. ADJECTIVES USED AS NOUNS

1. An adjective with the definite article before it, is often used to denote a class, the whole expression being treated as a plural noun.

> Blessed are the meek.—*Bible*
> The rich should pity and help the poor.
> Blessed are the pure in heart, for they shall see God.—*Bible*

2. Some adjectives have come to be used as nouns. Instead of *a nobleman* we say *a noble*; also *the nobles*. We speak also of *an imbecile*, *incurables*, *the invincibles*, etc. We say *catch cold*.

> He cannot keep this up for long, i.e. for a long time.

3. Such expressions as *the beautiful*, *the true*, *the good*, *the pure*, *the sublime*, *the coarse*, are used as abstract singular nouns. De Quincey says of Goldsmith that his feelings ' moved in the direction of the true, the natural, the sweet, the gentle '. Similarly, we speak of *the past*, *the present*, *the future*, meaning either *past time*, *present time*, *future time*, or *past events*, *present events*, *future events*. In poetical language, by *the deep* we mean *the sea*, *the ocean*.

> God knows the past, the present, and the future.
> An account of all your past will be required by God.
> There is far less disposition now to shirk the dark and disagreeable in human life, far more honesty in facing the actual and the inevitable.
> He breathed his last this morning at nine, i.e. his last breath. Thus the phrase means, *He died*.

4. Some adjectives put into the plural form become plural nouns. In conversational English, nouns are freely coined from adjectives in this way. We have examples in *goods*, *mortals*, *nobles*, *news*, *odds*, *sweets*, *greens*, *eatables*, *drinkables*, *movables*, *valuables*, *vitals*, *extras*, *worthies*, his *equals*, his *betters*, his *inferiors*. The word *belongings* denotes all the property one has, all that belongs to one.

He means to take all his movables to his new home, i.e. all his movable property.

The poor man's belongings were not a heavy burden.

The disease has fastened on his vitals, i.e. on those organs of his body which are essential to life.

Goods are any valuable things in one's possession.

When a man is convicted of treason, all his goods are confiscated to the State.

The term *goods* is very commonly applied to the commodities a shopkeeper has for sale. We often speak too of a *goods train*, i.e. a train which conveys wares that may be sold.

57. WHAT

1. *What*, when applied to persons, refers to one's calling, occupation, or profession. So that, *What is he?* means *What is his calling?*

What a man's father was, is a matter of no importance if he be honest.

2. In the introductory phrase ' I tell you what ', the word ' what ' is anticipatory and stands for the statement which follows. This phrase is used when a new thought suddenly strikes a speaker and he wishes to emphasize it.

I tell you what, the river is sure to be in flood and we shall not be able to cross.

3. ' He knows what's what ', is colloquial for ' he knows how to behave suitably in all circumstances '.

4. The expression *what with* is peculiar and means *partly with*. This phrase usually stands at the beginning of a sentence and generally speaking implies a multiplicity of things which constitute a hindrance.

What with writing letters, and lecturing, and attending to the duties of my office, I am so busy that I scarcely have time to eat.

The track, what with pack horses' feet and what with the wear and tear of five hundred years' rainfall, was a rut in which no horse could turn.

5. *What not* is sometimes used to cut short and complete an enumeration of several particulars when a full enumeration would be tedious or unimportant. It is therefore an abbreviating clause having a meaning similar to *et cetera*.

Battles, tournaments, hunts, and what not.—*De Quincey*

6. ' What of that? ' said in reply to a statement means ' What does that matter? ' Similarly, the colloquial ' So what? '

7. ' What though it be so ', means ' even if it be so '.

What though the field be lost, all is not lost.—*Milton*

This means, ' I admit that the battle waged is lost, yet our resources are not exhausted.'

58. One

While the simple meaning of ' one ' is, *a single individual, a unit,* the word has some peculiar idiomatic applications.

1. *One* is used as an indefinite pronoun or adjective. With this meaning it is frequently joined with *some, any, no, another.* In this sense, the word may have a plural form, *ones.*

> The great ones of the earth. Will some one please shut the door?
> Little children, love one another.—*Bible*
> I am the sister of one Claudio.—*Shakespeare*
> A quiet conscience makes one so serene.—*Byron*
> Send men to Joppa, and call for one Simon, i.e. a certain man called Simon.

This indefinite *one*, which has a plural, is in reality an old English noun: the numeral *one* has no plural form. The following exemplifies the numeral *one.*

> One day is with the Lord as a thousand years, and a thousand years as one day.—*Bible*

One day is also used of an indefinite time past or future.

> I met your brother one day last week.
> He will one day regret the course he is now determined to follow.

One preceded by *the* and followed by a relative is a demonstrative pronoun and stands for a definite individual.

> He is the one to whom I referred in my speech.

2. *One* is often used as a pronoun, to indicate a single individual of a kind already mentioned. When used in this way, it may have the plural form *ones.*

> The longest life, if a good one, is the best.—*Pope*
> Hand me today's newspaper; this is an old one.
> The shepherd has scores of white sheep and only three black ones.

All one, means, quite the same.

> That's all one to me. It is all one which road you take.

To be *at one*, is to agree, to be in harmony.

> Two men strove, and would not be at one again. The verb *atone* ' at one '=bring together, literally ' to make at one '.

In such sentences as,

> One wonders how he so suddenly got rich;
> One cannot but be annoyed at his impudence,

the word *one* really refers to the speaker himself. Rather than use *I*, which would look egotistic, he modestly softens it down into the indefinite *one*. So Byron's sentence quoted above.

One and all, means, all the individuals taken collectively.

> The islands one and all are subject to earthquake.
> The Russian sailors one and all were half drunk.

59. Some Negatives

In certain, notably Indian, languages, when a negative sentence is used, the word expressing the negation is commonly attached to the verb, and the nominative must be an affirmative expression; whereas in the English words, *none*, *no one*, *nobody*, *nothing*, the negative is already expressed, and the verb used with these is affirmative. In fact, *none*, *no one*, *nobody*, and *nothing* are used as nominatives, and things are predicated of them as though they denoted realities. They are also similarly used as objectives. The following expressions violate English idiom:

> There is not anybody in the house.
> Anyone does not know how the fire originated.
> He has not done anything to be ashamed of.

True, they could be

> There is nobody, *or* no one, in the house.
> No one knows how the fire originated.
> He has done nothing to be ashamed of.

The correct idiomatic usage of these words will readily appear if the student carefully considers the following.

> I care for nobody, no, not I,
>   And nobody cares for me.—*Song*
> Do nothing as if it were trifling.
> Perhaps it is safer to say nothing.
> None but the brave deserves the fair.—*Dryden*
> He went to Australia to search for gold, but found none.
> I asked the men what they wanted, but nobody made any reply.
> No one can read Charles Lamb without being charmed with his quiet humour and the beautiful simplicity of his style.
> Nothing annoyed him so much as want of gratitude on the part of those to whom he had done a favour.

60. Possessive Adjectives

There is an idiomatic use of Possessive Adjectives which may be best explained by a few examples.

> 1. Riding out one morning in September, I discovered a beautiful lake among the hills. In the end of the hot season I was back in the same district and meant to pitch my tent by the water's edge, but when I reached the place, *my* lake was gone, the hot season having dried it up.

This does not mean that the lake had come into my possession, but that on it my attention and hopes were fixed.

> 2. A professor addressing his students might say, 'Our subject today, gentlemen, is the literature of the Elizabethan period.'

By the phrase 'Our subject' he means, 'the subject to which we are to devote our attention'.

3.   We have another example in the following from an American poet.

> Who reach *their* threescore years and ten,
> As I have mine, without a sigh,
> Are either more or less than men—
> Not such am I.—*R. H. Stoddard*

Here there is a reference to ' the allotted span of life ', given by the Hebrew Psalmist in the Bible as threescore years and ten.

4.   In the following ' your ' has the sense of ' with which you are familiar '

> How long could *your* stout old oak-built man-of-war stand up against a modern ironclad?

5.   ' He missed *his* train ' means, he arrived too late to catch the train he intended to go by.

61. IT

1.   *It* as a pronoun stands for an antecedent neuter noun.

> Make me a cup of tea and bring it up here.—*Trollope*
> How much of the coarse web of existence owes its beauty to the idlest dreams with which we colour it !—*Jerrold*

2.   *It* is used to stand for a statement already made or about to be made. A succeeding clause represented by *It* is often introduced by the conjunction *that*.

> It is hard to say what should be done.
> How much cloth will it take to make me a coat?
> It is more blessed to give than to receive.—*Bible*
> It is now three months since my brother was married.
> It was very kind of you to come to see us.
> It was resolved that the meeting should close at ten o'clock.
> Depend upon it he will do what he threatens.
> You saw how well he took it when you praised his speech; here *it* stands for, your praising his speech.

If the student inverts these sentences, so as to express the same meaning while omitting the word *it*, the somewhat clumsy expressions resulting will show him how convenient is this idiomatic use of the impersonal pronoun. Here, for instance, are two of the statements inverted.

> To make me a coat, will take how much cloth?
> Since my brother was married, is now three months.

3.   *It* is used as a demonstrative before the verb *to be* followed by a noun or pronoun.

> It was the English, Kaspar cried,
> Who put the French to rout.—*Southey*

It was this boy who made the noise.
' Who was it that opened the door ? ' ' It was John.'

4. *It* is also used to represent state or condition in the most indefinite manner.

> After a voyage or two, so it befell, I was wrecked in the Wash.—*Kingsley*

5. *It* is used as an indefinite nominative for impersonal verbs denoting natural phenomena. Hence *it* is commonly used of the weather.

> It froze hard last night.
> It is a bright moonlight night.
> Is it raining?   No, it is snowing.
> It never rains but it pours.—*Proverb*
> It came on darker and darker.—*Dickens*
> If it is fine this afternoon, we shall go for a walk.

In this indefinite way, *it* is used of time as follows.

> ' What time is it ? ' ' It is half-past one.'

6. *It* is also used as an indefinite object after an intransitive verb, to represent a kind of cognate accusative.

> Let the dogs fight it out.
> Come and trip it as you go.—*Milton*
> The Lacedemonians, when their arms failed them, fought it out with their nails and teeth.
> To foot it.   To queen it.
> I will not permit him to lord it over me.
> One has to rough it in a new colony, i.e. has to put up with hardships and inconveniences.

The student will readily find other examples of idiomatic usages of this pronoun. In fact this is one of the most useful words in the language to get rid of unnecessary verbiage.

62. THERE

There is usually an adverb of place, but has also a peculiar idiomatic use. It is sometimes employed to begin sentences without any reference to place, and, when so used, is introductory, and has a kind of pronominal force: as in the following examples.

> There was not a cloud in the sky.—*Southey*
> There was a sound of revelry by night.—*Byron*
> It is evident to me that there is some mistake in this account.
> There was plenty to eat.

The excessive use of *there* in this way is to be avoided. If used too freely, it makes sentences weak and straggling.

63. Too

Too when used before an adjective commonly expresses excess beyond a certain supposed standard or limit of fitness. Thus,

> He is too proud to beg. The news is too good to be true.
> It is never too late to mend.—*Proverb*
> He knows too well how many of his own careful plans have failed, to be hard on others who have not succeeded.—*Nicoll*
> This book is too interesting to be treated with indifference, too good to be set down as bad, but also too bad for unqualified praise.

The common phrase, ' It's too bad ! ' is colloquial and expresses disapproval or indignation. Compare the modern, ' That's the limit '.

64. When and Where

A peculiar idiomatic use of these words should be noted. They are sometimes used with connective force as between sentences and are in such cases equivalent to *and then, and there*.

> I kept the horse till he was ten years old, when he became blind.
> I cast my eyes towards the summit of a rock that was not far from me, where I discovered one in the habit of a shepherd.—*Addison*

These examples show that these words *when* and *where* are sometimes used in composition like the Connective Relative.

CHAPTER IV

IDIOMATIC ADJECTIVE AND NOUN PHRASES

65. Several idiomatic phrases, each consisting of a noun and an apt appropriate adjective, are to be found in current English, many of which nevertheless are not explained even in good English dictionaries. In this chapter we propose to take up and explain some of these. Those we give, however, by no means form an exhaustive list: but they are expressive phrases in common use and should therefore be familiar to the student. We give them in the alphabetical order of the Adjectives.

And there are many short expressive Noun Phrases which require to be explained. These two sets of phrases form the subject of the next two sections.

66. PHRASES COMPOSED OF AN ADJECTIVE AND A NOUN

An able-bodied seaman is a skilled sailor, classed in the ship's records as A.B.

An absent-minded person is a person inattentive to what is going on around him at the moment.

Advanced in years, or **in life** means growing old.

Animal spirits. This expression denotes the natural cheerfulness and vivacity of healthy youth. **High spirits** is a similar expression, the opposite being **low spirits.**

Apple-pie order is perfect orderly arrangement.

An arch look is a sly, significant look.

Ardent spirits are strong alcoholic drinks, as brandy, whisky.

Armed neutrality is the condition of a neutral nation which is ready to resist by arms any aggression made against itself by either of two powers that are at war.

Argus-eyed. Argus was a fabled monster of antiquity, said to have a hundred eyes and set by Juno to watch Io, of whom she (Juno) was jealous. Hence the adjective has come to mean jealously watchful, so quick of eye that nothing can escape observation. But the word is applied in a slighting, resentful way. **Lynx-eyed** is having sight as keen as the lynx. This adjective also implies slight or resentment.

Augean stables. According to Greek mythology, Augeus, King of Elis in Greece, had a stable occupied by three thousand oxen, which had not been cleansed for thirty years. Hercules cleansed it in one day by turning two rivers through it. Hence to cleanse the Augean stables is to correct a great abuse, or to remove a nuisance or scandal which seemed irremovable.

Backstairs influence is influence exerted secretly and in a fashion not legitimate.

Bad blood is vicious temper, active enmity.

A bad time is an unfavourable, inopportune time; also, a miserable, uncomfortable time.

A bad tongue means an unhealthy tongue. **A foul tongue** is one given to uttering oaths or abuse; a sharp tongue, a sarcastic one.

To keep a civil tongue in one's head is to avoid rudeness.

A balance sheet is a summarized statement of account giving receipts and outlay in two parallel columns, and showing how the two columns agree in the total amount and what balance if any remains on either side.

Bated breath is a contracted form of **abated breath**. When a man from great anxiety or suspense or fear scarcely draws a full breath, it is said he speaks or sits with bated breath.

A bear garden is a phrase sometimes applied to a place where people are as fierce and angry in quarrelling as if they were enraged bears; a rude, turbulent assembly.

A besetting sin is a vice or sin to which a person has often yielded and into which, therefore, he readily falls: as, intemperance, laziness, passionate temper.

A man's better half is his wife. The phrase is colloquial.

One's better self: one's baser self. These mean respectively the higher part of one's nature, including conscience and good judgement; and the lower part of one's nature, including passions and appetites.

One's betters is colloquial, signifying one's superiors in rank.

The life beyond, is a term applied to the life after death, the life to which we shall pass on through death. Death is here regarded as a dark river: each person has to cross this: the life on the farther shore is **the life beyond.**

Blackmail is money extorted by threats or intimidation.

The black market is the illegal traffic in officially controlled goods.

A black sheep is a phrase used metaphorically for one who has a bad reputation in a company of people. Blackness in sheep is considered a defect or fault. The proverbial ' The black sheep of the family ' implies this idea.

Blank verse is poetry in which the lines do not end in rhyming syllables.

A blind alley is a narrow street or lane closed at one end.

A blood horse is a thoroughbred.

Blue blood is noble blood. Formerly it was held that the blood of a nobleman was blue as distinct from the red blood of the common people.

Blue Book is the name given to British official Parliamentary reports, so called because they are bound in blue covers.

The Blue Coat School is Christ's Hospital, a large public school formerly in, now near London. It is so called because the boys attending it wear a uniform with a blue coat.

Blue devils is a term given colloquially to depressed feelings (sometimes shortened to ' the blues '); also to *delirium tremens*.

Blue jackets (usually spelt as one word) are sailors of the British Navy. They wear jackets of blue serge.

The Blue Ribbon is a broad dark blue ribbon worn only by members of the Order of the Garter; hence, a member of this Order. A secondary meaning is, any token which marks the attainment of an object of high ambitious aims.

A blue stocking is a term applied colloquially to a literary lady. It was applied originally to a literary society comprising both men and women, one prominent leading man of whom wore blue stockings.

Board wages. Servants are often ' boarded ', that is, are fed in their master's house. When it is not so, the servants get higher wages and provide food for themselves. Such wages are called **board wages.**

Bodily fear is fear that hurt will come to one's person.

> He heard a noise in his house last night, but was in such bodily fear that he neither spoke nor moved.

The body politic is the collective body of a nation as politically organized, or as exercising political functions.

Bolt upright is perfectly upright.

> Awakened by the noise of robbers in the house, he sat bolt upright and called out ' Who's there? '

A born sailor, a born poet is one who seems naturally gifted with the qualities required for doing his work well.

A bosom friend is an intimate, trusted friend, one in whom you fully confide. **Fast friends** are friends who are firm and steadfast in their friendship, friends not easily alienated from one another. The term **close friends** is used with much the same meaning.

Boxing Day: see under Christmas box.

Boxing gloves are padded gloves used to cover the hands in boxing.

A brass farthing is a worthless thing.

Broad daylight is open, full daylight.

Broken English is imperfect English, such as a foreigner not well up in the language might use. The broken English the Chinese use is commonly called **pidgin** or **pigeon English.**

A brown study is a reverie.

> I startled him from his brown study.

The burial service is a religious service performed at the burial of the dead.

A burning question is a matter in dispute which urgently presses for settlement.

A cab stand is a place in a public street where cabmen and cabs (now usually taxi-cabs) stand waiting to be hired.

A capital crime is a crime legally punishable with death.

Capital punishment is the punishment of death legally inflicted. ' Capital ' is derived from Latin *caput*, the head.

The capital (town) is the head town of the country.

A capital sentence is one judicially pronouncing death upon a man as the punishment due to his crime.

A capital idea is an excellent, first-rate one.

The cardinal points are the four points of the horizon known as North, South, East, and West.

A carriage and pair is a carriage drawn by a pair of horses. So a **coach and four.**

The carrying trade is the trade which consists in carrying articles of commerce by sea from one country to another.

Cast iron is iron direct from the smelting furnace. Metaphorically it means inflexible: as, A man of cast iron will.

Casting vote. When the chairman of a meeting puts a question to the vote and the votes for and against the question are equal, he by giving a vote decides the matter. His vote given in these circumstances is called the casting vote.

A chicken-hearted fellow is a timid, cowardly fellow. The adjective **chicken-hearted** is used contemptuously.

The chief mourner is the nearest relative of a deceased person present at the funeral.

The Christian era is the period of time which dates from the birth of Christ.

The Christian name of a person is the name given in baptism as distinguished from the **surname** or family name. In the name ' Isaac Newton ', ' Isaac ' is the Christian name. The Christian name is applicable to the one person only; the surname, as *Newton*, belongs to all members of the same family. Sometimes there are two or more Christian names: as in William Ewart Gladstone, John Stuart Mill, the last name is the surname and the others compose the Christian name.

A **Christmas box** is a present of any kind made at Christmas. It may be money or any other article, and is not necessarily enclosed in a box. A Christmas box is usually given on the day after Christmas, that is, on the twenty-sixth of December, and hence that day is called **Boxing Day**.

Christmas Eve is the evening or day before Christmas, i.e. the twenty-fourth of December. So **New Year's Eve** is the last day of the dying year. Compare the phrase **to be on the eve of** doing a thing, i.e. to be on the verge of doing it.

A **Christmas tree** is a fir tree cut and decorated at Christmas with lights and toys at a children's party.

Circumstantial evidence. A murderer is sometimes convicted and adjudged guilty on circumstantial evidence, i.e. evidence which when sifted and put together leaves no room for doubt as to his guilt, even though no person saw him do the fatal deed. The testimony of an eye-witness would be **direct evidence.**

> There was no direct evidence in the case and the circumstantial evidence was not sufficient to attach guilt to him.

A **close-fisted man** is a stingy, niggardly, penurious man; a miser; close-fisted is used contemptuously. Contrast ' open-handed '.

A **close shave** is colloquially used, meaning, almost an accident.

A **close vote.** When votes are counted and found to be nearly equal, for and against, it is said there has been a close vote.

Closing hours. A shopkeeper's ' hour of closing ' would mean the hour at which he closes his shop any day. This term is sometimes applied to the last hours of a man's life on earth, the hours that close his life.

A **cold-blooded murder** is an unprovoked murder, a murder done deliberately without any cause to excite personal anger, hatred, or revenge; or done deliberately after passion has had time to cool down. Such a murder is often said to be committed in **cold blood.**

> Cold-blooded murders are occasionally committed for the sake of a paltry gain.

Cold comfort is something offered as comfort which instead of really soothing and consoling the sufferer is calculated only to increase the pain or produce irritation. The offer may be made with a kind intention, but in ignorance of what would suit the case, or it may be made with a secret wicked wish to vex and irritate the sufferer further.

> It is cold comfort to a man in deep affliction to tell him that it is his fate to suffer and that what can't be cured must be endured.

To have **cold feet** is to feel frightened.

To give one the **cold shoulder** is to show a person distaste for his company.

Cold war stands for unfriendly relations between countries, as distinguished from ' open ' or ' a shooting ' war.

A **cold manner** is behaviour wanting in ardour or warmth of kindliness, a manner without any enthusiasm.

A **highly coloured statement** or **story** is a statement or story set forth in very exaggerated terms so as vividly to strike the imagination.

Commanding presence. A man of impressive personal appearance is said to have a commanding presence.

A **commanding view** is a view from an elevated position, as a hilltop or tower, which gives a wide range of vision.

A **confirmed bachelor** is a man who has made up his mind never to marry.

A **cool head.** One whose nature is not easily excited is sometimes spoken of as having a cool head. A judge, for instance, needs to have a cool head, i.e. calm judgement.

A **cool** or **cold reception** is a reception in which no warmth of kindliness is shown by the host to the guest, a reception wanting in cordiality. Just as **cold** indicates greater intensity than **cool**, so a **cold reception** shows even less ardour and warmth of friendship than a **cool reception**. The opposite to both is a **warm** or a **hearty reception**. (A **hot reception** would be a hostile one.)

The delegates met with a cool reception.

A **corrupt passage** in a manuscript is a passage in which the words have been so carelessly written that it is impossible to decide what precisely the author wrote.

A **country dance** is a dance in which the partners are ranged opposite to each other in lines.

A **county town** is the chief town of a county.

Creature comforts are those things which minister to our bodily comfort and happiness.

Crocodile tears. Old travellers tell, though it is now known to be a fiction, that the crocodile sheds tears over its prey, as if the reptile wept for the victim it was going to destroy. Hence **crocodile tears** means affected, hypocritical tears; pretended sorrow.

Cross examination is examination of a witness in a court of justice by a lawyer opposing the side which brought forward the witness.

A **crying shame** or a **burning shame** is a phrase applied to something notoriously shameful.

A **curtain lecture** is a scolding reproof given by a wife to her husband in the privacy of the bedroom.

The Dark Ages is the term applied to a period of about a thousand years when learning was at a very low ebb in Europe say from the fifth century A.D. to the fifteenth.

Deathbed repentance is repentance professed by a person who believes he is about to die.

Delirium tremens is a terrifying disease brought on by the habit of excessive drinking. The words are Latin and mean ' trembling madness '.

A diamond field is a region in which diamonds may be dug up.

A diamond ring is a ring set with diamonds.

A diamond wedding. See under ' A golden wedding '.

Direct taxation. A tax is called direct when it is assessed upon the person who has to bear the burden of it, as income tax. A tax on an article of consumption, as salt, is called an **indirect tax**, because, though paid by the producer in the first instance, it really falls on the consumer.

A dizzy height is a very great height, to look down from which is enough to make one dizzy.

A dog cart is a light carriage with two seats back to back.

A dog-eared book is a book where the corners of the leaves have been turned down to mark particular pages.

A dog-in-the-manger policy. A churlish man is said to follow such a policy when he cannot himself use what another wants, and yet will not let that other have it. The allusion is to the fable of the dog who made his bed in a manger of hay, and would not let the ox come near to eat the hay.

The dog star is the star Sirius, the largest of the fixed stars. It is in the constellation Canis Major. The days when Sirius rises and sets, the hottest part of the year, are called the **dog days.**

A double-minded man is a man whose mind wavers between two or more courses of action, one whose intention is fickle and easily changed.

A down train is a train which starts from the principal terminus of the railway. A train going towards that terminus is called an **up train**.

A drawing-board is a board on which a person places his paper or canvas when drawing. So a **drawing-pencil**, a **drawing-pen** means a pen or pencil used to draw with. A **drawing-pin** is used to fasten paper to board.

A drawing-room. The word drawing is a shortened form of **withdrawing**. The **drawing-room** is the withdrawing room, the room to which company withdraws from the dining room. It also means generally a room used for the reception of company. The phrase secondarily means a company assembled in such a room.

The Queen held a drawing-room last Tuesday.

A **drawn game, a drawn battle** is a game or a battle from which both parties withdraw without either having won the victory: a game or battle equally contested.

Drinking water is water used for drinking purposes.

> These people get their bath water from the river and their drinking water from a large well outside the town.

A **drunken quarrel** or **brawl** is a quarrel or brawl between drunken people.

Dutch courage is courage excited by intoxicating liquor.

One's **dying day** or **dying hour** is the day or hour of one's death.

A **dying prayer** is the prayer uttered by a person about to die.

An early grave. To come to an early grave means to die prematurely.

Earth (or, land) **hunger** is covetous desire to possess territory.

Elbow room is opportunity for freedom of action.

> Only give him elbow room and he will succeed.

The **Emerald Isle** is a poetical name sometimes given to Ireland, because of the peculiar bright green of its pastures.

Engaging manners mean attractive manners, manners that draw the admiration of other people. The phrases **an engaging manner, an engaging address,** have similar meaning.

The **Eternal City** is a term sometimes applied to Rome. The ancient Romans believed that the gods had given them an empire that would have no end.

Extreme unction is a rite of the Roman Catholic Church in which a dying person is anointed with sacred oil by a priest.

A **Fabian policy.** Fabianus was a Roman general who, in his military operations against Hannibal, would not risk a battle in the open field, but harassed the enemy by ambuscades and in other ways. This method of campaigning earned for him the title of the Delayer. Hence a Fabian policy is a dilatory policy. The ' Fabian Society ' of socialists also seek their ends by slow and constitutional, rather than revolutionary, means.

A **fair copy** is a neat legible copy. It is commonly made from a **rough copy** or first copy.

A **fair essay** is an essay moderately good, not above mediocrity, not good enough to be plainly called **a good essay.**

One's **fair fame** is one's good name, or unblemished reputation.

A **fair hand** is writing which is easily read.

A **fair mark** is a target free from obstacles, unobscured.

Fair play and **foul play** are opposites. In the former there is no cheating or underhand play; in the latter there is. **Fair means** and **foul means** are also opposites.

Fair promise is reasonable ground for favourable expectation.

> These fields give fair promise of a good harvest.

The fair sex or **the fair**, is an old-fashioned name for women generally. Men were **the sterner sex**. **Woman** was also sometimes described as **the weaker vessel**.

Fair weather is cloudless, dry weather.

A fair weather friend is one who deserts you in difficulties.

A fair weather sailor is one who has never encountered a storm.

A fair wind is a favourable, propitious wind.

Fair words mean pleasing, courteous words.

A falling market. When prices are declining, there is said to be a falling market. Thus, if the price of cotton is getting lower, cotton dealers often hold over their stock rather than sell in a falling market.

Family likeness is similarity of features of the face, such as is often observed in persons of the same family.

A family tree is a chart showing the genealogy of a family.

A fancy price is an unreasonably high price put upon an article.

Fast colours are colours which do not fade or wash out.

Fast living is living luxuriously, dissipation, devotion to pleasure.

A fast man is an extravagant man; a spendthrift.

A fasting man is a man voluntarily abstaining from food.

A fatal blow is a blow causing death.

A fatigue party is a military term applied to a body of soldiers told off to do some duty in which they have no need to use arms.

Fellow citizens are citizens of the same city. So, **fellow townsmen**, etc.

A fellow creature is another human being.

Fellow feeling is sympathy.

Fellow labourers are persons working at the same work or in the same cause. **School fellows** are pupils attending the same school.

A fencing master is a master who teaches the art of fencing.

A field piece is a cannon.

The fine arts are the arts which depend mainly on the play of a refined imagination, as music, painting, sculpture, poetry, architecture. 'Applied arts' are those used in industry.

The fixed stars are those which maintain unchanged their relative positions in the sky. **The planets** seem to move among the fixed stars. The word **planet** means 'wanderer', and it is because of this habit of the planets that the fixed stars are so called.

A flowery style of writing is a style into which figurative language is rather freely introduced.

A flowing bowl or **cup**. Here **flowing** is a shortened form of **overflowing**, and therefore means copious, abundant.

A flowing mantle or **robe** is a mantle or robe that hangs loose about the person.

Flowing periods. This expression is applied to highly finished composition in which the rounded, polished sentences glide on or flow on pleasingly to the ear. **Period** in this expression means a well-rounded, vigorous sentence, as contrasted with a straggling, ill-constructed one. A **period** can also mean a full stop.

A **fly leaf** is a blank leaf at the beginning or end of a book.

A **fog horn** is a horn sounded in a fog to indicate that there is danger to any ship or train coming towards the place where the horn is sounded. It is commonly sounded on board ships in a fog to warn other ships off lest there be a collision; and at some parts of the sea coast, where fogs are frequent, there are fog horns at light houses and on rocks.

Folk lore means the traditional beliefs of a people.

A **forced march** is the march of any army or a detachment at its most rapid speed.

A **foregone conclusion** is an obvious one, resolved on beforehand, or determined before argument or investigation.

A **forlorn hope** is a desperate enterprise of which there is no reasonable probability that it will succeed. In military language, a forlorn hope is a body of soldiers told off to lead in an assault which is attended with great peril.

Forty winks is colloquial for a short sleep or nap taken during the day.

A **free lance.** The term was originally applied to a mercenary soldier, i.e. one who fought under any leader who hired him and not from love of country. Now used of a politician unattached to any party, or of a journalist not paid by any one paper.

A **free port** is a port where customs are not levied on imported articles of commerce.

Free trade is trade not interfered with by the imposition of customs or taxes.

French leave is absence without permission, or going off without intimation.

A **freshwater sailor** is a sailor who has made all his voyages in fresh water, i.e. in rivers or freshwater lakes, and has not been on a voyage on the open ocean. Hence the phrase has come to be applied to one who is a novice, one who is raw and unskilled at anything.

A **fruit stand** is a stall on which fruit is exposed for sale or exhibition.

Fugitive compositions are essays or articles in a newspaper or a magazine that are for the day and therefore soon pass from notice.

A **gala day** is a day of gaiety and festivity, a happy holiday.

A **gaming table** is a table used for purposes of gambling.

A **garbled quotation** is a mutilated extract from an author, an extract which perverts the author's meaning by reason of the omission made. So a **garbled statement** is a statement which professes to reproduce another person's words and yet misrepresents his meaning.

The George Cross is a decoration for bravery, instituted in 1940.

A going concern is a business in active operation.

The Golden Age is the primitive period of the human race, supposed to be characterized by purity and simplicity of manners and enjoyments; any period of brightness and prosperity.

A golden mean is a middle course or position between two extremes.

Golden opinions are very favourable opinions.

A golden opportunity is a highly favourable opportunity.

The golden rule is that which Jesus Christ gave to men, ' Do unto others as you would wish them to do to you ' (Matt. vii. 12).

A golden wedding; a silver wedding; a diamond wedding. When a husband and wife have lived together for twenty-five years, they hold festivities to celebrate their silver wedding on the twenty-fifth anniversary of their marriage day; in a similar way they celebrate their golden wedding on the fiftieth anniversary; and their diamond wedding on the sixtieth anniversary.

A good address is a polite and pleasant manner in approaching a person. Also, a house in a fashionable district.

Good breeding is polite manners formed by a good education.

Good cheer is applied to provisions for a feast.

A good deal: a great deal are phrases of frequent occurrence and generally mean, a considerable amount, much.

> This cost me a good deal of time and labour.—*Defoe*
> For a week past we have had a great deal of rain.—*Swift*

A deal in these phrases originally meant what a player received as his share when cards were distributed for a game. A ' square ' or ' raw ' deal mean, respectively, fair or unfair treatment.

Good Friday is the Friday before Easter Sunday.

To get into one's **good graces** is to obtain his favour or friendship.

A good hand at a thing is a person clever in doing that thing.

To write **a good hand** is to write in clear, legible penmanship.

Good humour is a cheerful state of mind.

Good land is fertile land.

Good manners is propriety of behaviour.

Good nature is natural kindness of disposition.

Good offices. To ask for a man's good offices is to solicit his intervention or recommendation.

A good Samaritan is one who befriends a stranger or friendless person in difficulties. The phrase is derived from the parable of the Good Samaritan. (See Appendix.)

Good sense is soundness of judgement.

Good society is a term descriptive of people considered to be polite and in good social position.

> We want to get into good society, not that we may have it, but that we may be seen in it.—*Ruskin*

Good spirits mean a cheerful and even hilarious state of mind.

A **gratuitous insult** is an insult not provoked, not called for by the circumstances, not deserved. The phrase is very condemnatory.

A **great gun**, or, more usually, **a big gun**, is a colloquial, slangish expression for a man of note, particularly a preacher or lecturer.

The great unwashed means the great mass of people

Greek fire is a kind of destructive combustible that burns under water, first used by the Greeks in war against the Turks.

The Greek Calends or **Kalends.** The calends was the Roman name for the first day of the month. There was no such term as the Calends in use among the Greeks; and hence at or on the Greek Calends came to be among the Romans a euphemism for **never**, a time that never would come. Hence, to pay a debt or do anything at the Greek Calends meant never to pay it or do it at all.

The green-eyed monster is jealousy.

A **greengrocer** is a dealer in vegetables.

A **greenhorn** is colloquial for a raw, inexperienced person.

A **green old age.** When an old man is cheerful, fresh, vigorous, undecayed, and has not grown out of sympathy with young people, he is said to enjoy a green old age.

A **green-room** is a room for actors off the stage.

A **ground swell** is a rough sea near the shore or in shallow water.

The Gulf Stream is a warm current in the ocean running from the Gulf of Mexico along the eastern coast of the United States and across the Atlantic towards Europe.

A **hair's-breadth escape** is an escape when *almost* overtaken by injury or disaster.

Half-hearted is having no enthusiasm for the business in hand.

Half mast. A flag is hung at half the height of a mast or flagstaff in sign of mourning.

Half pay is the pay an officer sometimes receives when not on active duty.

Hall mark is the official stamp of the Goldsmiths' Company of London or of other offices which test precious metals. It is affixed to gold and silver articles, to show their purity. Metaphorically it indicates genuine excellence.

The happy medium, or **mean**, is the middle course which avoids two inconvenient extremes.

A **happy expression** is an apt and pleasing one.

A happy suggestion is a clever, suitable suggestion, which shows the way out of embarrassment, and therefore produces a happy feeling.

Hard-boiled is used metaphorically to mean callous.

A hard drinker is one given to intemperance.

Hard fare is food coarse and insufficient in quantity.

Hard lines means a hard lot, a position or lot in which one has to endure hardships.

A hard saying is a saying difficult to understand, or a precept difficult to obey.

A haunted house is a house which superstitious people suppose to be frequented by a ghost.

A henpecked husband is a man habitually snubbed by his wife.

A herculean task is a work requiring very great effort for its accomplishment, a work which only a Hercules could perform.

A high flier is one who is extravagant in pretensions or manners. In Greek mythology, Icarus, flying from Crete with the aid of wax wings invented by his father, Dædalus, in his pride soared so high that the sun melted his wings and he fell into the sea and was drowned.

A high-flown sentiment is an extravagant sentiment.

A high-flown style is a pretentious style.

The Holy Scriptures. This name or epithet is applied to the sacred books of the Old and New Testaments, which make up the Bible. The term **scriptures** literally means **writings**; and the adjective **holy** is applied to these writings because they were inspired by the Holy Spirit of God, were written by holy men, and tend to promote holy living in those persons who accept and obey their teaching.

An honest penny is a small sum of money honestly earned.

The student turns an honest penny by delivering bread early every morning.

Hush money is a bribe paid to secure silence; money paid to prevail on someone to keep back information and to prevent a disclosure of unpleasant or compromising facts.

An idle or an **empty compliment** is a compliment which is meant to be hollow and without heartiness or sincerity. **Hollow compliment** means the same thing.

Indian file is one after another. **File** here means a row of men ranged after one another, and **Indian** here means North American Indian. **Indian summer** is another American expression for the spell of fine weather which occurs there in late autumn.

The iron age of the world is a supposed period in the past when men were harsh and rude in their intercourse; when there was little kindness of dealing between man and man.

An iron-bound coast is a rocky precipitous coast.

An iron hand is a harsh, severe hand; a tyrannical hand.

An iron will is a will not easily bent, an inflexible will, indomitable determination.

> Napoleon conquered by the force of an iron will.

A Jack Tar is a sailor.

A jail bird is a notorious offender who has often been in jail for his crimes.

A jaundiced eye is a prejudiced eye. A man is said to look at things with a jaundiced eye when he is determined to see only faults. The root of the prejudice is commonly either jealousy or hatred.

A knowing look is a significant look, indicating that the person looking knows more of a matter spoken of than is openly expressed.

A laconic speech is a short pithy speech; a bald statement of fact without any of the embellishments of oratory. Such speech the Spartan warriors, who despised oratory, were wont to indulge in; and as Sparta was the capital city of that province of Greece called Laconia, any abrupt, bald, pithy speech came to be called a laconic speech.

The Last Judgement is the name given to the final judgement of God at the end of the world.

The late Mr Brown, means, Mr Brown who has recently died. The **late** Governor of Madras is the gentleman who recently was governor, but has now vacated that office.

Laughing gas. The gas known as nitrous oxide is called laughing gas, because when inhaled it produces exhilaration and laughter.

Laughing jackass is the name of a bird, also known as the Australian kingfisher.

A laughing-stock is an object of ridicule, a butt for amusement.

> He talked nonsense and made himself the laughing-stock of his hearers.
> —*Macaulay*

A lay figure is a figure shaped like the human body which an artist drapes so as to have a model for drapery folds.

A leading question is a question so put to a witness as to suggest to him the answer which he is desired to give.

A leap year is a year of three hundred and sixty-six days. It comes every fourth year and in that year February has twenty-nine days.

Learned leisure is leisure devoted to the pursuits of learning.

The left bank of a river is the side to the left hand as you go *down* the river.

A left-handed compliment is one of doubtful sincerity, or ambiguous meaning.

Legal tender is coin or Government paper money which the law authorizes to be tendered in payment of debts.

Letters patent means an official warrant granting to a person the sole right to do some specified act, or enjoy some specified privilege. The words in this expression must not be reversed.

A **light-fingered person** is one given to pilfering, clever in small thefts. Thieves are sometimes called the **light-fingered gentry**.

Light literature or **light reading** is novels, tales, books, etc., that do not require much study to understand.

A **light sleeper** is a person easily awakened from sleep. The opposite is **a heavy sleeper**.

Live stock, the domestic animals kept on a farm, sheep, horses, etc.

Living rock is rock which has never been quarried, rock still in its original bed.

Lofty rooms are rooms that have a high ceiling, *not* rooms in the upper storey of a house.

Long clothes are clothes worn by an infant child.

One's long home or **last home** is a poetic term for the grave.

The long last sleep is applied to death.

Long-winded is tedious in speech or argument.

Low diet is a diet of simple food suited to a weak stomach.

Lynch law. A farmer named Lynch, of Virginia, in the United States of America, once punished a criminal without having him legally tried. He took the law into his own hands and was accuser, judge, jury, and executioner all in one. From his name came the term **lynch law**, which denotes the practice of punishing men for crimes where the punishment is inflicted by unauthorized persons and without judicial trial. **Mob law** denotes the same course when carried out by a mob.

Maiden name. A woman's maiden name is the surname she bore before she was married. For instance, Mary Smith is married to John Brown. Henceforth she drops her own surname and takes that of her husband and writes her name Mary Brown. This is the custom in regard to English names. And when anyone asks what Mrs Brown's maiden name was, the answer is, Smith.

A **maiden speech** is the first speech of a new member in a public body, as in a Town Council, or in Parliament. When a man in such circumstances makes his first speech, he is sometimes said to make his **début**. (This is a French word usually applied to the first appearance in society or on the stage.)

The main chance is the chief or principal opportunity. But the phrase is restricted to the opportunity of getting or making money. ' He has an eye to the main chance ', is said of a man who is very sharp and keen in his business transactions.

A **marriage portion** is a bride's dowry.

A mealy-mouthed fellow is a fellow so timid and sneaking that he is afraid to tell the truth in plain language, but speaks with feigned delicacy of speech. Tennyson speaks of one being ' nursed by mealy-mouthed philanthropies '.

The mercantile marine is a collective phrase, signifying all the ships engaged in commercial pursuits.

Merchant princes. Very rich merchants are sometimes so called.

Middle age is that period in a man's life when he is between about forty and sixty years of age.

The Middle Ages (note capital letters), the period extending from the decline of the Roman Empire to the revival of learning in Europe, say from the eighth to the fifteenth century A.D.

The Milky Way is a whitish belt of stars in the heavens. It is known in India as the heavenly Ganges.

A moral certainty is said of an event so likely to take place that its occurrence may be regarded as certain.

> This man lives so extravagantly that, if he does not soon rein in, his bankruptcy is a moral certainty.

Mother wit is natural shrewdness or sagacity.

Mountain dew is genuine Scotch whisky, so called from being stealthily distilled among the mountains of Scotland.

The naked eye is the eye unaided by any kind of instrument.

> Can anyone look on the noonday sun with naked eye?

A naked sword is a sword unsheathed.

A narrow escape is an escape effected at great risk, an escape involving exposure to serious danger.

Natural religion is knowledge of God derived from studying nature. It is commonly contrasted with **revealed religion** which is knowledge of God revealed to men.

The New World is the American Continent. It is contrasted with the Old World, that is, the Eastern Hemisphere.

The next world is the life after death.

A nine days' wonder is an unexpected occurrence which creates great interest for a short while and then drops out of notice.

An oily tongue is a flattering tongue, a tongue that glibly uses honeyed words of flattery. A person who uses soft, flattering language is sometimes said to have a **smooth tongue**.

An old maid is a woman who has never been married and is no longer young.

A one-sided statement or **view** is a statement or view which gives only one side of a case and is therefore only a partial statement.

Open country is a district of country free of trees where the view is undisturbed. Hence we also speak of **an open view**.

Open day is full, clear, diffused daylight, as distinguished from twilight. Hence a thing done publicly and without any secrecy, or attempt at concealment, is often said to be done in open day. Cf., too, the phrase: ' His mind is an open book.'

An open-handed man is a man generous with his money.

An open harbour is a harbour to which there is easy access.

An open-hearted man is a sincere frank man, not sly or cunning.

An open mind is a mind not yet made up. A man is said to have an open mind about a thing when he is waiting for further light before forming a definite opinion regarding it.

An open question is a matter for discussion and not yet decided.

An open secret is a secret that has oozed out and become known.

An open verdict is a verdict given when the guilt of the accused is left undetermined through lack of evidence. It is also applied to a verdict given in a case where it cannot be decided whether or not a crime has been committed. For instance, a man is found drowned and an inquest is held; but there is no evidence to show how the man got into the water, whether he fell in accidentally, or committed suicide in this way, or was pushed in by someone, and so the jury return an open verdict, and say, ' Found drowned '.

An opening speech is the first speech at a meeting. It is usually given by the chairman and is often prefatory to the principal speech given at the meeting.

Original sin is the innate depravity or proneness to evil which is in every man's heart.

A packed jury is one of men not unprejudiced.

Palmy days are prosperous times.

A paper knife is a blunt knife for cutting folded paper.

Parallel passages are passages in writings or books which closely resemble one another in thought and language.

Party spirit is enthusiasm common to a party of persons and binding them together; devotion to one's own party.

A pass word is a word privately agreed on beforehand to be given as a sign before one is allowed to pass.

The passing bell is a bell tolled at the hour of death. In superstitious times a bell was used to frighten away evil spirits from the human spirit as it was departing from the body.

Passing strange. The word **passing** here is equivalent to surpassing, and the phrase means, exceedingly strange. But the brief, terse, idiomatic form of the phrase must not be departed from. Similarly we have **passing fair**.

This news you have heard is passing strange.

A patron saint is a saint supposed to have a particular country or city or person under his or her especial guardianship. Thus St

George is the patron saint of England, St Andrew of Scotland, St Patrick of Ireland.

A **penny-a-liner** is a literary drudge or hack who writes for poor remuneration.

A **pious fraud** is a deception carried out under the plea of religion. It is justly regarded as doubly wicked because perpetrated in a holy name or cause.

Piping hot is quite hot, at great heat.

Plain sailing means generally, advancing without encountering obstacles or difficulties.

> Men do not find it all plain sailing when they settle down in a new country.

Poet Laureate is the name given to the poet chosen by the English sovereign and expected to write poems on great national occasions. The position is counted one of great honour and is commonly held for life. A small salary is attached to it.

Point blank is directly, out of hand. The metaphor is from the idea of a gun fired at short range.

> He gave a point blank refusal, i.e. he refused definitely and immediately.

A **practical joke** is a trick played upon a person by which it is sought to put him into a ridiculous position or show him in a ridiculous light. A practical joker sometimes gives grave offence and brings himself into serious trouble.

> Three men, as a practical joke, recently ducked a fourth in a mill pond; but unhappily the poor fellow was drowned in the operation. The three men were arrested.

The present day is a phrase applied to our own times as distinguished from former or future times.

A **private soldier**, or a **private** is one serving in the lowest rank of the army.

A **promising youth** is a young man whose character and conduct give reasonable ground for hope that he will yet become distinguished. It is in this sense of the word that Washington Irving uses **promise** in the following.

> My native country was full of youthful promise.

Proud flesh is flesh which grows as an excrescence in a wound or sore.

A **public house** is a house licensed for the retail sale of alcoholic liquors.

Qualified praise is restricted, modified praise. To say of a picture that it would look well if certain other pictures were not near it, is to give it qualified praise. The term **unqualified praise** is also found.

> This book is too interesting to be treated with indifference, too good to be set down as bad, and also too bad for unqualified praise.

A queer fish is a colloquialism for an eccentric person.

A quixotic project is a project as foolish and extravagantly romantic as those ascribed to Don Quixote. Don Quixote, the hero of a celebrated romance by the Spanish writer, Cervantes, is represented as engaging in all sorts of ridiculous and extravagantly romantic feats of gallantry.

A racy style is a highly characteristic or original style.

A rainy day in its metaphorical meaning is a time of adversity. A prudent man does not spend all he earns, but lays up something for a rainy day.

A ragged school was a free school for very poor children.

A random shot is a shot which is not aimed at any particular object, but which nevertheless strikes something. The phrase is used both literally and metaphorically.

> A man walking along the road was accidentally killed by a random shot fired by some sportsman.
> A student at an examination in attempting to answer a question he is not sure of, is sometimes said to take a random shot at the question; by chance he *may* hit the answer, but most probably he will not.

A random statement is a statement made without due consideration, a chance guess. It is generally implied by the phrase that the guess is not correct, or that the statement is far from the truth.

Raw material is material in the natural state to be used up in manufacture, material not yet worked upon by art. Hence raw cotton or raw silk is cotton or silk not yet spun or twisted.

> Bombay exports large quantities of raw cotton.

Raw recruits are men enlisted but not yet drilled to be soldiers.

Raw spirits are strong drink, e.g. brandy, undiluted with water.

Ready money is cash in hand, money available wherewith to make immediate payments.

A ready pen. A man who composes and writes quickly and easily, is said to have **a ready pen**, or to be **a ready writer**.

Real estate or **real property** is property in land or houses. All other articles of property are called **personal property**, as money, books, jewels.

A red letter day is an auspicious, fortunate day; so called because in the old Christian calendars the holy days or saints' days were marked with red letters, and the holy days were festival days.

Red tape. Official documents are generally tied with red tape, and so the phrase has come to mean excessive official formality.

A regiment nine hundred strong is a regiment having nine hundred soldiers.

The religious world is a phrase meaning all religious people.

A restless night. When a sick person cannot sleep but tosses uneasily on his bed at night, he is said to pass a restless night, i.e. a night giving him no rest.

A riding horse is a horse one keeps for exercise in riding.

A riding whip is a whip which one uses when riding.

The right bank of a river is the bank to the right hand as you go *down* the river.

A right hand man is one's chief helper or agent, a man whose active service one cannot do without.

The rising generation is that set or generation of young people who have not yet attained to manhood and womanhood, on whose shoulders will soon fall the burden of the world's work.

A river basin is a valley or tract of country through which a river flows and which it drains.

A river bed is the bottom of a river.

A rough guess is a guess made without careful calculation, one only approximately correct.

A round dozen is a full dozen. The term would be used when a dozen would be beyond expectation.

This man has a round dozen of children.

A round robin is a petition or declaration to which men attach their signatures in a circle so that it may not be known who of them is the leader.

The medical men signed a round robin unanimously agreeing upon the terms they would charge.

The ruling passion is the passion or motive which dominates a person's life, as the love of money, desire for popularity.

A saving clause is a parenthetical sentence which makes a reservation. For instance, Government, in granting someone a tract of land, might reserve the right to search for minerals. The clause in the deed of grant which specifically reserved this right would be the saving clause.

Scaling ladders are ladders by which soldiers, assaulting a fort, used to mount the walls.

Scot free is, exempt from payment, untaxed; and hence, unhurt, safe, without molestation. **Scot** formerly was the name of a tax or assessment. Hence **scot free** is literally, free from the scot or tax.

A screw loose is a colloquial expression, meaning that there is something wrong, usually *mentally* wrong.

Seasoned food is food spiced to render it more palatable.

Seasoned timber is timber so thoroughly dried that all the sap has gone out of it.

A settled conviction is a fixed permanent impression or belief, a conviction arrived at after mature reflection and now an abiding one.

Settled weather is clear, calm weather, weather free from storm for a considerable time. **Wet weather** is rainy weather.

Sharp practice is a recognized euphemism for knavery. The phrase is probably derived from the practice of some unprincipled lawyers who are at pains to manage their cases so as to secure for themselves as much money as possible.

A sheet anchor is the reserve anchor to which when cast out the sailor must mainly trust to prevent his ship being driven ashore by stress of weather. Hence the phrase has come generally to mean, the chief support, the last refuge for safety.

Sheet lightning is lightning in wide, extended flashes, spread out like a sheet. It really is the reflection of forked lightning, which is the name given to lightning which seems to dart from or split the sky.

A shooting box is a private house where a sportsman resides during the period when he is shooting game.

A shooting coat is a particular kind of coat which a sportsman wears when he goes to shoot game.

A shooting gallery is a place covered in where men practise shooting at a target.

A shooting licence is permission given officially by Government to kill game with firearms.

A shooting pain is a quick, sharp pain, coming suddenly like a shot.

The shooting season is the restricted time fixed by law for sportsmen to shoot particular game. The season for one kind of game is not always the same as for another.

A shooting star is a meteor.

A short cut is a direct, cross path which shortens the way.

A sick bed is a bed on which a sick person is lying.

Sick leave is leave granted on account of illness.

A sick room is a room in which a sick person lies.

A side issue is a question only indirectly akin to the question under consideration.

A side-line is work done apart from one's main work.

A side saddle is a riding saddle for a woman, so made that she can keep both her feet on the same side of the horse. Many women nowadays ride *astride*.

A siege train is heavy artillery intended to reduce fortifications.

A singing class is a class in which singing is taught.

Single blessedness is a term jocularly applied to the unmarried state.

Single combat is a struggle or combat in which there is but one person engaged on each side: a duel.

> History records instances of opposing armies staking the issues of a war upon the struggle between two champions chosen from the two sides and engaging in single combat in sight of both armies.

A sinking fund is a fund formed by setting aside a specified annual sum which will accumulate and in course of time wipe out a debt.

A sleeping draught is a draught of medicine taken to induce sleep.

A sleeping partner is a term applied to a partner in a business who has invested money in the business, but takes no active share in the management of it. He participates, however, in the profits and losses.

A slow coach is a colloquial term applied to a person who is slow in his mental or bodily movements, an inactive person who makes but slow progress; a dull, stupid fellow.

Small arms. Rifles, muskets, pistols, are called small arms as distinguished from cannon.

Small craft is a term applied to small boats, skiffs.

Small fry is colloquial for children or insignificant persons.

The small hours are the hours after midnight up to three or four o'clock.

Small talk is trivial conversation, gossip.

A smoking cap is a particular kind of cap formerly worn when smoking.

Social questions are questions about matters which affect the life of man as a social being, or as a member of society.

A society journal is a magazine which relates the news of fashionable people.

Society verses means entertaining poetry intended for the amusement of fashionable people.

Soft sawder or **soft soap** are colloquial expressions for flattery.

A sound beating is a thorough beating, a beating in which the strokes are laid on with force.

A sound sleep is a deep sleep.

Sour grapes. The fox in the fable seeing grapes on a vine high above him made many attempts to reach them, but in vain, and then said, ' They are sour '. Hence the expression is applied to a desirable thing which is not attainable and is on that account despised.

Spare time is unoccupied time, leisure time, time to spare.

Special pleading is the specious, unsound argument of one who sacrifices truth in order to gain a victory; in law it is the alleging of special, new matter which does not directly deny what is alleged on the opposite side,

A **stalking horse** is a figure like a horse, behind which a sportsman conceals himself from the game which he wishes to kill. Hence the phrase has come generally to mean a sham, a pretence or mask used to conceal a secret project.

> Hypocrisy is the devil's stalking horse, an affectation of simplicity and religion.

A **standing army** is an established permanent army, as distinguished from a body of fighting men called out only in an emergency.

Standing corn or **standing grain** is corn or grain in the field and not yet reaped.

A **standing joke** is a continuous subject for mirth or ridicule.

A **standing nuisance** is a continuous, permanent nuisance.

Standing orders are rules made by an organized body to regulate ordinary or routine business. So also, a **standing committee.**

Standing water is stagnant water, as distinguished from running or flowing water.

A **stand-up fight** is a contest in which the opponents face one another boldly. It may be applied to opponents in argument as well as to pugilists.

The Star-spangled Banner is the national flag of the United States.

The starting point is the point of departure in a race, the point from which a start is made. **The turning point:** sometimes a race is from a starting point, round a post away at a distance, and then back to the starting point. That distant post is the turning point. Metaphorically the phrase means the point upon which a disputed question turns and which decides the case: also, the point in the course of events, or in the progress of a disease, at which there begins a decided change. **The winning post** is the goal, the post to which the racer must go; and he who first reaches that post is the winner.

Stone blind is completely blind.

Stone deaf is completely deaf.

Stone fruit is fruit having a hard seed inside the pulp, as a peach, a plum or a mango.

A **storm signal** is a signal put up at appointed places on the sea coast to indicate that a storm is anticipated.

A **strait waistcoat** or **jacket** meant originally a garment of strong material, with long sleeves tied behind the back, formerly put on a lunatic to restrain him. To say of a man that he ought to be in a strait waistcoat, is a humorous way of saying that he ought to be restrained, for he does not know when to desist; he is most impulsive or passionate. ' Strait ' is an old word for ' narrow '.

A **strait-laced person** is one who has very rigid principles and manners, and who acts in a narrow-minded way.

Street Arabs is a term applied to destitute, homeless children, who wander about in the streets of towns as waifs of society. The name was doubtless first given to poor homeless children in the streets of London.

Strong drink is alcoholic drink, e.g. brandy, whisky.

Strong language is severe, angry language.

A **stubborn fact** is a fact which a person would like to get over or ignore, though circumstances do not permit of his ignoring it.

A **stump orator** is originally an American phrase for one who harangues people from the stump of a tree or any elevation. It is commonly applied to a man who makes electioneering speeches, in which he does not always adhere to strict truth, but is boastful and blatant; a blatant demagogue.

A **sun hat** is a hat worn to protect the head from the sun.

A **swan song.** The swan, though not a singing bird, was formerly believed to sing a sweet song before dying. So when a man just before death or retirement utters or publishes a statement, it is sometimes called his swan song.

Sworn foes are determined, implacable foes.

Sworn friends are persons among whom there is a friendship as firm as if they had sworn to love one another.

Tall talk is a colloquial expression for exaggerated language, especially language that is boastful.

A **thankless task** is a work for which, if you perform it, you will get no thanks or credit.

The three R's are reading, writing, and arithmetic. The phrase is formed from the alliterative beginning of these three words, the third word being often vulgarly pronounced as if the first letter were elided, *'rithmetic.*

A **time-honoured custom** is a custom which has been maintained for a long time.

Total abstinence is entire abstinence from the use of alcoholic liquor. They who practise this are called **total abstainers** or **teetotallers.**

A **towering passion** is a violent rage.

Trade winds are strong currents of wind near the equator which blow steadily in one direction for a considerable period.

Our transatlantic cousins is a name often used in Britain for Americans generally, inasmuch as they live beyond the Atlantic, and are many of them of the same kin as the British.

A **true bill** is the description given to an accusation which on a preliminary investigation is regarded as supported by evidence strong enough to warrant a trial in a court of justice.

An **untimely end** is premature death.

The upper ten means the aristocracy, the most fashionable grade of society. The term was first used in this sense in America, and applied to the fashionables of New York.

A utopian scheme. Utopia was the name given by Sir Thomas More to an imaginary island which had an ideally perfect government. Hence the term **utopian** has come to be applied generally to an admirable scheme or project that is fanciful, chimerical, incapable of accomplishment.

A vexed question is a question regarding which there has been much disputation without arriving at a decision.

The Victoria Cross is a decoration instituted about 1856 by Queen Victoria, given to officers and men in the British army, navy, or air force, but only for eminent valour under very great personal danger. The badge is a cross with the inscription on it, ' For valour '. It is much coveted as being the highest honour for personal bravery in the fighting services. One who has received it is called a **V.C.**

Virgin soil is soil which has never yet been cultivated.

A walking stick is a stick or staff which one keeps in his hand when walking.

A watering place is a seaside resort, or any place where there are medicinal springs.

A watery grave. One who comes to his death by drowning is said to have found a watery grave.

A well-read man is a man of literary culture, one who has read many good authors.

A wet blanket. A blanket saturated with water if put over a fire will slowly extinguish the fire. Hence the phrase has come to be applied generally to any person or anything whose presence damps or checks ardour or enthusiasm.

> All were full of fun and frolic before he came, but his entry into the room was a wet blanket to their mirth.

A white elephant. The elephant is an animal so hard to supply with food that he would soon eat all that an ordinary person possesses. It was said that when the King of Siam wanted to bring any of his courtiers to beggary, he presented him with a white elephant. Of course, the courtier cannot refuse a present given him by the king, nor can he refuse to keep it; the result is that he is soon a ruined man. Hence, to call a thing a white elephant, means that it is an unprofitable possession.

White heat is intense heat. Iron when hottest looks white. We also speak of a person being in a white heat when he is in extreme passion.

A white lie is an evasion, a harmless and non-malicious untruth.

A wild goose chase is a foolish, wild, unprofitable adventure, the pursuit of anything not knowing where it will lead one.

A winding sheet is a long piece of white linen or calico wound round a corpse before the corpse is placed in the coffin for burial.

A would-be philosopher is a person who dabbles in philosophy and would like to be considered a philosopher, but is not really one. So a **would-be poet**.

A young hopeful is an ironical term applied to a, generally naughty, boy.

67. Idiomatic Noun Phrases

Many expressive idiomatic phrases are composed of a noun and a prepositional adjunct, or a noun governed by another noun in the possessive case. We give a few of these.

The angels' song is the song sung by the angelic choir over the plain of Bethlehem, the night the infant Jesus was born. Its refrain is, ' Glory to God in the highest, and on earth peace, goodwill to men.'

An apple of discord is a subject of envy and strife. The origin of the term is the mythological story which tells that into an assembly of the gods, Eris—the goddess of discord—threw a golden apple on which was inscribed, ' For the fairest.' For this golden apple the goddesses Juno, Minerva, and Venus contended; it was adjudged to Venus.

The apple of one's eye is a thing delightful for a person to contemplate, and therefore very dear to that person.

Apples of Sodom are a kind of golden-coloured fruit found in the valley of the Dead Sea, but the taste is like ashes. Metaphorically, therefore, the phrase means, disappointed expectations, results which belie hopes, pleasures which have a sting.

The ass's bridge is a name playfully given to the fifth proposition in Book I of Euclid's Elements of Geometry. It is the first difficult proposition in the book, and schoolboys rarely get over it for the first time without stumbling.

A baker's dozen is thirteen.

The balance of trade is what makes up the balance between a country's exports and imports valued in money, or the difference in money between the exports and imports of a country. When the exports of a country, say in a year, exceed in money value the imports of the country for the same period, the balance of trade for that time is said to be *in favour* of the country, because more money comes in for the exports than is paid out for the imports. And on the other hand, when the imports exceed the exports in money value, the balance of trade is said to be *against* the country.

A beast of burden is an animal which draws or carries heavy loads, the horse, ox, camel, or elephant.

A beast of prey is a beast which lives by killing other animals and eating them, as the lion or tiger. So the eagle and vulture are **birds of prey**.

The bed of a river is the channel in which the water flows.

A bed of roses is an easy comfortable situation.

A bed of thorns is a very uncomfortable situation.

A bill of fare is a list of the articles of food provided for a meal.

Bill of health. A **clean bill of health** is a document signed at a port by the proper authorities, and given to the captain of a ship when about to sail, certifying that at the date of starting there was no infectious disease at the port which the ship left. The inference from this is, that when a ship gets a clean bill of health, she could not carry infection from the port of departure.

A bill of mortality is an official statement showing the number of deaths in a place within a given time.

A bird's eye view is a view seen from above as by a bird flying, a view taken in at a glance; hence a general view, not minute or detailed; also, a kind of perspective drawing in which the artist is supposed to be above the objects, and therefore to see them as a bird in the air would do.

We had a bird's eye view of the town from the college tower.

A bird of passage is a migratory bird, a bird which spends the summer in one land and the winter in another. Metaphorically, it is a person who roams from place to place.

Birds of a feather is a phrase applied to persons of like disposition, persons likely to act in the same way. ' Of a feather ' means of one feather, i.e. ' of the same plumage '. Hence the proverb: ' Birds of a feather flock together.'

The Board of Trade is a department of the British Government having charge of important functions regarding the nation's trade.

Body and soul is a phrase having the force of an adverb and meaning wholly, entirely.

He gave himself body and soul to the pursuit of pleasure.

The Book of Common Prayer is the authorized book containing the prayers and services used in the Church of England.

A breach of promise case is a case brought before a court of justice in which a woman charges a man with breaking his promise to marry her.

The burden of a song is the refrain, the part which occurs again and again in the song.

A burst of applause is a sudden breaking forth of applause. **A round of applause** is applause in which the whole circle or meeting joins.

A case in point is an apposite illustrative instance.

A cast in the eye is a slight squint.

Castles in the air (or a **Castle in Spain**) are visionary projects, imaginary schemes, projects having so slight a basis in the facts of actual life that they are never likely to be realized.

Charles's Wain is a name given to the constellation Ursa Major, the Great Bear. **Wain** here is a contraction for waggon. This striking object in the Northern hemisphere is also popularly called the Plough.

A cock and bull story is a silly, improbable story or rumour.

Contraband of war is a term applied to articles which by international law a neutral power may not supply to either of two powers at war. Such articles if attempted to be supplied, are liable to seizure and confiscation by either belligerent power.

A council of war is a meeting of officers in a time of war to discuss what steps should next be taken and what course followed.

The crack of doom is colloquial for the end of the world.

The crux of a question is the central point on which the issue turns.

Days of grace are days, commonly three, allowed for the payment of a bill, or other dues, beyond the date fixed for payment.

A diamond of the first water is a diamond perfectly pure and transparent. And the term is applied by metaphor to a reliable thing which is perfect of its kind. **A rough diamond** is a diamond uncut and unpolished. The term is used metaphorically of a person of unprepossessing exterior, but of sterling worth.

A drug in the market is a term applied to any commodity for sale for which there is no demand.

The ends of justice are the purposes for which justice is administered.

English; the English. The word **English** used alone is the English language. The phrase **the English** means the English people.

The three estates of the realm are the authorities that in the United Kingdom have jointly in their hands the legislative functions of the State—namely, the Lords Spiritual, the Lords Temporal, and the Commons. **The fourth estate** is a term sometimes applied to the Press. This expression indicates that the newspaper has come to be as powerful a leader and exponent of public opinion as any of the ordinary three estates of the realm.

The fall of man is the term applied to the sinning of the first parents of mankind—Adam and Eve—from their primeval state of innocence into a sinful state.

The field of vision is the whole space seen or looked at; especially the whole area seen through a microscope or telescope.

A fish out of water is a person in uncomfortable surroundings.

A flag of truce is a white flag indicating a desire for a temporary cessation of fighting and for a peaceful interview with the enemy.

Flesh and blood is a phrase denoting human nature. The phrase is not commonly used unless something hard to be endured is spoken of.

> Flesh and blood can bear it no longer.

A flight of stairs is a staircase.

A flourish of trumpets suggests a noisy ostentatious display.

A fresh lease of life. A man is sometimes said to have got a fresh lease of life when he recovers from a severe illness; it was feared he would die, but God has granted him a new term of earthly existence. The phrase is also sometimes applied figuratively to an arrangement which was likely to come to an end, but the force of which has revived.

A friend at court is a person well disposed towards you who can exert influence on those who have it in their power to benefit you.

The gift of the gab is colloquial for fluency of speech, loquacity. The phrase is slightly contemptuous.

God's acre is a cemetery, a burial ground.

Hammer and tongs is a colloquial phrase with adverbial force meaning vigorously, and sometimes violently.

A house of mourning is a term applied to a house in which one has died. In England usually a few days intervene between death and burial; during these days the term **house of mourning** is applied to the house.

> Many friends came together to the house of mourning to show their sympathy with the bereaved family.

The ins and outs of a thing is a phrase used colloquially to denote the full details of a thing.

A Jack of all trades is a person who can turn his hand to any kind of business. Commonly a **Jack of all trades** is not expert in any; hence the colloquial maxim, ' Jack of all trades, master of none '.

A Jack Tar is a British sailor. A sailor was formerly called a tar because his clothes were often smeared with tar.

King's evidence. Sometimes a number of persons are charged with a crime, but cannot be convicted for want of sufficiently strong evidence; if one of them confesses all and gives evidence which convicts the others, he is in consequence allowed to go free. Such a person is said to turn King's evidence; or in a Queen's reign it would be Queen's evidence; or he may be called an ' approver '.

King's evil is scurvy (scrofula). It is so called because in former times the touch of a king's hand was supposed to cure it. But we do not say Queen's evil.

The Queen's speech (or **King's**) is delivered by the Queen or by the Government in the Queen's name at the opening of the British Parliament.

The Land o' Cakes is a colloquial name for Scotland, applied no doubt because oatmeal cakes are a common kind of food there.

The land of the living. The phrase **the living** means those who are alive, and **the land of the living** is the place of living man, this earth.

The land of nod is the word often used by or to children for sleep.

The law of the land is the general, public, or common law of a particular country; also, the due process of law in a particular country.

A limb of the law is a colloquial name for a lawyer. (The police are the **arm of the law**.)

The lion's share is an unfairly large share. In Aesop's fable of the animals hunting, when the prey came to be divided, the lion took the greater part for himself.

The long and short of a thing is the whole of it tersely stated.

> The long and short of what I have to say to you is this, ' If you don't do your work as you ought, I will dismiss you.'

A maid of honour is a female attendant or companion of a queen or princess.

Man's estate is manhood.

A man in a thousand is a man so excellent that a thousand might be passed by before one could find his equal.

The man in the street is the ordinary inexpert man.

A man of letters is a man thoroughly acquainted with literature.

> The study of books is called literature and . . . a man versed in it is called . . . a man of letters instead of a man of books.—*Ruskin*

A man of parts is a man of more than ordinary talents.

A man of spirit is a courageous man.

A man of straw is a mere puppet or a man of no substantial means.

A mare's nest. The ancient Saxons supposed that what we call nightmare was produced by a demon or vampire called Mara sitting on the sleeper's breast. The vampire was believed to sit on hidden treasure as a hen on eggs, and the place where it sat was called its nest. In fact, however, the treasure existed only in imagination. Hence when anyone thinks he has made a great discovery, which afterwards turns out to be nothing, we say he has found **a mare's nest**.

The milk of human kindness is a phrase used by Shakespeare, meaning kindly or humane feeling.

A moot point is a point or question yet undecided, a question which may be debated, a point still open to discussion.

Neck or nothing is a colloquial adverbial phrase implying that a man is so reckless that he would rather risk his life than obtain nothing.

The Order of the Garter is the highest order of English knighthood.

A peal of laughter is a loud outburst of laughter.

Penelope's web. Penelope was the wife of Ulysses, King of Ithaca. Homer tells in the *Odyssey* that when Ulysses had been absent for several years at the Trojan war, and no news of him had reached Ithaca, many suitors came to Penelope and sought her in marriage. She had a web in her loom, and she put them off by saying that she would choose a new husband when she had finished weaving her web. But she was careful to unravel at night all that she had woven during the day, and thus deferred making any choice till at last Ulysses returned, when the suitors were all speedily dismissed. Hence **a Penelope's web** has come to be applied to some work which seems to be going on, and yet never comes to an end. Note that the name **Penelope** is a word of four syllables.

Pin-money is an allowance made to a lady for dress and other personal expenses, so called because originally granted to buy pins, which at one time were costly articles.

The pink of condition or **health** means the best possible. The expression is slightly jocular.

The Pope's Bull is a letter or edict of the Pope containing a decree or decision issued to the Roman Catholic Church, so called from *bulla*, the Italian word for *seal*, a seal being always attached to such a decree.

An Irish bull is a ludicrous expression involving commonly a contradiction in terms.

> An English nobleman speaking at a Farming Society dinner, advised the farmers to use iron ploughs, ' because they would last for ever and sell for old iron when they were done.'

The powers that be is an expression denoting those persons who are set in authority. The governing body in a college, in a hospital, in a railway company, or in a State, might be spoken of as ' the powers that be '. The phrase is found in the Bible.

The pros and cons of a question. **Pro** is the Latin preposition meaning *for*, and **con** is a contraction for the Latin preposition *contra*, which means **against**. **The pros and cons of a question** is a phrase used to denote the arguments urged for and against a thing.

> I have approached this subject with a desire to weigh the pros and cons connected with it.—*Tyndall*

A rope of sand. Of course a rope cannot be made of sand; but the phrase has come to be applied to a bond easily broken.

Rule of thumb. When an operation is performed according to practical experience, and not after proper thought, it is said to be done by rule of thumb.

Scylla and Charybdis. In the Straits of Messina, between Italy and Sicily, there is a rock on one side anciently called Scylla, and on the other a dangerous whirlpool called Charybdis. Sailors who gave Scylla a wide berth ran the risk of being drawn into Charybdis and destroyed: in avoiding Scylla they were in danger of falling into Charybdis. When a dilemma of this kind occurs, one might say, ' Take care that in avoiding Scylla, you do not fall into Charybdis.'

Signal of distress. When a ship at sea is in sore difficulty or danger, the sailors display a flag upside down: this flag is called a signal of distress.

The sinews of war is now generally understood to mean money required to carry on war or any arduous undertaking. Just as the body of an animal has no force without healthy sinews, so no difficult business or warfare can move on vigorously without the expenditure of money. The phrase may, however, be used in a wider sense.

> The bodies of men, munition, and money, may justly be called ' the sinews of war '.—*Raleigh*

The skin of one's teeth occurs in the Bible sentence, ' I am escaped with the skin of my teeth ' (Job xix. 20), i.e. escaped with loss of everything but life.

> The ship broke up; several were drowned; but four sailors managed to escape with (or, by) the skin of their teeth.

A skylight is a window in the roof of a house, facing upwards towards the sky.

A slip of the tongue is a slight mistake in speaking, a wrong word which slips out of the mouth before the speaker is aware and which he would know to be wrong on a moment's reflection. **A slip of the pen** is a similar mistake made by a writer.

A snake in the grass is a figurative expression for a secret foe, an enemy concealed from view; a sneaking, cunning person who openly pretends to be your friend and yet is in his heart a foe. To take one instance out of many: A man who, while pretending to be your friend, sets a spy to watch your house in the hope of seeing or hearing something against you, is indeed a snake in the grass, a person who has a good deal of the reptile about him.

Softening of the brain is a diseased state of the brain which is gradually fatal to life.

A soldier of fortune is a military adventurer.

A son of Mars is an old-fashioned expression for a soldier. Mars was the Roman god of war.

A step-mother. Suppose a widower who has children gets married; his new wife is the step-mother of his children by his former wife, and these children are the step-children of that new wife; step-sons and step-daughters.

A stone's throw is as far as one could throw a stone.

His garden is not more than a stone's throw from mine.

The sum and substance of an argument is the whole drift and meaning of it. Cf. ' the long and short ' above.

The three arms of the service, signify the artillery, the cavalry, and the infantry.

The Throne of Grace. This is a Biblical expression. The idea is that God is seated on a throne dispensing grace or gifts of mercy to those who seek Him by prayer.

The ups and downs of life is a colloquial phrase denoting the changes of life, varying states of prosperity and adversity.

The why and wherefore of a thing is colloquial for the whole and sole reason for a thing.

The wooden walls of England was a phrase used to designate the British Navy in an age when ships of war were built of wood.

68. Sometimes we find in easy colloquial English, adjectives made up of a few words. We have already explained a *dog-in-the-manger policy*. Other examples are,

This long-hoped-for journey.
This much-talked-of opening of Parliament.
A happy-go-lucky style of doing business, i.e. a haphazard mode, which may perchance turn out favourably.
Packets of very useful articles now come at a cheap rate to many an out-of-the-way place.
There was no open understanding between the two parties; and hole-and-corner conferences between them were despised.
These sketches picture in many cases modes and phases of life such as ordinary stay-at-home folks, and some travellers too, will find extremely difficult to realize.

Compound adjectives made up in the way shown above are often to be met with in conversation or in newspapers, and even in such books as are written in a chatty, easy style. The meaning is in most cases quite obvious.

69. There are certain adjectives that often go in pairs and the idiomatic order in which they stand should be fixed in the memory. The following are instances.

Ancient and modern	Bright or dark	Drunk or sober
For better (or) for worse	Cut and dried	By fair means or foul
	Dead and gone	Fair and square

Free and easy	High and mighty	Right and wrong
Good or bad	The long and short	Rough and ready
Great and small	More or less	Rough and smooth
Good, bad, or indiffer-	Null and void	Short and sweet
ent	Past and present	Slow and steady
High and dry	Rich and poor	Slow but sure
High and low	Right and left	Through thick and thin

70. Sometimes two nouns go together making an idiomatic pair. Note that in these pairs there is a fixed idiomatic collocation.

Alpha and Omega	King and queen	Profit and loss
Art and Science	Kith and kin	Rack and ruin
Bag and baggage	Knife and fork	Rank and file
Bow and arrows	Ladies and gentlemen	Rhyme or reason
Bread and butter	Land and water	Root and branch
Bread and cheese	Law and equity	Sheep and goats
Bread and milk	Life and limb	Sin and misery
A fair field and no favour	Light and shade	Skin and bone
Fire and sword	For love or money	Son and heir
Through fire and water	Male and female	Stocks and shares
Flesh and blood	Man and beast	Stuff and nonsense
Friend or foe	Man and wife	Sum and substance
Gods and goddesses	Master and man (*man* here=man-servant)	Sun, moon, and stars
Bound hand and foot	Men and women	Sword and shield
Hands and feet	Might and main	Tea and coffee
Over head and ears	Mistress and maid (*maid* here=maid-servant)	Time and tide
Heart and soul	Mother and child	Tooth and nail
Heaven and earth	Part and parcel	Town and country
Hill and dale	Pen and ink	Use and abuse
Hole and corner	Pen and paper	Virtue and vice
Horse and cart	Pins and needles	Watch and ward
House and home	Pipe and tobacco	Weal or woe
Houses and lands	Powder and shot	Wear and tear
Judge and jury		Wife and children
		Wind and weather

Here as in respect of idioms generally, it would be difficult to assign any reason why the foregoing expressions have the shape they have, and why a particular noun in the pair should be placed first rather than the other. We have to fall back on established usage. In some cases the second word is little else than a repetition of the first. *House* and *home*, *rack* and *ruin*, *wit* and *wisdom*. Sometimes the more important word stands first. *Master* and *man*, *man* and *beast*. Sometimes, where both words are not mono-syllables, the shorter is put first, to make the whole phrase pleasanter to the ear. *Hole* and *corner*, *town* and *country*.

71. We close this chapter with a section on generalized and collective words and phrases. Note the following.

The birds of the air	The denizens of the deep
The beasts of the field	The fish of the sea
The beasts of the forest	The lilies of the field

The word *bunch* is applied to several things, as fruit, keys, flowers; so that when we speak of a *bunch of grapes*, we must add the defining words *of grapes* to the word *bunch*, else it would not be known what the bunch consisted of. But a great many collective or generalized words need no such defining addition, but fully indicate by themselves the classes to which they apply. Thus, a *library* is a collection of books, and we need not say a library of books. So we have *fleet*, a number of ships under one commander; *crew*, the sailors of a ship; *choir*, a band of singers; *stud*, a number of horses kept by a single owner; *mob*, a crowd of riotous people; *rabble*, a throng of disorderly persons.

We also speak of a carpenter's *tools* and *workshop*; a surgeon's *instruments* and *surgery*; a chemist's *apparatus* and *laboratory*; a shopkeeper's *stock*; a farmer's *implements*; the *machinery* of a mill; the *works* of a clock; the *furniture* of a house; the *apparatus* of a school; the *contents* of a book; a pedlar's *wares* or *goods*; a lawyer's *documents*; a ship's *passengers*; a ship's *cargo*; the *rigging* of a ship; the *fittings* of an engine; *schools* and *colleges* would be grouped under the head of *educational institutions*.

The *rolling stock* of a railway is the collective name given to all the locomotives and carriages and waggons kept in working order on the railway.

The following correct expressions may also be noted.

A *shower* of rain
A *fall* of snow or rain
A *sheaf* of grain
A *sheaf* or *quiver* of arrows
A *regiment* of soldiers
A *posse* of police
A *stack* of wood
A *herd* of deer
A *shoal* of fish
A *flock* of geese
A *flock* of sheep
A *brood* of chickens
A *pack* of wolves or hounds
A *litter* of puppies
A *herd* of swine
A *flight* or *swarm* of locusts
A *swarm* of flies
A *swarm* of bees
A *flight* of birds
A *covey* of partridges
A *nest* of ants
A *herd* of cattle, i.e. cattle pasturing
A *drove* of cattle, i.e. cattle being driven
A *troop* or *squadron* of horse, i.e. of cavalry
A *crowd*, or *throng*, or *concourse*, or *multitude* of people

A *flight* of steps or stairs
A *bunch* of keys
A *bunch* of grapes
A *bunch* or *bouquet* of flowers
A *pair* of shoes
A *tribe* of Arabs
A *suit* of clothes
A *bundle* of hay
A *bundle* of sticks
A *group* of islands
A *series* of events
A *heap* or *mass* of ruins
A *heap* of stones or sand
A *clump* or *grove* of trees
A *cluster* or *galaxy* of stars
A *gang* of labourers
A *gang* of thieves or robbers
A *chain* or *range* of mountains
A *range* of hills or mountains
A *group* of figures in a painting
A *collection* of relics or curiosities

From these examples it will be seen what are the appropriate collective phrases to be used in many cases. But it will not do to mix up these expressions. While we correctly say, *a flock of sheep* and *a pack of wolves*, it would be wrong to say, *a pack of sheep* or *a flock of wolves*. Similarly it is wrong to say, *a heap of islands* or *a bunch of stones*.

CHAPTER V

IDIOMATIC COMMONPLACE COMPARISONS

72. It would be fortunate if the foreign student who wishes to acquire facility in using English idioms, could more frequently hear the conversation of educated Englishmen. Such a student for the most part has his attention directed to English books written in a fine, correct, polished style; and he thinks that when he converses in English, he should take what he has studied as a model for his conversational language. Now, the English of most books is formal, dignified, and sometimes rhetorical: the language of conversation among Englishmen is simple and straightforward, and avoids long or involved sentences and high-sounding expressions. Men carrying on a conversation in any language use words and phrases which by their vividness arrest attention. Hence short forms in expression and slight exaggerations in meaning, which would not be admissible in written prose, are allowable in conversation without risk of misunderstanding.

73. Englishmen in conversation often use striking comparisons to give flavour and piquancy to their intercourse, the comparisons being expressed in short pithy phrases. In conversational language, any lengthy comparison would as a rule be out of place. Many of these pithy phrases would hardly be met with in high-class literary compositions, but they may be found in novels, magazines, newspapers, books of travel, and generally in such writings as reproduce conversation. The following are instances.

As black	as coal	As brittle	as glass
,, black	,, ink	,, brown	,, a berry
,, black	,, jet	,, busy	,, a bee
,, black	,, midnight	,, changeable	,, the moon
,, black	,, pitch	,, changeable	,, a weathercock
,, black	,, soot	,, cheerful	,, a lark
,, blind	,, a bat	,, clear	,, a bell—said of tones
,, blind	,, a beetle	,, clear	,, crystal
,, blind	,, a mole	,, clear	,, day, noonday
,, bold	,, brass	,, cold	,, charity
,, bold	,, a lion	,, cold	,, a frog
,, brave	,, a lion	,, cold	,, ice
,, bright	,, day	,, cold	,, marble
,, bright	,, noonday	,, cold	,, a stone
,, bright	,, the light	,, cool	,, a cucumber
,, bright	,, silver	,, cunning	,, a fox

As dark   as midnight
,, dark   ,, pitch
,, dead   ,, a door nail
,, deaf   ,, a post
,, deep   ,, a well
,, dry   ,, a biscuit
,, dry   ,, a bone
,, dry   ,, dust
,, dry   ,, a mummy
,, dry   ,, a stick
,, drunk   ,, a lord
,, dumb   ,, a statue
,, easy   ,, ABC
,, fair   ,, a rose
,, fat   ,, butter
,, fat   ,, a pig
,, fierce ,, a tiger
,, firm   ,, a rock
,, flat   ,, a board
,, flat   ,, a pancake
,, fleet   ,, a deer
,, free   ,, the air
,, fresh   ,, a daisy
,, fresh   ,, a rose
,, gay   ,, a lark
,, gaudy   ,, a butterfly
,, gaudy   ,, a peacock
,, gentle ,, a lamb
,, good   ,, gold
(*Good* here = valuable.)
,, good   as a play
(*Good* here = delightful, amusing.)
,, graceful as a swan
,, grasping ,, a miser
,, grave   ,, a judge
,, greedy ,, a dog
,, greedy ,, a wolf
,, green   ,, grass
,, gruff   ,, a bear
,, happy   ,, a king
,, happy   ,, the day is long
,, hard   ,, flint
,, hard   ,, marble
,, hard   ,, a stone
(These comparisons would be used of material substances, as clay, wood, or they might be used of hard-hearted persons.)
,, harmless as a dove
,, heavy   ,, lead
,, hoarse ,, a crow
,, hot   ,, fire
,, hot   ,, pepper
,, hungry ,, a hunter
,, innocent ,, a dove

As large   as life, i.e. as he really is.
,, light   ,, air
,, light   ,, a butterfly
(This would be said of a person's disposition, *light* being here opposed to *grave*.)
,, light   as a feather
,, light   ,, thistledown
(*Light* is here opposed to *heavy*.)
,, like   as two beans
,, like   ,, two drops of water
,, like   ,, two peas
,, loose   ,, a rope of sand
(*Loose* here means incoherent, e.g. 'The lawyer's speech, instead of being a continuous argument firmly knit together, was loose as a rope of sand.')
,, loud   as thunder. ('The house fell with a crash as loud as thunder.')
,, mad   ,, a hatter
,, mad   ,, a March hare
,, merry   ,, a cricket
,, mute   ,, a fish
,, mute   ,, mice. (Mice can squeak, but carry on their depredations as silently as possible.)
,, obstinate ,, a mule
,, old   ,, the hills
,, pale   ,, death, i.e. as a dead person.
,, pale   ,, a ghost
,, patient ,, Job
,, patient ,, an ox
,, plain   ,, a pikestaff
,, playful ,, a kitten
,, plentiful ,, blackberries
,, plump   ,, a partridge
,, poor   ,, a church mouse
(A mouse that lives in a church gets very little to eat and therefore will not grow fat.)
,, poor   as Lazarus
(Lazarus is the name of a beggar mentioned in the Bible.)
,, proud   as Lucifer
,, proud   ,, a peacock
,, quick   ,, lightning
,, quick   ,, thought
,, quiet   ,, a lamb
,, quiet   ,, a mouse
,, rapid   ,, lightning

As red	as blood
,, red	,, a cherry
,, red	,, fire
,, red	,, a rose
,, regular	,, clockwork
,, rich	,, Croesus

(Croesus was a king of Lydia, renowned for his riches.)

| ,, rich | as a Jew |

(Formerly in England, the money-lenders were Jews.)

,, ripe	as a cherry
,, round	,, an apple
,, round	,, a ball
,, round	,, a globe
,, salt	,, brine
,, salt	,, a herring
,, sharp	,, a needle
,, sharp	,, a razor
,, silent	,, the dead
,, silent	,, the grave
,, silent	,, the stars
,, silly	,, a goose
,, silly	,, a sheep
,, slender	,, gossamer
,, slippery	,, an eel
,, smooth	,, butter
,, smooth	,, oil
,, smooth	,, glass. (This would be said of a hard substance.)
,, smooth	,, velvet, i.e. soft to the touch.
,, sober	,, a judge, i.e. *solemn*
,, soft	,, butter
,, soft	,, down
,, soft	,, wax
,, sound	,, a bell
,, sour	,, a crab, i.e. the wild apple.
,, sour	,, vinegar
,, steady	,, a rock
,, stiff	,, a poker
,, stiff	,, a post
,, still	,, death
,, still	,, the grave
,, straight	,, an arrow

As strong	as a horse
,, strong	,, a lion
,, stupid	,, a donkey
,, sure	,, death, i.e. as certain as death.
,, surly	,, a bear
,, sweet	,, honey
,, sweet	,, sugar
,, swift	,, an arrow
,, swift	,, lightning
,, swift	,, thought
,, swift	,, the wind
,, tall	,, a maypole
,, tall	,, a steeple
,, tame	,, a cat
,, tender	,, a chicken
,, thick	,, a cable
,, thick	,, hailstones
,, thick	,, blackberries, i.e. as plentiful.
,, thick	,, thieves, i.e. as closely bound.
,, thin	,, a wafer
,, thin	,, a rake
,, timid	,, a hare
,, tough	,, leather
,, tricky	,, a monkey
,, true	,, steel
,, ugly	,, a scarecrow
,, ugly	,, a toad
,, unstable	,, water
,, vain	,, a peacock. (See under *proud*.)
,, warm	,, wool
,, watchful	,, a hawk
,, weak	,, a baby
,, weak	,, a cat
,, weak	,, a kitten
,, weak	,, water
,, wet	,, a drowned rat
,, white	,, a sheet
,, white	,, snow
,, white	,, wool
,, wise	,, a serpent
,, wise	,, Solomon
,, yellow	,, a guinea
,, yielding	,, wax

To this list we must add certain commonplace comparisons which do not take the shape of the foregoing.

For instance, a lady with a sweet voice is said to sing *like a thrush*, or *like a nightingale*; a person is said to be *like a fish out of water* when he is out of his element and therefore ill at ease; one is said to be *off like a shot* when he starts off very quickly and unexpectedly; a person going *post-haste* is one going as fast as the post is carried; any person, or thing—as a train—moving forward very slowly, is said to go *at a snail's pace*; a man given to duplicity is said to have *as many faces*, i.e. *phases, as the moon*; the distance from one place to another is often said to be so many miles *as the crow flies*, i.e. in a direct line across the country.

And there are several other expressions used in such common comparisons as we are treating of.

To spread like wildfire.
To follow like a shadow.
To shake, tremble, or quiver like an aspen leaf.
He knows no more than a child how to do this.

She wept a flood of tears.
As merry as the day is long.

CHAPTER VI

VERBS AND NOUNS
WHICH IDIOMATICALLY GO TOGETHER

74. The English language has very many turns of expression in which from long usage certain nouns and verbs almost invariably go together.

For instance, a man may *take* a walk, *make* or *take* a journey, *acquire* knowledge, *cultivate* acquaintance, *enter* a profession, *win* prizes, *gain* a reputation, *profess* principles, *exercise* his gifts, *develop* his talents, *save* money, *bestow* alms, *relieve* distress, *grant* favours, *offer* services, *prepare* for a voyage, *disapprove of* a project, *pass for* a good scholar, *pass over* in silence, *seek* and *enjoy* repose. Again, water *flows* or *runs*, *freezes*, *boils*, *fills* a vessel or a pond, *quenches* thirst, *extinguishes* fire, *moistens* the soil, *nourishes* plants, *bears up* a ship.

Such phrases as these need no explanation, and our object at this stage is to put before the student a number of these expressions, the principal words in each being a noun and a verb which idiomatically go together.

75. The following list gives the verbs which denote the cries of several of the lower creatures.

Apes gibber
Asses bray
Bears growl
Bees hum
Beetles drone
Birds sing, twitter
Bulls bellow
Camels grunt
Cats mew, purr, caterwaul
Cattle low
Cocks crow
Cows low
Crickets chirp
Crows caw
Dogs yelp, bark, whine, growl, howl
Doves coo
Ducks quack
Eagles scream
Elephants trumpet
Flies buzz

Foxes yelp, bark
Frogs croak
Geese cackle, gabble, hiss
Goats bleat
Hawks scream
Hens cackle, cluck
Horses neigh, snort, whinny
Hounds bay
Hyenas laugh
Jackals howl
Kittens mew
Lambs bleat
Larks sing, warble
Lions roar
Magpies chatter
Mice squeak
Monkeys chatter, gibber
Nightingales sing, warble

Owls hoot, screech, scream
Oxen low, bellow
Parrots talk
Pea-fowl scream
Pigeons coo
Pigs grunt, squeal
Puppies yelp
Ravens croak
Rooks caw
Seagulls scream
Sheep bleat
Small birds chirp, twitter, pipe
Snakes hiss
Swans cry
Thrushes whistle
Tigers growl, roar
Turkeys gobble
Vultures scream
Wolves howl

76. When certain nouns are used in the accusative case after transitive verbs, each noun almost constantly prefers a particular verb, and as a rule does not idiomatically take any other synonymous verb. We now give a short list of transitive verbs indicating several of the nouns which they commonly take after them in the accusative case. Prepositional verbs are treated in a separate chapter.

Bear (to carry, endure), a burden, arms, a sword, sway, a badge, a name; a date; witness, testimony; spite, grudge; cold, heat; bear the brunt of;* bear a hand (=give assistance); bear the charges or cost of (=pay the expenses of); bear me company (=go with me); bear the name of a thing; bear a punishment; bear oneself proudly, nobly.

Bear (to bring forth or produce), fruit, apples; children, young; money invested or lent bears interest.

Bend, a rod, a bow; one's knee; one's will.

Bend the twig and you bend the tree.—*Proverb*

Bind, grain, a sheaf, a prisoner; a book; the conscience; the edge of a carpet or garment; bind oneself to do a thing; bind oneself as an apprentice. Frost binds the earth. Certain drugs bind the bowels. A tyre binds a wheel. Attraction binds the planets to the sun.

Break, a stick, glass, a rope, a chain, a lock, a seal, a link; a set, i.e. a set of china, a croquet set; a promise, a vow, a resolution, faith, a treaty, the law; silence, the peace; one's fall, one's fast; break news to a person;* break cover, break ground;* break the neck, the back, the heart, one's leg, one's arm; break a joint in bricklaying. Great losses are sometimes said to ' break a bank ', i.e. to render it unable to meet its liabilities.

The last straw breaks the camel's back.—*Proverb*

Bring, any article that can be carried, as wood, coal, a burden; bring one honour; bring an offering, a present; bring a lecture to a close; bring an action or a suit at law against a person; bring a work to an end. **Bring** is also used with several infinitives after it.

The post or a messenger brings news.
He soon brought the guns to bear on the fort.

Build, a nest, a house, a ship; hopes, a reputation.

Buy, an article that may be sold, as a horse, a book, grain; buy honour with flattery.

* The student will find the section where the phrase is explained in the Index at the end of the book. Further references to the Index will be similarly marked with an asterisk.

Carry, a burden, cargo; a measure, a motion, a point, a resolution, news; a fortress, i.e. capture it by assault; carry captive; carry all before one;* carry matters with a high hand;* men able to carry arms; carry war into a country; and many other phrases. Will this colt carry me?, i.e. is it strong enough to bear me?

Cast, anchor, lots; cast a horoscope, i.e. to reckon it; cast one's eyes towards; to cast in a foundry, as metal, wheels, cannon. The snake casts its slough (pronounced *sluff*). Birds in moulting cast their feathers.

Catch, fish, a rope, a branch, a ball, a bird, a thief; cold, fever, small-pox; infection; the spirit of an occasion, a melody; catch one's ear, one's eye; catch a glimpse of or glance of; catch a Tartar;* catch a train.*

Climb, a hill, a mountain, a wall, a steep place, an ascent.

Close, a letter, a book, a bargain; a list, one's hand, a box, a parcel, a door; close the ranks of an army.

Collect, money, rents, taxes; materials, votes, news, letters, statistics, information; an army; shells, specimens.

Cut, paper, cloth, a rod, a rose, wood, glass, a cord, a canal; standing corn; the hair, the nails, the flesh; cut a notch in wood; to cut a person (*colloquial*), i.e. to drop acquaintance with that person; to cut capers, i.e. to play pranks, to frolic; cut a figure;* cut the Gordian knot.* A child cuts teeth, i.e. the teeth pierce through the gums and appear.

Desert, a friend, one's country, a cause, one's colours.

Deserve, praise, credit, a reward, thanks; punishment, blame; good or bad treatment. A workman deserves his wages. They deserve the treatment they get.

Dig, the ground, a garden, a field; a hole, a pit, a trench, a grave, a well, a mine; a foundation, i.e. a trench in which to lay a foundation of masonry.

Do. This verb is fully treated of in other places.*

Draw, a cart, a load, a tooth, a bow, a curtain; a line, a figure, a picture; a fowl; blood, breath, water; tears, groans, a long face; a bill, a deed, a will, a cheque, interest; draw money from the bank; draw a letter from one's pocket; the sword, a moral, a conclusion, an inference. The magnet draws the needle, i.e. attracts it. (See also Section 26.)

Drink, any liquid, as water, milk, wine, nectar, poison, medicine; drink the health of, or to the health of.

Drive, any animal, as a camel, cattle; a carriage, an engine; a bargain, a trade; a nail. To drive one mad. The wind drives the ship along. The engine drives machinery. Steam or water drives the mill.

Eat, any kind of food or fruit, as bread, beef, venison, rice, figs, a mango, dates, one's dinner; eat one's words;* eat humble pie.* The tiger eats its prey. Cattle eat grass, straw, hay, grain.

Exercise, a horse, troops; discipline, control, authority; caution, patience; exercise one's gifts.

Feed, cattle, a horse, a flock, bees, a bird, a child; feed an engine with water; feed a furnace with coal. Springs feed ponds. Several small streams feed the river.

Feel, pleasure, pain; feel (=perceive by the sense of touch) a stone, one's pulse; feel the force of, feel one's strength, feel one's way; feel the want of, feel an interest in, feel the weight of. Make them feel the authority of the law.

Fill, any vessel, as a pot; an office, a post, a vacancy. The wind fills the sails. Air fills a balloon. The people filled the hall. The Speaker fills the chair of the House of Commons. Fill a letter with news. The lecturer's voice was too weak to fill the hall.

Find, anything lost, as a key, a book, a document, a child; time, leisure; find fault with; find food for an army; find (=discover) gold, the bottom; find means or courage to do a thing; a verdict, a true bill of indictment. He finds his son in money and clothes, i.e. he supplies his son with money and clothes; find quarters, i.e. find temporary residence.

> She could hardly find courage to enter.—*Thackeray*
> Livingstone found tribes in Africa that had not before been heard of.

Follow, an example, a precedent, a leader, a guide, a track, the fashion; the hounds, a trade; follow suit.

Forget, any article, as a paper, an umbrella; a promise, a kindness, an injury; to forget a thing supposed to be fixed in the memory, as a lesson, the name of a person or place or thing; to forget a person, i.e. it is so long since you saw him that you could not now recognize him; to forget oneself, i.e. to commit an oversight, or to be guilty of something unworthy of one's character.

Form, an opinion, a resolution, an attachment, an alliance, a plan; classes, a company, a band of marauders, the majority, the Cabinet; form part of. The Indus forms a delta.

> 'Tis education forms the common mind.—*Pope*

Forsake, a nest, a friend in need, one's home; rats forsake a ship; forsake the path of virtue.

Gain, money, a reward, a prize, a victory; time, knowledge, dominion, power; a case at law; gain ground.* To gain the day is to be victorious in a contest.

Get. This verb is fully treated of elsewhere.*

Give, anything that may be a gift, as a ring, a watch, a book, a shawl; help, a helping hand, a ride, a drive, a price, a prize, medicine, a drink; an opinion, judgement, credit, security; praise, thanks, offence, tit for tat; the alarm, a hint, an inkling of, notice, warning, advice, a rebuke, a scolding, a shock; an answer, a reply; give way,* place, room for; give cause for complaint, trouble; evidence, an impression, permission, authority, powers; give a shout, i.e. to utter a shout; give rise to, occasion to or for, preference to, effect to, ear to, heed to, vent to; give tone to;* give loose rein to;* give a false colouring to;* give battle, quarter,* a broadside;* give chase=to pursue; give the right hand of fellowship. His manner gave me the impression that he was not sincere.

Grind, grain, meal, coffee, grind the poor or grind the faces of the poor, i.e. oppress them grievously.

> Laws which grind the poor.—*Goldsmith*
> Ye grind the faces of the poor.—*Bible*

Grow, fruit, as grapes, mangoes; grain, as wheat, rice. **Grow** as a transitive verb is, to cause to grow, to raise, cultivate, produce. This farmer grows sugar-cane.

Have, anything that one possesses, as a house, a farm, cows, abilities, capacity, talents, authority, powers; room, possession of; an appointment, riches, influence, patience, liberty, credit, trouble, health, hope, pity, beauty, leisure, time, a neat figure, a desire, a wish; a quick eye, a good understanding; a cold, a fever; a taste for, a regard for, a hold of, care of, an interest in, a claim upon; effect; dealings with; have a sense of shame; have work to do.

Hear, any noise or sound, a report, a whisper, a footfall, a rumour, a shout, a voice; words, a song; hear evidence; hear a person, a witness, i.e. listen to what he says; hear a case, i.e. judicially, as a judge would. The infinitive without **to** follows **hear**. Hear a man speak, hear a lion roar, hear a bird sing.

> I am anxious to hear what you have got to say.
> List if thou canst hear the tread of travellers.—*Shakespeare*

Hold, anything that can be seized by the hand, as a rope, a branch; an opinion; a view, a fort, a post, an appointment; an examination; hold the plough, i.e. drive or manage the plough; hold a meeting, a session, a festival, deliberations; hold a council, a parliament, a court; hold one's breath, one's peace, one's tongue, one's ground, one's hand; hold a jug by the handle; hold a horse by the bridle or mane; hold a cord with your teeth; to hold one's own, i.e. maintain one's present position; hold one responsible; hold him guiltless = regard him as guiltless.

By what tenure does this man hold his farm?
Broken cisterns that can hold no water.—*Bible*
The sea holds the secret of many a shipwreck.
She would have held her own among those stupid people.—*Thackeray*
This argument will not *hold water*, i.e. will not bear examination, is not a valid argument.

Keep, goods, money; a secret, a vow, a promise, faith; silence, the peace; guard, watch, i.e. to watch; a book, a fast, a festival; a horse, sheep; keep boarders, i.e. entertain or have the care of boarders; keep house, i.e. have the charge of a house; keep a school, shop; keep company with, i.e. associate with; keep one's ground, one's footing; keep hold of a thing; keep the field;* a term at the University; a loose or tight rein; keep pace with, i.e. go as fast as; keep an eye on; keep a thing in mind, i.e. remember it; keep a sharp look-out;* keep body and soul together;* keep the wolf from the door.*

He has promised to keep the appointment open for me, i.e. to keep it unfilled till I am ready to take it.

Knit, a stocking; knit one's brows, i.e. to frown.

Lay, a foundation, bricks in a wall; a plan, a trap, a snare, ambush; lay hold of, lay hands on, i.e. seize; lay a telegraph cable; lay a tax on imports, a duty on wines; lay a wager, i.e. stake or hazard a wager; lay a charge against, lay a thing to one's charge; lay one's mind to a thing; lay siege to, i.e. besiege; lay wait for, i.e. lie in ambush for; lay oneself open to, i.e. expose oneself to; lay heads together, i.e. consult together; lay a thing to heart, i.e. feel it deeply; lay a ghost; lay a mine. A hen lays eggs. A shower lays the dust. A servant lays (=arranges) the table for dinner.

Lead, a camel, an army, a gang; lead the way, i.e. act as guide; lead a busy life, an easy life; lead a person wrong, lead a person a life, i.e. cause that other person to spend or pass a troubled, wearisome life; lead a child by the hand, a horse by the bridle; lead people captive, i.e. carry them into captivity.

Lead a quiet and peaceful life in all godliness and honesty.—*Bible*
What a life he used to lead his wife and daughter.—*Dickens*

Learn, a lesson; a language, as Latin, a science; a game, as chess; learn the way to do a thing; learn a poem by heart, i.e. commit the poem to memory; learn tricks.

Leave, a legacy; leave the room, home, one's house, one's father; leave school, i.e. cease to attend school as a scholar; leave one's mark on a thing; leave no trace of; leave one's moorings; leave footprints on the sands of time; leave no stone unturned; leave a good name behind, i.e. a good reputation after death.

When did the vessel leave port?, i.e. when did she start on her voyage?

Lend, any article that may be borrowed, as money, a spade, an umbrella, a book; assistance, lend a hand or a helping hand, i.e. assist; lend one's name or support or influence to a project; lend one's ear (=listen) to a discourse.

Light, a fire, a candle, a torch, a match, a lamp, a bonfire; light the streets of a town.

Load, a ship, a boat, a cart; any beast of burden, as a horse, a camel; load the table with food; load one with presents; load a gun= put a charge into the gun; load the stomach with food=eat too much.

Lose, any article of which one has had possession, as a glove, a pencil, a sheep, a coin, a watch; time, one's life; caste, rank, favour with, credit, reputation, one's chance; an appointment, one's position; lose one's way, i.e. miss one's way, go astray; lose ground, i.e. fall behind; lose oneself or lose one's head, lose self-respect, self-control; lose one's memory; lose one's bearings; lose one's reckoning, i.e. become flurried, confused, bewildered; lose heart or courage, i.e. become discouraged; lose one's case in a court of law; lose sight of a thing; lose a battle, lose men in a battle=by the men being killed; lose a leg, as by amputation or by its being shot away; lose an eye=lose the power and use of the eye by its being put out.

He lost his companion in the crowd.

Love, any person; a pet creature; music, painting; love one's own, i.e. one's own relations or possessions.

Love the Lord thy God with all thy heart.—*Bible*
Thou shalt love thy neighbour as thyself.—*Bible*

Make, a speech, a proposal, a promise, a request, an assertion, a remark, a suggestion; a fuss, a row, confusion, a noise, a disturbance; a will; a record, a copy, a sketch, an outline; a change, a complaint, a charge, an effort, an attempt, an experiment; an engagement, an appointment; a road, a railway, a canal, a journey, a voyage, one's escape; a bargain, an offer, an objection; a grimace; interest, friends, progress; make way, i.e. to advance; make faces, i.e. make grimaces; make music, melody; terms, peace; make amends, i.e. give adequate compensation; make short work of;* make game of, a fool of, fun of, light of; make haste, speed; make a rush for; make an end of; use of; a point of; make hay, money, i.e. to earn, or acquire money; make profit in trade; make no difference; make choice of, i.e. choose; make an allusion to; make love to a person; make ends meet; make one's appearance, i.e. to appear, to present oneself; make oneself agreeable or obnoxious; make a name for oneself,

i.e. acquire a reputation; make one's mark; make one happy,
miserable; make one acquainted with, i.e. cause him to know;
make common cause with, i.e. to join oneself to, to become
partners with; make a clean breast of;* make one do a thing,
i.e. cause or require him to do it; make atonement, i.e. atone.
A carpenter makes a cart; a smith makes a plough; a tailor
makes clothes; a poet makes verses.   To make a bed is to prepare
the bed for sleeping upon.   To be made king, is to be appointed
king.   To make a thing one's god, i.e. to regard it as one's god.
He makes the sum to be eighty-five pounds, i.e. he has counted
up the sum and finds it to be eighty-five pounds.   The ship
made ten knots, i.e. the ship passed over ten nautical miles in
an hour.   The ship made the harbour at six o'clock, i.e. the ship
reached the harbour at six o'clock.   I made it easy for him to go.
(See Index for further phrases.)

> A good son makes a good husband.
> He made his appearance before dinner.
> How poor a martyr I should have made in those days.—*Lamb*
> Its distance from any town or market made it an inconvenient situation.
> —*Lamb*

Open, a door, a window, a shop, a school, a dispensary; a box, an
  oyster, a debate, a discussion, a correspondence, a negotiation;
  the eyes, the mouth, the hand, a letter; the bowels; a canal.
  To open one's mind is to reveal one's secret thoughts.
Pass, an examination, a town on a journey; pass an island or a ship
  on a voyage; pass a counterfeit coin, i.e. put it into circulation;
  pass the evening, i.e. spend the evening; pass the wine, i.e. hand
  on the wine to the next person at table; pass a day with a friend;
  pass (=go past) a landmark.   The Bill has passed both Houses
  of Parliament.   It would be well if Government would pass
  a law against infant marriages.   A judge passes (=pronounces)
  sentence of death.   The river Thames passes Windsor.
Pay, money, a debt, a bill or account, taxes, tribute, dues, wages;
  pay a shopkeeper his bill; pay a labourer his wages; a visit,
  a compliment, respects, a visit, attention to, deference to,
  heed to, regard to; pay one's way;* to pay one back in his own
  coin, is to retaliate.
Play, a fiddle, a tune; tricks, pranks; a comedy; any game, as
  cricket, chess; play the fool, i.e. act like a fool; play the man,
  the spendthrift, the madman.   Play the part of Hamlet; play
  second fiddle=take a secondary or subordinate place; play
  truant.*
Put, a thing into its proper place; put life into; put a stop to; put
  an end to a discussion, to a nuisance; put a stone on the road, an

obstacle in one's way; put one's foot down; put one's foot on shore; put a limit to one's outlay.

Raise, a window, a shout, a rebellion, a standard, an army; taxes, money; a question, a difficulty, an objection; the price of a thing; a smile, an alarm, a report; raise the spirits; raise the heat of a furnace, the temperature of a room; raise the dead; raise wheat, rice, horses; to raise a siege, is to relinquish an attempt to take a place by siege; to raise a blockade, is to withdraw the ships or forces which maintained the blockade; raise the wind.*

Read, a book, a letter, any writing, a will, a placard; read one's writing, i.e. decipher his penmanship; read a dream, a riddle = solve it, interpret it; read another person's meaning = understand it; read music, figures, signals; read character; read between the lines = detect the underlying meaning; a gipsy reads a hand.

Receive, a letter, a parcel, money, rent, wages, information, news, notice, warning, admission, stolen goods, an impression, a proposal, honour, a welcome, support, strength, a visit; receive a friend, a visitor.

Remove, goods, an obstruction, an error, a landmark, an objection.

Peter the Great removed the seat of government from Moscow to St Petersburg. It was beyond the power of medicine to remove the disease.

Ride, an animal, as a camel; ride a hobby;* ride a race; ride a long distance, i.e. travel a long distance by riding.

See, any visible object, as one's face, a tree, the stars; a flaw, a mistake, an error; a ghost; one's meaning, one's way; to see land;* to see the light.* I have come to see you, i.e. to pay you a visit.

Set, a table, a chair; a trap, a snare; set foot on; set fire to a thing, set a thing on fire; one's heart on; set a broken limb; set an example; set eyes on, i.e. see; set (=adapt) words to music; set (=put in due order) a clock, a razor, a saw; set (=fix) a price on a horse; set sail, i.e. unfurl sail; set oneself against, i.e. oppose; set a scheme on foot, i.e. start a scheme; set the teeth on edge, i.e. affect the teeth with a sharp grating sensation; set a prisoner free; set a price on one's head; set one on his legs again, i.e. replace him in a position where he may get on, said of a man broken down by misfortune.

The accident set him thinking. Set your affection on things above.

Show, anything visible, as a picture, a house; signs of, fear, kindness, courage, discretion, one's mettle; a bad temper; one's face; show a place on a map; show the way, i.e. point out the road; one's colours, i.e. show to what party one belongs; show the way to do a thing; show a horse, i.e. exercise him so as to show his paces;

show fight, i.e. show readiness to fight; show a bold front, show determined opposition; a clock shows the time.

Show him the room where he is to sleep.

Shut, a door, a gate, a letter, a shop; one's mouth, one's eyes.

Sow, seed; a field, land; discord; sow the seeds of rebellion.

Sow dissension in the hearts of brothers.—*Addison*

Sow one's wild oats, is to lead a dissipated life in one's youth.

Spend, money, time, a day, strength, energy, one's resources.

He spent all he had in trying to perfect his invention.

Spill, any liquid, as water, milk, ink, blood.

Spin, cotton, wool, flax; a thread; a top; to spin a yarn, is to tell a tale.

Spread, a sheet of anything, a carpet, a sail, a tent, a table-cloth; a report; a disease, infection, manure, plaster. Trees spread their branches; birds spread their wings.

Spring, a mine, a trap; spring a leak, i.e. begin to leak, said of ships.

Start, a question, an objection, a doubt, a difficulty; start (=cause to start) a race, a train, a hare, opposition; a newspaper, an enterprise.

Strike, a blow; any object to which a blow may be given, as a man, a dog; to strike a match is to ignite it; to strike a bargain is to conclude a bargain; strike (=take down) sail, a flag, a tent; strike the mind with surprise; it strikes me, that, etc., means, it occurs to me that, etc.; to strike hands on, is to make an agreement on; to strike terror into, is to terrify suddenly; to strike work, is to leave off work in order either to compel an advance of wages, or to prevent a reduction of wages. A tree strikes its roots deep; the clock struck ten; strike an average.

Take, anything that may be laid hold of by the hand, as a pen, a brush, a hat, a leaf of paper; a seat, a walk, a drive, a ride; a photograph, a step, steps, precautions, measures, trouble, pains, revenge, satisfaction, refuge, control, food, a glass of milk, poison, medicine; one's ease, rest, a course, one's own course, time, offence, shame to oneself, warning, advice, alarm; a cold, a fever, a stand, shape, leave, one's departure; aim, flight, captive, heed to, a fancy to, a liking for, exception to, credit for, pleasure in, delight in, charge, charge of, care, care of, the direction of, hold of; account of, the place of, advantage of, the liberty of, possession of, the place of, the part of, part with, part in, an interest in, pride in; take the way to a place; take a leap in the dark;* take a thing for granted; take the reins, i.e. assume the direction of; take a census; take the field;* to take a thing in hand, is to undertake it; to take, or take up, arms, is to begin war.

Teach, a person, a class, a school; a subject or lesson, as English, geometry, music, composition, sewing, writing; teach manners, obedience, honesty.

Tell, a tale, a story, the truth, a lie, a falsehood; one's future; one's fate; tell me all you know.

> Tell us all about the war,
> And what they killed each other for.—*Southey*

Throw, a stone, dust, dice; a cannon throws a shell; a fire-engine throws water on a burning house; a man throws his antagonist in wrestling; a horse throws his rider.

Turn, wood or ivory in a lathe, as the legs of a table; turn a wheel; turn a handle; turn a mill; turn one's head or body; turn (=reverse) a coat; turn cattle from the road; turn a ship from her course; turn one's attention to a subject; turn the course of a river; turn a thing to good account; turn black to white; turn French into English, prose into verse, sense into nonsense, good into evil; to turn a corner, is to go round a corner; turn the scale; to turn the flank of the enemy's army, is to pass round and take up a position behind it; to turn one's coat, is to change to the opposite side, to become a turncoat; to turn one's back, is to flee; to turn one's back on, is to forsake; to turn tail, is to retreat ignominiously; to turn a somersault; to turn the edge of, is to make blunt; to turn the arguments of an opponent upon himself; to turn a thing to advantage, is to take advantage from it; to turn a deaf ear to, is to refuse to listen; to turn a cold shoulder to, is to ignore.

Use, a book, a chair, a knife, a plough, time, means, efforts, exertions, precautions; a supply of anything, as food, salt, water; use flour for bread, potatoes for food, water for irrigation, paper for printing; to use one's fists, to box or fight with the fists; use words correctly; use (=treat) a beast cruelly; use (=treat) one well or ill.

Wear, clothes, as a coat, a hat, shoes; wear (=dress in) silk, or broadcloth; a crown, a sword, an ornament, honours; wear a channel, i.e. by attrition; wear a smile on the countenance.

> A constant drip will wear a hole in a stone.—*Proverb*

Weave, a web, linen, stockings, silk, cotton, yarn; weave words into verse (poetic).

Win, a prize, a scholarship, money, a game, a race, a battle, honour, a crown, a stake; to win golden opinions, is so to conduct oneself as to win the admiration of others.

CHAPTER VII

IDIOMATIC ADJECTIVE PHRASES, COMPOSED OF AN ADJECTIVE OR PARTICIPLE AND AN APPROPRIATE PREPOSITION

77. English has many idiomatic expressions formed of an important word and a preposition following it. We now take up phrases formed of an adjective and an appropriate preposition, giving examples to show the usage. Ignorance of the appropriate prepositions to be used in such cases is a fruitful source of errors of idiom. We include several participles often used as adjectives. A participle commonly takes after it the same preposition as the verb does from which it is derived. The skilled teacher will here find abundant material for school exercises.

Abhorrent to. Slavery is abhorrent to a humane man.

Abounding in, with. Rivers abounding in fish. English is a language abounding with idiomatic turns of expression.

Abreast of. Keep abreast of the progress of scientific study.

Absorbed in. She sat on the ground absorbed in her grief. He looks like a man absorbed in plans for making money.

Acceptable to a person. His present was not acceptable to me.

Accessory to. This man was accessory to the crime.

Accompanied by. He came here accompanied by a friend.

According to. The building is according to the architect's plans. According to, is often regarded as a compound preposition, but according is then strictly speaking a participle.

Accountable for a thing, **to** a person. Every man is accountable to God for everything he says and does.

Accruing to. The profits accruing to him from the business.

Accurate in his calculations.

Accused of a crime, **by** a person. Three men were brought into court accused by this farmer of theft.

Accustomed to. It is hard to drive a bullock not accustomed to the yoke. The work of the office will be easy when you get accustomed to it.

Acquainted with. I am not well acquainted with your brother. Before a man speaks on any subject, he should at least be acquainted with it.

Acquitted of. He stands acquitted of all intent to injure you.

Adapted for, to. School-books adapted to the capacity of children. Crops adapted to a shallow soil would thrive here. This machine is ill adapted for its professed purpose.

Addicted to. Can you reclaim a man addicted to drugs?

Adequate to. The supply of provisions is not adequate to the wants of the garrison.

Adjacent to. These two men's farms are adjacent to each other.

Adorned with. Adorned with flowers. A house adorned with paintings.

Affixed to. The syllable -en affixed to an adjective often forms a verb, e.g. broad, broaden.

Afflicted at, by, with. She is greatly afflicted at the loss of her child. He has been much afflicted by this sad news. Poor man, he is sorely afflicted with rheumatism.

Afraid of. Why should you be afraid of a ghost? I hope you are not afraid of work.

Aghast at a sight.

Agreeable to. The plan was not agreeable to his wishes. The acquaintance he formed became far from agreeable to him.

Akin to. I regard it with a feeling akin to contempt.

Alarmed at, by, for. You were alarmed at the crash. Alarmed by rumours of war. He is alarmed for the safety of his brother.

Alive to. He is not at all alive to the danger he is in.

Allotted to. He likes the place allotted to him in the procession.

Ambitious of. How pitiable to see this infirm old man so ambitious of a name for wealth.

Amenable to. Is this foreigner amenable to the laws of the country?

Angry with a person, **at** a thing, or **because** of a thing. Your conduct is enough to make your master angry with you. Why be angry at a stone if you stupidly stumble over it? He is angry with her for having broken her promise.

Animated by. He is animated by a genuine love of art.

Annoyed at a thing; **with** a person for a thing. He was annoyed with you for your persistency. I was annoyed at my mistake.

Anxious about, for. John is anxious about his success in the contest. Most men are anxious for the advancement of their children. **Anxious** is sometimes followed by the infinitive, e.g. I am anxious to point out your errors.

Apart from. He sat apart from the other men.

Applicable to. Your criticisms are not applicable to the subject.

Apprehensive of. He is apprehensive of the future.

Appropriate to. Music appropriate to the occasion.

Ashamed of. He looked quite ashamed of his folly. Are you not ashamed of your company?

Associated with. I should not like to have my name associated with his in any business whatever.

Astonished at. He seemed quite astonished at your zeal.

Attentive to. A pupil should be attentive to his teacher. No one was more attentive to his duty than he.

Averse to. How averse he is to work!

Awake to. He is not awake to his opportunities.

Aware of. I was not aware of your intention.

Away from the point, **away from** home, **away from** one's post.

Bare of. Some parts of the country are very bare of trees.

Based upon. A slanderous story based upon idle rumour.

Belonging to. He stole a horse belonging to this gentleman.

Beloved by, of. A boy greatly beloved by *or* of his father.

Bent on. The two boys are off, bent on mischief.

Beneficial to. Regular exercise is beneficial to health. Stability of government is beneficial to any nation.

Bereaved of, or **bereft of.** He is a lonely old man bereft of all comforts. Bereft of reason, i.e. insane. She is bereaved of her husband and all her children.

Beset with. An enterprise beset with difficulties.

Blended with. The prevailing colour in the carpet is green blended with blue.

Blessed with good health; **blessed with** a healthy family.

Blind in one eye. **Blind to** one's own defects.

Boastful of. How boastful he is of his little prize!

Born of parents; **in** or **at** a place; **in** a condition. A child born of an intelligent mother. Born in Brussels. Born in poverty and sin. Born at a village in Denmark. A project born of sedition ought not to be countenanced.

Bound for. A ship bound for Melbourne.

Bred in, to. Born to wealth but bred in poverty. These people are bred to silk-weaving.

Burdened with. His last days were burdened with many cares. He is burdened with a large family.

Busy at, with. They are all busy at work. The girl is busy with her knitting.

Capable of. Is the child capable of understanding this?

Careful of. It is a duty to be careful of one's health.

Careless about, of. Careless about the risk he runs. Careless of consequences.

Cautious of. Be cautious of giving offence.

Celebrated for. A city celebrated for its healthy situation.

Certain of. He felt quite certain of success.

Characteristic of. It is characteristic of the man to be thrifty.

Clear of. The ship has got clear of the rocks. He is now clear of all business difficulties. The town is clear of cholera.

Close by, to. His house is close by mine, or close to mine. The wolves came close to the tent.

Clothed in, with. Clothed in fine linen. Clothed with authority.

Clumsy at. She is clumsy at drawing water.

Cognisant of. For a time he was not cognisant of my presence.

Commensurate with. A salary commensurate with his abilities.

Common to. Sentient life is common to man and beast.

Comparable with, when a common point of resemblance is indicated; **comparable to,** when one thing is taken as an illustration of another. In point of health, the coast is not comparable with the town. The grades of caste in Hindu society are comparable to layers of strata.

Compatible with. It would not be compatible with the public safety to let criminals off with a slight punishment.

Complained of. The nuisance complained of has been removed.

Composed of. Water is composed of oxygen and hydrogen.

Concerned about, for, in. We are quite concerned about our father's illness. He is greatly concerned for the safety of his grain. These two men were concerned in the business.

Conducive to. Good ventilation is conducive to good health.

Confident of success.

Congenial to. Leisure for study is congenial to his tastes.

Conscious of a thing. He was conscious of the presence of a thief in the room.

Consecrated to. A monument consecrated to the memory of the brave.

Consistent with. Conduct consistent with his professions.

Conspicuous for bravery.

Content with. A frugal man is content with little.

Contented with. Be contented with the lot God assigns you.

Contiguous to. Iran is contiguous to Afghanistan.

Contrary to. This has turned out contrary to my expectations. His opinions are directly contrary to yours.

Convenient for, to. This house is not convenient for me. It is not now convenient to me to write a letter.

Conversant with. He is conversant with recent books of travel. Geology is a science I am not conversant with.

Convulsed with laughter.

Corresponding to, with. I found an old coin corresponding to one figured in this cyclopaedia. He found two sculptured arms of marble corresponding with each other.

Covered with shame. A body covered with a cloak.

Covetous of. He is covetous of distinction.

Crowned with. His efforts have been crowned with success. Crowned with glory and honour.—*Bible*

Crushed to death; crushed to pulp. **Crushed with** grief. **Crushed by** superior force.

Cured of a disease, **of** a bad habit. Only a few are cured of leprosy.

Deaf to all entreaty, to advice, to reason.

Deficient in. He is deficient in geometry. His speech was indeed deficient in fluency.

Delighted with. How delighted the child is with his toys!

Dependent on. The old cripple is altogether dependent on the earnings of this little boy.

Deprived of his property.

Derogatory to. It is very derogatory to a judge that he should take bribes.

Descriptive of. A book descriptive of the cities of Italy.

Deserted by. Gautama, deserted by his fellow-ascetics, sat down dejected under a Bo tree.

Deserving of praise.

Desirous of. A soldier desirous of fame. He is desirous of obtaining a good situation.

Destitute of. The fellow is destitute of all sense of shame. Destitute of the means of subsistence.

Destructive of. Intemperance is destructive of health and ruinous to moral character.

Detrimental to. His enmity is detrimental to your interests.

Devoid of. He is a man devoid of all fine feeling.

Different from. The Parsee's hat is very different from the turban.

Diligent in his business.

Disagreeable to. It is disagreeable to me to hear such things.

Disappointed in, of, with. I was disappointed in my clerk when I got to know him. I was disappointed of my expected rise in pay. I was disappointed with the book when I had bought it.

Disgusted at, with. Disgusted at the sight of the opium-smoking den. We were disgusted with his vulgarity. Disgusted with college life.

Displeased at, with. Why should you be displeased at the fun of the children? He is greatly displeased with you.

Displeasing to. His manner was very displeasing to me.

Distasteful to. Travelling is distasteful to the old man.

Distinct from. These families are distinct from one another.

Due to. What are earthquakes due to?

Dull of hearing, **of** comprehension.

Eager for, in. Eager for fame, for praise. Eager in the pursuit of science. **Eager** is sometimes followed by the infinitive. Eager to get on in the world.

Easy of access, of attainment.

Eligible for. Is this boy eligible for a scholarship?

Eminent for piety, eminent for learning.

Endowed with. He is endowed with strong will.

Endued with. He is a man endued with fine talents.

Enraged at, with. He is enraged with you for speaking against him. The bear is enraged at his keeper.

Envious of. Be not envious of your neighbour's attainments.

Equal to. He was equal to the occasion. This angle is equal to that. Will the boy be equal to such a task?

Essential to. Truth and purity are essential to moral character.

Exclusive of. This book cost ten shillings exclusive of postage.

Exempt from. The very poor should be exempt from taxation. No one is exempt from suffering and decay.

Exhausted with toil, with anxiety.

Expert at, in. Expert at accounts. He is expert in hunting up evidence.

Expose to danger, to the fire of the enemy.

Expressive of. His looks were expressive of gratitude.

Faithful to the trust reposed in him; to one's engagements.

False to. He has proved false to his professed principles. Never be false to your promises.

Familiar to, with. His name is familiar to me. Nothing but patient study can make one familiar with English idioms.

Famous for. Tyre was famous for its commerce. This clergyman is famous for eloquence.

Fatal to. The wound is likely to prove fatal to him. This battle was fatal to his cause.

Fatigued with his journey.

Favourable for, to. The wind is favourable for setting sail. A sunny aspect is favourable to good health.

Fearful of. He is fearful of the results of his rashness.

Fit for, to. This bread is not fit for food. I want a building fit for a dispensary. This shirt is not fit to wear.

Flushed with success, with victory.

Foiled in an attempt.

Fond of. Children are fond of sweets. I was always very fond of picking up old stories.

Forgetful of one's promises; forgetful of advice.

Fraught with. The enterprise is fraught with danger.

Free from restraint; from care, danger, molestation.

Friendly to. He will not join the association, but he is friendly to it.

Fruitful in. A noble life, fruitful in kind deeds. Fruitful in expedients. Fruitful in resources.

Full of. He started out full of hope. A bag full of sand. A man full of himself, i.e. vain, conceited, having a high opinion of himself.

Gifted with. He is not gifted with eloquence.

Given to, is to be devoted or addicted to. I am sorry to say this man is given to the use of drugs. This youth is given to study.

Glad of. I am glad of an opportunity of obliging you.

Good at, for. He is good at mathematics. Admittedly the Suez Canal has been good for the commerce of both East and West.

Grateful to a person, **for** a thing. He feels grateful to you for the kindly interest you have taken in him. Always be grateful for kindness.

Grown over with, is to be covered with a growth of. His garden is grown over with weeds.

Guilty of. He is found guilty of manslaughter.

Hard of hearing; hard of heart.

Heedless of. He rushed on, heedless of consequences.

Held in. A man held in high esteem. This fellow is held in contempt by all who know him. Your horse does not like to be held in, i.e. to be restrained or held in check.

Hidden by, from. A cottage among the trees, hidden from view; a flower hidden by leaves; a toy hidden by a child.

Hopeful of. He is quite hopeful of success. He has begun the work of reform and is hopeful of accomplishing much.

Hostile to. I always thought him hostile to you.

Hurtful to. Immoral actions will be and ought to be hurtful to your good name.

Ignorant of. How can I appear ignorant of his doings? No one should remain ignorant of the commands of God.

Ill of, with. The poor man is lying very ill **of** fever, or ill **with** fever.

Illustrative of. His lecture is meant to be illustrative of the way in which an epidiascope is used.

Imbued with. Let the minds of the young be imbued with the love of purity and truth.

Impatient at, for, of, under. Impatient at the unexpected delay. Impatient for the arrival of my friend. Impatient of restraint or control. Impatient under a burden.

Important to. This document is important to your case.

Impressed on, with. Let the nobleness of truth be early impressed on him. Deeply impressed with a sense of wrong.

Incapable of. This man is incapable of falsehood.

Incident to. How many ailments are incident to childhood!

Inclusive of. This sum covers the cost inclusive of postage.

Inconsistent with. This proposal is inconsistent with your plan.

Incumbent on. It is incumbent on all citizens to obey the laws. Do the duties incumbent on you.

Indebted to a person **for** a thing. I am greatly indebted to you for your help.

Independent of. He is independent of all help from me.

Indifferent to. A Buddhist seeks to be indifferent to pleasure or pain.

Indignant at, with. Instead of feeling complimented by the offer, he is indignant at it, and with the manager for making it.

Indispensable to. Clearness and precision are indispensable to a good style of writing.

Inferior to. I do not acknowledge myself inferior to him. His essay is not inferior to yours.

Infested with. I never saw a place so infested with rats.

Informed of. Keep me informed of his movements.

Inhabited by. A village inhabited by thieves.

Injurious to. Intemperate habits are injurious to health. Instability of government is injurious to the best interests of a country.

Innocent of. Beyond question he is innocent of the crime.

Instead of. Let Richard come instead of him.

Intent on. He was so intent on his book that he did not observe my approach.

Interested in. He seems interested in your success.

Intimate with. Are you intimate with this gentleman?

Involved in, with. He soon got involved in serious difficulties. How did you come to be involved in this lawsuit? Were any other men involved with him in that crime?

Inured to. These are men well inured to hardships.

Irrespective of his merits, i.e. not taking them into account.

Irritated at, by, with. Do not be irritated at this disappointment. These men are irritated by being kept so long exposed to the sun. I was irritated with him for not replying at once to my letter.

Jealous of. Do not be jealous of another man's success. John has got the appointment, but you need not be jealous of him.

Kind to. Be kind to the poor. God is kind to men. If you are kind to others, they will in turn be kind to you.

Laid up with, is to be confined with some ailment to one's bed or one's room. He is laid up with influenza.

Lame in. A man lame in one leg.

Lavish of, in. He is lavish of money. Lavish of praise. Lavish in his expenditure.

Level with the ground.

Liable for, to. Is a man liable for his son's debts? He is liable to imprisonment for a month.

Loaded with. He came out of the examination loaded with honours.

Lost to. He is lost to all sense of shame.

Loyal to. A good citizen is loyal to the government.

Mad with rage, with disappointment.

Made of, from. A chariot made of wood. Paper made from rice straw.

Married to a good wife.

Mindful of. It is well to be mindful of your promises.

Moist with. A cloth moist with dew.

Moved at a sight, **by** an entreaty, not easily moved **from** his purpose; moved **to** tears; moved **with** pity.

Natural to. It is natural to man to err.

Neglectful of duty.

Negligent in work.

Notorious for. He is notorious for smuggling. The town is notorious for daring thieves.

Obedient to. The servant must be obedient to his master.

Obnoxious to. The sight of him is obnoxious to me.

Observant of. Be observant of the rules of your office.

Occupied in, with. The vultures were occupied in tearing the carcass of the camel. The whole day was occupied with trifles.

Odious to. The minister has made himself odious to the prince.

Opposite to. Whose house is opposite to the hospital?

Overcome by, with. Overcome by stronger men. Overcome with fatigue.

Overrun with. A garden overrun with weeds.

Overwhelmed with. He seemed overwhelmed with confusion.

Painful to. This news is very painful to my mother.

Pale with fear, pale with fasting, pale with envy.

Parallel to. This line is parallel to that.

Partial to. This man is always partial to his friends.

Peculiar to. This is a custom peculiar to the Mongols. This style of architecture is peculiar to the Moors.

Pernicious to. Bad company is pernicious to good morals.

Pertinent to. These remarks are not pertinent to the subject.

Pleasant to. Sweet music is pleasant to the ear.

Popular with. A colonel popular with his regiment.

Possessed of. He is a man possessed of great wealth.

Praised for. Milton is praised for the majesty of his poetry.

Preferable to. Poverty with honesty is preferable to wealth got by unfair means.

Prefixed to. The syllable **un-** prefixed to a word often reverses the meaning of the word: do, undo; wise, unwise.

Prejudicial to. This will be prejudicial to your best interests.

Preparatory to. He studied logic preparatory to entering the college.

Previous to. He left previous to your arrival.

Prior to. This event was prior to the battle of Panipat.

Productive of. Industry and economy will be productive of good results.

Proficient in mathematics; proficient in office work.

Profitable to, for. Are protective duties in the long run profitable to a country? The book will prove profitable for the public to read.

Prompt in. He is always prompt in replying to letters. Prompt in complying with my orders.

Prone to. The heart of man is prone to folly and evil.

Proper for. This work is not proper for you. Quinine is a proper remedy for fever.

Proportionate to. Rewards should be proportionate to merit.

Proud of. He is proud of his parentage. The boy is so clever that his father is quite proud of him.

Quick at, in, of. The dog is quick at hearing. The boy is quick **at,** or **in** working sums. Quick **of** understanding.

Radiant with beauty. A young woman radiant with smiles.

Ready at figures. Ready **for** action. Ready **in** answering.

Reduced by, to. He had had his pay reduced to a hundred pounds a year. His salary has been reduced by ten pounds a year. His illness has reduced him to a skeleton.

Regardless of. I never met a man so regardless of remonstrance. A feast got up regardless of expense.

Regretted by. His death is a loss regretted by all.

Relative to. I have read all that the author says relative to the constitution of our law courts.

Relevant to. His speech was not relevant to the question.

Remarkable for. The Duke of Wellington was remarkable for early rising.

Renowned for. He is renowned for wisdom.

Replete with. He made a speech replete with good sense and humour.

Reposed in. Never belie the confidence reposed in you.

Repugnant to. All harshness is repugnant to his feelings.

Responsible for a thing **to** a person. We are all responsible to God for the gifts he has endowed us with.

Rid of trouble, of debt, of an undesirable companion.

Sacred to. The heart should be a temple sacred to God alone.

Sanguine of results; sanguine in one's expectations.

Satisfied with. He is quite satisfied with his income. I have not been at all satisfied with his conduct recently.

Secure against, from. A place secure against attack. Treasure secure from robbers.

Seized with. Seized with a panic, the men flung down their arms and fled from the place.

Sensible of. He is quite sensible of his danger.

Serviceable to. Here is a letter of introduction which I hope will prove serviceable to you.

Short of money; short of supplies. A garrison short of provisions.

Sick of, at. He is sick of hard work. Sick of waiting. Sick at heart.

Significant of. An historical festival is commonly significant of some past event accounted memorable.

Similar to. The coin you showed me is similar to this one.

Skilful in debate, **in** rowing.

Sorry for. I am sorry for his failure.

Startled at a crash, an explosion, sudden bad news.

Starved to death; starved **with** hunger, **with** cold. (**Starve** once meant to die *any* manner of death.)

Strange to. This custom is strange to me.

Struck with the appearance of a thing; to be struck with fear, with alarm. He was struck with it as a piece of accurate description.

Studded with. She wore a head-dress studded with diamonds.

Subject to. All things earthly are subject to decay. A girl subject to fits of epilepsy.

Subsequent to. A time long subsequent to the king's death. I got his reply subsequent to the date of my second letter.

Successful in. I hope you will be successful in business.

Sufficient for a purpose.

Suitable for, to. This block of marble is suitable for a statue. These ornaments are not suitable to her station in life.

Suited for, to. He is not suited to the post. His speech was admirably suited to the occasion. His acting was not suited for the part.

Superior to. He is superior to all meanness.

Sure of. He felt sure of the appointment.

Surprised at, by. Why should you be surprised at this action? They were surprised by the appearance of two soldiers.

Surrounded by. He is very happy at school surrounded by his friends.

Susceptible of. ˙He is susceptible of deep feeling.

Suspicious of. Men even of the same tribe are often suspicious of one another.

Sympathetic with, towards. He showed himself sympathetic with my difficulties.

Temperate in. Be temperate in speech as well as in eating and drinking.

Thankful to a person, **for** a benefit. Be thankful to God for all His gifts. I feel very thankful to my old friend for giving me this appointment.

Tired of, with. He is tired of doing nothing. Tired with his ride. Also, tired to death, i.e. excessively wearied.

Tributary to. Several rivers are tributary to the Ganges.

Troublesome to. The deer are troublesome to these farmers.

True to. Be true to the trust reposed in you. A servant true to his master's interests.

Uncared for. The children are left uncared for.

Unfit for. The meat is unfit for human food.

Unheard of. Unheard of difficulties. Tribes before unheard of.

Unknown to. A man unknown to fame. His handwriting is unknown to me.

Useful to a person, **for** a purpose.

Vain of. A girl vain of her pretty face. An orator vain of his powers of persuasion.

Versed in. He is well versed in the science of optics.

Vexed at, with. I am vexed at my brother's absence. Do not be vexed with me. Vexed with care.

Void of. This man seems void of common sense.

Weary of his burden, weary of wandering.

Worthy of. His eloquence is worthy of a better cause. A crime worthy of severe punishment. The labourer is worthy of his hire.

Zealous for, in. A servant zealous for his master's honour. Be zealous in a good cause.

78. We now give a mixed set of examples of idiomatic phrases composed of an adjective or participle and an appropriate preposition following. These are for the most part collected from such standard authors as Defoe, Dickens, Thackeray, Trollope, Swift, and Lamb. We put them in the alphabetical order of the adjectives.

He returned accompanied by a very sprightly young friend.
He has become acquainted with his son's doings.
A land afflicted with drought.
She could make herself agreeable to her benefactors.

They were alarmed about him at home.
Alone in a strange place.
Alone with a friend.
They were highly amused with the scene.
She was amused by the lady's talk and not ashamed of her company.
Anxious about my own danger.
Her brothers were very anxious about her.
His position was one beset with difficulties.
A man bred to the bookbinding business.
So long as his age and infirmities will leave him capable of business.
It must be quite clear to every reader that, etc.
He crept closer to his master.
Conscious of their powers.
Conscious of everything that is passing around you.
Consistent with his dignity.
Content with a humble position.
It was my lot to have been daily conversant with the persons then in power.
Covered with dust.
It was very cruel of you to laugh.
Secret plottings, besides being dangerous to the State, are hurtful to the community.
She had been deaf to all that passed.
A child dear to its mother.
Decked with costly jewels.
Deprived of the benefit of his instructions.
Deprived of the sight of both eyes.
Deserving of all praise.
The Queen found them very desirous of a secure and honourable peace.
It proved not altogether displeasing to him.
A mill driven by water.
Drowned in debt.
Drowned in a cask of wine.
Struck dumb with fear.
Eager for praise.
He felt himself pretty easy about his adversary.
He was very easy in mind about his brother's absence.
He will be faithful to his promises.
Familiar with the family.
I want a teacher familiar with trigonometry.
Familiar probably to us all.
Far from his intention.
A trench filled with stones and sand.
Filled with hope and fired with ambition.
Not fit for use.
Flushed with indignation.
Fond of music.
Fond of playing with fire.
Free of debt.
Free from danger and quite out of reach of the water.
To get free from prison.
The regret of a recent separation was fresh in his mind.
A tank full of water.
Youth is full of hope.
Her heart full of sorrow and her body full of pain.
Rather more than was good for him.

Gratified at thinking over their triumphs.
If I have been guilty of any mistakes, they must be of small moment.
Harassed with perplexing circumstances.
Impressed with the belief that, etc.
To her the Duke is chiefly indebted for his greatness and his fall.
Such men as were perfectly indifferent to any religion.
Indignant at the treatment they received.
The father seemed to grow more indulgent to his son than ever.
Houses inhabited by people of the poorest class.
He was originally intended for a trade.
Irritated by the loss of power.
Drive him mad with terror.
Too numerous for recital.
Overborne by oppression.
Overcome with emotion.
Perishing with hunger.
Pleased with the compliments which were paid him.
Proficient in the art of teaching.
He was proud of his own skill.
Livid with rage.
Eyes red with weeping.
Relative to his own son's affairs.
She was woefully sad at leaving school.
Safe from danger.
A province scourged with locusts.
Shorn of all outward prosperity.
Silent with regard to her marriage.
Deer startled with the baying of hounds.
She was starved to death.
Subsequent to your coming.
An army badly supplied with ammunition.
Surprised at the sight.
Swayed by the speeches of agitators.
Thrilled with triumph.
Very tired with his walk.
Tired of his companion.
Not troubled with much compunction of conscience.
As the needle is true to the pole.
True to nature.
Prove herself worthy of the attention bestowed on her.
Writhing with anguish.

CHAPTER VIII

IDIOMATIC PREPOSITIONAL PHRASES AND ADVERBIAL PHRASES

79. We now take a chapter on idiomatic Prepositional Phrases and Adverbial Phrases. These two run into each other, many expressions which are prepositional in form being adverbial in meaning.

Prepositions form but a small class of words in English, but they enter so frequently into combination with other words that they help to make up many of the idiomatic expressions of the language. Many delicate shades of meaning are expressed by prepositions. For instance, when a man is out of debt, it is true to say of him that he is not in debt; and yet the expressions *not in debt* and *out of debt* are not exactly equivalent. To say that a man is *out of debt* implies that he has been in debt, but has now got rid of it; whereas to say that a man is *not in debt* implies nothing about his previous position: he may have been in debt and have got rid of it, or he may never have been in debt at all.

Some of the English prepositions are simple words, as *at, by, from, to, with*; others are compounds, as *before, into, upon, without*; while a few were originally participles of verbs, as *concerning, during, pending*.

There are also several phrases which in composition serve the purpose of prepositions, as *on account of, in front of, at variance with, out of keeping with*. These phrase-prepositions are commonly made up of a preposition and a noun followed by another preposition.

A preposition attached to a verb often gives a new meaning to the verb: as, *get, get up, get on*; *laugh, laugh at*. These prepositional verbs we reserve for treatment in the next chapter. Several prepositional phrases, moreover, are found only with some part of the verb *to be*, and when joined to that verb give an expression which in reality is equivalent to a new verb. Such instances we shall consider in a separate chapter.

80. We now take ordinary prepositions and set before the student a number of idiomatic phrases of which they form an important part. As a general rule, no preposition but the one given can stand in the same collocation. For instance, in *He is at* *liberty to go*, we must not alter the preposition *at* into any other. Nor will it do to introduce a new word into a prepositional phrase while we seek to preserve the idiom and the same meaning. For instance, we cannot change *I have a brother at sea* into *I have a brother at the sea*. The latter expression indeed has a meaning, but it is quite different from that of the former one.

In this connexion what the student needs particularly to notice and fix in his memory is what particular preposition stands in a particular phrase, for, as is usual with all idioms, the idiomatic turn of expression must not be altered.

81. It must be remembered that the examples given below by no means exhaust the application of the prepositions.

About, about the hour, i.e. near the hour; it is now about five o'clock; about six miles, i.e. six miles or a little more or a little less; about the size; a discussion about (=concerning) the origin of evil; to ride about the country; to go about the town; tell us all about the war.

About is really an adverb in the following: About three thousand men were killed; the rent of this house is about twenty pounds a month.

In such phrases as **about to go, about to die, about to write,** the word **about** signifies **ready to, on the point of, in the act of.** They were about to be married.

Above, above one's head; the balloon rose above the clouds; above your comprehension; above the grasp of reason; a man above (=superior to) all meanness; a man not above his business, i.e. not too proud to do anything and everything which the proper carrying on of his business requires him to do; he is above asking a favour; to live above one's means, is to spend more than one's income can afford; a thing done above-board, is a thing done openly, without any secrecy or underhand dealing.

In many expressions **above** signifies more in quantity or number than, more in degree than. The population of this city is above a hundred thousand; a man above suspicion, i.e. so excellent that no one would suspect him; to speak above one's breath is to speak in a tone as faint as a whisper. In the sick-room we scarcely spoke above our breath.

The phrase **above all** means, chiefly, before any other consideration. This expression would be used when a speaker, after having mentioned a number of things, wishes to state something further which is of still greater importance. ' Be cleanly; be sober; be honest; but, above all, be truthful.'

For the phrase **over and above**, see under **Over.**

Across, across the road; a bridge is laid across the river; ships sail across the ocean; the road lies across the moor; a chain across the bows of a ship; a rope stretched across a lane; he threw the burden across his shoulders; the horse galloped across the cornfield.

After, after dinner; after ten o'clock; after consultation with; after an interval of three hours; a longing after immortality; after such behaviour, i.e. in view of; a painting after Reynolds, i.e. after the style of Reynolds; to make a thing after a model; he comes here day after day; after dark, i.e. after it has become dark. How are you after your journey? What is he after? i.e. What does he want?

There is the phrase **after all.** After all, what does it matter whether he comes or not? i.e. everything being taken into account, what does it matter whether he comes or not?

Against, against the rule; against the laws; against orders; to go against the wind; against the tide, the current; against the grain;* to swim against the stream; to go against the enemy; to vote against a motion; to vote against one's own interests; to lean against a wall; to hope against hope;* to work against time, i.e. to work to finish within a given time.

Over against means opposite to. An island over against the mouth of a river.

Along, along the seashore; along the valley; the men marched along the highway. **Along with** conveys the idea of companionship a little more fully than **with.**

Amid, Amidst, amid danger; amidst the horrors of the battlefield; this book was written amidst many interruptions; he persevered amidst many difficulties.

Among, Amongst, among friends; hid among the trees; among the people; he fell among thieves; amongst the reasons I have to give, there is this important one.

To divide among: see under **Between.**

Around, around the hearth; to travel around the country, i.e. to travel about from one part of the country to another.

As to. For **as to** as a preposition, see under **To.**

At, at fault; at liberty; at one's ease, at leisure; be at sea;* at random; at noon; I woke at daybreak; at Christmas; help is at hand; the boy is at school; I met him at dinner; he studied at the university; sick at heart; they are at variance, i.e. they disagree; be at daggers drawn;* be at a loss;* keep him at arm's length; they galloped at full speed; the question at issue; he is not at home; he is standing at the door; at a distance; jackals prowl about at night; the ship rides at anchor, or is at anchor, or is lying at anchor; this bank draft is payable at sight; I have no money at present; I am at your service, i.e. I am ready to serve you in any way you mention; my horse is at your disposal; he is busy at farming; a seat at the council board; at all events; at all hazards; at any rate; at a standstill; at the foot of the hill; at first sight; I took it in at a glance or at the first glance; at the first blush (=first glance); to lend money at interest; the interest is at four per cent; he sells cloth at a dollar a yard; these nations were at war but now they are at peace; watching the boys at play; the men are at work; she shuddered at the sight; I rose at his command; at this news she fainted; the quarrel is at an end; I did not expect such treatment at your hands (=from you); to be at large, i.e. to be unconfined; at the sword's point; at the point of the bayonet; to set at nought, i.e. to treat as nothing, to despise; a good hand at a thing; we reached home at the same time; I fell at his feet; this was repaired at my expense; the citizens are at the mercy of their conqueror; a fortress surrenders at discretion; you will find an index at the end of this book; a man at his wit's end, i.e. so puzzled that he knows not what to do; at death's door or at the point of death; at the back of the mountain; he was sitting at his desk; he was alarmed at the news; I can call up his form at will, i.e. I can recollect his appearance whenever I wish; at the top of one's voice, means as loud as one can shout.

At once usually means immediately, but occasionally has the sense of simultaneously. He was at once frank and honest.

There are also the phrases **at all, at least, at most, at best, at last, at length, at the longest.** He never was in debt at all. Give me at least an hour of your time. At most his subscription will not be over twenty shillings. He cannot live more than three days at best. In spite of many hindrances they have at last succeeded. After a tedious voyage we at length reached our destination. Tell the servant to come at once. Life at the longest is but a span.

Athwart, athwart the path; a cable athwart the bows of a ship; athwart the ship's course.

Before, before one's face; before one's eyes; before the fire; a dainty dish to set before the king; they stood before the prince; he appeared before the magistrate; I wrote a letter before breakfast; the case came before the committee; a ship running before the wind; he came before the time, i.e. before the fixed time; we shall visit you before Christmas; the fleet anchored before Alexandria.

The adverbial phrase **before long** means, soon, before a long time has elapsed.

Behind, behind one's back; the sun is now behind a cloud; hidden behind the door; a regiment behind the hill; the train is behind time, i.e. after the stated time; he has been behind the scenes;* the dog walked close behind you; he left nothing behind him but his good name, i.e. at his death he left nothing but, etc.; what is behind his proposal? i.e. what secret scheme is to be brought forward after his proposal is carried ?

Below, below the table; shares below par; a composition below average; his leg is broken below the knee; below the rank of a duke; to strike below the belt; he is below the standard height for a soldier.

Beneath, beneath notice, i.e. too trifling to be worthy of notice; he is beneath contempt; such conduct is beneath the dignity of a gentleman, i.e. it is so base that no gentleman would stoop to it; he lies beneath this stone; brutes are beneath man in the scale of creation.

Beside (=by the side of), beside the well; a garden beside the river; beside the fire; a hut beside the wall of the city; the bride stands beside the bridegroom; he stood beside his father's grave. Beside (=aside from) our present purpose; beside (=aside from) the mark.

To be beside oneself, is to be out of one's senses.

Besides (=distinct from, in addition to), besides all this; besides these arguments I have used, there is another, etc.; he has two children in the house besides his own.

Besides is also used as an adverb, meaning, moreover.

Between, between friends; between ourselves; he sat between Charles and me; between two fires; between the scenes in a play; between sunrise and sunset; between the hours of twelve and three o'clock; the Straits of Dover lie between France and England; between this and the end of the month, i.e. between this time and the end of this month; war between the French and the Chinese; Crewe is on the railway between London and Liverpool; he tried to mediate between the parties; let there be no quarrel between us; there is an understanding between them.

The second syllable of **between** is of the same root as **twain,** i.e. **two.** Hence to **divide between,** implies two; whereas **to divide among,** implies more than two. There is therefore a distinction between **He divided the apples between the boys** and **He divided the apples among the boys.**

Beyond, beyond limits; beyond the sea; beyond the stars; a hill beyond the village; beyond doubt; beyond expectation; beyond reach; beyond the mark; beyond the power of medicine to cure him; the life beyond the grave; the scene was beyond description, i.e. it is not possible to describe it; he went in beyond his depth, i.e. he went into water where it was so deep as to cover his head; the stars are beyond number; this is a luxury beyond my income, i.e. my income is not such as to admit of my buying this luxury.

But (=except), all consented but you; he gave me all the books but one.

By, to open a door by force; to light on a thing by chance; to travel by land or by water; to go by rail or by steamer; by fits and starts; to read by moonlight, or by the light of a lamp; a mill driven by water, or by wind, or by steam; to tell the time by the sun; it is seven o'clock by my watch; to go by the pond; a house by the city wall; to sit by oneself, is to sit alone; all by myself, is quite alone; to know men by name; I caught him by the shoulder; to take time by the forelock;* to hold a horse by the bridle; to get a letter by post; to pay a bill by (a bank) cheque; to be taken by surprise; to learn poetry by heart; a poem by Milton; a letter written by a schoolgirl; Lisbon was destroyed by an earthquake; a city destroyed by fire, or taken by violence; he will be here by nightfall; by this time the moon had risen; profits made by trade; a room twenty feet by ten; too long by two yards; greater by half; he is older by five years than John; by degrees; by main force; by all means; by hook or by crook;* by his side; to sell cloth by the yard, eggs by the dozen, grain by the bushel or ton, cotton by the bale, snuff by the ounce; to do things by halves; killed by traitors; they sleep side by side; by force of circumstances, means compelled by one's circumstances.

One by one, day by day, house by house, drop by drop, piece by piece, mean, each one, each day, house, drop, piece, severally.

By is the preposition of adjuration. By all that we hold dear.
By and by is an adverbial phrase meaning, soon, after some time.
By the by is equivalent in meaning to **in passing.**

Down, down stairs; to run down the hill; to swim down the river; tears ran down his cheeks; I went down the pit; I looked down the shaft of the mine.

During, during the late king's reign; during the battle; during his lifetime; during the space of a year; during the holidays.

Except, Excepting, all the countries except England; I have examined all the papers except two; I have read all, excepting his application.

For, good for food; ready for battle; this book is for you; he has bought food for his children; a house for sale; crying for mercy; for a time; the boy has been ill for a week; looking for aid or help; crying out for fear; he hangs down his head for shame; he could not speak for sorrow; he left for school an hour ago;

I know this for certain; it is easy for you to learn your lesson; to sell for money; I sell these at three for a shilling; what did you pay for your hat?; to flee to a castle for protection; to flee for one's life, i.e. in order to save one's life; lame for life, i.e. during the remainder of one's lifetime; the soul will last for ever; she is brave for a woman, i.e. she must be pronounced brave when it is borne in mind that she is a woman; left for dead, i.e. believed to be dead; I took you for your brother; I would not part with it for any money; he would not give it up for all the world; this is for the general good; some toil for money, others for fame; he works for bread; he works for praise; placed there for safety; for this reason; to ask a question for information; to read for amusement; to go out for a walk; for God's sake hear me; every man for himself; he came with me for company; a fight for life; to take for better for worse;* pray for kings and for all in authority; he started for Bombay on Monday; tit for tat; to take amiability for piety is to take glass for diamonds; were it not for his poverty I would dismiss him at once; but for your coming, I should have been very lonely; these two essays are word for word alike; for (=in spite of, notwithstanding) all his wealth, he is not happy; for anything I know, the man is dead.

From, away from home; far from the fire; Delhi is a long way from Bombay; a letter sent from London; a young man from the country; figs come from Afghanistan; safe from danger; free from care; I have known him from childhood; I have known him from a boy, i.e. from boyhood; from my youth up; from the creation of the world; from his experience; released from his vow; rescued from the enemy; he did it from gratitude and not from fear; he has authority from the government; a brand plucked from the burning; saved from a watery grave; all men are sprung from Adam; light comes from the sun; a lamp hanging from the ceiling; separate the good from the bad; I judged from this testimony; he drew the sword from its scabbard; this is far from being the case; to rise from the ranks.

From first to last; from door to door; from side to side; from hand to mouth; from youth to age; from heaven to earth; from pole to pole; from grave to gay; from bad to worse; from the cradle to the grave.

In, in the house; in parliament; in the village; a well in the garden; in a place of danger; in a maze; in his presence, or absence; in the distance; to look a man in the face; in the background; in heaven; in the sun, i.e. in the sunshine and not in the shade; in the van; in the open air; in the thicket; in the dark; in a corner; an estate in Chancery, i.e. under Government care; walk in front;

in summer; in an unguarded moment; just in time; in danger; in pain; in joy; in sight; in store; in stock; they came in state; he is in a difficulty; to put a law in force; they are scattered in flight; up in arms; in haste; in a deep sleep; to converse in a whisper; they walked in silence; in earnest; to pay in advance; to end in nothing; the work in hand; vile men are in power; hold them in check; have them in subjection; pray for all in authority; in the power of the enemy; the child is in love with his toy; he is over head and ears in debt; involved in ruin; well read in mathematics; triangles in all respects alike; in case he should decline the offer; three in every four of these mangoes are spoiled; Sir Richard Temple was then in office as finance minister; in honour bound; in all probability he will come; in round numbers there were five hundred; keep in mind; put in mind; work in harmony; in exercise; not in use; in the end; to take in good part;* a man in a thousand; in the main; put in order.

The adverbial phrases **in all, in general, in fact, in truth, in a word, in brief, in short, in fine, in vain**, are quite common. **In the long run** means, ultimately. **In the mean time** is while waiting; in an interval of time. **In the mean while** has the same meaning.

Into, come into the house; I followed him into the garden; to fall into the river; led into error; forced into compliance; let into the secret; to look into a book, or room; burst into fragments; pour water into a vessel; a stream runs into another; to turn Spanish into English; to turn prose into poetry; to resolve water into its constituent gases; water is convertible into vapour; children frightened into fits; carbon enters largely into the composition of material substances; fly into a passion; he has got into difficulties.

Into is used chiefly after verbs, participles, and adjectives.

Near, to sit near the fire; to be near the door; near your father; the village is near the seashore; to be near the heart; he is near death.

Of, a man of courage; a flock of sheep; a crown of gold; the capital of Spain; a native of Zanzibar; men of Athens; the Book of Proverbs; the sacred book of the Moslems; the people of the Middle Ages; as a matter of course; of use; of value; of little or no account; of importance; this is of no consequence; a course of mathematics; the place of honour; a man of mark; a Master of Arts; the price of wheat; the force of the wind; the bridge of the nose; a tenth of the remainder; hard of hearing, i.e. dull in hearing; he will, of necessity, do this; to have right of way; to be short of provisions; to cure a man of fever; the murder was committed within a mile of the town; they went of their own free will; they are all of one mind.

Of old, is formerly; **of late**, is recently; **of course**, is by consequence, in the ordinary way.

Off, an island a little way off the coast; he fell off the scaffolding; I caught him off his guard; the responsibility is off my shoulders; the wind almost lifted me off my feet; the men are off work, i.e. not working; to do a thing off-hand, i.e. at once, and without study or preparation.

The adverbial phrase **off and on** is explained in Section 84.

On, on land; on board; a ship on the rocks; a book on the table; a hat on one's head; a monkey on the roof of the house; a cart on the road; a berry on the tree; a sick man lying on a couch; rain falls on the earth; the sun shines on the fields; Benares is on the Ganges; a tree on the hill; leaning on his staff; to play on an instrument: on a harp, on a guitar; this village is on your way; the ship is on the way to Japan; to go on foot, or on horseback; on a proper footing; to be put on one's mettle, i.e. to be incited to do one's best; on one's good behaviour; on 'Change, is on the Exchange; business on my hands; goods on hand; goods on sale; a picture on view; on an average; a map on a large scale; a house on fire; on the one hand; on each side; on your part; remarks on a subject; on a public occasion; on no account; on further reflection he rejected the offer; the moon is on the wane; to set the teeth on edge; he will give the ground on certain conditions; to lend money on good security; to pay on demand; he had pity on her; something on my mind; on you be the blame; testimony given on oath; on the breaking out of war he left the country; on inquiry I found, etc.; on the supposition that, etc.; on the move, is in motion, or ready to move; a bird on the wing, is a bird in flight; to arrange things on a certain plan; to stand on tiptoe; to live on terms of friendship with a person; his hair stood on end; at work for ten hours on the stretch, i.e. continuously, without cessation; to be on duty, is to be occupied in the discharge of one's duty; to take a thing on trust, on trial; on the whole, i.e. taking the whole circumstances into consideration; he dined on venison.

On a sudden (or, all of a sudden) means suddenly; **on the alert**, is in a state of watchfulness or activity; **on high**, is in an elevated place; **on the spot**, is immediately, without moving away.

Out of, out of use; out of favour; out of reach; out of one's power; out of the way; out of step; a remark out of place, is one not pertinent to the subject in hand or made at an inopportune time; out of fashion; out of date; out of all reason; out of repair, i.e. in a condition needing repair; a clock out of order, is one not in proper order; a musical instrument out of tune; a book out of print, i.e. all the printed copies of it have been sold; out of doors, is outside the house; out of hearing, is beyond the reach of hearing; out of sight; time out of mind, is beyond the reach of memory; out of rank; a limb out of joint; delivered out of danger; plants grow out of the earth; he paid me out of his pocket money; to do a thing out of kindness; out of fear; a quarrel arising out of a trifle; to go out of one's way to oblige another; out of trim, is not in proper trim, or order; to be out of temper, is to be out of good temper, or in bad temper; the seed was sown out of season, i.e. not in the proper season; out of breath, is breathless, panting for breath; to be out of one's depth, is to have got into too deep water; out of sorts is slightly unwell, or out of order; to be out of pocket five shillings, is to have expended five shillings; out of one's mind, or out of one's wits, is insane; out of debt, is no longer in debt. An out-of-the-way place, is a place hard to get to. To do a thing out of hand, i.e. immediately, straight off. To put someone's nose out of joint, is to earn his jealousy.

Over, the clouds are over our heads; a canopy of smoke over the city; over the hills; the river runs over the rocks; the water is all over the field; over the country; to look over one's shoulder; to have power over property; he has many advantages over you; God over all; over head and ears in love; my income is not over my expenditure; to tumble head over heels; to stay over night, i.e. till the next day; to keep grain over winter, i.e. till the winter is past; to show me over your house;* to buy a house over one's head.*

Over enters into several compound words, frequently with the meaning of excess, as overcharge, overcautious; also with the idea of spreading, as overcast, overflow; and sometimes with the idea of reversal, as overturn.

Over and above, meaning besides, is used sometimes prepositionally, often adverbially. Over and above this consideration, there is another I wish to mention.

The adverbial phrases over again and over and over are explained in Section 84.

Past, past hope; past recall; a disease past cure; past recovery; a statement past comprehension or past belief; past feeling; past shame; past endurance; past control; past four o'clock; of a man just dead we might say, he is past our care, or past our help.

Round, a voyage round the world; the planets move round the sun; a wall round the garden; a gallop round the race course; a walk round the town; to wind a cable round a windlass; the courtiers stood round the prince; to get round a person.*

Since, since the crusades; he had been ill since Monday.

Through, through the gate; he went through the door; he bored a hole through the door; a shell passed through the ship's side; the balloon went up through the clouds; through the wood; deer roam through the forest; fish move through the water; the bird flew in through the window; through the ages; through the valley of the shadow of death; to go through fire and water for a person, is to go through the most terrible difficulties; to go through thick and thin, is to go through difficulties great or small as they arise; all through the year; through life, is during the whole of life; he escaped through the swiftness of his horse; he got this post through influence and not through industry; he obtained his request through a friend at court; to look through a book, is to peruse it hastily.

Throughout, is compounded of **through** and **out**. Throughout the year, is during the whole year.

To, he went to his house; where does this road go to? It leads to London; they escaped safe to land; go to bed; go to rest; add this to that; a speech addressed to a large audience; to say a thing to one's face; this will come to an end; it stands to reason; to sing to the harp; brought as sheep to the slaughter; to bring a lecture to a close; the pudding is done (=cooked) to a cinder; give the picture to your mother; your duty to your parents; thanks be to God; pray to God alone; all that they did was piety to (=as compared with) this; beaten to (=as far as) death; flattered to his ruin; they assembled to the number of five hundred; given to social pleasures; pleasant to the view; pleasing to the eye; sweet to the taste; ready to your hand; to his honour be it spoken; rising to wealth and honour; looking up to heaven; leave that to me; is he your cousin, or what is he to you?; he entered on a quarrel to his cost; keep a secret to oneself; an argument to the point, is a pertinent argument; a farm left to you by your father's will; the house is not to his mind, i.e. not as he would like it; to take to wife; to their joy the door was wide open; nothing to the purpose; to all intents and purposes; to all appearance, i.e. apparently; the odds are as two to one; three is to nine as eight to twenty-four; they fought to the last man=as long as there was a man left; to the full, is to the fullest extent; he was conscious to the last=till the moment of death; from first to last; from day to day; from time to time; from beginning to end; from end to end; from age to age; from year's end to year's end; from hand to mouth; a thing descends from father to son.

Up to and as to are used as prepositions. **Up to** means, as far as; and **as to** means, with regard to. He does his work up to the measure of his ability. A horse up to my weight, is a horse strong enough to carry me. He has misgivings as to the future.

To the last, to the contrary, are intelligible phrases. **Today, tonight, tomorrow, to and fro**, are adverbial expressions explained in Section 84.

Under, under a tree; a cellar under the house; a cell under ground; a post under government; to be under arms; under water; under cover; I arrest you under a warrant from the court; a ship under sail; a ship under way, i.e. having already started on her voyage; under a load; under heaven; there is nothing new under the sun, i.e. in all the world; under fire, i.e. exposed to the enemy's fire; a man under trial; a prisoner under sentence of death, is a prisoner on whom sentence of death has been passed; a bill under discussion; a measure under consideration; under this head we may mention, etc.; to act under compulsion; soldiers under orders to march; under these conditions I will do the work; to speak under one's breath, is to speak very softly or in a whisper; to live under oppressive rule; he is under a vow of celibacy; under an impression, a misapprehension; under necessity to do a thing; under suspicion; to be patient under pain, misfortune; he would not sell his horse under a hundred pounds; I inherited this under my father's will; he is under age, i.e. under full age, he is a minor; to do a thing under the rose, is to do it secretly, in a manner which forbids disclosure; given under my hand and seal; he travelled under the name of John Smith; under foot, under one's feet; under lock and key; how many hands has this overseer under him?

Up, to go up stairs; to walk up a hill; to swim up the stream; he has gone up country, generally means, he has left the town.

Up to, for **up to** as a preposition, see under **To**.

Upon, a book upon the table; a spring upon the top of the hill; a ship upon a reef; a bundle upon the head; a burden upon the heart; a boat upon the lake; the moon shining upon the surface of the lake; it is upon record that he did so and so; I refuse upon principle to do this; to stand upon the same footing; to be put upon one's trial; upon one's good behaviour; upon his word; take the road upon the left; to stand upon one's rights; once upon a time; upon occasion; upon full consideration, he would not go; upon this, means hereupon; upon the whole, i.e. everything being considered.

Upon, compounded of **up** and **on**, is less used than formerly: its place is now almost always taken by the simple preposition **on**, (e.g. on the whole), with which it is for the most part interchangeable.

Distinguish between **upon** and **above**. Do not say, The zenith is a point in the heavens directly **upon** our heads, but directly **above** our heads, or **over** our heads.

With, go with him to the market; to travel with a companion; there were two men with him; there is no living with such people; ground dug by the gardener with a spade; a street paved with brick; fed with rich food; they plot with bated breath; he passed the examination with great credit; walk with haste; these considerations have no force with him; with all one's might and main; he came with his dog and his gun; with the ancients, poetry and legend passed for history; it is a custom with the Hindus to burn their dead; to weary one with a long complaint; I am with (=in harmony with, in conjunction with) you in this business; side by side with; with that he drew his sword, i.e. immediately after saying or doing that, he drew his sword; with (=notwithstanding, in spite of) all his wealth he is not happy; with one exception everything passed off pleasantly; he wrote with this intention; it rests with you to decide the matter; he does his work with a will, i.e. most willingly; with telling effect, means, most effectively.

Within, within a circle; within reach; within range; within easy distance; within the target; within a mile; within the boundary; within the lines; within an hour; within the month, i.e. before the present month expires; it is within your power; keep your expenses within your income, i.e. do not spend more than you receive; keep within doors, i.e. keep inside your house, do not go out; he is within call, i.e. he is so near that he can hear if you call him; during our conversation he was within hearing, i.e. he was so near that he could hear us converse.

Without, he escaped without damage; he is without help; he is without wife or child; without success; he would like to live without labour; to die without hope; a soldier without arms; without recourse to strong measures; we cannot do this without you; to settle a dispute without an appeal to law; this cannot be done without a division of the property; he will come without fail; without a doubt the ship is lost; come without delay; to act without precaution.

82. Several phrase-prepositions or prepositional phrases consist of a preposition and a noun followed by another preposition. Most of these are so simple as to require no explanation, and would be translated into another language by a single word. We give some prepositional phrases commonly used.

At the end of	In favour of	In harmony with
At home in, i.e. perfectly familiar with	In front of	In keeping with
	In honour of	On account of
At the side of, i.e. beside	In hope of	On behalf of
At the top of (one's voice)	In place of	On the brink of
	In prospect of	On the eve of
At variance with	In respect of	On the face of
Because of	In lieu of	On the ground of
By force of	In search of	On the part of
By means of	In spite of	On the point of
By reason of	Instead of	Out of harmony with
By the side of, i.e. beside	In view of	Out of keeping with
	In the character of	Out of proportion with or to
By virtue of	In the event of	
By way of	In the face of	Under the character of
For fear of	In the hope of	Under the name of
For the purpose of	In the name of	With the help of
For sake of	In the rear of	With the hope of
For want of	In the sight of	With the intention of
In behalf of	In the teeth of	With the view of
In case of	In order to	With a view to
In common with	In proportion to	With an eye to
In consequence of	In regard to	With reference to
In course of	In accordance with	With regard to
In defiance of	In connexion with	With respect to

There are also double prepositions, such as *over against, from above, from out of,* etc.

I saw a tiger come rushing out from among the bushes.

83. PARTICULAR USAGES OF A FEW PREPOSITIONS

I. **With** and **by.** Distinguish between **with** and **by** when brought into contrast. *By* is used before a noun denoting the agent, and **with** before a noun denoting the instrument.

The prisoner was bound with a chain by the jailer.
This letter was written by a clerk with a steel pen.
The field was ploughed by the farmer with his neighbour's plough.

II. **In** and **into.** Generally speaking **in** expresses rest in a place, while **into** indicates motion towards a place.

You sat in your room; he followed me into the garden.
Carry this parcel into the house. Roses grow in the garden.
His horse strayed into my field. He fell into the pond.
I walked into his field. I can't walk in the park.

Certain peculiar phrases to be learnt by heart are:

To set in motion.	To fall in love.
To put in motion.	To fall into decay.
To put in force.	To take into consideration.
To put in *or* into practice.	To turn Greek into English.
To take in tow.	To change water into wine.
To take in hand.	To make up goods into parcels.

III. **In** and **within** with phrases of time. Foreign students often mistake the idiomatic meaning of **in** in such phrases as,

> The messenger will come back in an hour.
> I expect a letter from my father in a week.

They think that **in** here means *during the course of*, whereas it means *after the lapse of*. To say that the messenger would return during the course of an hour, the idiomatic form would be,

> The messenger will come back within an hour.

IV. **At the same time** and **In the same time**. Note also the distinct meanings expressed by these.

> You started from Madras and I from Bombay, and we reached Calcutta at the same time, i.e. we arrived at the same hour.
> We reached Calcutta in the same time, i.e. the same space of time was spent by both in making the journey to Calcutta.

V. **For.** Some peculiar uses of **for** deserve special notice.

1. The sentence, *I took you for your brother*, means, *I thought it was your brother, whereas it was yourself.* So that *took* really here means *mistook*. The expression, *They left him for dead*, means, *They, believing that he was dead, left him.*

2. We have the idiomatic expression, *He is tall for his age*, i.e. he is taller than most boys are at his age. The expression would be used of a growing boy. **For** may be similarly explained in

> She is strong for a girl. This is a rich town for its size.
> For its extent, Russia is a poor country.

3. **For** in the clause *for anything I know*, means in spite of, notwithstanding.

4. In such idiomatic expressions as

> He may go where he likes for me. He may go to Hongkong for me,

the preposition **for** signifies, *notwithstanding*; so that *for me* in these sentences indicates that I do not care in the slightest where he goes. But such phrases are used contemptuously.

5. *The thief ran for all he was worth*, means, ran as hard as he could.

VI. **To.** The following has a very noticeable meaning of **to**.

> They rose to a man and left the room.

This means that they all, down to and including the last man, rose and left the room.

VII. We can correctly say, *by day*, *by night*; *in the day*, *in the night*; and also *at night*, but not *at day*.

We say, both *day by day* and *day after day*; *night by night* and *night after night*.

84. Adverbial Phrases

At all is a phrase expressing emphasis, found chiefly in negative or interrogative sentences.

Will he not come to see us at all?

Again and again has the meaning of, often, repeatedly, with frequent repetition.

At large. To say that a dog or a prisoner is **at large** means that he is unconfined.

The phrases **at first, at last, at length**, have been given under the preposition **at**.

The phrase **a little** is often used adverbially of either time, space, or degree. Wait a little, i.e. for a short time. Go forward a little, i.e. a short way. His writing is a little better, i.e. somewhat better.

By and by means soon, after a little while.

By and by the rest of my family came on board.

By the by means incidentally, in passing.

In **far away**, the word **away** intensifies the meaning of **far**.

Far and near, far and wide, are quite intelligible; but the order of words in these phrases should be fixed in the memory.

Few and far between. The poet Campbell's line, *Like angels' visits, few and far between*, has popularized this phrase.

Windows were in those days so few and far between that the folks inside remained quite unaware of what was going on outside.

First and foremost is also easy, but the order of words should be noted.

For long is a short way of saying *for a long time*.

It seems unlikely that unbroken/peace should ever in this world continue for long to be the lot of man.

For the better, indicates improvement. The weather, the invalid, etc., has taken a turn for the better.

In short, in brief, in the long run, etc., are given under the preposition **in**.

The adverbial phrase **in time**, in such expressions as *The cheat is in time found out*, means, in the course of time, eventually.

Now and then, is occasionally, sometimes.

Off and on. For instance,

He has been working here off and on for five years, i.e. he has been sometimes working and sometimes not, but altogether it is five years since he began work here.

Often and often means, very frequently.

Once, with a past tense, has sometimes the meaning of formerly, at one time in the past.

She was once able to sing well. Sandwich was once an important port.

At once is soon, without delay; also, at the same time.

> Go and do the work at once.   They all rose at once.
> He urged me to begin at once.

Once again is another time, one time more.

Once and again is repeatedly, at repeated times. Strictly speaking this phrase means *one time and then a second time*. Milton says that Noah from the ark ' a dove sent forth once and again to spy '.

Once for all means finally, as a certain and final thing not to be repeated.

> I tell you once for all that this must be done.
> He [Buddha] forsook once for all his home, his kindred, his kingdom, and every worldly possession.
> It is better on the whole that the controversy between the landlords and the peasants should be fought out once for all.

Once more is one time more, one occasion further.

Once upon a time, is once in a time indefinitely past.

Out and out means completely, altogether, to the fullest extent, without reservation.   This expression is colloquial.

> This horse is out and out the best one you ever had.

Over again means another time, a second time, once more.

> We must begin the whole business over again.
> I had a great deal of work to do over again.

Over and above.   We have seen that this phrase is sometimes used as a preposition.   And it is often an adverbial phrase, meaning, besides, moreover, furthermore.

Over and over, also **over and over again**, mean repeatedly, very often, again and again.

Through and through is thoroughly, entirely, completely.

> He has been caught in the rain and is wet through and through, i.e. his clothes are saturated with rain.

To and fro is backwards and forwards.

> He walked to and fro about the room, evidently in a perturbed state of mind.

To in *today*, *tonight*, means *this*.   *Tomorrow* is the day following this day; *the morrow* means the day after a particular past day mentioned in the narrative, and therefore means the day following *that* day.

We have also the idiomatic phrases,

> All (the) day long, meaning, through the whole day.
> All my life long,   „   throughout my life.
> All the year round,   „   through the whole year.
> All the world over,   „   over the whole world.
> The wide world over, „   over the whole world.

And caused the golden-tressed sun
All the day long his course to run.—*Milton*

The ideas of justice and righteous equality are dear to men the wide world over.

85. Miscellaneous Phrases

1. **All but,** means, all except; also, almost but not altogether.

The shipwrecked people were rescued all but one.
The man was all but blind.
Their strength was all but worn out.
The elections are all but over.
He was all but ruined through the failure of the bank.

2. **All moonshine.** When it is said of a statement that it is all moonshine, the meaning is, that the statement is a foolish, idle, untrue, statement. For instance, a man does some peculiar action and assigns a special reason or motive for it; but it afterwards turns out that his real motive was something quite different from the assigned one. In such a case we say that his alleged motive was all moonshine.

He said it was his desire to get his photograph taken that made him go to England; but that, you may be sure, was all moonshine; he would never take such an expensive journey without a more important object.

3. **Anything but.** The meaning of this will appear below.

I soon had reason to think that my friendship was anything but disagreeable to her, i.e. that it was quite agreeable to her.
He was likely to prove anything but an acquisition.

4. **Fast asleep; sound asleep; in a sound sleep.** These are equivalent and signify a state of deep sleep. Note the words which here go idiomatically together.

The child was fast asleep in his mother's lap.
The boys were found lying under a tree in a sound sleep.

To **go to sleep; go off to sleep; get to sleep; fall asleep.** These are equivalent.

Children should go to sleep when they are put to bed.
He had scarcely swallowed his dinner when he went off to sleep.

5. **To the best of my belief; the best of my recollection.** When a man is called on to relate any facts he knows, as for instance in giving evidence in a court of justice, he tells truthfully all he can remember, and says, ' To the best of my recollection, these things are exactly as I have stated'; or 'to the best of my belief he was not angry '. **To the best of my recollection,** means, so far as I am able to remember the facts. **To the best of my belief,** means, so far as I have grounds for believing.

6. **Behind the scenes.** The scenes here mean the fittings of a stage in the theatre. Persons in front of the scenes see what is openly acted; persons behind the scenes know all about the management of the play. Hence, *to be behind the scenes* has come to mean, to be aware of how a thing is managed, to be aware of the motives for certain conduct.

> The secretary of the company has been dismissed, and having been behind the scenes, he has made some strange revelations as to the way in which the business is managed.

7. **Between two fires.** If two parties are firing at each other, any person getting between them is exposed to the fire of both, and is therefore in an awkward and dangerous position. Hence *to be between two fires* has come to mean generally, to be assailed on different sides by contending difficulties of a very disagreeable or risky nature.

> These two neighbours had a bitter dispute and a mutual friend was asked to arbitrate between them; but his award pleased neither party and now each attacks him as if he were his enemy. He feels it hard to be placed between two fires after he honestly tried to mediate between the disputants.

8. **In a body.** To say of a company of men that they went **in a body** to a place or a person, means that they went together, animated by one intention.

> Twenty delegates from the workmen on strike went in a body to the Mayor and asked permission to hold a public meeting in the Town Hall to discuss their grievances.

9. **On foot.** *To set out on foot* is to start for a place walking. *To go on foot* to a place, is to walk to it, as distinguished from riding or driving.

> This man made the whole journey to Benares on foot.

To **set foot on** or **in**, is quite intelligible.

> He will never set foot on American soil.
> As soon as he sets foot in my house, he will find a state of things very different from what he expects.

To **set on foot.***

10. **By force of circumstances.** When a man's circumstances require or oblige him to do a certain thing, we say he is compelled to do it **by force of circumstances**.

> His plan was too expensive to carry out, and so he was obliged by force of circumstances to abandon it.

11. **Wide of the mark; beside the mark.** When an archer shoots at a mark and his arrow goes aside so as to strike a place away from the mark, he is said to shoot wide of the mark. So in discussion, to

use irrelevant arguments, is to reason beside the mark, or beside the point.

His reasoning is impressive, but altogether wide of the mark.

12. **Next to nothing**, is almost nothing, scarcely anything, the nearest approach to nothing.

The rats have attacked the bread, and there is next to nothing left.

13. **Or so; more or less.** We have already seen that *about* when joined to an expression of number indicates that the number specified is generally correct, but does not pretend to be exact or precise. In the same way, ' Fifty or so ', means ' About fifty ', i.e. Fifty, or a few below fifty, or a few over fifty. And the expression ' Fifty, nore or less ', has the same meaning.

' What is this man's age, do you think ? ' ' Sixty-five or so.'
I asked a farmer how much wheat he expected his field to yield, and he said, a hundred and fifty bushels, more or less.

14. **Out at elbows** is a phrase we may notice. When a man's coat gets shabby and torn at the elbows, he is literally **out at elbows**. But the phrase is applied metaphorically to a man in broken-down circumstances, one who has become poor and possesses little or nothing.

It is not the business of the government to collect the bad debts of every out-at-elbows landlord.

15. **Part and parcel.** This phrase is applied to a thing which is a component part of a specified whole.

Individuals must regard themselves as part and parcel of a larger whole.

16. **Of a piece**, means of the same sort, as if broken from the same block, similar, alike. This phrase is commonly followed by *with*, and often implies something disagreeable or bad.

This mean act of his is quite (or, all) of a piece with his conduct generally.

Piecework. When people work for wages, expecting to be paid according to the quantity of work done and not according to the length of time spent, they are said to do **piecework**. A man employed to *work by the day* is not anxious to work hard, for whether he does much or little, he has earned his day's wage when the day is done; but a man who does piecework will work hard because the more work he does, the more wages he will receive. The work of a contractor is piecework: he gets so much for the whole work.

Apiece is one by one, singly.

There were thirty-two beggars, and I gave them a penny apiece.

17. **No matter; never mind.** No matter means generally, it is of no importance, of no moment. **Never mind** means pay no heed

or regard. Note the exact order of the words: we must not sa *no mind, never matter*.

> Never mind the common people.
> No matter about the rain: come at once.

18. **A storm in a teacup,** is a phrase sometimes used derisively to indicate a great fuss about a trifle.

> We have had a storm in a teacup since you left. The whole village was in violent commotion for a week because a stranger caught a fish in the river.

19. **Through thick and thin** is a colloquial phrase. meaning through all obstacles and difficulties.

20. **The thin end of the wedge.** When a man in cleaving wood uses a wedge, his efforts are first directed to getting the thin end of the wedge inserted; once he has this firmly in, he will soon cleave the log. So a skilful debater tries to get in some general principle, which, once admitted by his opponent, will in the end overturn his opponent's arguments. So again: the efforts of reformers are in the first instance directed to get in the thin end of the wedge.

21. **Just the thing; the very thing.** These are equivalent and mean, exactly the thing required or desired.

> You may talk as you please, but this appointment is just the thing.
> For some time I have been looking out for a good house and have at last found one which is the very thing.

22. **To one's taste; to one's liking. One's taste** or **one's liking** here means, what one wishes, or would find pleasure in.

> This house is not to his taste, i.e. he does not like it.
> The book you sent me was quite to my taste.
> John's way of doing things is not at all to my liking.

23. **With might and main** means, with all the energy that one can command. **Main** formerly meant the same thing as **might,** so that here the meaning is intensified by repetition.

> Our boat was caught in a strong current, but the rowers rowed with might and main, and soon we got into safe waters.

24. **With** or **against the grain, the stream, the current, the tide.** To cut wood with the grain, is to cleave it in the line or direction in which the fibres of the wood lie. The opposite is, cut across the grain, or against the grain. To go or swim or sail with the stream, the current, the tide, i.e. in the direction in which the water is flowing. *Against* is here the opposite of *with*.

These phrases have a metaphorical application. When a man allows himself to drift along with the current of public opinion and falls in with the course of things around him, he is said to go with the tide, or the current, or the stream.   If he resists, he goes against these.

> Virtue often requires that a man should set himself against the customs practised around him, and makes him go against the tide; but the end is worth the struggle.

25. **Not worth his salt.** This is said of a good-for-nothing fellow, not worth his keep in salt.

> From the testimonials the man showed me, I thought he must be a skilful carpenter, and I gave him a piece of work to do, but soon found that he was not really worth his salt.

26. **Like a fish out of water.** Water is the natural element for fish to be in.   A person is like a fish out of water when he is not in a congenial element.

27. **Null and void.** This adjectival expression means, invalid, valueless, no longer in force.   The one adjective here only repeats and intensifies the meaning of the other.   An offer which is intended to hold good for a specified time becomes null and void when the time expires.   An agreement becomes null and void when the conditions attached to it are broken.   A lease of a house intended to run for twenty-one years, becomes null and void when the specified term of twenty-one years has expired.

86. We close the chapter with a miscellaneous collection of examples of prepositions, prepositional phrases, and adverbial phrases, showing how these are used in composition.   Anyone can enlarge the list to an indefinite extent.   Most of the examples below are from well-known standard authors.

> He put her in mind of her promise.
> Visitors came to the place out of curiosity.
> With an eye to business.
> Does the tiger lie in wait for its prey?
> She woke up with a smile.
> He persevered in the face of all obstacles.
> Through thick and thin she followed him.
> At this horrible sight, his cheeks turned white with fear.
> Poems that have been read the wide world over.
> A public breakfast, dinner, tea, and supper all the year round.
> I still had hopes to return and die at home at last.
> You may have your choice for me.
> Shelter from the heat of the sun.
> One boy who was tall for his age.
> I went out every day with my gun.
> The Sabbath was made for man.—*Bible*
> To kill two birds with one stone.*
> Faithful found among the faithless.—*Milton*
> Speak with the master of the house.
> He had taken his seat by the fire.
> I could now walk, quite up to the wreck.

Sold to a life of slavery for daily bread.

Silent with regard to her marriage.

He would go all over the world with me.

A philosopher with a taste for music.—*Thackeray*

'Tis not in mortals to command success.—*Addison*

The system was rather expensive at first.

His mind was thus perfectly set at ease.

I did not care to go out of sight of the boat.

He keeps the lease of his property under lock and key.

I knew we were far enough out of their reach.

England, with all thy faults, I love thee still.—*Cowper*

This evil lies at the root of the general discontent.

It was out of her power to accept the offer.

A bird in the hand is worth two in the bush.—*Proverb*

He desires me to say once for all that, etc.

His house is not quite a mile from this place.

During his lifetime.

Poverty was the best defence against pillage.

It would be to no purpose to speak to my father.

Desperate with hunger and reckless with misery.—*Dickens*

He is on a visit at his old tutor's.

For fear of being buried alive.

Quite out of cash.

If he had no money to bequeath, he has left a good name behind him.

It appeared to be among the papers I had with me in Germany.

Greece is apparently on the brink of war.

A female relative of my mother's had come on a visit to our house.

A man who had often to flee for his life did not care to encumber himself with baggage.—*Creighton*

You think I must be over head and ears in love with Mirah.   Quite right, so I am.—*George Eliot*

He began to ply his oar without further remark, and they went along swiftly for many minutes without speaking.—*George Eliot*

It is entirely beyond my power to take part in the celebration at Liverpool on the 20th.

Unseen amid the throng.—*Milton*

But for him it never would have taken place.

To see that there are no mistakes in point of fact.

He would have turned them to good account.

Over against this church stands a large hospital.

The servant placed lights on the table by him.

The secret was destined to come out before long.

Few of the Esquimaux can count to ten.

He looked all over his desk for it without finding it.

They sat down in ranks by hundreds and by fifties.—*Bible*

She went off for the purpose of fetching her sister.

George would have parted from Amelia at any rate.—*Thackeray*

Darkness dies pierced through and through with light.

Go along with me.   I should be set at liberty.

Pious reflections are out of place in mere story books.—*Thackeray*

I dined privately with a friend on a herring and a chicken.—*Swift*

They had a conversation in English with the judge about the school.

A clever man with a great propensity for running into debt.

Why are we never quite at our ease in the presence of a schoolmaster?—*Lamb*

The principal of the college expelled him for what after all is but a trivial offence.

The plain was not above two hundred yards broad and about twice as long.

He lay like a warrior taking his rest with his martial cloak around him.—*Wolfe*

I saw the Prime Minister walking in the park with the Foreign Secretary.

He uttered these words in a feeble voice, but they were overheard at once.

Time out of mind, strength and courage have been the theme of bards and romancers.—*Thackeray*

After all, the conditions under which we do our work are of little consequence, if only we earnestly aim at doing it well.—*Andrews*

I will buy with you, sell with you, talk with you, walk with you; but I will not eat with you, drink with you, or pray with you.—*Shakespeare*

A professional gentleman, with a bluish nose, and his face tied up for the benefit of a toothache, presided at a jingling piano in a remote corner.—*Dickens*

I saw a man clothed in rags, standing in a certain place, with his face from his own house, a book in his hand, and a great burden upon his back.—*Bunyan*

CHAPTER IX

VERBS FOLLOWED IDIOMATICALLY BY PREPOSITIONS; COMPOUND VERBS MADE UP OF A SINGLE VERB AND A PREPOSITION OR ADVERB FOLLOWING

87. Certain Verbs when followed by certain Prepositions or Adverbs become compound verbs bearing a new signification. For instance, *to carry* is to bear; *to carry through* is to accomplish; *to cry* is to shout, bewail, lament; *to cry up* is to praise, extol; *to chime* is to sound like bells; *to chime in with* is to agree with; *to give* a problem, is to propound a problem; *to give up* a riddle, is to abandon all attempts to solve a riddle. Other common examples are, *to laugh at*, meaning to ridicule; *to fence in*, meaning to enclose with a fence; also the intransitive verb *to get on*, meaning to progress or succeed.

Certain of these compound verbs have more than one preposition added to the simple verb: as *bear up against, come in for, come up with, fall in with, look up to, look down upon, make off with, put up with, stand up for*. And we have such compounds as *do away with, make away with*.

88. The added preposition in these verbs has really become an adverb united to the verb. The new compound verb thus formed, is in most cases transitive, but not always. For instance, *get on, go on, run on, run out* (=expire, e.g. of a lease), are intransitive.

These compound verbs are sometimes called Prepositional Verbs. We have already used the term for convenience; but inasmuch as the added preposition is in reality an adverb closely united to the verb and modifying it, the term Prepositional Verb is not satisfactory. Nor is the term Compound Verb distinctive, for this term is applied to a compound word used as a verb, as *back-bite, cross-question*. We suggest the term *Phrase Verbs*. We have the analogy of Phrase Prepositions applied to such expressions as, *along with, by means of, on account of, with regard to*.

Those authors who in the main write in 'Anglo-Saxon' English (see Section 11) make frequent use of Phrase Verbs. The writings of Charles Lamb are particularly rich in apt examples of the use of such verbs.

89. Again, many verbs are followed by certain prepositions where these prepositions cannot be accounted part of the verb.

And the same verb may take different prepositions after it, with, of course, a new shade of meaning in each case. For instance, we agree *with* a person, we agree *to* a proposal; a man sinks *in* mud, or sinks *into* the sea, or sinks *upon* the ground, or sinks *under* a burden.

It is sometimes difficult to say whether the preposition or adverb which follows a verb is to be regarded and parsed as part of the verb, or as a separate word introducing a new phrase. It is sometimes said that the test of a prepositional verb is found by turning the verb into the passive voice, and so changing the other parts of the sentence as to make the new sentence express the same meaning; if then the preposition still clings to the verb and cannot be separated from it, that verb and preposition make up a prepositional verb. For example,

This man walled in a garden.
A garden was walled in by this man.

Here the preposition clings to the verb in the passive voice as in the active.

This test is derived from the circumstance that only transitive verbs have a passive voice. The rule, however, though apparently easy and though applicable in most cases, is by no means an infallible one, for some Phrase Verbs being intransitive have no passive voice.

A better test is found in the circumstance that a single word may often be substituted for a Phrase Verb: as, *ridicule* for *laugh at*; or the Phrase Verb can be translated into another language by a single word.

90. In regard to these Phrase Verbs, grammarians do not all hold the same view. As this book, however, is meant to be a practical help to the student, we shall not enter in detail into the arguments of the grammarians and shall not attempt to separate our treatment of (*a*) the preposition as part of the verb, and (*b*) the preposition as idiomatically following the verb, but bearing an essential part of the meaning of the verb.

91. We content ourselves with two examples of the difficulty involved.

To go to Bombay on business. To carry on business in Bombay.

In the first, the expression *on business* is a distinct phrase quite separable from *go*, and indicates the purpose of going. But in the second example, the words *on business* do not constitute a distinct phrase separable from *carry*. It is quite plain from the meaning that the whole verb is not *carry*, but *carry on*. If the student reads the first example, pausing a little after *go*, thus *to go—*

on business, he finds he has added to the simple idea expressed by
to go another simple idea expressed by *on business*, and has arrived
without any confusion at the complex idea expressed by the whole
phrase *to go on business*. But let him try the same method with
to carry—on business, and he will see at once that the verb here is
not *carry* but *carry on*, and that *on* cannot be here regarded as a
preposition introducing a phrase.

92. Certain prepositions when joined as adverbs to verbs
serve to make the verb express greater completeness than if the
simple verb stood alone. *Up* is notably one of these. *To use
provisions*, is to make use of provisions; *to use up provisions*, is
to use them till the whole supply is exhausted. *The ship has broken
up*, is equivalent to *the ship has broken to pieces*; comparing this
with *the ship has broken*, we see at once that *up* has added the
idea of greater completeness. *Off* and *away* are often added as
adverbs to verbs, to intensify the meaning and add greater completeness. *Cut off, run away, cast off*; cancer *eats away* the flesh.
On often adds the idea of continuity. *Run on, work on, read on,
write on*. *Into* often indicates gradual change to something different.
*Glide into, grow into, lapse into, merge into, pass into, run into,
turn into*.

But these prepositions or adverbs add a different idea with other
verbs: as, *ride up, set off, keep away*.

93. PREPOSITIONAL OR PHRASE VERBS
AND VERBS IDIOMATICALLY FOLLOWED BY PREPOSITIONS

Abide by a statement, a decision; abide **in** or **at** a place; abide
with a person. The latter two of these are rarely used now,
though common in earlier English. **Abide** is also used transitively without a preposition, somewhat colloquially, in the sense
of, **bear** or **tolerate**.

> He must abide by the contract.
> She could not abide Master Shallow.—*Shakespeare*
> Today I must abide at thy house.
> Abide with me.—*Bible*

Abound in, with.

> A land abounding in springs and streams of water.
> This country used to abound with snakes.

Absolve a person **from** a promise.

Abstain from food, **from** indulgence, **from** luxuries.

> Abstain from all appearance of evil.—*Bible*

Abstract a thing **from**.

> To abstract money from a safe, articles from a parcel, salt from water.

Accede to a request, **to** terms proposed by another, **to** the conditions or terms of a treaty.

Accommodate a friend **with** a loan or **with** lodgings; accommodate ourselves **to** our position or circumstances.

Account for a thing; account **to** a person **for** a thing.

> His intemperance accounts for his poverty.
> You must account to your master for the money you have received.

Accrue to.

> But little profit accrues to any one from this business.
> Advantages accrue to society from the freedom of the press.

Accuse a person **of** an offence, as of treason, of theft, of breach of trust, of deserting one's friends.

Accustom oneself **to.**

> He who accustoms himself to fraud in little things, needs only the opportunity to practise it in great things.

Acquiesce in an opinion, **in** a proposal.

Acquit a person **of** a charge.

> I acquit him of all design to defraud me.

Acquit is also used reflexively. To acquit oneself well or ill, is to do one's part well or ill.

> The lawyer acquitted himself poorly in this case.

Act for is to act on behalf of.

> The solicitor who had been acting for him.

Act from, out of. Here **from** and **out of** point to source or motive.

> He acted from fear rather than from a sense of duty.
> He acted out of regard for your father's good name.

Act under. Here **under** implies subjection, submission, or representation. To **act under** orders, implies submission to orders; to **act under** compulsion, is to act being overborne by something, being in subjection to it; to **act under** a misapprehension, is to act through submitting to the misapprehension; to **act under** pretence of a thing, is to act while making that thing a cloak to conceal the real nature of your action.

Act upon or **on** means, exert an influence upon, affect.

> Heat acts on bodies and causes them to expand.
> The gastric juice acts upon the food we swallow.
> By gravitation the sun and the planets act and react upon one another

To act upon or **on** has also the meaning of, to act trusting to, or relying on.

> The police, acting upon the information they had received, caught the robbers dividing their spoil.

Act up to, means, act according to, in proportion to. To **act up to**

one's engagements, is to fulfil them; to **act up to** one's advantages, is to act in proportion to one's advantages.

> The brake did not act up to the engine driver's expectations.
> Many are convinced that they ought to abandon superstitions, but they have not courage to act up to their convictions.

Adhere to one's party, **to** principles of truth and honour.

Admit of; admit a person **to** or **into**.

> His conduct admits of no extenuation.
> They have admitted me into their club.
> Why will they not admit you to the examination ?

Advise (in commercial usage = inform) a person **of**.

> I have advised him by letter of the loss of the ship.

Affix a seal **to** a document; affix a syllable **to** a word.

Agree on, to, with.

> He agreed to all the proposals we made.
> I agree with you in the opinion you have expressed.
> This food does not agree with me, i.e. this food does not suit me.
> After much discussion, they have at length agreed on the terms of partnership.

Aim at, means, aim in the direction of; also, set one's heart on **a** thing with the view of securing it.

> The huntsman aimed at the lion and fired, but missed him.
> He is aiming at the professor's chair.
> He aims at being considered a poet.

Alight at, from, on.

> He alighted from the carriage at the railway station.
> The birds alighted on the ridge of my house.

Allot a thing **to** a person.

Allude to a statement, an occurrence, a person.

> This is not the man to whom I alluded.
> The circumstance he alludes to is well known.
> (cf. *refer* below; *refer* is more definite than *allude*.)

Anchor off a place, means, cast anchor near the place.

> The British squadron anchored off Alexandria.

Answer for, to; answer **to** a person **for** a thing.

> Every man must answer for his actions to God.
> Let his neck answer for it, if there be any martial law.—*Shakespeare*
> In Indian mythology, Mata answers to (=corresponds to) the Venus of the Greeks.

Apologize to a person; apologize **for** a thing.

> I must apologize to you for not replying to your letter at once.

Appeal to a person; appeal **to** a higher court; appeal **to** one's benevolence, pity, sense of right. Appeal **against** a decision **to** a higher court.

Apply to a person; apply **for a** thing.

> He has applied to the banker for a loan.

Appoint a person **to** a situation.

Appropriate a thing **to** oneself, or **to** one's own use.

Approve of.

> What right-minded man can approve of fraud even in little things?

Arbitrate between two parties **in** a dispute.

> He was asked to arbitrate between two merchants in a dispute about the short delivery of some goods.

Argue with a person; argue **for** or **against** or **about** a thing.

> He argued for an acceleration of the mails.
> He will argue against the making of a new canal.
> Do not argue with a newspaper editor; he can always have the last word.

Arrive at, in, from.

> They arrived in an open car.
> When does the mail train from Paris arrive at Marseilles?

Ask about a thing; ask **after** a person, is to inquire from another how that person is. We ask a person **for** a thing; we ask a thing **from** a person. Ask **of** is an old form, no longer used.

> He never asked me for anything. He never asked anything from me.
> If any of you lack wisdom, let him ask of God.—*Bible*

Assent to a proposal, a stipulation.

Associate with people of good character.

Atone for. Who can atone for the sins of men?

Attend to counsel or advice; attend **on** or **upon** a person.

Attribute his losses **to** his gross carelessness.

Avail oneself **of** a holiday to visit the seaside.

Back out, means, withdraw from an engagement or contract.

> He would like to back out of the contract, but we cannot allow it.

Back up (colloquially), means, to support, to sustain.

> This man is always ready to back up his friends.

Bark at. What are the dogs barking at?

Bask in. He basked in her favour like a beggar in the sun.

Bathe in water, **in** the river, **in** the sea; also, to be bathed in tears, in perspiration.

Bear, means, to carry; also, to endure; also, to bring forth young.

Bear down, is to overthrow or crush by force—said of opposition.

> He has been able to bear down all opposition.

Bear down upon. This is used of a force or warship moved forward to attack an enemy.

> A Spanish frigate bore down upon the Arab *dhow*.
> The cavalry bore down upon the enemy's right flank.

Bear off or **away**, is to carry off as a conqueror.

He bore off the prize: or, bore away the palm.

Bear out, is to establish, confirm, corroborate.

If the evidence bears out the charge, the man will be convicted.

Bear up. This is intransitive and means, to endure, to be firm, to persevere in endurance.

Is it easy to bear up when one is beset with difficulties on all sides?

Bear up against trials, is to endure or undergo trials without being overwhelmed by them, to resist successfully.

The bridge cannot long bear up against the force of the current.
It is surprising how well he bears up against (*or* under) his misfortunes.

Bear upon or **on**.

Our guns were brought to bear upon the enemy's batteries.
Your remarks do not bear on the matter in hand, i.e. do not apply to it, are not pertinent to it. The noun is also used in this sense. Your remarks have no bearing on the question.

Bear with, means, to tolerate, to be indulgent to.

I could not bear with his violent temper.
Bear with me while I point out a mistake you have made.

Beat about, is to search for by various means. Hence the common phrase, **to beat about the bush**.

A man comes to me with a request, but before stating it he enters into a long explanation, until, growing weary of his tediousness, I say, ' You need not beat about the bush; come to the point at once.'

Beat against. The waves beat against the shore.

Beat back, is to compel to retire. The flames beat back the firemen. A huntsman might beat a tiger back into a thicket.

Beat down, is to subdue, to crush; also, by repeated efforts to make a seller lower his price.

I will beat down his foes before his face.—*Bible*
I beat down the price of the car to a hundred and twenty pounds.

Beat into, is to instil into a dull mind by repeated instruction.

Beat off, is to repel an attack, to drive back by force.

They beat off the enemy.
It is not easy to beat off a swarm of wasps if they attack you.

Beat out. To beat out gold, is to hammer it into a thin plate. **To** beat out wheat from the ear, is to thresh it with a stick or a flail.

Take a stick and beat out the seed from these pods.

To be dead beat is to be thoroughly exhausted.

Beat up is, to suddenly disturb a quarry (=an animal hunted) or an enemy; also (colloquially) to thrash.

Beat up for recruits, is to go about to enlist recruits for the army, accompanied in old days with a drum.

Beat upon, is to strike upon repeatedly or continuously.

> The rain descended, and the floods came, and the winds blew, and beat upon that house, and it fell.—*Bible*

Become of, means, to be the fate of, to happen to.

> No one seemed to care what had become of me.

Beg of or **from** a person; beg **for** bread, **for** money.

> I beg of you to keep perfectly still.
> From whom did you beg this money?

Belong to.   Does this book belong to you?
Bequeath to.

> His uncle has bequeathed to him five thousand pounds.

Bestow upon or **on.**

> He bestows great attention on his garden.

Betake oneself **to.**

> To what district has he betaken himself?
> They betook themselves to their villages.

Beware of evil company; beware of forming bad habits.
Bind a burden **on** the camel's back.
Bind over, is to oblige by bond to appear in court; to place legal restrictions upon.

> This man has been bound over to keep the peace for six months.

Bind to, with.

> He bound the prisoner to a stake with a strong rope.
> I tell you this in confidence and bind you to secrecy in the matter.

Blame for.   He blames you for neglect of duty.
Block up, is to impede by an obstruction in the way.

> A piece of rock has fallen and blocked up the path.
> A ship ran aground in the Suez Canal and blocked up the traffic.

Blot out, is to erase.

> Blot out what you have written on your slates.

Blow down, is to throw down by the force of the wind.

> The storm yesterday blew down several large trees.

Blow off steam, is to allow steam to escape from an engine.   Sometimes applied colloquially = to blow off energy.

> I took a long walk last night to blow off steam after a long day at the office.

Blow out, is to extinguish by a puff of breath or wind.   The verb **put out** is used for extinguish **by any means.**   You may **put out** a candle or lamp by blowing it out, or by any other means:

you **blow out** a candle by a puff of breath, or the wind may **blow it out.**

To *blow out a man's brains*, is to shatter his head by shooting.

Blow over, is to pass away without injurious effect.

The squall speedily blew over.
There is sometimes opposition to the re-marriage of widows; but let those who favour this wise and kindly reform maintain their ground and the opposition will in time blow over.

Blow up, is used both transitively and intransitively, and means, to explode; also, to destroy by explosion; also, to inflate a balloon. **Blow up** and the corresponding noun are also used colloquially meaning, to give a sound scolding to, to rate soundly.

There were seventy men in the mine when it blew up.
He placed a bag of gunpowder in position and blew up the bridge.
You are sure to be blown up for coming late to your work.

Blow upon, is to bring into discredit or disfavour.
Blush at, for.

She blushed at the mention of her lover's name.
I blush for the vices of my countrymen.

Boast of.

One boasts of his wealth; another of his learning.
It is natural that we should boast of our Constitution.

Boil. **To boil potatoes** or any other article of food is to cook the potatoes, etc., by boiling. **To boil the kettle, the pot,** is to apply heat to the kettle or pot till the liquid in it boils. There are places where they say 'cook the kettle'. This is wrong, it should be, **boil** the kettle.

Boil away, is to evaporate by boiling.

I boiled the cauldron till the water boiled away.

Boil down to, is to be reduced to, amount.

Their evidence boiled down to this . . .

Boil over. When water in a vessel, boiling violently, runs over the edge of the vessel, the water is said to boil over; and, strangely enough, the vessel is said to boil over. And the verb is applied metaphorically to strong feeling.

If you put on more fire the pot will boil over.
You should not have allowed the milk to boil over.
The persecution of the Jews was as fierce as it was a few years ago, and the European press boiled over with indignation.

Boil up, i.e. begins to rise in boiling.
Border on or upon.

Burma borders on India.
His excited, frenzied utterances bordered upon madness.

Brag of one's successes, **of** one's possessions.

Break away, is to free oneself from restraint and get away.

> You held the horse by the bridle, but he reared and broke away.

Break away from restraint, **away from** a person restraining.

> The child broke away from all discipline.

Break down, is to come to a stop through something breaking.

> The train broke down, i.e. something connected with the train broke, so that further progress was for the time impossible.
> We had a breakdown on the way.
> He has had a nervous breakdown.

This phrase verb would also be used of a series of interdependent mechanical arrangements, as of a postal service.

> Sometimes in wild parts the post breaks down, causing inconvenience to travellers.
> He broke down in the midst of his speech, i.e. he failed to go on.

Break in a bullock, is to accustom him to the yoke. **To break in a horse,** is to train him and accustom him to do work. To **break in a door,** is to force it open.

Break in upon, is to interrupt by a sudden violent and unexpected appearance.

> The police broke in upon the robbers when they were in a lonely place dividing their booty.

Break into, is to enter suddenly and forcibly; to change into.

> No man has a right to break into his neighbour's house.
> His cattle broke into my field of wheat and did much damage.
> To break into a run, is to change from walking to running.
> To break into song, is to begin singing.
> To break into a conversation, is to interrupt it.

Break a person or **animal of,** is to cause to be rid of, to cause to abandon. To break a person of a bad habit.

Break off, is to separate by breaking; also, to stop, to desist. It is used metaphorically of an engagement, negotiations.

> He broke off in the middle of his story.
> He broke off a branch from the tree and threw it into the river.
> These two young people were to be married, but the young woman changed her mind and now the engagement is broken off.

Break open, is to open with force or violence.

> He broke open the box and carried off its contents.

Break out, is to burst forth, to appear suddenly; also, to escape from restraint.

> The thief broke out of prison and escaped.
> The sun broke out and brightened all the landscape.
> Cholera has broken out among the pilgrims at Mecca.

A fire broke out in the lower story and soon the whole building was in flames.

He broke out into a fury of language which we will not repeat.—*Thackeray*

This man has been ill for months and now his whole body has broken out into sores.

Break over.

The waves broke over the pier.

The cattle broke over the fence into my field.

Break through.

The robber broke through the wall of the house.

Break up, is to break in pieces; also, intransitive, to come to an end, to disperse, to dissolve.

The stranded ship broke up in last night's storm.

When does the ice break up at Vladivostock?

The meeting broke up in great confusion.

He broke up a strong box for fuel to cook his dinner.

The conspiracy was strong, but the prince was able to break it up.

A school is said ' to break up for the holidays ', i.e. it closes for the holidays.

Break with, means, to cease to be friendly with.

John was your great friend a month ago, but you now seem to have broken with him altogether.

Bridge over a road, or a river, is to put a bridge across it; hence, to reconcile two parties that have been at variance.

It is not easy to bridge over an arm of the sea.

There is a good deal of bad feeling between these two men; can you do nothing to bridge over their differences?

Bring about, is to cause to happen. It is the causative of **come about**. The same meaning is expressed by the phrase, **bring to pass**, which is the causative of **come to pass**. The phrase **to bring about** often implies skilful planning and arranging.

To bring about a reconciliation.

The king tried to bring about the peace.

Bring down, is to cause to come down, to humble; to shoot down.

To bring down proud looks.

As if Oliver were some bird of rare plumage that he had skilfully brought down.—*Dickens*

Bring forward, is to produce, or introduce to notice; also, to cause to advance.

The proposal he brought forward seemed a foolish one.

The rain will bring forward the young crops.

Bring in, is to collect; also, to produce as the result of sale.

A vigorous effort must be made to bring in all arrears of revenue before the end of March.

How much will the auction bring in, do you suppose? Perhaps three hundred pounds.

Bring off, is to convey away; also, to rescue, to achieve success.

A lifeboat goes to a sinking ship and brings off all the people.
The brigands attacked the police and brought off their comrade.
The merchant brought off the deal.

Bring on, is to cause to begin.   To bring on an action at law; also, to originate, to induce.   To bring on a disease.

Dirt often brings on disease.
Intense pain had brought on delirium.

Bring out, is to expose, to bring to light.

The investigation is sure to bring out some surprising things.

Bring over, is to convey across.   To bring passengers over a ferry in a boat; also, to persuade to change sides.

The king tried to bring over the rebels by offering a free pardon to all who would lay down their arms.

Bring a person round or **to**, is to cause him to recover.

He has stood the operation well, and good nursing will bring him round.
The man had fainted, but the stimulant brought him to.

To bring a ship to, is so to manage the sails or engine that the ship is made stationary.

Bring to.

The matter was brought to my notice.

Bring under, is to subdue, to reduce to obedience.

The minstrel fell, but the foeman's chain
Could not bring his proud soul under.—*Moore*

The rebels must be utterly brought under before there will be peace in the kingdom.

There are also such expressions as **bring under one's notice.**

Bring up.   1. To **bring up a child**, is to rear or train him.

Your uncle has his family to bring up.
The way in which they have been brought up.

2. To **bring up the rear**, is to close the line of march; to constitute the rear rank, to be in the rear in a procession.

In the march to the Town Hall, the police will bring up the rear.

Brood on or **over**, is to muse on, to consider long and anxiously.

You should not brood on your misfortunes.

Burden with.

A wise government will avoid as much as possible burdening the country with taxes.

Burn out or **away**, means, transitively, to consume by burning; intransitively, to burn till the fire exhausts itself.

I watched the fire till it all burnt out *or* burnt away.
In ancient times, barbarians burnt out with hot irons the eyes of those they took captive in war.

Burn up, is to consume completely.

Burst forth, is to issue forth suddenly, as flames.

> Tears, such as angels weep, burst forth.—*Milton*

Burst into tears, into a fit of passion, or of laughter.

Burst out laughing, crying, etc.

> He burst out crying like a child.

Burst upon, is to issue forth suddenly and with violence.

> The news burst upon him like an earthquake.

Call at one's house, is to come to the house and inquire after the inmates. A train **calls at** a station.

> This ship does not call at Aden.

Call down, will be intelligible from the following.

> To call down the shaft of a mine, is to shout, directing the voice down the shaft. To call down blessings or curses on one's head, is to appeal to God to send blessings or curses on one's head, to pronounce blessings or curses on him.

Call for has different meanings.

> To call for a friend, is to call at his house that he may accompany you.
> His crimes call for punishment, i.e. demand punishment as a matter of justice.
> A collector calls for reports from his assistants, i.e. he requires his assistants to send in reports to him.

In the following nursery rhyme we have a common meaning of **call for**, namely, to require to be brought.

> ' Old King Cole was a merry old soul,
> And a merry old soul was he;
> He called for his pipe and he called for his bowl,
> And he called for his fiddlers three.'

Call forth, is to evoke, to require the exercise of.

> This is a task that will call forth all his energies.

Call in. 1. To call in friends or neighbours, is to invite them to come together. 2. To call in a professional man, is to send for him in his professional capacity.

> A lawyer is often called in to write a man's will.
> Your father is very ill; you should call in a doctor at once.
> Among Christians, a clergyman is often called in to speak words of comfort in times of sorrow.

3. Government is said to call in currency notes when it withdraws them from circulation.

4. To call in accounts or debts, is to ask for payment of those accounts or debts, to collect the sums due.

> Some business houses call in their accounts every three months.
> It is a most vexatious thing in business to have old debts to call in.

Call off, is to summon away; to divert (the attention).

> The crash called off my attention from the burning house.
> My dog barks at a beggar; I no sooner notice this than I call the dog off.

Call on or **upon,** is 1. To pray to, to invoke. 2. To pay a brief visit to. 3. To require authoritatively, to order.

> Of what avail is it to call on gods that are only imaginary gods ?
> I hope to call on you at your office at three o'clock today.
> You will be called upon in the court to give evidence.
> Parliament will be called upon next session to undertake important legislation.

Call out, is 1. To cry aloud or shout. 2. To require authoritatively to come forth. 3. To challenge to fight.

> To call out the militia, is to require the militia to get under arms.
> The bell-man is calling out something, but I cannot hear what it is.
> He called his opponent out, but the fellow was too great a coward to come.

Call over, is to recite particulars in order, as names on a class roll, articles on a list.

Call to a person, is to address him in a loud voice. The phrase implies that the person addressed is at a distance. **To call out to** is similar in meaning. **To call to** is used also of the lower animals. A man is said to be **called to the bar** when he is admitted as a barrister.

> The dove calls to her mate.
> I saw a man on the opposite side of the river, and called to him, but he showed no sign that he heard me.
> Sheldon Amos was called to the Bar at the Inner Temple.

Call up. To call up a person you wish to speak to by telephone, is to summon him by telephone to receive your message. Men are ' called up ' for military service.

Care for or **about.**

> He did not care about wealth.
> I don't care for tea, means, I do not like tea.

Carp at. He is in a mood to carp at anything I say.

Carry a thing **about,** is to retain it with you as you go from place to place.

> This man carries about toys and small books for sale.
> It is not safe to carry a loaded pistol about in your pocket.

Carry away, is to bear off; also, to captivate.

> The raven carried away a silver ring.
> The soldiers were carried away by the martial music.

Carry a judicial sentence **into** execution.

Carry off, is to bear away; also, to kill.

> These manufacturers carried off a prize medal at the late Exhibition.
> Cholera has carried off half the people of the village.

Carry on, means to promote, manage, conduct, continue.

> The conversation was carried on in a low tone.
> What business does this man carry on ? He is a grocer.
> For more than twenty years she has carried on a system of imposture.

Carry on, is sometimes used intransitively and colloquially, meaning, to behave wildly; to play pranks, as schoolboys might do.

Carry out, is to execute directions given.

> A dutiful son likes to carry out his father's dying wishes.
> He had no longer any doubt about his ability to carry out the plan.

Carry through, is to accomplish a work; also, to sustain. **Carry out**, refers mainly to directions about the doing of a work; **carry through** (=accomplish) rather refers to the whole work, and implies difficulty or delay.

> Perseverance and pluck will carry a man through many difficulties.
> A general has much anxiety in carrying through the operations of a long campaign.

Cast about for, is to look for, be on the watch for.

> He will cast about for an opportunity of taking revenge on you.

Cast aside, is to reject, to throw aside as useless.

> Do not cast aside the love of truth or the fear of God.

Cast away, is to throw away, to give up.

> Soldiers in flight usually cast away their heavy baggage.

Cast down, is to throw down; to humble; also to depress or to deject —commonly in the passive voice.

> God has power to cast down and to raise up.
> He was much cast down by his dismissal.

Cast in one's lot **with**, is to resolve to share with him in weal or woe.

> I intend to cast in my lot with him.—*Bunyan*

Cast off, is to discard, abandon, put off, disburden. **Cast-off clothing**, is clothing which has been worn so long that the owner has put it aside to wear it no more. In the latter case **cast-off** is a participial adjective.

> In London many lower-class Jews deal in gentlemen's cast-off clothing.

Cast oneself on, is to entrust oneself or one's case to, without reserve.

> I was at fault, and I cast myself on his clemency.

Cast out, is to reject, to expel.

> The Jews cast him out of the temple.
> An outcast is one driven from his home or country, one expelled from society; a vagabond, a degraded person.

Cast up, is to reckon, to calculate.

> Will you please cast up this column of figures for me

Catch at, is to endeavour to snatch or seize suddenly, the phrase being used of a material thing and also metaphorically
To catch a thing, is to lay hold of it; **to catch at** a thing is, to make an attempt to seize it.

> A drowning man will catch at a straw.—*Proverb*
> A man fell overboard; he caught at a rope thrown to him, but missed it and sank.
> They catch at every opportunity to make money.

Catch up, is to snatch or take up suddenly; to come up with, to overtake.

> He caught up the nearest stone and threw it back at once.
> You catch up a companion in a walk, or in his studies, when he has got ahead of you.

Caution against, is to warn against.

> You cautioned me against their charms.—*Swift*

Cave in, is colloquial for, to yield, to acknowledge oneself beaten.

Cavil at, is to raise frivolous, captious objections against.

> Many cavil at religion, and yet will not fairly and carefully examine it.

Cease from strife, cease from agitation.

Cede to, is to surrender to, to yield up to, resign to. The term is used of nations and the action of their rulers.

> France was once compelled to cede to Germany the important provinces of Alsace and Lorraine.

Charge against, with. A man charges his memory **with** a thing. We charge a man **with** a crime; and we charge a crime **against** a man.

> I charge this man with receiving stolen goods.
> He declined to charge his memory with so many details.

Charge for, to.

> I say to a bookseller, ' What do you charge *for* this book ? ' i.e. ' What is the price you sell it at ? '
> A shopkeeper from whom I buy an article for which I do not pay at the time, charges that article *to* me in his books.

Cheer up, is used both transitively and intransitively.

> I gave him a drink to cheer him up.
> I cheered up at the good news.

Chime in with, is to agree to, to correspond to.

> He just chimes in with the opinion of any one near him, and seems to have no mind of his own.

Clamour for.

> The starving crowd are clamouring for food.
> The people clamoured for vengeance on the landlords who had so ruthlessly oppressed them.

Clear away, is used transitively, meaning to remove; and intransitively, meaning to disperse or dissolve.

> A railway embankment falls in and men are set to work to clear away the soil from the line.
> The clouds cleared away and the stars shone very brightly.

Clear a person **of** or **from** an accusation or imputation.

Clear off, is used of the weather in the following way.

> The clouds have cleared off and it is now fine.

Clear off! or **Clear out**! is also a way of saying, ' Go away.' 'Be off.

Clear out, is also to empty. To clear out a room, a stable.

Clear up, is to become bright. When the cloudy sky has become clear, we say that it has **cleared up**. To **clear up** also means, to tidy up a mess, to make clear what before was obscure.

> If the weather clears up in the afternoon, we shall go for a drive.
> Her face cleared up as she read the document.
> This book has cleared up many difficulties for me.
> The time is nearly at hand when all doubts as to the policy of the Liberals will be cleared up.

Cling to.

> The tendrils of the vine cling to the trellis work.
> The party will cling to their leader very determinedly.

Commonly **cling to** implies effort in the one who clings, and means to hold fast, especially by winding round or embracing. The phrase thus differs from **adheres to**, which does not imply effort. A postage stamp **adheres to** or **sticks to** a letter—not **clings to**. But a child clings to its mother; the monkey clings to the branch; a man clings to hope.

Close down. A shop is said to have ' closed down ' when it has stopped business.

Close up. Up here denotes completeness.

Close with, means to agree or assent to, to accept; also, to engage in combat.

> You should close at once with the offer.
> The two men closed with each other in a wrestling encounter.

Coincide with.

> The triangle ABC coincides with the triangle DEF.
> The date of the fall of Granada coincided with that of the establishment of the Inquisition.—*Prescott*

Come about, is to happen, occur, take place. The causative of **come about** is **bring about**. To **come to pass** has the same meaning as **come about**, and the causative of it is, to **bring to pass**.

> How did this state of things come about ?
> John Knox, judging from a man's character, said that he would die on the scaffold; and the event came about as he had predicted it.

Come across, is to meet with accidentally, to alight upon, to discover, to happen upon.

Searching in the library, I came across an old forgotten manuscript.

Come after, is to follow as in a line of succession.

What king came after George III of England ?

Come at, is to get within reach of, to attain to.

Nothing could come at me from the outside.
I saw the fruit on the tree, but it was too high for me to come at.

Come away, is to leave, to depart. If I say to you, ' Come away from this place,' the words imply that I wish you to leave it **in company with me**; but if I say to you, ' Go away from this place,' the words imply that I wish you to depart but *not* with me. So that the former expression implies that I also am leaving the place while the latter does not.

Come before a person, is to come into his presence.

None should come before the king in rags.

Come by, is: 1. To come by way of or by means of. 2 To gain, obtain, acquire.

This parcel came by rail and not by air.
He would not tell me how he came by his watch.
The rogues have fallen out, and honest men may come by their own.—
Kingsley

Come down, is to descend; or metaphorically, to be humbled.

Cotton came down at Bombay yesterday, i.e. became cheaper.
A torrent of rain came down and damaged the crops.
He has come down in the world, or come down in his fortunes, i.e. he is
poorer or less honoured than he once was.

There is an idiomatic colloquial use of the phrase **come down**. If a man treats his guests to a splendid entertainment, it would be said of him, ' He came down handsomely '. Or, ' He came down with a generous subscription '.

Come in, has the idea of coming near, coming to one's hand. Hence the term **income**. Also, to enter; also, to come into use, to become fashionable.

The mail has come in early this morning.
The tide is coming in, i.e. there is a flood tide.
When did the fashion of wearing tall hats come in ?, i.e. begin ?
In the race this horse came in first, i.e. was first at the winning post.
At what time of the year does the tobacco crop come in ?, i.e. at what time
is it ripe ?
This family has forty pounds coming in monthly, i.e. the monthly income
of the family is forty pounds.

Come in for, is to have a chance of participating in, to be heir to; also, to receive.

He was in London for the Coronation, and came in for all the festivities.

This man has come in for a good deal of property through the death of a near relative.

If this boy carries on his pranks much longer, he will come in for a sound beating.

Come into.

The marquis will come into the estate on his father's death.

Come near, is to approach, to get within reach of.

As soon as I came near him, I saw what he was doing.

Come of, means: 1. To become of. 2. To issue from.

Poverty often comes of idleness.

Luther came of (=sprang from) a noble race.

Nothing came of his proposal, i.e. it led to no result.

Come off, is to fare, to emerge; to take place.

When does the concert come off ? The concert came off well.

The British army came off victorious in South Africa.

When the expression **come off** is not a compound verb, **off** indicates separation.

He bent down his head and his hat came off.

The ring will not come off his finger.

Come on, is to advance; to begin to occur; also, to thrive.

The dragoons came on to the attack. The rain came on.

The plants are coming on, i.e. are growing well.

Come out, is to become public, to appear, to transpire; to reappear; also, to eventuate.

Several new books have come out this year.

The truth was now obliged to come out.

It came out that she was aware of the facts all the time.

The moon has come out, i.e. has emerged from the clouds.

The calculations have come out right.

Come out of, is to get clear of.

He has come out of all his difficulties.

Come out with a thing, is to disclose it unexpectedly.

Come over, is to pass from one side to another; to overspread; also, to come into one's mind.

A troop of Arabs came over to us from the enemy.

A look of terror came over the sweet smiling face.—*Thackeray*

A great longing came over me to see her again.

Come round. The literal meaning is plain. Secondary meanings are: 1. To recover from illness, to revive. 2. To change gradually to an opposite opinion.

The ships of Holland came round the Cape of Good Hope.

This man has had a severe illness but is coming round again.

He showed violent opposition at first, but when the scheme was fully explained, he came round to our view.

Come to, is: 1. To arrive at as a result.   2. To amount to.   3. To recover from a swoon.

> To come to a decision; come to an understanding; come to terms; come to a standstill; come to an agreement; come to grief; come to blows; come to the point; come to light.
> What will all this agitation come to ?
> The amounts you have spent will come to a large sum.
> This man will never come to much, i.e. will never attain to anything important.
> He looked as if he had just been all but choked and had that moment come to.—*Dickens*

Come up, is to shoot up above the ground; also, to approach or overtake.

> The seed never came up at all.
> They shortened sail to let me come up in my boat.

Come up to, is to conform to, to be equal to.

> The yield of the mine did not come up to our expectations.
> This book comes up to my idea of what a school book ought to be.

Come up with, is to catch up with, to overtake.

> A man on horseback will quickly come up with a traveller on foot.

Come upon, is to find or meet with accidentally.

> He came upon the announcement in the newspaper.
> The farmer in digging a well came upon a vessel containing old coins.

Compare to, with.

> Burke compared the parks of London to the lungs of the human body.
> We may compare Cicero with Demosthenes and decide which was the greater orator.

Compete with a person, **for** a thing.

> These young men competed for the silver medal.
> Holland once competed with England for the mastery of the high seas.

Complain of a thing, **to** a person, **against** or **of** a person.

> He complains of a pain in his chest.
> O loss of sight, of thee I most complain.—*Milton*
> I have to complain against him because of his rudeness.
> Now, Master Shallow, you'll complain of me to the king.—*Shakespeare*

Comply with, is to assent to, to yield to.

> They will not comply with the demands of the prince.
> They forced him to comply with their request.

Conceal a thing **from.**

> The trees concealed the deer from view.
> Do not conceal your intentions from me.

Concede to, is to yield to, to grant.

> Better concede to him all he asks.
> A right of way has been conceded to him.

Condemn to, for. A judge condemns a man **to** a certain punishment **for** a certain crime.

> He was condemned to imprisonment for robbery.

Conduce to. Proper ventilation **conduces to** good health.

Confer (=consult) **with** a person, **about** or **regarding** a thing; confer (=bestow or grant) a favour **on** a person.

> She returned to confer with her husband.—*Lamb*
> The men of the village conferred together about sinking a new well.
> The King conferred large privileges on the barons in return for their services.

Confide in a person; confide a thing **to** a person.

> Do not confide your secrets to everyone.
> I confided in him and he has not deceived me.
> It is rare to find a friend in whom you can always confide.

Conform to.

> Why conform to a custom when the custom is bad ?

Connive at, i.e. disregard, wink at, is used of a blameworthy thing.

> Never be guilty of vice yourself and never connive at it in others.

Consist in, of.

> The strength of this man's cause consists (=stands, remains fixed) in the justice of it.
> The atmosphere consists of (=is composed of) certain gases mixed together in definite proportions.

Consult with.

> Consult with your brother before you decide.

Contend with or **against** an opponent, **for** or **about** an object. When the struggler seeks to gain the object for himself, he is said to contend **for** it. To contend **about** a thing is general in meaning and does not imply a desire to secure the object for oneself.

> Do not contend with a passionate man.
> This gentleman means to contend for a seat in Parliament.
> What did Prussia and Austria contend about in their last war ?
> In the American Civil War, the North contended against the South.

Converse with a person **on** or **about** or **regarding** a subject.

> What were you conversing with the gentleman about ?
> I conversed with the traveller on various topics and found him well informed on all.

Convince one **of.**

> He is now convinced of the truth of the report.
> You cannot convince him of having done wrong in the matter.

Cope with, i.e. manage.

> Your opponent is too skilful for you to cope with him.
> He is not able to cope with the difficulties of his position.

Correspond as by letter **with** a person **about** a thing; correspond (=resemble, agree) **to, with**.

> The wing of a bird corresponds to the arm of a man.
> I corresponded with him about his business prospects.
> My recollections do not exactly correspond with yours.

Count on or **upon**, is to rely on or upon, to confidently expect.

> The admiral counted on assistance from the land forces.
> To count on one's help; count on some one lending you a hundred pounds; count on one's co-operation; count on her sympathy, etc.

Count out a meeting, is to bring a meeting to a close by counting the numbers and finding that there is not a quorum present. This is applicable only to business meetings where a certain number at least must be present to constitute a quorum; unless a quorum is present, no business can be legally transacted. A boxer is said to be **counted out** when he fails to rise in time after a fall.

Crave for, is to yearn for, to beg earnestly for.

> A man in sorrow craves for sympathy.
> She craved for her husband's life on her bended knees.

Creep into, is to steal into unnoticed.

> An error often creeps into a book through a printer's mistake.
> Sophistry often creeps into works of so-called argument.

Crow over, is colloquially used for, to exult over a vanquished adversary, to boast. The term is derived from the practice of a cock crowing exultantly after he has beaten another cock.

> He crowed over me because he had got a pony and I had none.

Cry down, is to decry, to depreciate, to make little of.

> The success of the English was cried down by her foes.
> Men of dissolute lives cry down religion, because they would not be under the restraints of it.—*Tillotson*

Cry for. To cry for a thing, is to cry with the object of getting it, to desire; also, to cry because of it.

> An infant crying for the light.—*Tennyson*
> This woman cries for the slightest thing. The child is crying for its toy.

Cry out, is to shout out, to clamour.

> The disciples cried out for fear.—*Bible*
> The report of a gun was heard and my companion cried out that he was shot in the leg.

Cry out against, is to complain loudly against, to raise a loud voice in opposition to.

> The people cry out against the high taxes.
> The peasants cry out against the tyranny of their landlords.

Cry to, is to call aloud to; also, to implore or entreat with a loud voice.

> The flamingo cries to its mate.
> The people cried to the king for bread.

Cry up, is to praise, to extol, to make much of.

> This man cries up his own wares as the best in the fair.
> The quack's pills are cried up as a remedy for all ailments.

Cure a person **of** a disease.

> No medicine can cure a man of discontent.

Cut across. To cut across a field, is to take a short course across a field. **To cut wood across the grain,** is to cut it across the line in which the fibres of the wood lie.

Cut down, is: 1. To fell. 2. To diminish. 3. To kill.

> He has cut down the old palm tree.
> A man does not like to have his salary cut down.
> Cholera cut down many in this village last year.

Cut in, is to join in, as in conversation, or a game of cards.

Cut off, is to separate; also, to kill, to destroy. **To be cut off,** when said of a person, means to die.

> He cut off the pigtail from the Chinaman's head.
> The tide coming in cut off all retreat.
> How many men are cut off in the prime of life ?

To cut off with a shilling, is to disinherit by naming one in a will and leaving to him the merest trifle. This usually refers to a person who expected a large legacy.

Cut out, is to shape by cutting; also, to remove by cutting. To **cut out** smoking, is to stop the habit.

> A tailor cuts out a coat from the roll of cloth.
> This block of marble was cut out of Italian quarries.
> He is a reformed character, having cut out drinking altogether.

To be cut out for a position, is colloquial for, to have qualities fitting oneself for that position. The primary meaning of **cut out for** seems to be of cloth cut out for a garment.

> I was never cut out for a magistrate.
> Caste did not allow a man to take up an occupation which his talents showed him to be cut out for.

Cut up, is to cut to pieces; to injure, as by severe criticism; to hurt one's feelings or cause grief and pain.

> The butcher cut up the animal he had slaughtered.
> The news of his father's death has cut him up greatly.
> The reviewers mercilessly cut up his book.

Dash against. The waves dash against the shore.

Dash down, is used transitively and intransitively.

> The water dashed down the precipice.
> Dash down yon cup of Samian wine.—*Byron*

Dash in pieces, is to break in pieces.

Dash off, used intransitively, means to rush off violently; transitively and colloquially, to write off quickly; also, to sketch hastily.

> The horse dashed off down the street.
> He dashed off three letters in half an hour.

Dash over.   The waves dashed over the sides of the ship.

Dawn on.

> It dawned on me that the story I was reading was not history but a romance, i.e. the idea grew up gradually in my mind.   The idea is at first a glimmer and by degrees it grows clearer and stronger—as morning dawns.   An idea striking one suddenly is said *to flash on* one.

Deal by a person, is to treat him either well or ill, to behave towards him.

> This gentleman deals well by his clerks.

Deal in, is to trade in.   From this meaning comes the noun, **dealer,** meaning trader.

> This merchant deals in silk goods.

Deal out, is to distribute.

> A judge should deal out equal justice to all.

Deal with, is to trade with, to have to do with; to treat well or ill; also, to treat of.

> I will not deal with this shopkeeper at all.
> This book deals with questions of Political Economy.
> Magistrates are cautious of how they deal with offenders.

Decide on; also, decide **for** or **against.   Decide** is also followed by the infinitive.

> He has not decided on his course yet.
> The case was decided against him.   Does he decide to go or to stay ?

Declare against or **for.**

> The French Senate has declared for peace.
> The Municipality has declared against building a new bridge.

To declare oneself, is to express openly what one thinks.

Deduce from.

> Euclid deduces the truths of geometry from a few definitions and postulates.

Defend against.

> I should defend my friend against all attacks.
> The resolute garrison defended their city against a beleaguering host.

Defer to the opinion of wiser men.

Delight in.

> I delight in the law of God.—*Bible*
> It is not right to delight in vicious courses.

Deliver from. Deliver **up** a thing **to** a person.

> Deliver us from evil.—*Bible*
> Today he delivered up charge of his office to his successor.

Depend (=rely) **on** or **upon.**

> I depended on his coming at seven o'clock.
> Depend on God for all mercies and blessings.

Deprive of. A man is deprived of a thing he would like to keep.

> They are deprived of their rights as citizens.
> Paralysis has deprived him of the use of his right arm.

Desist from an attempt, **from** a course of action.

Despair of success, of gaining anything, etc.

> He despairs of winning a scholarship.

Deter from.

> Nothing should deter you from choosing the true and doing the right.

Deviate from, is to turn aside from.

> Never deviate from the straight path of virtue.

Devolve on or **upon.**

> It will devolve on you to manage this school.

Die away, by, of, out.

> The effects of the late agitation have died away.
> Men die of hunger, of cholera, of inflammation of the lungs, etc.; men
> die by the sword, by pestilence, etc. What did this man die of ?
> In these degenerate days the practice is dying out.

Differ about, from, in, with.

> Men differ in opinion about his conduct.
> I differ with you as to the precise meaning of this word.
> In what respect do the planets differ from the fixed stars ?

Dig out articles or persons entombed by the falling of a house.

Dig up the soil in one's garden, is to turn it over by digging. Also, dig up old coins, i.e. turn them out of the ground by digging, to exhume.

Dip into. To dip into a volume, is to read it here and there at random.

> You will never get much profit from a philosophical treatise by merely
> dipping into it occasionally.
> Dipping into this volume of travels, I noticed a passage which shows
> that the author is a Radical in politics.

Disagree with, is not to agree with; also, to be unsuited to.

> The patient is so weak that solid food disagrees with him.

Disapprove of a plan, **of** conduct.

Discriminate between.

> A judge will discriminate between different degrees of crime.

Dispense with, to.

> You can easily dispense with (= do without) his services.
> He dispenses (= deals out) equal justice to all.

Dispose of, is to sell, to get rid of; dispose (=incline) a person **to** a thing.

> He has disposed of all his chattels.
> Sad news disposes him to melancholy.

Dispute about, with.

> These men have disputed about their landmarks.
> Several places dispute with Smyrna the honour of being the birthplace of Homer.

Dissent from an opinion.

Dissuade from an attempt, from a course of action.

Distinguish between two; distinguish one **from** another.

> The light is so dim that I cannot distinguish one object from another.
> Death does not distinguish between the rich and the poor; it comes alike to the peasant and the prince.

Divert from, is to cause to turn aside from.

> It is not easy to divert a stream from its course.

Divest of clothes, arms, equipages; divest one **of** his rights, etc.

Divide between two, **among** more than two; divide **into** parts.

> Divide the apple between the two children.
> How can I divide a shilling among ten beggars ?
> He divided his farm into three equal portions.

Do away with, is to put away, to remove, to destroy, to nullify.

> The British Government wisely did away with *suttee*.

Do for, is to suit instead of, to serve the purpose of.

> This place would do for a gymnasium.
> Take this piece of muslin; it will do you for a turban.

To do for often colloquially means, to disappoint, to ruin, to put an end to.

> This man's case is done for. You are done for.
> At the examination he made several glaring blunders in spelling, and that did for him, i.e. that prevented him from passing.

Do into. We speak of **doing** a fable **into** poetry, doing a story **into** verse, where **do into** means, to change into the form of.

Do one **out of** a thing, is to deprive him of that thing by cheating or cunning.

Do up a parcel, is to pack up a parcel. To **do up** a room, is to put it into order. **To be done up,** is to be exhausted—said of a person, or of an animal—as a horse.

Do with, is to make use of, to employ; also, to dispose of.

> What did the man do with his bundle ?
> He has got a telescope, but does not know what to do with it.
> What am I to do with this troublesome fellow ?, i.e. How am I to get rid of him ?
> What does he do with himself all day ?, i.e. How does he occupy himself all day ?

Do without a thing, is to dispense with it, to manage without it.

Domineer over, is to lord it over, to treat harshly.

Draw aside. I am said to draw a person aside when I induce him to come apart with me for private conversation.

Draw back, is to recede; to withdraw.

> I have vowed sacrifice to God and I cannot draw back.
> He will not draw back from what he has promised.

Draw down, is to attract from above.

> A metal rod draws down the lightning.
> Wickedness will draw down punishment from a righteous God.

Draw for, is used of drawing tickets or numbers at a lottery, and a man is said to **draw for** the prize, i.e. he draws a ticket in the hope of getting the prize.

Draw in, is to retract, to bring inside, to pull in, to inveigle.

> The snail draws in its horns; the camel draws in its tongue.
> I put my hand out of the window and drew in a bunch of grapes.
> The villagers were readily drawn in and the conspiracy grew strong.

Draw near, is to approach.

> As Autumn draws near, the cornfields show signs of ripeness.
> Draw near to God with humble heart and pray to Him with sincerity.

Draw off, is to withdraw, to take away, to abstract.

> He has drawn off a gallon of water from this cask.

Draw on or **upon.** One is said to **draw on** or **upon** a banker when he issues a cheque in order to get money from the banker. The verb **draw on** also means, approach; also, entice, allure.

> As the time drew on, all stood in readiness.
> He drew the animal on till he brought him into a trap.

Draw out, is to extract, prolong. To **draw out a person,** is to elicit his opinion or views, to induce him to tell you his thoughts.

> He drew out his remarks to a great length.
> He drew out his sword and would have killed himself.—*Bible*
> He was a taciturn person, but I managed in the end to draw him out.

Draw out of, is to withdraw from, to retire from.

> You cannot draw out of your engagement now.

Draw to, is to feel attracted to.

> The man was so genial, I was drawn to him at once.
> If evil consisted merely in ignorance, men would be drawn to virtue as soon as it was explained to them; but, alas! how many know their duty and yet do not do it.

Draw up, is to compose in due form, to draft; also, to arrange in order, as a body of troops, to marshal. To draw up a petition, a will, a memorial, a remonstrance.

> Nelson drew up his warships opposite Alexandria.
> i drew up a statement of my affairs in writing.
> The barons drew up the Magna Charta setting forth their claims.

Dream away the hours, is to pass them in idle reverie.

Dream of.

> More things are wrought by prayer than this world dreams of.—*Tennyson*
> There are more things in heaven and earth, Horatio, than are dreamt
> of in your philosophy.—*Shakespeare*

Dress up, is to adorn by dressing, to clothe gaily or fashionably.

> I just now met your brother dressed up in fine style.
> This little girl wants her mother's cape in which to dress up.

Drive at, is colloquial for, to aim at, to intend.

> I listened attentively to his long rambling speech, but could not make
> out what he was driving at.

To let drive at, is to aim a blow at.

> The rogues let drive at me.

Drive in a nail, or stake. To drive in an idea, is to succeed by great
effort in getting the idea into the brain of a stupid person.

Drive on, is to drive further.

> Our cab had to stop because of a commotion in the street, and it was
> ten minutes before we could drive on.

Drive out, is to banish, to expel. When said of cattle, it means
either to drive afield, or to drive beyond a boundary.

> Drive out the sheep to the meadows.
> The Swiss assembled and drove out the invaders of their country.

Drop in, is to visit casually.

> I dropped in at the club on my way home.

Drop off. Fruit drops off a tree. Also, decrease in numbers;
drop off to sleep, i.e. to fall asleep.

> The audiences for this play have recently dropped off.
> There are no apples on this tree: all have dropped off.

Drop out. To drop out, said of a soldier, is to leave the ranks.

> As they marched, a few got sunstruck and dropped out.

Dwell (=reside) **among** people **at** a place, **in** a country. To dwell
on or **upon** a subject, is to speak of, or to ponder over it at some
length.

> Do not let your mind dwell on these troubles.
> In his speech he dwelt on the importance of prompt action.

Eat into, is to corrode. Rust eats into iron.

Eat up. Up here expresses completeness.

> The larger the capital sunk in the modern factory, the more urgent is it
> that there should be no stoppage of work; for, when work stops,
> interest is eaten up.

Egg on, is to instigate, to urge on.

> What or who egged you on to fight with a professional boxer?

Eke out, is to supplement what is scanty so as to have enough.

> He eked out by his wits an income of barely fifty pounds.—*Macaulay*

Embark in, on. Embark on board a vessel; embark in a new business speculation.

> This is a kind of business in which I would not embark my capital.

Emerge from water, from obscurity, from a place of hiding.

Encroach on.

> The sea has encroached here on the land.

Engage in battle, in controversy, in business; to be engaged in writing a letter.

Enjoin on.

> I enjoin this on you as a solemn duty.

Enlarge on or **upon,** is said of a man making a long speech on a particular subject.

> The lawyer enlarged upon this part of the evidence and treated it as of great importance.

Enter is followed by **into** and **upon.**

> You enter into an engagement, into conversation, into an alliance, into a contest, into a contract, into a discussion, into possession.
> You enter upon a work, upon a course, upon a lawsuit, upon a war.
> Lead enters into the composition of pewter.

Entrust a person **with** a thing; entrust a thing to a person.

> I entrusted a hundred pounds to him to take to the bank.
> I entrusted him with a hundred pounds to take to the bank.

Escape from jail, from control, from punishment. In the phrase **escape my notice,** no preposition is needed.

Excel in painting, music, mathematics, running.

Exchange a thing **with** a person **for** an equivalent.

> Will you exchange pencils with me ?
> I exchanged a copy of Milton with my cousin for a copy of Wordsworth.

Exclude from the privileges of membership.

Explain a thing **to** a person.

> I wish to explain this matter to you.

Expostulate with.

> I did not expostulate with the driver at the fare he charged me.

Exult at success; exult **over** a fallen foe.

> It is natural for him to exult at his son's success.
> You have triumphed over James this time, but you need not exult over him, for he may beat you next time.

Fall among, is to come among accidentally.

> A certain man fell among thieves.—*Bible*

Fall away, is to become lean; to revolt; to apostatize; to fade.

These cattle have quickly fallen away in flesh.
The whole province has fallen away from the king.
How can the soul . . . fall away into nothing?—*Addison*

Fall back, is to recede.

We charged and the enemy's front line fell back.

Fall back upon, is to have recourse to some expedient formerly found helpful, but not yet tried in the case in hand.

Fall down, is: 1. To fall from a higher position.   2. To prostrate oneself in worship.

Jack fell down and broke his crown.
He fell down from a tree into which he had climbed.
The wise men fell down and worshipped the infant Jesus.

Fall in, is to fall from above into a hollow or open space below; also, when soldiers are being marshalled they are ordered to **fall in,** i.e. to get into line.

The sides of the pit fell in and buried two men.
The captain ordered his men to fall in at once.

Fall in with, is: 1. To meet with accidentally, to come upon by chance.   2. To agree with, to concur with.

In my journey I fell in with two pilgrims going to Rome.
The weak-minded boy quickly fell in with the plans of the burglar.

Fall into a pit, a trap; fall into conversation.

A tourist he knew fell into conversation with him.

Fall off, is: 1. To drop, as fruit from a tree.   2. To become detached. 3. To diminish.   4. To decline from former excellence.

Love cools, friendship falls off, brothers divide.—*Shakespeare*
The subscribers to this newspaper have fallen off
This newspaper has fallen off; it is not what it used to be.

Fall on or **upon,** is: 1. To drop on, to descend on.   2. To attack.

A constant drop falling on a stone will wear a hole in it.

Fall out, is: 1. To drop out.   2. To happen, to befall.   3. To quarrel or wrangle.   4. To leave the ranks (of soldiers).

When civil dudgeon first grew high,
And men fell out, they knew not why.—*Butler*
In his sleep he let the money fall out of his hand.
It so fell out that no guard was on duty that night.
Accuse each other of cheating when they fall out in money matters.—
Thackeray

Fall out with a person, is to quarrel with him.

Fall through, is to miscarry, to fail, to come to nothing.

As neither of us would give in, the bargain fell through.
Eventually the project, which seemed so near realization, fell through.

Fall to, is to apply oneself to, to begin eagerly to do a thing.

> The author fell to writing again.
> Ulysses's soldiers, elated with the spoil and the good store of provisions which they found in that place, fell to eating and drinking, forgetful of their safety.—*Lamb*

Fall under, is to come under; also, to be ranged under.

> To fall under a category or class; fall under one's notice or displeasure.
> The village you speak of does not fall under my jurisdiction.

Familiarize oneself with a book, a business, a science, modes of agriculture, etc.

Fasten on, to, with.

> The leech fastened on his arm at once.
> The fisherman fastened his net to the side of the boat.
> He fastened the door with a strong lock.

Fawn on or **upon,** is to court favour by low cunning, like a dog; to flatter meanly so as to win favour.

> They fawned on him and ate his dinners and drank his wines till he had nothing left, and then they ridiculed him for his folly.

Feed on or **upon.** Both transitive and intransitive.

> His dog feeds on mutton bones.
> Leaving thy trunk for crows to feed upon.—*Shakespeare*
> He feeds his horse on corn and beans.

Feed with. To feed cattle with turnips and hay; to feed an engine with water; to feed a furnace with coal; the spring feeds the canal with water. To be **fed up with** is a slang expression meaning, to be tired of.

> I have fed you with milk and not with meat.—*Bible*

Feel for, is to have sympathy for; also, to try to touch, to grope for.

> A humane man will feel for others in their suffering.
> I felt for the book in the dark room, but could not find it.

Ferret out, is to search out by patient efforts; to follow out till one finds, as a ferret does its prey.

> The lawyer will not rest till he ferrets out all the information he needs.
> The swindler has hid himself, but the police are sure to ferret him out before long.

Fight against, for, with.

> England and France fought against Russia in the Crimean War.
> A fourth man unbound the Dane and bade him catch up a weapon and fight for his life.—*Kingsley*
> To fight with thee no man of arms will deign.—*Milton*

Fight out, is to continue fighting till a definite end is reached.

> The controversy should be fought out once for all.

Fill in a map or picture or piece of embroidery, is to insert the details of the work after an outline has been made.

Fill out, is to distend by inflation.

Fill up, used transitively, means, to make quite full; used intransitively, it means, to become quite full.   To **fill up** a cheque or a form, is to insert the appropriate words or figures in the blank spaces.   To **fill up** an appointment, is to fill it by appointing someone to it.

> A man fills a post, i.e. he himself holds it.
> A man fills up a post, i.e. he appoints another person to it.
> You fill up a cask with water.   (*Up* here denotes completeness.)
> The Suez Canal would soon fill up with mud if not regularly dredged.

Fill with, is both transitive and intransitive.

> The doctor filled the bottle with medicine.   Her eyes filled with tears.

Find a person **in** clothes or expenses, is regularly to provide him with these things.

Find out, is to detect; to discover.   **Out** with this verb is sometimes equivalent to absent, away from home.

> He was unable to find out the answer.
> Be sure your sin will find you out.—*Bible*
> Virtues in plants which I could not find out.—*Defoe*
> I called at his office yesterday, but found him out.

Fire away, is to continue firing with guns.   As slang, it has the meaning of, to begin.

> All right, fire away with your questions.

Fire on, is to attack with firearms or cannon.

Fire a person **with,** is to animate or inspire him with.

> This fresh outrage is enough to fire one with rage and revenge.

Fit out or **up,** is to equip, to furnish with useful articles.

> How soon will the ship be fitted out for her trial trip ?
> He is busy fitting up his house for friends and guests.

Flare up, is to shine out with sudden splendour, to give out a dazzling light.   Also, to suddenly grow angry or irritated, to burst into a fit of passion.

Fling aside, is to cast aside with vehemence.

> The carpenter angrily flung aside his tools and would work no longer.

Fling away, is to throw aside vehemently or violently, to discard.

> The madman flung away his watch and his purse.
> Cromwell, I charge thee, fling away ambition.—*Shakespeare*

Fling down, is to throw down violently.

> The pedlar flung down his pack at my door and walked off.

Fling off, is vehemently to throw aside, to cast off hastily and with force; to beat off.

> He flung off his coat and leaped into the river.
> He flung off his antagonist thrice.

Fling up, is vehemently to throw up. To fling up a design, a scheme, a plan. Some disparagement is implied in this verb.

Fly at, is to rush upon suddenly, to spring towards; also, to attack suddenly with angry, biting words.

> The dog will fly at a man's throat. The cat flew at the mouse.
> I have made a very mild suggestion and all at once you fly at me with bitter reproaches as though I sought to injure you.

Fly away. Away indicates completeness here.

> If the bird is let out of its cage, it will certainly fly away.

Fly into, is used literally and figuratively.

> A dove flew into my house on the day of the eclipse.
> As soon as she saw the contents of the letter, she flew into a passion.

Fly off, is to depart hastily. **Fly off at a tangent.** *

> As we came near, the parrots rose and flew off.
> He flew off to the station in the hope of catching the train.
> As his cycle went down the hill, the tyre of one of the wheels flew off.

Fly open, is to become open suddenly or with violence.

> He touched a spring and the drawer flew open.

Fly out, is to rush out.

> The child opened the door of the cage and the bird flew out.
> A cry of ' Fire ' was raised and all the people flew out of the house.

Free oneself **from** or **of,** is to release or disengage oneself from. Also, free a person or thing **from** or **of**.

> Free the prisoner of his fetters.
> If the misguided youth would free himself of his bad companions he would soon improve his own position.
> Proper sanitary measures would soon free the district from cholera.

Fret at, or **about,** is to chafe at. What is the child fretting at?

Furnish a thing **to** a person; furnish a person **with** a thing.

> You furnish food to the hungry, medicine to the sick.
> You furnish a family with provisions, and a servant with money to buy articles for you.

Gain on or **upon,** is to encroach on, to come up nearer to.

> The second horse in the race gained on the first, i.e. was overtaking him.
> Two boys go to school and are put into the same class; one outstrips the other at first; but by patient study the second gains on his companion and passes him.

Gain over, is to win over a person from the opposite side.

> Rulers often try by a judicious distribution of favours to gain over hostile tribes.

Get. This verb is followed by more prepositions or adverbs than almost any other.

Get about, is to go about, to move from place to place.

> It is a relief to a man who has been ill to get about again.
> The storm is so severe today that it is impossible to get about.

Get above. **Above** here indicates **higher than**, either literally or figuratively.

> John has got above James in the class.
> He has now got above his misfortunes.

Get one's head above water. *

Get about, is to go from place to place; also, to circulate.

> He has quite recovered and able to get about.
> A rumour has got about that he is going to resign his appointment.

Get ahead, is to outstrip others in a race or competition; also, to get in front, to advance, to prosper.

> It is the diligent student who gets ahead and wins prizes.
> In the regatta, the *Penelope* soon got ahead of all the other yachts.

Get along, is to proceed, to advance; to fare, to prosper; also, to live pleasantly together.

> He seems to be getting along well in his business.
> Schools get along but poorly enough in backward countries.
> These two brothers never could get along.

Get among, is to attain to the position of being among.

> It was easy to see, from his beaming face, that he had got among congenial companions.

Get at, is to reach, to attain to.   The phrase implies effort.

> Our object in this inquiry is to get at the truth.
> When the fox could not get at the grapes he said they were sour.
> It is no easy thing to get at the meaning of every idiom in English.

Get away, is to leave, to escape, to get free.   To **get away with**, is to succeed, or achieve something with impunity.

> When one has business on hand it is hard to get away from home.
> He was really as guilty as his partner, but managed to get away with it.

Get back, is to return; also, to receive back.

> He has just got back from his long journey.
> I have got back the articles that were stolen from my house.

Get before, is to arrive in front of, to arrive further forward.

> The bay horse soon got before the others in the road.
> Do not let your companion get before you in learning.

Get behind, is to fall into the rear, to lag, to get into a backward position.   It is the opposite of **get before**.

> A man gets behind in business, i.e. he does not succeed and therefore is not able to meet the claims upon him.
> A man gets behind with his rent, i.e. he is unable to pay his rent when it becomes due and it accumulates as a debt against him.

Get between, is to arrive between.

> A body of police got between the opposing mobs.
> When the moon gets between the earth and the sun, there is an eclipse of the sun.

Get beyond, is to go out of the reach of, to go outside a limit.

> The sailor climbed up on the rock and got beyond the reach of the waves.
> The young man went into the river to bathe, but, getting beyond his depth, he was carried off by the current.

Get down, is to descend from a higher position to a lower.

> They have climbed up the precipice; but how will they get down ?

Get forward, is to proceed, to advance.

> I hope these boys are getting forward with their education.

Get in, is either intransitive, meaning, to enter; or transitive, meaning, to bring in, to receive as the result of collecting.

> I went to your house today, but could not get in, i.e. enter it.
> A railway guard seeing passengers waiting to enter the carriage says, ' Get in.'
> A man gets in debt; a general gets in information of the enemy's movements; a collector gets in reports from various districts.

Get into, is to attain to a position in.

> This new reform is fast getting into favour with the people.
> It would be well if the blind could be got into an institution where they would be cared for and taught.
> A man gets into a carriage, into difficulties, into debt, into favour.

To **get into trouble,** i.e. to fall into trouble; to **get a person into trouble,** is to bring another person into trouble.

Get near, is to approach.

> It will be dangerous if the ship gets near the rocks.
> The crush was so great I could not get near the platform.

Get off, is to dismount; also, to escape, to become free from. It is also used transitively. To **get off goods,** is to sell them, to get rid of them by sale, or to dispatch them.

> He cannot get his coat off.
> He got off his bicycle and went into the house.
> I have just got off a hundred bales of cotton to England.
> The traveller was very busy all day, but got off by the evening train.
> The ship has stuck on a bank, but they hope to get her off at full tide.
> If this fellow was imprisoned for but one week for so grave an offence, he got off cheap, i.e. he escaped with a very slight punishment.

Get on, is to advance, to succeed, to fare; to put on; also, to live pleasantly together.

> He cannot get his boots on.
> How is your son getting on at school ?
> How can an idle spendthrift hope to get on in the world ?
> This husband and wife cannot get on together.

Get on with. To **get on with a person,** is to find him agreeable. To **get on with a work,** is to get forward in doing it.

Get over, is to overcome, to surmount. To **get over** an illness, is to survive it, to recover from it.

The boys got over the garden wall and escaped.
You have got over all your difficulties, have you not ?
The habits of a lifetime are not got over immediately.
This man never got over the death of his son, i.e. never quite overcame the shock which his son's death caused him.

Get out, is to escape, to get or set free, to go outside.

The woman fell into the well and could not get out.
The jailer must take care that no prisoner gets out.

To get a person out, is to procure escape for him, to extricate him.

Get out of, is to escape from, to get free from, to go outside of.

I got out of bed.
It is easier to get into debt than to get out of it.
The squirrel ran up a tree and got out of my reach.
She was anxious not to let the children get out of her sight.

Get round a person, is colloquial for, to wheedle or prevail with him; also, to circumvent him by deception or flattery.

He will try to get round the money-lender and thereby meet his present commitments.

Get through, is to pass through; also, to finish a thing, to accomplish a work. To **get through an illness**, is to pass through it and to recover from it.

Does the doctor think the sick man will get through ?
These labourers are getting through their work slowly.
John has got through the examination, i.e. John has passed it.

Get through with a job, is to finish it up, to accomplish it completely.

Get to, is to reach, to come close to, to attain to.

I resolved if possible to get to the ship.
When do you get to your destination ?
He made me promise that I would go to see them when I got to England.
Is Zanzibar an easy place to get to ?, i.e. Is it easy to get to Zanzibar ?
    The former of these is the idiomatic form of the question.

Get up, is to rise, as from a seat or bed; also, to ascend. **Get up** is also used transitively, meaning, to make ready, to prepare, to arrange for; also, to set on foot, to establish.

He got up and locked the door.
He fell down on the road and was too weak to get up.
It does not matter how early you rise if you do nothing when you get up.
Who is going to get up the concert ?

To **get up** a subject, is to master it, to acquire a thorough knowledge of it. To get up a commotion, is to stir up or cause a commotion. To get up a concert, is to arrange for it. This book is well got up, i.e. is well arranged, printed, and bound. The **get up** of a play, means the arrangements of a play. A **person's get up**, is his or her costume, style of dress, equipment. A **got up affair** or story, is a concocted affair or story.

The programme is got up in an attractive style.
Efforts to get up a Home Rule agitation among the cool and hard-headed Scots have not hitherto proved very successful.

Give away, is to make over to another, to transfer, to part with altogether. **Away** indicates completeness.

The father gave his daughter away in marriage.
He never gave away a farthing in his life.

Give back, is to restore, to return what you receive.

Please give me back the atlas you borrowed from me.
I gave him back tit-for-tat, i.e. I treated him as he treated me.

Give in, is to tender, to hand in, to make known; also, to yield, to submit.

He has given in his adherence to the Liberal party.
He was compelled to give in, i.e. to yield.
As neither of us would give in, the bargain fell through.—*King*
After many years of honourable service, the Head Clerk has given in his resignation.

Give in to, is to submit to, to agree to, to yield assent to.

He gave in to the wish of the majority.
The old gentleman must give in to him.

Give off, is to emit, to exhale. It is said of odours or vapours.

Some flowers give off their richest fragrance at night.

Give out, is to announce; to emit; also, to send out, to give to be done outside.

The jessamine gives out a sweet perfume.
He gave out that he was going to England.
This lady gives out her sewing, i.e. gives her sewing to be done by some person away from her house.

Give over, is to transfer, to hand over from one to another. **Make over,** has much the same sense.

He gave over charge of his office to his successor today.

Give up, is to abandon or relinquish finally; also, intransitive, to fail utterly.

I gave up possession of my house today.
We have given up all hope of our father's recovery.
The lawyer said his client would not give up his claim to the property.
The horse gave up through sheer exhaustion and we had to stay there all night.
He had given the ship up for lost and was surprised to hear she had reached port.

To **give up a riddle,** is to cease attempting to answer it.

To **give up the ghost,** is to die, to yield up one's spirit in death.

Give a person up, is to relinquish all hope of his coming, or of his recovery, as the case may be; to deliver up; also, to abandon oneself to.

She gave herself up to her own forebodings.—*Thackeray*
He gave himself up to all kinds of low vices.
We waited dinner for you till seven and then we gave you up.

Glance at, is: 1. To take a hasty look at.   2. To touch on lightly, as in a speech.

He glanced at the stranger's face.
This newspaper article glances at our relations with China.

Glance over, is to look at or look into hastily, to peruse casually, as, to glance over a book, letter, or catalogue.

Glory in, is to boast of, to be proud of; also, to delight in.

He glories in bloodshed and slaughter.
Let not the wise man glory in his wisdom.—*Bible*

Gloss over, is to cover over or embellish so as to conceal faults or deficiencies.

The joiner tried to gloss over the little cracks in the work box by the judicious use of wax.
He made a long speech, eulogizing the gentleman's career, and glossing over those actions which had not been pleasing to the people.

Go about, is to move from place to place; also, set to work at.

He went about doing good.
There is a tiger going about the country.
I go about in black, i.e. dressed in black clothes.
'Go about your business', is said contemptuously to a person who is pestering you and whom you wish to be rid of.

Go abroad, is to go to a foreign country; also, rarely, to become public.

The man you speak of went abroad ten years ago and no news of him has since come.
A story went abroad to the effect that this woman had committed suicide by jumping into a well.

Go across, is to cross, to go from one side to the other.

I have been where the railway goes across the Nile.

Go after, is to follow, to pursue, to apply to.

The dogs went after the wounded deer.
God commanded, saying: 'Go not after other gods.'
The spendthrift first spent his money; then his jewels went after his money; and so on till he was in beggary.

Go against, is to resist, to go contrary to, to be disagreeable to; also, to march to attack.

The German army went against Paris.
It goes against my wishes to leave the country.
In splitting wood, do not try to go against the grain.

Go ahead, is to advance, to get before others, to prosper.

The Americans pride themselves in being a go-ahead people.
In the boat race, though all started together, the Collegians' boat soon went ahead.

Go along with, is to accompany. **Along** strengthens the idea of companionship in **with** here.

> He started on his journey and two servants went along with him.

Go aside, is to turn to the side, to deviate, to swerve; to go a little way off.

> Never go aside from the path of truth and rectitude.
> They went aside from the crowd and conversed together in private.

Go at. To go at a thing, is said of going towards an obstacle and overcoming it. It also means to attempt to do a thing. **Go at** is also used colloquially for, to attack.

> The horseman went at the wall and cleared it, i.e. went towards the wall and leaped over it.
> The soldiers went at their work in brisk style.

Go away, is to depart, to go off, to leave.

> Is the epidemic likely to go away when the hot spell ends ?
> Trade has gone away from Goa since Bombay rose into importance.

Go back, is to return to where one came from; also, to retire, to recede, to withdraw.

> The steamer arrived from England a week ago and goes back tomorrow, i.e. starts on her return voyage tomorrow.
> Our country is going back, i.e. is not progressing.

Go between, is to go in the midst of two, to lie or pass between one place and another; also, to mediate, to interpose between two parties. An intermediary or middleman is often called a **go-between.**

> This road goes between two high walls for a mile.
> The post goes between Calcutta and all parts of India.
> John acted as a go-between for the two parties.

Go beyond, is to go outside a boundary or prescribed limit.

> Arabi Pasha was not allowed to go beyond the limits of Ceylon.
> The professor in his lecture went beyond the capacity of his audience.
> In the auction, many articles went beyond their value, i.e. were sold at prices above their value.

Go by, is to pass near, to proceed by way of or by means of, to follow; also, to elapse, when used of time. To **go by a name,** is to be known by that name.

> The railway from London to Liverpool goes by Crewe.
> He went by the directions contained in the guide-book.
> This room goes by the name of The Study.
> He meant to go by rail and not by steamer.
> Lamb calls a certain picture of a lady ' my beauty ', and adds that this is ' a foolish name it goes by among his friends '
> A week went by without the culprit being secured by the police.

To **give one the go-by,** is to avoid him, to pass him by without notice:

> Some songs to which we have given the go-by.

In times gone by, means, in past times, usually times long past.

Go down, is: 1. To descend, to sink, to go below the horizon. 2. To fail, to come to nothing. 3. To be swallowed. 4. To be accepted without opposition. 5. To get lower in price. 6. To leave a university.

> Like ships that have gone down at sea,
> When heaven was all tranquillity.—*Moore*

Go downstairs and get supper ready. The pills would not go down.
They went down the river, i.e. towards the sea.
The ship went down in six fathoms, i.e. it sank.
Silk is going down, i.e. is becoming cheaper.
This story will not go down, i.e. people will not believe it.
The undergraduates are due to go down today.

Go for, colloquially, is to attack.

To **go for nothing**, is, to be useless, of no efficacy.

Go forth, is to depart, to issue from; also, to become public.

A rumour went forth that the Prince was poisoned.
A great cavalcade went forth from the town to meet the Governor.

Go in, is to enter.

A servant opened the door and we went in.

Go in for, is to enter as a competitor with the hope of gaining; also, to be in favour of, to advocate, to take as one's object.

All sensible Hindus should go in for the abolition of caste.
He goes in for cricket, football, and all other manly sports.
I've decided to go in for a new suit.

Go into, is to enter into; to treat of.

He went into the garden and picked some grapes.
The gentleman said he would go into the problem in his next lecture.

Go off, is to leave, to depart. When used of firearms, it means, to explode, to be discharged. Other meanings appear below.

She went off to fetch the book.
The pistol went off before he knew.
If a spark were to reach the gunpowder it would go off at once.
He went off into a passion, i.e. he suddenly became angry.
He went off in a passion, i.e. when he went away he was in a passion.
The goods go off today, i.e. will be dispatched today.
This fruit is going off rapidly, i.e. is going bad.

Go on, is to continue, to progress; to be put on.

Let him go on and finish his work.
This coat would not go on, i.e. could not be worn.
Our mirth and uproar went on.—*Lamb*

Goings on, a phrase denoting strange or blameworthy behaviour.

Go on with a work, is to continue at it, to keep on doing it.

While others are idling their time, this student goes on steadily with his studies.

Go out, is to go outside, to become public; to cease to burn. When said of the tide, it means to recede, to ebb.

> He keeps to the house and will not go out.
> Does the life of a man go out like a candle ?
> The tide has gone out, but will soon turn.
> Do not let this silly story go out to everybody.
> And life itself goes out at Thy displeasure.—*Addison*

Go out of, is to go outside of.

> All the lepers went out of the city.
> If a man wishes to go out of his country, why should he not ?

Go over, is to pass across a limit; to pass from one side to another, or from one thing to another; to look into, to peruse; to examine, to review.

> He went over a great many points in his speech.
> Two regiments of infantry went over to the enemy.
> The Magistrate goes over all his district every year.
> He carefully went over the whole account, item by item.
> Few countries will allow travellers to go over their frontier without producing a passport.
> I went over the house, i.e. I went into every part of the house and looked at the whole of it.

Go through, is to pass through to the other side; to endure to the end; to examine from beginning to end.

> I cannot go through these letters in an hour.
> We went through a dark wood and met no person on the way.

Go through with, is to continue doing a thing till it is completed, to go to the end, to perform or execute thoroughly.

> I felt I should never settle to anything with resolution enough to go through with it.—*Defoe*
> The great defect with reformers is that they content themselves with *talking* about what should be done; and even when they believe it right that certain things ought to be done, they are afraid to go through with them.

Go to, is to go or reach as far as. To **go to** a person, is to approach him, often with the idea of applying for something or of receiving something. To **go to the dogs** is to be ruined.

> Does this railway go to the coast ?
> Take this letter and go to the Magistrate for instructions.

Go up, is to arise, to ascend.

> She went upstairs. Two men went up in a balloon.
> Cotton has gone up, i.e. has risen in price.
> The boat was going up the river, i.e. towards its source.

Go up and down, is to go here and there, to go from one person to another; also, to go up and down a stair or steps, to go up and down the shaft of a mine.

Thou shalt not go up and down as a talebearer among thy people.—*Bible*

Jacob in his dream saw a ladder with its foot on the earth and its top in heaven, and the angels of God went up and down upon it.

Go up to, is to ascend to, approach quite near to, go close to.

Go up to the statue and read the inscription.

I went up to him boldly and asked him what he had to say against me.

Go upon, is to act or proceed according to.

Is this the principle you always go upon ?

In his whole argument, he went upon the assumption that his client was perfectly innocent.

Go with, is to accompany; also, to agree with.

Can a singular verb go with a plural noun ?

If you go with fools you must expect to be treated as a fool.

We let the boat go with the current, i.e. as the current bore it.

Go without, is to be or remain destitute of.

He has gone without his dinner, and yet he goes on with his work.

A poor man has to go without many things which a rich man regards as almost necessaries of life.

Grapple with, is to enter into contest with, resolutely and courageously.

He grappled with the thief in the dark.

Grapple with your difficulties and trust in God.

Grasp at, is to catch at, to try to seize.

Did Cromwell ever think of grasping at the crown ?

As he fell, he grasped at a hanging chain and missed it.

Grieve at, for, over.

The maidens grieved at my concern.—*Cowper*

I grieve for him: he has met with a sad loss in the death of his only son.

You grieve over your loss.   He grieved over his dead friend.

Grind down, is to oppress grievously.

The peasantry were ground down till no spirit was left in them.

Grow from, is to spring from; also, to advance from.

Some plants grow from seed and some from cuttings.

The business of the firm grew from very small beginnings.

Grow in, is to increase or advance in respect of.

The Prince grew in popular esteem.

May he grow in wisdom as he grows in years.

Grow out of, is to spring from, as a plant from the soil, or as a branch from the trunk; also, to advance beyond.

I saw a plant growing out of a crevice in the wall.

These wars have grown out of commercial considerations.

If a youth has unhappily contracted bad habits, he should strive to grow out of them.

The child has grown out of his clothes, i.e. he has grown so big that his clothes are now too small for him.

Grow to, is to gradually attain to, to become by increasing.

> I cannot fancy to what this agitation will grow.
> Many a boy educated here has grown to eminence.

Grow together. One's skin or flesh if cut, is said to **grow together** when it adheres and unites by growth. The bark of a tree if cut is said to **grow together** when it reunites by growth.

Grow up, is to arise gradually; also, to attain to manhood or womanhood, to arrive at maturity.

> An intimacy grew up between the old lady and me.
> She will be a nice girl when she grows up.

Grow upon, is used of habits, and means, to increase in power over, to acquire greater mastery over.

> The habit of taking drugs has been growing upon the schoolmaster.

Grumble at.

> He grumbles at his lot instead of resolutely facing his difficulties.

Guard against, from.

> Be careful to guard against mistakes in your composition.
> The Lord guard you from all dangers.

Hand down, is to transmit in succession, as from father to son, or from one generation to another.

> Why follow the traditions handed down to us by our fathers ?
> These diamonds have been handed down in his family for generations.

Hand in, is to give in, to tender. You hand in an application, a resignation; you hand in a letter at an office, i.e. you give it in by hand and go away.

Hand into, is to help into by means of your hand.

> To hand a lady into a carriage.

Hand on, is to pass a thing on to another by hand, to transmit, to pass on to posterity.

> The letter was not for me and I handed it on to the next clerk.
> Boys stand in a row at play: the first boy takes a ball and hands it on to the next, and he hands it on to the third, and so on till it comes to the last boy.

Hand out, is to bring out a thing from some place and put it forward with the hand.

> The shopkeeper handed out his goods and the carrier took them away.
> I handed them out five shillings, i.e. I drew the money from my pocket and gave it to them.

Hand over, is to deliver over to another, to give over by hand.

> He has resigned and will hand over charge of his office today.
> I bought a horse and handed over the price of it to the Afghan.
> The French police handed over the swindler to the English officials.

Hand up, is to deliver up.   The idea of higher authority is implied.
The lawyer handed up the lease to the judge.

Hang about, is to loiter near a place.

> Two suspicious looking fellows were seen hanging about the village last evening.

Hang back, is to be reluctant to go forward, to incline to retire.

Hang down, is said of the head when one keeps his head bent down a little with his face towards the ground.

> The servant hung down his head with shame.

Hang on, is to continue clinging to something. A boy hangs on to a cart moving along, i.e. clings to it.   To hang on to a person, is to resort to him often, in hope of receiving benefit.   To hang on in this sense is contemptuous.   A ' hanger-on ' is one who clings as a parasite to a person, place, or society.   To hang on or upon a speaker's words, is to pay the closest attention to his words.

> Let him hang on by the ladder for a few minutes till relief comes.

Hang out a sign or banner, is to display or unfold it.

Hang over, is to overhang, to suspend over; also, to be delayed or postponed, to be put off.

> The discussion of this case can easily hang over till next meeting.
> He held on by a branch and hung over the precipice without fear.

Hang together, is to be consistent.

> These two assertions do not hang together.

Hang up, is to suspend from something high; to defer the settlement of a thing.

> Let him hang up his hat in the hall.
> The judge adjourned the case, so that the matter is now hung up till next sessions.

Hang upon a speaker's words.

Hang a room or wall **with** drapery or pictures.

Happen on, to.

> Walking into the country, I happened on (=came unexpectedly on) a band of gipsies.
> I hope nothing has happened to (=no misfortune has occurred to) my friend.

Have on, is to wear, as clothes.

> He had on a purple turban.   She had on a pretty silk dress.
> I had no shoes on when I met the gentleman.

Have it out with a person, is to carry on a contest or argument till it ends.

Have a person up, is to cause him to be brought before a court of justice.

Hear of, out.

> Everybody has heard of the applause that distinguished his maiden speech.
>
> Hear the speaker out, i.e. hear him to the end of his speech.

Hedge in, is to enclose with a hedge; also, to encompass, to embarrass.

> The farmer hedged in a piece of ground and turned it into a garden.
>
> He tried to hedge you in with his arguments.

Help forward, is to assist in promoting, to advance.

> Help forward every good project you can.
>
> Drink helps many a man forward to ruin.
>
> The absconding of the cashier with several thousand pounds helped forward the failure of the bank.

Help on, is to assist to put on, to continue to assist.

> I helped him on with his coat, i.e. I helped him to put it on.
>
> Who would not help on female education in India ?

Help out, is to extricate, to assist in freeing from; also, to aid in completing a thing.

> The tutor will help you out of your difficulties in geometry.
>
> If the sheep has fallen into a pit, should you not help it out ?
>
> He did not seem able to finish the work himself, and so we helped him out with it.

Help one over, is to help him to surmount.

> Help the boy over his first difficulties in chemistry.

Help one to, is to assist him in obtaining; to supply or furnish with. To **help oneself to,** is to take a portion to oneself, and therefore is sometimes used as a euphemism for, to steal.

> Shall I help you to some sweets ?, i.e. Shall I give you some sweets ? Please help your friend to a glass of milk.
>
> A man came into the shop, and finding no one there, helped himself to a quantity of sugar, i.e. stole the sugar.

Help one up, is to raise him, to assist him in rising.

> A woman was knocked down in the street and a soldier helped her up.

Hem in, and sometimes **round,** is to surround, to restrain, to encompass with obstructions.

> At Metz the French were so hemmed in by the Germans that there was no escaping.

Hide from.

> I shall not hide the truth from you.

Hint at, is to allude to, to indicate by a hint.

> In his speech he dwelt on the importance of education and merely hinted at the need of giving teachers good preparatory training.
>
> This book is on astronomy, and yet it does not even hint at the possibility of discovering new comets or other heavenly bodies.

Hit against, is to clash against.

Hit off, is to describe accurately or happily.

> Swift has hit off this part of the Scottish character.
> You exactly hit off the nature of this association when you call it a mutual praising society.

To hit it off, is to get along together agreeably.   It is here impersonal.

> My father and I never could hit it off in my youth.

Hit out, is to strike out with one's fists.

Hit upon or **on,** is to come upon by chance, to light upon.

> The author of this book has hit upon an important discovery.

Hold back, is to keep back, to conceal; to restrain; also, to remain behind.

> If I had not held him back, he would have beaten you soundly.
> When others are attempting to reform, why do you hold back ?
> When a man is called on to give evidence, he should hold back nothing.

Hold by a thing, is, having caught hold of it, to cling to it; to adhere to a thing.

> He held me by the arm, by the hand, by the coat, etc.
> To hold a horse by the bridle, a bullock by the tail, etc.
> When the handle of a bucket breaks, there is nothing else to hold it by.
> The son always held by his father's advice.

Hold forth, is to exhibit, to put forward; also, to harangue, to declaim.

> She held forth her child to the holy man and asked him to bless it.
> He held forth on politics for an hour at the meeting last night.

Hold in, is to restrain; to restrain oneself.

> If the horse had not been held in, he would have cleared the fence.
> He was so tempted to laugh that he could scarcely hold himself in.

Hold off, is to keep at a distance, to avoid connexion with, to stay away, to be slow to do a thing.

> If the rain holds off, we can go for a walk in the afternoon.
> Cotton is falling in price, and buyers hold off, i.e. buyers are slow to buy.
> A ship holds off from the shore, i.e. the ship is sailing along the shore, but keeps away from the land.

Hold on, is to continue to proceed in, to continue holding or clinging to; to proceed.   The phrase usually expresses more or less of determination.

> The good ship held on her course.
> Trade is dull at present, but if this millowner can hold on for a few months longer, better times will come.
> The poor fellow clung to the spar as long as his arms had strength; and when he could hold on no longer, he uttered a cry and sank beneath the waves.

Hold out, is to offer, to extend; to refuse to yield; to continue; to endure, to continue to suffer.

She held out her hand.

The King held out to Esther the golden sceptre.—*Bible*

A garrison can't hold out against starvation.

The garrison held out gallantly for forty days and then capitulated.

He said he could hold out to me no hope of a rise of salary.

Our daily consumption of water is so great that the supply cannot hold out
longer than a month.

Hold over, is to delay, to postpone; to retain; to keep before.

The judge said he would hold over your case till the next sitting of the
court.

The threat of dismissal has been held over him for a month and yet he
does not mend his conduct.

Hold to, is to abide by; to cling to, to continue in.

Do you still hold to your intention of going to Australia ?

This man holds to his first statement, notwithstanding that several persons
contradict him.

Hold together, is to remain united or unbroken.

The chair is so rickety that it will not hold together.

This Insurance Company cannot long hold together.

Hold up, to keep up; to remain unbroken; to support; to present
prominently; also, not to rain—said of the weather.

The horse holds up his head well.

The boys held up a large blue banner.

A critic often holds up a book to ridicule or contempt.

The boy was held up to, or held up before, the whole school as an example
of neatness and diligence.

If the weather holds up, I shall be glad.

To **hold up a train** or coach, is for robbers to stop it.

Hold with, is to side with, to agree with.

I hold with you that it is better to be forgiving than censorious.

Surely you hold with medical opinion that cleanliness makes for good
health.

Hope for.

We hope for better times.

Readers must hope for no such romance.—*Thackeray*

Hunt down, is to follow or chase till caught; to overbear by
persecution.

The soldiers will not leave off pursuit till they have hunted down the rebel
leader.   These hounds will soon hunt down the stag.

Many a good man has been hunted down by rivals till for sake of peace
he has left them in full possession of the field.

Hunt for, is to search for.   Sometimes, it is **hunt about for**, or
hunt after, instead of **hunt for**, the meaning being the same.

What were you hunting for in the newspaper ?

Did he find the man he was hunting for in the fair ?

You might as well hunt for a needle in a bag of hay, as search for a lost
child in the wood.

Hunt out | is to search diligently for and find.   The phrases imply
Hunt up | difficulty in the search.   **Hunt up** is the expression
more frequently used.

> We see children perpetually running from place to place to hunt out
> something new.—*Burke*
> Hunt up all the information you can about the explosion, and let us send
> an account of it to the newspapers.
> There is a gentleman in the library hunting out, or hunting up, materials
> for a lecture on Indian astrology.

Hush up, is to suppress, to keep concealed, to maintain silence
concerning.   This phrase verb is often used when people strive
to keep a bad thing secret by silencing the persons who could
give information about it.

> The tale is hushed up now.—*Hood*
> It was whispered that a man had been murdered, but a few pounds
> hushed the matter up.

Hence the expressive term **hush-money**: see above, p. 63.

Impart to. He will impart no information to anyone.

Impose on or **upon.**

> Why should you let this fellow impose upon you ?
> I impose on you the task of looking after this child.

Impress a thing **on** a person; impress a person **with** a thing.

> Impress early on him the love of truth.
> I wish you would impress him with the importance of prompt action.

Impute a thing **to.**

> In public speaking never impute motives to anyone.
> A student imputes his failures to his misfortune rather than to the want of
> diligent preparation.

Indulge in: indulge oneself **with.**

> He indulges in smoking to an amazing extent.
> I am sorry to say he indulges himself with wine.
> Most men are more willing to indulge in easy vices than to practise
> laborious virtues.—*Johnson*

Infer from.

> What do you infer from this man's hesitating manner ?

Inflict punishment **on** an offender.

Inform against, of.

> Telegrams from England inform us of a rise in the price of silver.
> A man came to the Magistrate and informed against Smith, i.e. laid an
> accusation against him.

Inquire of the person asked; **about, after,** or **concerning** the object
of inquiry; **into** a subject, a matter, a cause; **for** a thing sought.

> I went to inquire after his health.
> He is gone to inquire for a letter at the Post Office.
> The Magistrate will inquire into the causes of this riot.
> Inquire of the first man you meet which way you should take.

Insist on.   He insists on being paid the full sum.

Intercede with a person **for** or **on behalf of.**

> He will intercede with the manager for you, or on your behalf.

Interfere between, in, with.

> England did not interfere between France and Germany.
> I will let no man interfere with me in my private affairs.

Intermeddle with.

> Why should you intermeddle with other people's disputes ?

Intervene between.

> I will not intervene between them in their quarrel.
> A long period intervened between these two events.

Intrigue with.

> The police intrigued with the rebels.

Introduce to, into.

> Let me introduce my brother to you.
> He introduced into the problem a fresh consideration.

Intrude into a place, **into** a matter that does not concern you; **upon** or **on** a person, **on** or **upon** one's time.

Invest a thing **in**; invest a person or a thing **with.**

> He is ready to invest his money in these new shares.
> The Queen invested him with the honour of knighthood.
> The speech of the barrister invested the inquiry with a new interest.

Invite to.   I wish to invite some friends to a concert.

Involve in, with.

> Extravagance often involves men in ruin.
> Take care lest, in dealing out punishment, you involve the innocent with the guilty.

Issue from.

> Profits issuing (=accruing) from land.
> Water issued from the rock in a tiny stream.
> The troops issued from the fort and attacked the besiegers.

Jeer at.   Never jeer at a man because he is unfortunate.

Jest at.   Do not jest at sacred things.

Jog on or **along**, is to continue going at a slow pace.

> The old man and his ass jogged along to the fair.

Join in.

> All joined in and we gave the Governor a cordial welcome.
> For a time he kept aloof from our games, but now he joins in.

Join in with, is to unite with, to take part in.

> He refuses to join in with us and prefers to act independently.

Join with me in the expenses of the trip.

Join to.   He has joined a pleasing manner to a virtuous life.

Join up, is to enlist.

Judge by.

> Judging by his testimonials, I think he will suit the post.

Judge of.

> She is wise if I can judge of her.—*Shakespeare*
> I cannot judge of these things till I examine them carefully.

Jump at, is to accept or close with eagerly.

> He is ready to jump at any proposal that may be made to him.

Jump to a conclusion, is to rush to it hastily and without due consideration. The phrase is commonly used when a conclusion hastily reached turns out to be a wrong one.

> When the census was first taken in India, many people jumped to the conclusion that it was for the purposes of taxation.

Keep at, is to continue doing.

> If he will only keep at his work, he will soon finish it.

Keep back, is to reserve or conceal; to restrain; to impede.

> I will keep nothing back from you.
> I would have been here sooner, but the rain kept me back.

Keep down, is to hold in subjection, to prevent from rising.

> It will take a strong force to keep down the mountain tribes.
> This man is active and should rise in the world, but his large family keeps him down.

Keep from, is to abstain or refrain from.

> He could not keep from the use of tobacco.
> If he would only keep from bad company, he might yet do well.

Keep in with, is to continue to agree with, not to quarrel with.

> He will keep in with the paymaster if he possibly can.

Keep off, is to ward off, to remain at a distance.

> These curtains are meant to keep off mosquitoes.
> To keep the ship off shore was impossible.—*Kingsley*
> ' Keep off the grass ' is a notice often displayed in parks.

Keep on doing a thing, is to continue doing it.

Keep out, is to cause to remain outside, to hinder from entering or taking possession.

> These warm clothes should keep out the cold.
> They have shut the door and mean to keep us out.
> I have bought a farm, but the seller keeps me out of it.

Keep to, is to adhere to, not to deviate from.

> Always keep to your word, to your promise.
> In his speech he kept strictly to his subject.
> Whatever the rule is, you may be sure he will keep to it.
> I kept to my tent.
> They keep to the custom of having their marriages only in May.

Keep together, is not to part asunder.

> They agreed to keep together during the evening.

Keep under, is to hold in subjection; to control or restrain.

> Everyone should keep his appetites and passions under.
> It is the duty of the government to keep these plundering tribes under.

Keep up, is: 1. To maintain, to prevent from falling. 2. To continue, not to cease. 3. To remain unsubdued. 4. Not to be confined to bed.

> These props will keep up the house.
> He kept up acquaintance with her.
> My father still keeps up; he is loth to take to bed.
> I do not know how he keeps up under his misfortunes.
> To *keep up appearances*, is to continue to maintain things in the same state as before, so far as outward appearance is concerned. (This would commonly be said of one who had met misfortunes or losses and wished to refrain from showing this openly.)

Keep up with, is not to fall behind, to maintain a position as far forward as, to keep pace with.

> Can America keep up with Britain in the building of ships ?

Kick against, at.

> Some men seem happy only when kicking against authority.
> It is better to fall in with these arrangements than to kick at them.

Knock about, is to travel here and there without any definite aim or fixed business.

Knock against.

> The casks rolling about on deck knocked against one another.

Knock at.   I knocked at your door for a quarter of an hour.

Knock down, is: 1. To fell, to overturn. 2. To assign to a bidder in an auction by a stroke of the auctioneer's hammer.

> He struck his opponent a heavy blow and knocked him down.
> The auctioneer knocked down the field glasses to me at five shillings.

Knock off, is to cease from, to desist from (colloquial).

> My health compels me to knock off work.

Knock on the head (colloquial), is to frustrate.

> Your action has knocked his plans on the head.

Knock out, is 1. Totally to disable one's opponent. 2. To make (a plan) hastily.

Knock up, is: 1. To arouse by knocking. 2. To be fatigued; to be wearied out with labour.

> Knock me up at five in the morning, please.
> The horses were beginning to knock up under the fatigue of such severe service.—*De Quincey*

Know of.

Do you know of any man who has horses to sell.

Knuckle under, is colloquial for, to submit, to own oneself **beaten,** to cave in.

Labour under.

The disability under which he laboured.

Land at, in.

On his way to England, he landed at Malta and saw the sights.
Extravagance will soon land a man in debt.

Laugh at. Laugh to scorn (scorn being in this phrase a noun).

I soon learned to laugh at fairy stories.
She laughed to scorn the notion of a nunnery.—*Kingsley*
If they laughed at him, they would laugh at her for choosing him.—
Kingsley

To **laugh in one's sleeve** at a person, is to be secretly amused at him.

Lay about one, is to deal blows on all sides.

Lay aside, is to put away, not to retain; also, to discontinue.

He laid aside all reserve and spoke boldly.
We have laid aside the use of many good old English words.

Lay a thing **before** one, is to present it for his consideration.

It is our intention to lay these papers before the Governor.

Lay by the heels, is to capture and confine in prison.

Lay down, is to resign, to renounce, to relinquish, to surrender; also, to propound, to set forth.

To lay down a burden you carry; lay down a commission or office; lay down one's arms; lay down one's life on behalf of one's country; lay down a proposition; lay down the law.

Lay in, is to store up, to provide beforehand.

The governor of the fortress has laid in a good store of provisions.

Lay on, is to apply blows with force; also, to supply gas or electricity or water.

Taking up a stick, he caught the boy and laid on vigorously.
This house has no electricity laid on.

To **lay it on,** is colloquial for, to do anything to excess, particularly praise, so that it amounts to flattery.

To **lay one's hand on a thing,** is to find it when wanted.

To **lay hands on,** is to seize, to take hold of with violence.

Lay out, is to expend; to exert; also, to dispose in order—said of a garden, or of preparing a corpse for burial.

He laid out two shillings in the market.
It is foolish to lay out all your strength on this.
The gardens and grounds were laid out by an expert.
They carefully laid out the corpse, i.e. they dressed the corpse in grave clothes and placed it in a lying position.

Lay oneself **out for**, is to work keenly for.

> The police officer made a careful inquiry and laid himself out for a conviction.

Lay (=impute) **to** one's charge; lay (=take) **to** heart.

Lay under obligation, under contribution, under restraint.

Lay up, is to store up for future use.

To **lay up** a ship, is to place her in a dock, as for repairs.

> The miser lays up wealth; but who will spend it ?
> Lay up for yourself treasure in heaven.—*Bible*

Lead aside from.

> Let nothing lead you aside from the path of duty.

Lead away.

> He caught the bridle and led the horse away.
> Let no strolling orator lead you away from loyalty.

To **lead** someone **by the nose**, is to make him do what you want.

Lead into, is to introduce to, to bring into.

> He is sure to lead you into error.
> He led the regiment into the fight.

Lead off, is to lead away; also, to go first, to begin.

> The captain led off his team.
> Who is to lead off in the debate ?
> The Earl and Countess led off the dance.

Lead on, is to continue leading.

> He led on his forces in gallant style.

Lead on to, is to continue leading as far as.

> Gambling often leads on to other vices.

Lead out.

> He led out the lady to the dance.
> The groom is leading out the horse, i.e. from the stable.

Lead to.

> There is a shaded walk at the foot of the garden which leads to a bridge over the stream.

Lead up to, is to lead as far as.   To **lead up the garden**, is to entice further than was intended.

> His arguments led up to a startling conclusion.

Leak out, is to escape by leakage; also, to ooze out, to become known in a clandestine way.

> The water is leaking out of this cask.
> The whole plan of the campaign has leaked out and now the enemy has got to know it.

Lean against, on or **upon, to.**

> The old man was leaning on his staff.
> There is a beam leaning against the wall.
> I always like to lean to the side of mercy.

Leave things about, is to let things remain out of their proper place; to be untidy.

Leave alone has two meanings.

> Leave me alone !, i.e. don't interfere with me.
> Are you going to leave me alone ?, i.e. going to desert me.

Leave off, is, when used transitively, to desist from, to put aside; intransitively, to cease.

> I am going to leave off fishing.
> Leave off a garment; leave off strife; leave off work.
> Leave off now and return to work in the morning.

Leave out, is to omit.

> In copying this paper, be careful not to leave out any words.

To leave to oneself, is to leave alone, leave unaided or uncared for.

> The next day he bade his men sit still and look on and leave him to himself.—*Kingsley*

Lecture on.

> The professor will lecture today on the Solar System.

Let alone, is to allow to remain without interference.

> Let this useless scheme alone.

Let down, is to lower, to permit to sink or fall, or, of a person, to fail a friend.

> She let down the bucket into the well.
> I thought I could rely on him, but he let me down.

Let in, is to admit, to allow to enter; also, to insert, as a joiner would insert a piece of wood into a space formed for it.

> The child stood at the door knocking and crying, ' Let me in.'
> This boat lets in water.   (This is the opposite of *leak.*)

Let into, is to suffer to enter, to admit.

> They would not let him into the meeting.
> He will not let you into the secret of making fine porcelain, i.e. he will not make the secret known to you.

Let off, is to suffer to go free, to release.

> To let off a gun, is to discharge it; to let off an arrow, a squib; to let off anything kept in confinement, as a prisoner from a jail.
> I ought to fine you for this breach of rules, but I will let you off this time, i.e. I will let you escape without punishment this time.
> You promised to help me today, but as your father wants you at home, I will let you off, i.e. release you from your promise.
> To let off steam, is to allow steam to escape.

Let out, is to suffer to escape; to lease or hire; to extend or enlarge, to loosen.

> He lets out his car on hire.
> He has opened the gate and let out the sheep.
> To let out rope or cable on board a ship; to let out the folds of a garment.
> To let the fire out, is to allow the fire to die out.

Lick up. Up here is intensive, and indicates completeness.

> The dogs greedily licked up the creature's blood.

Lie by, is to be deposited with, to lie aside unused; also, to intermit work, to rest.

> He had a manuscript lying by him.
> They will lie by during the heat of the day.
> This old ship may be allowed to lie by till the wintry storms are over.

Lie down, is to go to rest, to lay the body down.

> Let me lie down; I am very weary.
> He lay down on the couch and was soon fast asleep.

Lie in one, in one's power, is to be in the power of; to depend on.

> As much as lieth in you, live peaceably with all men.—*Bible*
> He will do what lies in his power to secure the appointment for you.
> Success lies in diligence and vigilance.

Lie on, is to remain.

> Goods lie on a shopkeeper's hands, i.e. remain with him unsold.

Lie over, is to be deferred to a future time.

> A bill or account lies over, i.e. it remains unpaid.

Lie to. A ship is said to **lie to** when those navigating her bring her to a stop in her course.

Lie under, is to remain under, to suffer, to be subject to.

> Why should I lie under an imputation of falsehood when there are no grounds for it ?

Lift up, is to raise, to exalt, to swell.

> The cripple fell down and there was no one near to pick him up.
> Lifted up with pride.—*Bible*
> Nation shall not lift up sword against nation.—*Bible*

Light on or **upon,** is to alight upon, to chance to find.

> The bee lights on this flower and on that.
> Here we lit on the lost treasure.

Light up, is to illuminate; also, to become cheerful.

> It will take six lamps to light up this room.
> His face lighted up when he saw me.

Listen to.

> She would sit for hours listening to the songs of the birds.

Live at a place. I always thought this man lived at Naples.

Live by hard honest labour.

Live down, to maintain such a course of conduct as to subdue or eradicate. To live down opposition to oneself, to live down an evil rumour about oneself.

> Her whole life has been such as to belie every idle report, so that she has lived down all suspicion of her character.

Live for, is to devote one's life to, to live in the hope of securing.

> Many a man has lived and died for his country.
> This man lives for nothing else but to gather money.
> ' I live for those who love me, for those who know me true.'

Live in a country, a condition.

> How long did you live in England ?
> These people live in squalor and misery.

Live on or **upon.**

> What do monkeys live on ?   Horses live upon grass and grain.

Live up to one's income, is to spend all that one gets.   To **live up** to one's principles, is to put them into practice.

Live with a friend, or a relative.

Live within one's income, is to spend less than one's income, not to spend beyond one's income.

Long after or **for,** is to greatly desire.

> I long for an opportunity of seeing you.

Look about, is to look on all sides.   To **look about one,** is to be on the watch.

Look after, is: 1. To take care of.   2. To look towards one who is moving away.

> He left me in charge, chiefly to look after his garden.—*Defoe*

Look at, is to direct the eye towards.   **Look at** implies less of deliberation than **look on.**

> He stood looking at the picture for a long time.
> The young thieves . . . looked uneasily at each other.—*Dickens*

Look away, is to turn one's gaze in another direction.

Look back, is to cast a retrospective glance.

Look down on or **upon,** is to treat with indifference or contempt.

> He is so proud of his promotion that he looks down upon all his former friends.

Look for, is to search for; to wait for patiently, to expect.

> We shall look for you tomorrow.
> I looked for better conduct at his hands.
> He has lost his keys: let the caretaker look for them.
> I look for important news by the next mail from England.

Look forward, is to look before one.

Look forward to, is to expect with pleasure.

> I am looking forward to your visit.

Look in.

> I knocked at the door but there was no answer; I then looked in at the window but could see no one.
> The carpenters are at work in the house down the street; I wish you would look in as you pass and see how they are getting on.   ' Look in ' here and in such expressions, means ' go in ' and does not mean, to look in from the outside.

To **look in,** sometimes means to pay a short friendly visit.

Look into, is to examine or inspect closely; to have a direction towards.

> After what you have said, I shall certainly look into his conduct.
> An auditor should look into all the accounts and all the securities.
> When we look into the works of nature, how marvellous are the evidences of skill and design.
> A window looking into some pleasant little gardens.—*Dickens*

Look on or **upon,** is to direct the eye towards; to be a spectator; also, to regard or consider. **Look on** implies more of deliberation than **look at.**

> I'll be a candle-holder and look on.—*Shakespeare*
> I looked on Virgil as a succinct, majestic writer.—*Dryden*
> I now look upon all these stories as mere idle tales.—*Lamb*
> Our carriage was looked upon with some envy by our poorer neighbours. —*Lamb*
> A ' looker-on ' or ' onlooker ' is a mere spectator.

Look out, is: 1. To look outwards. 2. To be on the watch. 3. To choose, to select. 4. To search out. 5. A cry of warning.

> He looked out his address in the directory.
> She looked out stealthily through the blind of the window.—*Kingsley*
> Look out ! here comes that ruffian.

Look out for, is to be on the watch for, to expect.

> The eagle is looking out for prey.
> You may look out for squalls in the Mediterranean.

Look out of a window, out of a cave, etc.

Look over, is to examine. To look over one's accounts.

Look through, is to see to the other side; also, to examine, to peruse, to understand perfectly.

> Look through this book and tell me what you think of it.
> Looking through a hole in the door, I saw a man on the ground asleep.

Look to, is: 1. To look towards. 2. To watch, to take care of. 3. To resort to in the hope of obtaining something.

> Look well to thy herds.—*Bible*
> The creditor may look to the guarantor for payment.
> Look to God in all your perplexities.

Look up, is: 1. To direct the look upwards. 2. To search for and find. 3. To have an upward tendency—said of prices or of things commonly sold. 4. To pay a visit to.

> Hearing a shout, he looked up and saw a boy standing on the cliff.
> Look up this word in your dictionary.
> Consols are looking up; the price of cotton is looking up.
> Look me up when you come to Bombay.

Look up to a person, is to respect him, to regard him with esteem.
Look up to, is the opposite of, **look down upon.**

Lord it over, is to domineer.   **It** is here impersonal.

Why should you let this man lord it over you ?

Make after, is to run after.

The constable made after the thief.

Make away with, is to put away, to remove in an underhand manner; also, to kill, to destroy.

He has made away with five thousand pounds.
For long this tribe made away with their female children.
The two young princes were made away with during the night.

Make for, is to move towards; also, to tend towards, to tend to the advantage of.

The thief made for the gate of the city.
Follow after the things which make for peace.—*Bible*

Make of, is to understand, to regard, to esteem.

He is unable to make anything of this telegram.
I know not what to make of this news, i.e. I am puzzled to know how to regard it.

To be made of, is to be composed of, as a chariot made of iron; this paper is made **of** or **from** rice straw.

Make off with, is to run away with, to carry off surreptitiously.

He has made off with my books.

Make out, is: 1. To discover, to decipher, to find out.   2. To prove, to establish by evidence or argument.   3. To write out.

He cannot make out the meaning of this passage.
I think the barrister made out his case very clearly.
He was instructed to make out an account of all the sums paid.
I was too ignorant to make out the Latin inscription.

Make over, is to transfer to another person.

He has made over all his real property to his eldest son; his personal property he makes over to his other children equally.

Make towards, is to go in the direction of.

The swimmer made towards the right bank of the river.

Make up, is: 1. To put into form.   2. To reconcile or compose. 3. To supply what is deficient.   4. To compensate or make good.   5. To adjust or settle.   6. To **make up one's mind,** is to determine or come to a fixed resolution as the result of deliberation.   7. To dress so as to suit some character in a play, as an actor would.

These men have happily made up their quarrel.
It will not be easy to make up all their accounts.
He made up a package of books and sent it off by train.
Why should you expect Government to make up your loss ?
She made up her mind to dismiss the servants.
We have collected some money, but a few shillings are still wanting to make up the requisite sum.
Making up one's mind to meet courageously what comes, is the secret of taking heart.

To **make up a prescription,** is to compound the medicine, the ingredients of which are written in the prescription.

Make up for, is to compensate for.

> This foolish book of witch stories had no pictures in it; but I made up for them out of my own fancy.—*Lamb*

Make up to, is to approach; to ingratiate oneself with.

> He made up to us boldly and asked who we were.
> The clerk was apt to make up to his employer.

Make it up with, is to settle one's differences with, to become friendly again with.

> Hating strife, I made it up with him, and now we are friends again.

Meddle with, and sometimes **in.**

> He hardly ever meddled with politics; his interests lay elsewhere.

Mediate between.

> England tried to mediate between France and China.

Meet with, is to light upon, to encounter.

> He has lately met with serious losses in trade.
> She had met with no small kindness.
> A man never knows what he may meet with in the forest.

Melt away, is to dissolve and vanish.

> The snow and ice have all melted away.
> All her anger melted away.

Mourn for. The queen mourned for her son.

Murmur at, against.

> Is it wise to murmur at adversity ?

Muse on or **upon,** is to think on closely, to study in silence.

> He mused upon the new situation.
> I muse on the work of Thy hands.—*Bible*

Object to, is to oppose in words or argument.

> He does not object to this proposal.
> I object to party politics being dragged into this discussion.

Occur to, is to come into one's mind.

> It never occurred to me that he was only acting a part.

Offend against.

> There was nothing in his speech to offend against good taste.

Originate in a place, or **in** a thing, as a cause.

> The fire originated in the coach house.
> The riot originated in a petty squabble.

Originate with a person.

> With whom did this scheme originate ?, i.e. who began it ?
> The idea of lowering the tax originated with the Governor.

Pack away an article, is to pack it up and put it away in a safe place for preservation.

Pack off, is to send off quickly and unceremoniously.

> He packed the beggar off.

Pack up goods; pack up a parcel.

Palm off, is to impose on fraudulently.

> He tried to palm off a horse on me; but luckily just when I was going to close the bargain, I found that the horse was blind.

Part from (usually of persons), **with** (usually of property), is to say good-bye to, to relinquish.

> She knows I mean to part from her.
> He did not part with the hat which he had stolen.
> She read the letters over, but could not part with them.

Pass away, is to disappear, to vanish; also a euphemistic expression for, to die.

> His difficulties have passed away.
> My father passed away last night at twelve o'clock.

Pass by, is to go or pass alongside of; also, to disregard, to omit, to overlook.

> I passed this essay by quite inadvertently.
> ' I passed by his garden and saw the wild briar.'

Pass for, is to have the reputation of, to be regarded as.

> He passes for a learned man in our little community.
> The Government currency notes pass for money.

Pass from, is to leave, to get away from.

> Let us now pass from this; we have discussed it long enough.

Pass into, is: 1. To go into.   2. To change by gradual transition to, to blend together, as two colours, in such a way that you cannot say precisely where one ends and the other begins.

> When does a boy pass into a man ?   He passed into his house.
> In a rainbow, the colours pass into one another.

Pass off, is to vanish; to happen; also, to impose on by fraud.

> The rain has passed off.
> He was caught trying to pass off counterfeit coin.
> The entertainment passed off well, i.e. was a success.

Pass on, is to proceed.   **Pass** sentence of death **on** a murderer.

> Let us now pass on to another branch of our subject.

Pass out, is (1) to graduate, or (2) to faint.

Pass over, is to come and depart; to pass by, omit; overlook.

> I passed over many candidates and chose this one.
> A frown passed over his countenance as he read the letter.

Pass through, is to go through to the other side; pass through an experience.

> The water passes through this pipe.
> He passed through the crowd without molestation.
> He has passed through college without learning much.

Pass under, is to go beneath.

> The Romans made their captives in war pass under the yoke.

Pay away money, is to disburse it.

Pay down, is to pay ready money when an article is bought.

Pay for, is to give an equivalent for; to bear the cost of; be punished for.

> I pay for all I buy.
> He has paid dear for his whistle.
> Men often pay for their mistakes with loss of wealth.

Pay off, is to recompense and discharge.

> He paid off the ship's crew.

Pay out. To pay out cable, is to slacken it and allow it to run out of the ship till as much has run out as is necessary.

To **pay one out for,** is to punish by way of taking revenge (colloquial).

> ' Why are you so anxious to pay him out for this supposed insult ? '

Perish by the sword, is to die in battle.

Perish with hunger, with cold.

> We were all perished, i.e. greatly upset, with hunger.

Pick off, is to take away with a sudden movement, as to pick off the enemy by sharp-shooting.

Pick out, is to select, to choose, to separate.

> I have picked out the bad potatoes from the basket.
> He has tried to pick out all the purple passages from this poem.

In painting, **pick out** means, to relieve with lines of a different colour.

Pick up, is to take up—often said of a small thing.

> You pick up a pin; a bird picks up a worm.
> He picks up a livelihood, i.e. obtains it by taking advantage of chance opportunities.

A person who has been ill is said to **pick up** when he is getting back his strength.

Pin a man **down** to a statement, is to compel him to abide by it when he is seeking to modify it.

Pine away, is to languish, to droop; also, to wear away through pain of body or distress of mind.

Pine for, to grieve for, to languish through desire for.

> She pined for her husband's return.

Pitch upon, is to choose.

> I have pitched upon a site for my house.

Play off, is to set one person against another for one's own advantage.

Play on or **upon.**

> Play on a musical instrument, as a harp, a violin.
> The fire engines played on the flames, i.e. discharged water on.
> The setting sun plays on their shining arms and burnished helmets.—
> *Addison*

To **play on** words, is to use them in a witty way.

To **play upon** one's fears, is to impose on one by taking advantage of his fears.

Play with, is to engage in fun with; also, to trifle with.

> Let me go and play with the children.
> It is dangerous to play with fire.

Plead with a person **for** a thing.

> She pleaded with the king for her husband's life.

Plot against.

> What should be done to men who plot against the prince?
> Those ruffians are plotting against the liberties of the nation.

Plough in, out, up.

> To plough in seed, is to cover it by ploughing.
> To plough out or up a crop, is to turn it out of the ground with the plough.

Pluck away, is to pull away, to separate by a twitch.

Pluck down, is to pull down, to demolish; to bring to a lower state.
The idea of suddenness is conveyed by the expression.

Pluck off, is to tear off, to pull off with a jerk.

> To pluck off a rose from the tree.

Pluck out, is to draw out suddenly; to tear out.

> To pluck out a feather from a bird.

Pluck up, is to tear up by the roots; also, to gather up.

> To pluck up shrubs; to pluck up spirits or courage.

Plunge in, into.

> The horse plunged into the river and swam across.

Ply between.   A boat plies between two ports.

Ply a person **with** flattery, or with questions, is to press praise or questions on him, generally with an ulterior object.

Point out, at, to.

> His speech pointed to a few common abuses.
> Now must the world point at poor Catherine.—*Shakespeare*
> It is easy to blame a man and to point out his errors.
> Point out this town on the map.   He pointed his rifle at the hyena.

Ponder on or **over.**

> He sat pondering over (or on) the advice he had received.

Pounce on or **upon.**

> He is ready to pounce upon you if you make a single mistake.

Pray for a person or a thing; pray **to** God.

> Neither pray I for these alone.—*Bible*
> Pray daily for your absent friends.

Prefer to.

> I prefer dates to raisins.
> He prefers honest poverty to a high position obtained by questionable means.

Prefix to.

> If you prefix *en-* to *trap*, you form the verb *entrap*.

Prejudice one **against.**

> His rudeness of manner prejudiced me against him.

Prepare for.

> The sailors began to prepare for a rough night.
> He is diligently preparing for the examination.

Preserve from.

> The Lord preserve you from all evil.
> I wish you could preserve this fruit from spoiling.

Preside at, over. Preside at a banquet; preside over a meeting.

Prevail against, on, over, with.

> None of these considerations prevailed over his prejudices.
> If you cannot influence him, I cannot hope to prevail with him.

Prey upon.

> What does the kite prey upon ?
> His discontent preys upon his life.

Proceed against, from, on.

> Light and heat proceed from the sun.
> In any inquiry, be careful to proceed on right principles.
> I am constrained to proceed against him in a court of justice for the recovery of this debt.

Protect from.

> A wide hat protects his head from the sun.

Provide against, for, with.

> A wise man provides against emergencies while he can.
> The garrison being well provided with food can stand a long siege.
> A father should provide for the education and upbringing of his children.

Pry into, is to inspect closely. This phrase verb usually implies reproach.

> He must needs pry into a secret which certainly does not concern him.—*Kingsley*

Pull down, is to demolish, to destroy, to humble.

> He has begun to pull down the house.
> It is easier to pull down than to build up.
> One is not sorry to see the proud pulled down.

Pull off, is to separate by pulling.

> He pulled off his coat and began to work.

Pull out.

> Pull out the pin.
> The train pulled out of the station.

Pull one **through** (colloquial), said of both doctor and patient.

> The doctor will pull him through, i.e. will make him recover.
> This poor fellow will, I hope, pull through, i.e. will recover.

Pull together, is to agree, to work together in harmony.

> If the brothers would only pull together they would succeed.

Pull up, is to pluck up; also, to draw the reins, to halt.

> Why did you pull up these young plants ?
> He pulled up at my door.
> He pulled up his horse and dismounted.

Punish a person **for** a fault or a crime.

> How should a servant be punished for pilfering ?

Push down, is to overthrow by pushing.

> The bullock pushed the boy down.

Push off, is to move away.

> The sailor pushed off from the shore.

Push on, is to urge or hasten forward.

> The rider pushed on at a rapid pace.—*Scott*

Put about.

> They put the ship's head about, i.e. they turned or changed the course
> of the ship.
> To put one about, is to cause him inconvenience.

Put (it) **across,** is to succeed in anything.

> I thought he would fail, but he contrived to put it across.

Put away, is to renounce or discard; also, to put things in their
proper place.

> To put away a wife, i.e. to divorce her.
> These are bad practices which he should put away.
> Put the books away, i.e. put them where they should remain when not in
> use.

Put back, is: 1. To hinder or delay.   2. To restore to the original
place.   3. To move backward, as the hands of a clock, so as
to make the clock show an earlier hour.

> Put back this book in the place where you got it.
> My watch was ten minutes fast so I put it back.
> In England, cloudy weather often puts back the ripening of the grain.

Put by, is to lay aside; also, to lay up in store.

> He took off his hat and put by his walking stick.
> When your salary is good, put by something against contingencies.

Put down, is to deposit, to suppress or extinguish; also, to snub,
or slight designedly.

> To put down a burden; put down an insurrection; put down an impudent
> person.

Put down one's foot (colloquial), is to show determination in the face of opposition.

Put forward, is to cause to advance; to move forward, as the hands of a clock, so as to make the clock show a later hour.

> He will put forward his son as a candidate at the next election.
> My watch was slow and I have put it forward to the correct time.

Put in, is to insert, to introduce among others.

> He talked so fast that I could not put in a word.
> Be careful to put in (=present) your claim soon.

Put in at. Sailors are said to put in at a port when they call at it on their voyage.

> The tenth day they put in at a shore where a race of men dwell that are sustained by the fruit of the lotus-tree.—*Lamb*

Put in for, is to offer oneself for; to lay claim to.

> Several candidates have put in for the headmastership.
> I mean to put in for a share of the profits.

Put off, is: 1. To lay aside. 2. To turn one aside from a purpose or demand. 3. To postpone. 4. To push or start away from shore—said of a boat.

> He put off his shoes before going into the house.
> I went to him for help, but he put me off with a frivolous excuse
> Never put off till tomorrow what you can do today.—*Proverb*
> Perhaps I'd better put off my visit till tomorrow.
> It is a fool's trick to put off what you must do in the end.
> They got into a boat and put off at once.

Put on, is: 1. To invest oneself with. 2. To assume. 3. To inflict or impose on. 4. To charge upon or impute to. 5. To urge forward. 6. To apply.

To **put on** clothes, a hat, shoes, spectacles, etc.

To **put on** airs, is to assume proud airs.

Why should all the blame be **put on** him?

To **put one on** his mettle, is to rouse him to do his part.

To **put on** the screw, is to exert pressure on a person with an ulterior purpose. To extort a confession or promise, to extort money.

Put out, is: 1. To eject, as to put out an intruder. 2. To extinguish, as to put out a fire, a lamp, a candle, a torch. 3. To stretch forward or extend, as to put out the hand. 4. To place at interest, as to put out money at interest. 5. To confuse, disconcert, or annoy. 6. To publish, as to put out a pamphlet, a book. 7. To shoot, as the bush puts out buds.

> The barbarians caught him and put out his eyes.
> He was put out by their interruptions.

Put out of use, is to cause that a thing be used no longer. To put out, is: 1. To dislocate; 2. To annoy. To put it out of one's power to do a thing, is to put it beyond his power to do it. To put a knife out of a child's reach, is to remove it beyond his reach, to put it where he cannot get it.

> The medicine given him soon put him out of danger.
> It would be a kindness to the dying dog to shoot him and put him out of pain.

Put one in authority **over** men.

Put up, is: 1. To lodge. 2. To pack away. 3. To lay aside or put away. 4. To offer for sale.

> He stopped reading and put up the paper.
> The shopkeeper has put up the goods in two parcels.
> We shall be happy to put you up when you come to town.
> The auctioneer has just put up a pair of porcelain vases.

Put one **up to,** is to incite or instigate.

> Who put you up to this mischief?

Put up with, is to endure without resentment or opposition. To put up with a person, sometimes means to stay at his house for a time.

> I could not put up with his insolence.
> People in poverty have to put up with hard fare.
> He will put up with the Smiths at their villa.

Qualify for.

> He had qualified himself for office.

Quarrel over a thing; quarrel **with** a person.

> Do not quarrel with your neighbours.
> These men have quarrelled over the price of a load of hay.

Rail against or **at,** is to reproach, scoff at.

> He would rail at the world for its neglect of his genius.—*Thackeray*
> It is useless to rail against your master or against his orders.

Rail in, is to enclose with a rail.

> He has railed in a piece of ground for a flower garden.

Rake up a quarrel is to revive it; to rake up an old story about anyone, is to call up and repeat the story—the word being used of a disparaging story.

Rank with.

> What poet of any country can rank with Shakespeare?

Reason with a person, **about** a thing.

Rebel against authority, against a prince, against the State.

Rebel at harsh treatment.

Recede from, is to retreat, withdraw.

> Tides receding from the shore.

Reckon on or **upon,** is to depend on.

Reckon with, is to settle accounts or claims with; to call to account.

> He will have to reckon with me before this business is finished.

Recoil from.

My whole nature recoils with horror from such a deed.

Recompense one **for.**

I cannot recompense you for all the trouble you have taken.

Reconcile one **to**; reconcile one thing **with** another.

How can you reconcile this statement with what you said yesterday

Recover from a swoon, an illness, the effects of a shock.

Reduce to.

To reduce a sergeant to the ranks, is to degrade him to the rank of a private.

Reduce a man to poverty, or to a skeleton; reduce shillings to pence; reduce marble to powder; reduce mutineers to subjection.

Refer to (cf. **allude** above).

This author begins by referring to the early history of India.

The Local Court has referred the whole case to the High Court.

Reflect on or **upon**, is: 1. To throw back beams on. 2. To consider carefully. 3. To cast reproach on.

This essay reflects great credit on the writer.

I hope he will carefully reflect upon the advice you gave him.

I do not reflect in the least on the memory of the late king.

Refrain from tears, reproach, anger, strife.

Reign over an empire, a dominion, a country, a nation.

We will not have this man to reign over us.—*Bible*

Rejoice at, in, over, on account of.

No one rejoiced at (*or* in) their success more than she.

Relate to, is to bear upon, to concern.

Bring me all the papers that relate to this business.

Relieve from any burden or distress, as toil, duty, pain.

Rely on or **upon** one's help, one's judgement; or on a person.

I can always rely on you in any difficulty.

Remind of.

His face reminds me of his father.

The death of friends should remind us of our own end.

Remonstrate with a person **for** or **against** a course he has taken.

Remove from.

This man removed from Madras a month ago, i.e. changed his place of residence from Madras.

Render to, into.

What shall I render to the Lord for all His gifts to me ?

To render (=translate) German into English.

Repair to, is to go to, to betake oneself to.

The soldiers repaired to the market and began a riot.

Repent of the sin of wrong doing.

> During his sixty days in prison, he will have ample time to repent of his latest exploit in petty larceny.

Reply to a letter.

> He replied to the insinuation in a vigorous speech.

Reprimand a person **for** a fault.

Reproach a person **for** a mistake, for, or with, a fault.

Rescue from danger, from enemies, from destruction.

Resolve on or **upon.**

> He means to follow out the course he has resolved on.

Resolve often takes the infinitive after it.

> He resolved to send his son to the hospital.

Resort to.   Never resort to mean tricks to serve your end.

Respond to.

> Accuse men of sin and each one's conscience responds to the charge.

Rest on or **with,** is to be founded or based on, to devolve on.   To rest **on one's laurels,** is to stop trying for further successes.

> His whole theory rests on a wrong assumption.
> It does not rest with me to do this work.

Restore to.

> It delighted him to restore the lost child to its mother.
> He means to restore this building to its early grandeur.

Result from a cause; result **in** an effect.

> How can peace of heart result from a life of sin ?
> This marriage is likely to result in much happiness.

Retire from business, from public life, from a contest.

Retire into private life, into a monastery, into a cave.

Retire upon or **on** a pension.

Revert to.

> I shall not revert to this subject further.
> When the lease expires, this house reverts to the landlord.

Ride at.

> Ships ride at anchor.
> He rode at the fence, but his horse shied and would not take it, i.e. he rode towards the fence intending to jump, but his horse turned aside and refused it.

Ride down a person, is to treat him in an insolent, overbearing manner.

Ride out.

> A ship rides out the gale, i.e. survives the gale, is not destroyed by the gale.

Ride to hounds, is to ride out to hunt with hounds, as in fox-hunting.

Rig out, is to furnish with apparatus or tackle (said of a ship); also to dress up.

Rob one of.

> By lying he would rob me of my good name.

Root out or **up**, is to pull up by the roots, to destroy.

> He rooted up all the trees on his farm.
> It is vain to attempt to root out heresy by force.

Rout out, is to force or fetch out.

> I routed him out of bed at dawn.

Rub down a horse, is to clean him by rubbing, to curry him.
To **rub down** a thing, as by filing, is to make it smaller.
Rub off rust, rub off an impression, rub off rude manners, rub off awkwardness.

> The king's head is nearly rubbed off this coin.

Rub on or **along**, is to get through life with difficulty.

> The poor men intend to rub along very much as they did before.

Rub out, is to erase, to obliterate.

> Indiarubber rubs out pencil marks.
> What can rub out the stain of blood ?

Rub up, is to polish, to burnish, to brighten.

> Let the saddler rub up the harness.
> The servant has rubbed up the silver plate.
> To rub a person up the wrong way, is to irritate him by your speech or manner.

Rule out, is to exclude.
Rule over an empire, over a people, over a tribe.
Run after, is to follow, to try to catch; to try to find; to follow in a crowd.

> The boy ran after the carriage.
> Locke speaks of ' running after similes '.
> It is strange that people should run after this demagogue.

Run against a person, is to come into contact or collision with him, as in the dark. Figuratively it means, to come into collision with him in speech or action. A ship runs against a rock. To run against a stone wall, is to rush obstinately and senselessly against difficulties which are evidently insurmountable.

Run at, is to attack.

> The bull ran at the farmer.

Run away, is to flee; to bolt—said of a horse.

> The horse took fright and ran away.
> The soldiers threw down their arms and ran away.

Run away with, is to convey away speedily, to make off with; to assist in eloping.

> He lets his feelings run away with his judgement.
> This fellow ran away with his neighbour's daughter.

To **run away with** a notion, is to persist in following a wrong or foolish notion.

Run down, is to chase till the quarry is exhausted and caught; also, to censure, to decry, to disparage. Other meanings are given in the examples.

> To run down a stag.
> To run down a ship, is to strike her and sink her.
>   ' Which made his brethren of the gown
>   Take care betimes to run him down.'
> The clock has run down, i.e. the spring which kept the clock in motion has exhausted itself and the clock has therefore stopped.

Run in, is to enter running. Or, colloquially, to take into custody. Also, to get an engine into proper condition by working it.

Run into debt, into danger. This phrase verb implies heedlessness, want of due consideration.

Run off, is to resist or break loose from control and run away; to flee.

> The thief heard a noise and ran off.

Run on, is to be continued; to talk incessantly; also, as a term in printing, meaning to carry on or continue in a line without any break or without making a new paragraph.

> In her talk she ran on so that no one could get in a word.

Run out, is to waste, to be wasted, to become poor; to expire, as a lease; to leak or trickle.

> The lease of these houses runs out at Christmas.
> If land is cropped and not manured, it will soon run out.
> The water is running out of the canal.

Run over, is: 1. To ride or drive over. 2. To overflow or over leap. 3. To glance over or examine in a cursory manner.

> His car ran over a dog. The train ran over the embankment.
> You have filled the cask till it is running over.
> The water is running over the sides of the canal.
> Run over this batch of papers and tell me what you think of them.

Run through, is: 1. To pierce. 2. To waste or to expend. 3. To examine hurriedly.

> He ran the mad dog through with a bayonet.
> This man has run through his whole fortune.
> I had to run through the book in an hour.

Run to. Vegetables run to seed, i.e. instead of developing the produce for which they are valued in a juicy state, they shoot up and yield flowers and ultimately seeds; hence, to become useless, to go to waste.

Run up, is to grow, to enlarge by additions; also, to put up quickly.

Seeing a ship on the horizon, we ran up a flag of distress.

Run up a house, i.e. build it quickly and in a flimsy manner.

To run up an account, is to buy articles on credit and have the shopkeeper charge them in his book against the buyer. A person buying in this way is said to run up an account.

Save from.

To save a house from the flames.

They saved the girl from drowning.

Scoff at religion, at sacred things.

Search for a thing lost, or a thing not readily found.

Search into all the details of a subject.

Search out, is to seek till found, as, to search out the truth.

See about a thing, is to look after it, to attend to it.

See off, is to accompany one to a place of starting, and wait with him till he takes his departure.

He found a crowd of two or three hundred people waiting to see him off.

See through, is to discern; to penetrate; to watch to the end.

A wise man will see through fine pretensions.—*Tillotson*

See to, is to look well to, to attend to.

It rests with you to see to this business.

Seek after or **for,** is to follow, to endeavour to find.

He professes to seek after *or* for wisdom and truth.

Seek out, is to find with pains.

Send away, is to dismiss; to dispatch, as a message, a parcel.

Send him away; he is a nuisance.

Send by, is to send by way of or by means of.

Send me an atlas by book post.

Send for, is to send a message requiring or requesting to come or be brought.

I sent for the doctor without any delay.

He sent for an ambulance and took her to the hospital.

He (Hamlet) was sent for by the queen, his mother, to a private conference.—*Lamb*

Send off, is to dispatch. Send off goods, letters.

Troops were being sent off to the Continent.

Separate from. To separate wheat from chaff.

Serve out, is: 1. To distribute. 2. To serve the full period of time agreed upon.

To serve out provisions to soldiers.

An apprentice serves out his time, i.e. serves his master to the end of the term agreed upon. We also say, an apprentice serves his time; but ' serves out ' expresses completeness.

Serve up, is to present food to be eaten.

He served up a fine dish of lobsters.

Set about, is to begin, to apply oneself to.

> I recommend you to set about your business without delay.

Set one thing **against** another, is to set them in contrast.

Set apart, is to reserve, or separate to a particular use.

> One day in seven is set apart as a holy day.

Set aside, is to disregard, to annul.

> He set aside all objections and granted my request.

Set down, is: 1. To cause to alight. 2. To record. 3. To censure, to slight, to humiliate.

> This insolent fellow needs someone to set him down.
> The Magistrate set down in writing all the statements I made.
> I made the ferryman set me down at the landing stage.

Set forth, is to manifest, or exhibit, to proclaim.

> He set forth his views with clearness and force.

Set in, is to begin.

> The rain set in. A soft sea breeze set in at midnight.
> To set in order, is to adjust or arrange.

Set off, is 1. To depart. 2. To decorate or embellish. 3. To place over against as an equivalent.

> They mean to set off when the moon rises.
> Words . . . set off by the graces of utterance and gesture.—*Macaulay*
> The evils which are to be set off against the many blessings of popular government.—*Macaulay*

Set on or **upon,** is to incite, to urge on; to attack.

> It is wicked to set on boys or dogs to fight.
> Two dogs set upon the poor old beggar.

Set out, is: 1. To depart, to start on a journey. 2. To display.

> He set out on his travels.—*Thackeray*
> He set out his case with all the grace of a rhetorician.

Set to, is to attach to or affix; also, to begin to apply oneself to.

> Let these men set to work at once.
> He has set his seal to this document.
> Set spurs to a horse. Set people to work.

Set up, is: 1. To erect or elevate. 2. To establish. 3. To put forward. 4. To begin a new business. 5. To put in power. 6. To make prosperous. 7. To raise a shout. 8. To arrange type for printing.

> They have set up some stones as landmarks.
> John Osborne, whom he had set up in life.—*Thackeray*
> It is very wicked to set up false witnesses and get men to swear for money.
> He determined to set up a public house.
> Barbarous tribes often set up their greatest warrior as king.
> His success in business has quite set him up again.
> The printer has set up but four pages of your manuscript.

Set up for, is to put oneself forward as, to establish oneself as, to pretend or profess to be.

> Do you mean to set up for a philosopher ?
> I was now set up for a Guinea trader.—*Defoe*

Settle down, is to become quiet, to establish oneself.

> These turbulent tribes have at last settled down to habits of industry.
> To settle down in such a fair land and call good acres his own.—*Kingsley*

Settle on or **upon,** is to confer upon by grant.

> He has settled on his only daughter an annuity of a thousand a year.

Sever from.

> To sever the head from the body.

Shake off sleep, drowsiness, nervousness, etc.

> A snake fastened on Paul's hand at Malta, but he shook it off and felt no harm.

Shake out a folded garment, a banner.

Shake hands **with** another.

Ship off, is to dispatch by ship.

> He has shipped off a large lot of cotton to England.

Show off (transitive) is to make a show of, to display or exhibit in an ostentatious manner.

> She has gone to church to show off her new dress.
> The draper will show off his goods to the best advantage.

Show off (intransitive), is to put on a fine appearance in order to excite admiration.

> The dandy walked on the promenade just to show off.

Show over, is to show every part of.

> She showed Rebecca over every room of the house.—*Thackeray*

Show up, is to expose; to hold up to ridicule or contempt; also, to usher or conduct one upstairs.

> If he provokes me further I shall show him up.
> What pleasure you find in showing up people's mistakes !
> Show the visitor upstairs.

Shrink from contact with the leper.

Shudder at a dreadful sight, carnage.

Shut in, is to enclose, to confine. To shut in a flock of sheep; also, to interrupt the view.

Shut off steam, is to prevent the passage of steam to the engine by shutting or closing the throttle.

Shut out, is to exclude, to deny admission to.

> A tightly shutting window should shut out the rain and the wind.
> The Norman, after a while shut out from France, began more and more to feel that England was his home.—*Trench*

Shut up, is to confine or imprison; to close or fasten the entrance to. Also, to cause a person to say nothing more (colloquial).

> I shall shut up the shop tonight.
> The keepers have shut up the prisoners for the night.

'Shut up!' is used colloquially and contemptuously for 'Stop talking!'

Side with, is to take the part of, to embrace the opinions of.

> He has always sided with the Tory party.

Sin against God; sin against light and love.

Sink beneath or **under** the waves, under a load, a sorrow.

Sink in the mire, in the morass, in a whirlpool.

Sink into the sea, into evil habits, into obscurity. Sink into the mind, is to enter the mind and become fixed there.

Sit down, is to place oneself in a seat.

> He sat down and began a long story.

Sit for a portrait, is to sit so that an artist may take one's portrait. Sit for a constituency as a Member of Parliament elected to represent it.

Sit on a person, is to snub him, to treat him in an overbearing way, to slight him designedly.

Sit out, is to sit till all is done. To sit out a lecture is to remain seated till the lecture is ended. This might be said of one who remained to the end of a dull, uninteresting lecture.

Sit over the fire, is to sit crouched near to the fire.

> The noise of footsteps . . . roused the merry old gentleman as he sat over the fire.—*Dickens*

Sit up, is to rise from a recumbent position, to assume the position of a person seated; to refrain from lying down.

> This poor fellow is too weak to sit up.
> He had to sit up all night, i.e. he did not go to bed all night.
> We woke him and he sat up and began to talk incoherently.
> He sat up till three o'clock in the morning, i.e. he did not go to bed till three.

Sit up with a sick person, is to refrain from going to bed so as to be able to attend upon the sick person.

Sleep away the time on a journey; sleep away the hours.

Sleep off, is to recover from by sleeping. To sleep off intoxication, is to sleep till the effects of intoxication have passed away; sleep off sickness, sleep off fatigue.

> Go, sleep off your wine.—*Kingsley*
> Sleep off the fatigue of today, since tomorrow will bring work for itself.

Slow down, is to gradually diminish speed, to lessen activity.

> A train slows down coming into a station.
> You cannot continue studying so hard; you must slow down.

Smart under pain, under a rebuke, a yoke, tyranny.

Smile at, on or **upon.**

> She smiled at the compliment and turned away.
> Fortune has smiled upon him since I last saw him.

Snap at, is to endeavour to seize suddenly and eagerly, to accept eagerly.

> He snapped at the offer I made him.
> The dog snapped at the thief and caught his leg.
> To snap one's fingers at, is to treat with contempt.

Snap off, is to break off or bite off suddenly.

Snap up, is to catch up a thing hastily.

Sneer at, is to show contempt by a particular expression of countenance.

> To sneer at Dobbin about the accident of birth.—*Thackeray*
> Taught by a woman who loved him, he could listen to humiliating truths which he would otherwise have sneered at.—*Kingsley*

Speak for one, is to urge his claims, to be spokesman for him.

Speak of or **about.**

> Ulysses spoke of the men and the cities that he had seen.

Speak out or **up,** is to speak louder.

Speak with a person, is to converse with him.

Spin out, is to prolong to a tedious length.

> He spun out his lecture till his audience was wearied.

Spread abroad, is transitive and intransitive.

> A tree spreads abroad its branches.
> The telegram speedily spread abroad news of the war.
> Evil reports usually spread abroad very rapidly.

Spread out, is transitive and intransitive.

> The merchant spread out his carpets before the lady, hoping she would buy one.
> As I stood on the hill top, a beautiful panorama lay spread out before me.

Spread over.

> The plague has spread over many provinces.

Spring at, is to attempt to reach by a leap.

Spring in, is to enter in haste, as with a bound.

Spring a mine **upon,** is to give a shocking surprise to.

Spring up, as seed.

> An attachment has sprung up between them.

Spy out.

> He came to spy out the nakedness (=poverty) of the land.

Stamp out, is to thrust down forcibly so as to destroy the power of, to crush.   To stamp out a plague, a rebellion.

Stand against, is to withstand, to resist.

> No king could stand against Alexander.

Stand aloof, apart, aside, have similar meanings.

Stand back, is to retire, withdraw.

Stand by, is to be near, to defend or support, to agree to.

> The stag stood by the edge of the stream.
> If we stand by each other, we shall most likely beat them.—*Macaulay*
> Men who stand by their country and do their duty without fear or favour.
> —*Trollope*
> Let us ask this man what the creature is and I will stand by what he
> shall say.—*Macaulay*

Stand for, is to present oneself as a candidate for; to be in the place of.

> At the last election, he stood for Manchester.
> In the Roman numerals, C stands for one hundred.

Stand off, is to remain at a distance, to keep aloof.

> Seeing men in hostile attitude on the cliffs, the captain stood off from the
> shore.

Stand on, is to attach importance to, to insist on, to be a stickler for. To stand on ceremony, stand on one's dignity.

Stand out, is to project, as a promontory; persistently to oppose.

Stand out against, is persistently to oppose or refuse to yield.

> He stood out against all our efforts to persuade him.

Stand to, is: 1. To be ready, e.g. to ply oars. 2. To abide by, as a contract, a promise, one's word. 3. To be consistent with.

> It stands to reason that if the canal should burst, it will be where the sides
> are weakest.

Stand up, is to rise from a sitting posture, to be on one's feet.

> The men stood up as we came near.

Stand up for, is to defend, to vindicate, to maintain.

> I mean to stand up for my rights.
> Are you going to stand up for this scoundrel ?

Stare after, is to gaze with staring eyes on a person going away from you.

Stare at.

> She stared at me wildly as if she were out of her mind.

Stare one in the face. An impending disaster is said to stare one in the face when there seems to be no escape from it.

> The provisions ran out and death stared the garrison in the face.

Start for, is to set out with the aim of reaching a place.

> When did he start for Australia ?

Start off, out, is to set out, as on a race; to depart.

Start up, is to rise up suddenly; to come suddenly into notice or importance.

> The monkeys started up and scampered off.
> A new cotton-spinning company has started up here.

Stave off, is to delay (transitive), to put off.

> We hear of daring speculators cooking the accounts of mercantile companies, in order to stave off the evil day.

Stay away, is to remain absent for a long while.

Stay in, is to keep indoors.

Stay out, is to remain outside the house.

Stay up, is not to go to bed; also, to remain in an elevated place.

> I went to bed at nine, but these fellows stayed up till twelve.

Stay with one, is to put up at his house.

> I stayed with a doctor when I was in Ceylon.

Steer for, is to steer towards with the hope of reaching.

> He took the helm and steered for the harbour.

Step aside, is to go a little distance to one side.

Step in, is to enter, to walk in.

Step into a house; step into an inheritance, i.e. to come suddenly and unexpectedly into it.

Step out, is to walk with lengthened or quickened step.

Step up, is to increase the rate or volume of, as, step up a man's pay.

Stick at, is to hesitate, to have misgivings about.

> He will stick at nothing to accomplish his purpose.

Stick by, is to adhere closely to, to uphold.

> Stick by your friends and they will stick by you.

Stick out (intransitive), is to project; stick out (transitive) is to thrust out.

Stick out for a thing, is to insist on it (colloquial).

Stick to, is to adhere perseveringly to.

> He will stick to his party to the last.

Stick up, is to stand on end, to have an upright position.

Stick up for one, is to defend him (colloquial).

Stoop to. He never stooped to acts of dishonesty.

Strike at, is to try to hit, to aim a blow at.

> He struck at me, but I avoided the blow.
> These proposals strike at the liberties of the people.

Strike down. He is struck down with cholera.

Strike for, is to start on a course for, to try to attain to.

> The spinners have struck for higher wages.
> The slaves are banding together and mean to strike for freedom.
> (A *strike* by employees is a refusal to work except on certain terms.)

Strike in, is to come in suddenly, to interpose suddenly.

> He struck in and joined in the fray.
> He struck in and took part in the chorus.

Strike into a path, is to turn aside to the path and walk in it.

Strike off (=erase) a name from a roll, strike off (=print) copies of a book; strike off (=cut off by a blow) a man's head with a sword.

Strike out, is to erase; to contrive; to deal a blow; to begin to swim.

> He took a pen and struck out two paragraphs from his essay.
> This merchant aims at striking out a new course of business.
> He struck out for the shore.

Strike up, is to cause to sound; to begin to sing or play as a musician.

> Strike up the band.
> The band struck up ' God Save the Queen '

Strip a person **of** clothes, of authority.

Strive about, against, for, over, with.

> Strive for the truth; strive against temptations; strive about *or* over a small matter.
> Strive not with a man without cause.—*Bible*

Struggle about, against, over, under, with.

> He has been struggling against *or* with adversity all his life.
> The poor boy struggled hard against the current but was carried off.
> Struggle about *or* over a trifle; struggle under difficulties.

Submit to.

> Submit to authority, to the Government, to pain, to privation.
> Submit a question to a lawyer, submit a case to arbitration.

Subscribe to.

> To subscribe to an opinion is, to profess one's adherence to it.
> To subscribe to a good cause is, to give a donation for its support.

Subsist on.

> The shipwrecked sailors subsisted on nuts and roots which they gathered in the woods.

Succeed to.

> The marquis will succeed to the dukedom at his father's death.

Sue for, is to make legal claim for.

> He sued for damages to the extent of five hundred pounds.

Supply to, with.

> Supply food to the poor; supply the poor with food.

Sweep away the dust from the door, sweep away abuses.

Sweep the seas **of** pirate ships, or **of** submarines.

Sweep the dust **off** the table.

Sweep out a room, is to remove the dust from the floor with a brush.

Sweep up the dust into a heap.

> The wind swept up the sand into a mound.

Take after, is to imitate, to resemble.

> This boy takes after his father.

Take away, is to remove, to deprive one of. To **be taken away,** sometimes means to die.

> Take away the thorns from the path.
> By forbidding him to sell books, you have taken away his living.
> This statement is enough to take away my breath.

Take back, is to withdraw.

> I take back all I've said.

Take one **by the throat,** is to seize him by the throat.

Take down, is to bring down; to pull down; to record. To **take one down,** is to humiliate one who has been proud or boastful.

> To take down a scaffolding, take down a wall, a house.
> To take down a book from the shelf. To take down from dictation.
> He took down the man's evidence most carefully.

Take for.

> I took him for a priest, i.e. I thought he was a priest.

Take from, is to deprive of; to subtract.

> Take four from seven and three remain.

Take in, is 1. To enclose with a fence. 2. To include or comprise. 3. To comprehend. 4. To contract. 5. To admit or receive. 6. To receive regularly. 7. To cheat, to deceive, to gull—often used in this last sense in the passive voice.

> He has taken in a piece of ground for a garden.
> This map takes in Egypt, Nubia, and Abyssinia.
> The boys could not take in his meaning.
> Your coat is too large: get the tailor to take it in.
> This vessel takes in water. You have been taken in by sharpers.
> I take in a daily paper and a monthly magazine.
> To *take in hand* is to undertake.

Take off, is to remove; to mimic, to ridicule.

> He used to take his boots off.
> Did you not see that he was only taking you off ?

' **Take yourself off** ' is equivalent to ' Go away ! '

Take on airs, is to assume foolish or proud airs (cf., **put on airs,** above); **take on** (=undertake) a duty, more work; **take on** (colloquial) is to grieve violently.

Take out, is to extract, to remove, as, a tooth, a stain.

> To take it out of one is to get compensation from him, or to revenge oneself upon him.

Take over responsibility, take over charge of an office, take over stock in a shop.

Take to, is to apply to, to resort to; to be fond of.

> Men of learning, who take to business.—*Addison*
> She had taken to superstition in her old age.—*Kingsley*
> These two schoolboys took to each other from their first meeting.

Take up, is: 1. To lift or raise.   2. To engross or occupy.   3. To answer.   4. To begin where another left off.   5. Take up a person's cause, is to charge oneself with it.

> He took up a pen and began to write.
> These boxes take up a large space.
> The copying of these letters took up the whole day.
> He was vehement in his challenge and no one took him up.
> When one girl ceased the chant, another took it up.
> They forced Ulysses . . . against his will to take up his night quarters on shore.—*Lamb*

Take up with a person, is to begin to be friendly with him, to begin to keep company with him.

To be taken up with, or **taken with,** is to be pleased with, to be captivated by.   **Taken up with** also means, occupied with.

> I am quite taken with this author's style.
> My time is taken up with a lot of trifles.

Take upon oneself, is to assume, to undertake.

> He took upon himself to say that the officer was a thief.

Talk about or of.

> He talked of war and glory.
> Now let us talk about something else.
> Who asked you to talk about my affairs ?

Talk at a man, is to talk to someone else in the man's presence in order to hurt him.

Talk away, is to continue talking freely.

Talk down a person, means to silence him with incessant talk.   To **talk down** to a person is to speak to him condescendingly.

Talk a person **out** of his intentions or plans, is to persuade him to abandon them by showing him the futility of them.

Talk over, is to deliberate on, to discuss; to criticize; to persuade.

> They talked over the scheme till midnight.
> When the visitor left, the family talked him over, i.e. freely criticized him.
> Before he left, the family had talked him over, i.e. persuaded him to change his ideas.

Talk to, with, is to converse with.

> She talked to him of modesty and humility.—*Kingsley*
> Swift liked talking with thoughtful literary ladies.

Tamper with, is to meddle with, to trifle with, to make little experiments with.

> It is dangerous for boys to tamper with gunpowder.
> To tamper with a conspiracy is to spread it.

Tear away from, off, out, up.

> Slave dealers ruthlessly tore children away from their parents.
> The enraged elephant tore off branches from the trees.
> He tore up the letter and threw it away.

Tear down, is to dismantle, to destroy fiercely; also, intransitive, to rush violently along.

> To tear down a building, a reputation.
> The horses stampeded and tore down the street.

Tell about or **of,** is to mention, to narrate or describe.

> Tell me about this ship.
> The time would fail me to tell of Gideon, and of Barak.—*Bible*.

Tell against a person, is to prove adverse to him.

> In an investigation, a new fact becomes known, which tells against a suspected or accused person.

Tell one thing or person **from** another, is to distinguish.

Tell off, is to count, to divide; to select and appoint to some special duty. Also, colloquially, to reprimand.

> The superintendent told off six policemen to watch the burning house.

Tell over beads, as a monk might do in saying his prayers.

Tell upon, is to affect, to have an influence on.

> Sleeplessness is sure to tell upon his health.
> General education is beginning to tell on the people's mode of living.

Tend to, is to incline to. Idleness tends to poverty.

Think about, of.

> He thinks of competing for a scholarship.
> This takes some time to think about.

Think on or **upon** a subject, is to meditate or muse on it.

Think out a scheme, is to consider it carefully and study it till it is completely formed.

Think over, is to meditate upon, to consider.

> She was left alone to think over the sudden and wonderful events of the day.—*Thackeray*

Throw about books, is to fling them here and there, and leave them in disorder. To throw about money, is to waste it, to squander it.

Throw away, is to lose by neglect or folly; to reject.

> The lunatic threw his watch away.
> He has thrown away a fine opportunity.

Throw back, is to retort.

Throw down, is to overturn or destroy, as a wall or pillar; to fling down.

Throw in a word, is to interject a word; to throw in an extra article, is to add one without charging for it

Throw off, is to cast off, to expel, to discard. Throw off a disease, throw off all sense of shame.

Throw oneself on or **upon,** is to rely upon as a suppliant would; also, to dash upon, make an onset upon.

> I throw myself on your clemency.
> They threw themselves on the enemy.

Throw open the doors, is to give admission.

Throw one **over**, is to get rid of him, to abandon him.

Throw out.

> To throw out an observation, is casually to give utterance to it.
> The Bill was thrown out, i.e. was rejected by Parliament by vote.

Throw up, is to resign; to cast up; to eject from the stomach.

> This man has thrown up his appointment.
> The soldiers threw up an earthwork.
> The lawyer, finding himself deceived by his client, threw up the case.

Thrust at, away, off, from, on (=urge), **out, through.**

> He thrust at me with a spear.
> The citizens thrust them out of the city.
> I tried to help him but he thrust me away

Thrust down, is to push down vigorously.   To thrust a thing down one's throat, is to compel him to hear—said usually of reproach or severe criticism or blame.

Thrust oneself **in,** is to intrude.

Tide over, is to surmount; to cause to overcome.

> A little money lent him would tide him over all his difficulties.

Tire one **out,** is to weary or fatigue him excessively.

> This old veteran could tire out the most robust sportsman.

Touch at, is to come to and go off without tarrying.

> Do the mail steamers touch at Aden and Malta ?

Touch off, is to sketch hastily, or to give finishing touches to.
To touch off a portrait.

Touch on or **upon,** is to treat of slightly in a discourse.

> In his lecture on geology, he touched on the subject of climate.

Touch up, is to repair or improve by giving slight touches; to burnish.

> Let the saddler touch up the harness.
> Ask the master to touch up your picture.

Trade in, with.

> England trades with India in tea, wheat, rice, and cotton.

Trade on, is to take advantage of another through special knowledge.

> I traded on his good nature to get what I wanted.

Train up, is to educate.

> Train up a child in the way he should go; and when he is old he will not depart from it.—*Bible*

Trifle with, is to treat lightly, to mock, to play the fool with.

> To trifle with sacred things; trifle with one's feelings; trifle with one's opportunities.

Triumph over enemies, over obstacles.

Trump up a charge or a story, is to devise or fabricate it, to make it up unfairly.

Trust in, to.

> Trust in the Lord and do good.—*Bible*
> I trusted to his coolness and skill, and he did not fail me.

Trust a man **with** money.

Try on a coat, is to put it on to see whether it fits or not. Similarly, one will **try out** a new car.

Try over a piece of music, is to play it through on an instrument for the first time.

Turn about, is to face in the opposite direction.

Turn a person **adrift**, is to throw him on his own resources.

Turn against, is to become hostile to.

Turn aside, is to avert; also, to deviate.

> Never turn aside from the path of rectitude.
> How can a wicked man hope to turn aside the judgement of God ?

Turn away, is to dismiss; to avert; also, intransitive

> He has turned away three applicants.
> Wise men turn away wrath.—*Bible*
> The sight was sickening and I turned away.

Turn away from, or turn **from** an evil purpose; turn men away from conspiracy.

Turn back, is to return; also, to drive back.

> Can any force turn back the incoming tide ?

Turn down a page, is to fold it back. Turn down a street, is to leave the street you are walking in and turn aside into another street. To turn down a scheme is to reject it.

Turn in, is to bend inwards; to enter a house for a short visit; also (colloquial), to go to bed.

Turn into.

> Turn Persian into English. Turn sacred things into ridicule.

Turn off taps, lights, etc. To dismiss; also, to change the course.

> I mean to turn this servant off. The road turns off to the right.

Turn on gas, water (in pipes), electric light, music (as in the radio). Also, to face a person with hostile intent.

Turn out, is: 1. To expel. 2. To put to pasture. 3. To produce as the result of labour. 4. To result or eventuate. 5. To bend outwards. 6. To make tidy. 7. To get up. 8. To assemble.

> Don't turn me out of doors to wander in the street.—*Dickens*
> Let them turn out all the cattle to pasture.
> How much yarn can this mill turn out in a day ?
> Do you think the crops will turn out well this year ?
> The officer ordered the guard to turn out.
> If my story turns out good enough, I shall send it to a publisher.
> Turn out a room, a drawer, is to clean it thoroughly and leave it tidy.

Turn over.

>To turn a matter over, is to consider it.
>
>To turn a log over, is to roll it over.

Turn to.

>Turn to God for mercy and help.
>
>In his sorrow he turned to drink and brought himself to ruin.

Turn up, is to come to light, to transpire, to happen.

>We know not what may turn up tomorrow.
>
>An article lost *turns up*, i.e. it is found accidentally when no one is thinking of it. A visitor *turns up* (=arrives unexpectedly). A boy runs away from home and no trace of him is left; five years later he *turns up* somewhere else as a railway porter, i.e. five years later he is recognized by persons who had known him before he ran away.

Turn upon, is to hinge upon.

>His whole argument turned upon the validity of a document.

Unite with.   Oxygen unites with hydrogen to form water.

Vie with.

>In a trading nation, the younger sons may be placed in a way of life to vie with the best of their family.—*Addison*

Vote against, for.

>Ten men voted for the motion and three against it.

Wait at table, is to attend at table as a servant (waiter) when a meal is being taken.

Wait for, is to await, to remain in expectation of.

>I thought you were only waiting for encouragement.
>
>Shall I wait for you here ?, i.e. wait here till you come to me ?

Wait on, is: 1. To attend a person as a servant would.   2. To visit on business.   3. To follow as a result (poetical).

>May I wait on you at your office tomorrow and show you some articles I have for sale ?
>
>Poverty waits on idleness and extravagance.

Wake from sleep, from stupor, from a reverie.

>That calm and peaceful rest which it is pain to wake from.—*Dickens*

Wake up, is to wake from sleep.

>She woke up with a smile.—*Thackeray*
>
>Wake up to one's responsibilities, one's danger.

Walk about, away, back, walk **by** (=according to) a rule; **down, forward, in, off, on, out, over, past, through** a house (=go from room to room of a house), **up, up to.**   These are so easy as not to need exemplification.

Wash away, off, out, is to remove by washing; or, to be capable of removal by washing.

>Will the ink-stain wash out ?
>
>There was blood on my sword, but my servant washed it off.

Wash against, down, in, up.

> The sea washed against the promenade.
> Sailors wash down the decks of a ship.
> The tide washed in some broken spars.
> To wash up, generally, is to clean table utensils after meals.

Wash overboard, to carry overboard by the force of a wave sweeping into a ship.

Watch for the dawn, for a friend coming, for a letter.

Watch over, is to take care of, to guard.

> Trust in God and He will watch over you.

Wear away, off, on, out, up.

> Friction wears away the impression from coins.
> As the day wore on, we became more anxious.
> His wife was nearly worn out with her labours.—*Trollope*
> To wear out a coat, is to wear it till it can no longer be worn.
> To wear out one's patience, is to exhaust his patience, to be so dilatory as to make him impatient.
> A visitor is said ' to wear out his welcome ' when the friends he visits grow impatient with him as a guest and wish him gone.

Wear well. A person or a garment is said to wear well when he or it is not much affected by time.

While away time, to spend it idly or pleasantly. Pope uses ' while away this life '.

> Nowhere is so pleasant to while away a few idle weeks at, as one or other of the universities.—*Lamb*

Wind about. The road winds about to avoid the hills.

Wind off, is to unwind from.

> She wound off the silk from the ball.

Wind up has different meanings.

(1) To wind up one's affairs, is to bring them to a final settlement or adjustment.

> These partners are breaking up partnership and mean to wind up the business of the company without delay.

(2) To wind up a clock or a watch, is to wind the spring round its axis, so as to put the clock or watch in order for regular motion. Metaphorically, **wind up** is applied to the feelings, and means, to raise by degrees to an intense pitch.

> I wound up my watch last night at nine.
> The feelings of men had been wound up to such a point [by the trial of the seven bishops], that at length the stern English nature, so little used to outward signs of emotion, gave way, and thousands sobbed aloud for very joy.—*Macaulay*

Wink at, is to avoid taking notice of.

> I can wink at his faults no longer.
> The judge, who was a shrewd fellow, winked at the minor offence.

Wipe away, off, out, up, is to remove by wiping or rubbing; to clear off.

> Wipe off dust; wipe out debt; wipe away a stain; wipe up spilt ink
> Much is being done to wipe out the memories of past misrule.

Wish for, is to desire to have, to long to attain to.

> This is as useful a book as you could wish for.
> No matter how rich a man becomes, he will never say that he has nothing left to wish for.

Withdraw from.

> You cannot honourably withdraw from the contest.

Work against, is to work in opposition to; work against time.*
Work away, is to continue working.
Work at, is to be engaged upon.

> I worked at my lesson.

Work into, through, is to penetrate laboriously.

> The miners will work their way into the rock till they have worked through to the other side.   Work through difficulties.
> Work oneself into favour.   (This generally implies cunning, sneaking.)

Work for wages.   Work for a kind master; for one's family.
Work off debt, is to get rid of it gradually by sustained efforts.
Work on, is to continue working; also, to influence.

> Let the men work on till sunset.   They tried to work on her fears.

Work a thing **open,** as a locked box of which the key is lost— is to apply all methods to the lock with repeated efforts till the box opens.

Work out, is to effect or produce a result; to solve, as a problem; to exhaust by working, as a mine.

> He worked out his own salvation.
> Are the diamond fields in South Africa worked out ?

Work to an end, is to conduce to that end or purpose.
Work up, is to excite; to use up materials in work; to elaborate.

> He worked himself into a great passion.
> They will work up all these stones in building the bridge.
> This writer has worked up his story well.

Work with persons or things.

> The other clerks will not work with this one.
> The powers and instruments with which he works are public.—*Gladstone*

Worm a secret **out of** one, is to draw it out cautiously, as by confidential questioning; to pretend to be a friend and, under that guise, to induce a man to tell you what is in his heart.   This phrase verb implies the condemning of such a practice.
Worm oneself **into** favour, is to insinuate oneself into favour.

Yearn for, is to desire with eager longing.

Every man yearns for sympathy in sorrow.

Yield to, is to submit to, to comply with, to bend one's will to, to give way to; also, to surrender.

Yield to one's wish, to fate, to reason, to mercy.

It is clear after a careful study of this chapter that these prepositional or phrase verbs are very numerous in English. They are characteristic, moreover, of the best writers.

They abound also in good conversational English. The student will find instances of this in abundance in well-written novels or stories which largely reproduce or represent conversations as among well-educated people.

CHAPTER X

IDIOMATIC VERBAL PHRASES HAVING THE VERB *TO BE*

94. Many prepositional and other phrases in English are used for the most part with the verb *to be*. We give a number of idiomatic verbal expressions formed in this way. There are many more.

To be about to do a thing, is to be going to do it.
To be after, is to be in pursuit of, in search of.

> The bailiffs are after him.
> ' What's he after ? ', i.e. in what scheme is he now interested ?

To be against, is to be adverse to, not to be in favour of.

> I am against the proposal.

To be dead against, is more emphatic than **to be against**.
To be for doing a thing, is to be in favour of it.

> Some were for trying to run the witch down.—*Kingsley*

To be in, is to be at home, to be in the house; to be present.

> Is your father in ?, i.e. is he at home, or in his office.
> What a place to be in is an old library !—*Lamb*
> ' He is sure to be in at the death', would be said of a hunter who would be close to the hounds when the quarry—say, a fox—was caught.
> Labour is in, the Tories out, i.e. in office, out of office, as the majority party in Parliament.

To be in for a thing. A prisoner is in for theft, i.e. in prison for theft. A student is in for his degree, i.e. in at the examination for his degree. This man is in for losses, i.e. is exposed to or involved in losses. This boy is in for a good sound beating from his father, i.e. he will surely get such a beating.

> This young man is to be married next month; so his father is in for a lot of expense.

To be in for it. Here the word **it** is indefinite. This phrase is colloquial for, to be involved in or committed to something that will bring down some disaster, as punishment, blame, or loss. Hence the proverb, ' In for a penny, in for a pound '—which has much the same meaning as ' As well be hanged for a sheep as a lamb '.

To be in with, is to be friendly with, to have the favour of a superior.

> He wishes you to think that he is in with the Governor.

To be off, is to be away, to put aside; to go away, to go off.

> His hat was off.   His shoes are off.
> He is off to England, i.e. he is in the act of going or is already gone off.
> They were all off to Chatham.
> The boat race is off, i.e. it is not to take place.

Be off!' as an imperative, means 'begone!' and is usually a contemptuous command.   Sometimes the form is, 'Be off with you!' or simply 'Off with you!'

> 'Be off! you wretch; off with you at once!'

In the saying, 'To be off with the old love and on with the new', **to be off**, means, to be rid of, to have put aside.

To be on, is said of anything put on or attached to the body, as clothes, armour, spectacles, boots.   What's on? means, what's happening?

> My spurs were on an hour ago.
> His cap was on and his shoes were off.
> The concert will be on at 8 o'clock.

To be out, is not to be in the house; also, said of the tide at ebb; said also, of a fire or light, meaning, to be extinguished; also, to be mistaken (colloquial).

> My brother is out.
> The candle is out; the fire is out; the lamp is out.
> You are out in your guess.
> To be out in a game, is to have been ruled out of it.

To be over, is to be above in authority; to go abroad through; also, to have ceased or come to an end.

> The story was all over the town in half an hour.
> The dream of success was over.
> When the eating was over, the drinking began.
> No improvement in business is looked for until the holidays are over.

It is all over with, or **all up with**, a person', means, 'he is done for', i.e. he is about to die and no remedy can cure him.

To have been to a place or a person, is to have gone to see it or him; to have visited it or him.

> He had been to the manager.
> They had been to the panorama of Moscow.—*Thackeray*
> 'Have you been to London lately?'

To be up, is to be out of bed; to have risen; to be in a position of prominence; to have expired—said of time.

> The sun is not up yet.   He is up at five every morning.
> The time is up, i.e. the allotted time has expired.
> The rebels are up, *or* are up in arms, i.e. are in insurrection.
> The game is up, i.e. success is now impossible.
> He is up to anything, i.e. he is ready for any trick or adventure that may be suggested.
> To be up to the eyes in work, is to be very fully occupied.
> To be up to the ears in debt, is to be greatly burdened with debt.

To be up to, is to be equal to; also, to be acquainted with.

> This man is up to all the tricks of the trade.
>
> The train is up to time, i.e. has arrived at the appointed time.
>
> Do you think the horse is up to my weight ?, i.e. strong enough to carry a man of my weight.

To be above doing a thing. When a man's self-respect or sense of moral right will not permit him to act in a certain way, he is said to be above doing so.

> You should be above all meanness and fraud.

To be up and doing, is to be actively engaged; contrasted with loitering.

> A farmer must be up and doing in spring if he would reap in harvest

To be well up in a subject, is to have mastered it thoroughly.

95. The verb *to be* joined to certain adverbs gives expressions which are applied to health.

To be well, is to be in good health; the opposite is, **to be ill,** or **to be unwell.** In the phrase, **to be pretty well,** the word **pretty** means moderately, expressing a less degree than **very.**

To be better, is to be convalescent; or to have recovered from illness.

To be worse, is to be more unwell.

> Is your father quite well ? He has been ill, but is better now.

To be oneself again, is to be in one's normal state of health after illness.

> Last night you were in such a passion that you seemed to have taken leave of your wits; I am glad to see you are yourself again today.
>
> ' You are not yourself ', means, you are not in your usual state or mood.

96. To be well off, to be badly off, to be ill off, to be better off, to be worse off, are expressions applied to one's circumstances or position in life, the meaning being evident. **To be well to do,** has the same meaning as to be well off

> The merchant is pretty well to do.
>
> He is worse off than before.

97. The present or past tense of *to be* is sometimes followed by the infinitive of another verb—often the passive infinitive; and this idiomatic construction commonly expresses necessity, capability, appointment, or determination.

> He was to leave for England a month ago.
>
> The marriage is to take place on Monday next.
>
> From the place where we stood no village was to be seen.
>
> This work is to be done before evening, i.e. must be done.

98. Adjectives are often joined predicatively to the verb *to be*. Hence we have,

To be abreast of	to be blind to	to be destitute of
,, afraid of	,, content with	,, equal to
,, alive to	,, deaf to	,, worthy of

and many others. Some of these have notable peculiarities.

To be aware, or **to be aware of,** is to know. The first form is followed by **that**; the second by an objective noun or its equivalent.

> He is not aware that his friend is ill.
> He is quite aware of his friend's illness.

To be bitten. This phrase has sometimes the meaning of, to be cheated or deceived. So we have the phrase **the biter bit** or **bitten,** i.e. the man who meant to cheat others has himself been out-witted and cheated. So Pope has the expression, ' The rogue was bit '.

To be born with a silver spoon in one's mouth, is a colloquial expression meaning, to be born in affluent circumstances, to be a rich man's child.

> Struggles develop sturdy character. Those who are born with a silver spoon in their mouth rarely accomplish any of those great and good things which require force of character.

To be born under a lucky star. This phrase has descended from the time when people believed in astrology. It was thought that certain stars brought good fortune, and if one was born under such a star, he was sure to be fortunate in life. Though the belief in such things is exploded, the phrase remains; and when a man has a stroke of good fortune, it might be said of him that he was born under a lucky star.

In addition, we have the following from astrology.

> His star is in the ascendant.
> This was an ill-starred expedition.
> Under what evil star was this project born ?

The word **disaster** comes from the same source. It is derived from the Greek words **dys**, bad, and **aster**, a star. So, too, we have the phrase **to thank one's stars.**

To be equal to an occasion, is to be competent to act suitably to the occasion, to be able to cope with a difficulty that has arisen, to be competent to meet an emergency.

> He is not quite equal to the task.
> The orator was not equal to the occasion.

To be near, is to be stingy, parsimonious.

> I never thought he was so near till I saw how he dealt with his son.

To be past cure, past mending, past recovery.

> The doctor declares that his patient is past recovery, i.e. that the patien will die.
> This old car is past mending.

To be posted up in a subject, is to be well acquainted with it. When the phrase is used without any subject being mentioned, the meaning is, well informed generally.

> Here is a statement regarding Xerxes I don't understand, but let us ask the professor; he is well posted up in Persian history.

To be shaky, is to be in an enfeebled or tottering condition. The phrase is sometimes applied to a bank or firm supposed to be not able to discharge its liabilities. It is also used of one who has a feeling of great uncertainty about a result.

Men withdraw their money from a bank when they suspect it to be shaky.
' Will he pass his degree examination ? '   ' He is shaky enough about it.'

To be sick of a thing, is to be wearied and disgusted with it.

To be little worth or **to be worth little; to be not much worth,** or **to be not worth much.**

All that he did for me was not worth much.
My time or labour was little worth.—*Defoe*

To be worth while. Sometimes **worth the while,** or **worth one's while. While** is here a noun. A thing not worth while attempting, is a thing upon which it is not worth spending the **while** or the time which the attempt would require.

It is worth while your trying the experiment.
Learning Latin is not worth his while, for all the use he will make of it.
It will be well worth your while to consider this offer, i.e. this offer may be of advantage to you, and is therefore worth your consideration.

To be worth its weight in gold, is said of something extremely valuable. Occasionally the phrase is applied in praise of a person who has performed some work of great value.

In the desert a bottle of water is often worth its weight in gold.
This medicine cured her son and she counts every drop of it worth its weight in gold—or, she counts the doctor who gave her the medicine worth his weight in gold.

99. To be of advantage, or **be to** or **for one's advantage, to be of service, to be of no avail.** The meaning of these phrases will be clear from the following:

His well-meant efforts were of no avail.
It may be of service to others.
This will soon cease to be of any service at all.
A free press is of great advantage to a loyal people.
It should be to his advantage that he has made this discovery.

100. *To be* is used with other adjectival adjuncts.

To be the better for, the worse for, is to be in a better or worse condition because of.

His clothes are the worse for wear, i.e. are getting shabby.
He is the worse for drink.
The schoolmaster is much the better for his holiday.

To be easy in mind. Sometimes, we have **the mind is easy.**

Now my mind will be easy.
She is quite easy in mind about the whole affair.

To be ill at ease, is to be disturbed in mind.

> A thief must be ill at ease when he sees a policeman approaching.
> One is often ill at ease when he has to meet a superior and is uncertain how he may be received.

To be lost, or **dead, to all feeling** is to be so callous as to be past feeling; to be utterly hardened and heartless.

> I once heard of a youth who was so dead to all right feeling, that he would not pay for medicine for his sick father.

To be lost in the clouds. When a man gets into unintelligible speculations, or becomes inextricably involved in an argument, we say, he is lost in the clouds, or he has lost himself in the clouds; he is in a fog. These phrases are commonly applied to a confused and confusing speaker whose thoughts are so hazy, so wrapped in clouds of mental confusion, that he cannot set forth his meaning clearly.

To be open to bribery, is to be willing to take a bribe.

To be caught napping. This is said of a watchman or sentinel found asleep when he should be watching, he is caught taking a nap or short sleep. Hence the phrase is applied to one who though usually quick and on his guard, is nevertheless deceived on a particular occasion.

To be caught red-handed, is to be caught in the act of committing crime.

To be set upon a thing, is to desire it greatly, to be bent on doing it.

> She is set upon going to the continent next week.

To be wide awake, is to be so fully awake that one's eyes are wide open; hence, to be well aware of what one is doing, to be ready and watching for anything that may happen, to be on one's guard so as not to be deceived or cheated.

To be all ears, is to be a very attentive listener. The phrase is often used of a person who is trying hard to overhear a conversation which he is not supposed to hear.

To be no more, is to be no longer among the living.

> Jenny was no more: she had died in the interval.—*Lamb*

To be nowhere, is colloquial for, to be so far behind in a competition as to be not worth taking into account, to be in a position of no importance whatever.

> He was nowhere in the examination, being last on the list but three.

101. The use of *to be* with some noun adjuncts is noteworthy.

To be an authority on a subject. When a man is known to be so fully acquainted with a subject that his opinion on it commands respect, or is considered decisive in any doubtful question, he is said to be an authority on that subject.

Huxley is an authority in natural science, and anything but an authority on metaphysical or religious matters.

To be no chicken, is to be no longer young.   This is colloquial and rather contemptuous.

To be Greek, or **double Dutch, to one,** means, to be as unintelligible to one as an unknown tongue.

His enunciation was so bad and his voice so low, that the speech he made was all Greek to me.

To be a good hand at, is to be skilful in, clever at.   We can also say, **a capital hand at, an excellent hand at, a crack hand at,** and we also have opposites of these, such as, **a poor hand at, a bad hand at, a wretched hand at.**

You can hardly fancy what a capital hand she is at embroidery.
Jack may be a crack hand at wood-carving, but he is a wretched hand at painting.

To be a host in oneself, is literally to be equal to a host, i.e. a great many persons; and hence, to be a person of great powers or attainments.

Napoleon was to his soldiery a host in himself.
You will not want for fun so long as Charles is in your party; he is a host in himself.

To be master of the situation. The situation here, means, the circumstances of a case as they now are; and to be **master** of the situation, is to be in a position to decide by one's influence and action what the result shall be.

To be a nobody, is to be a person of no importance, to be sprung from no family of importance, to have no connexions of important position.

The prime minister is the real ruler and the prince is a mere nobody.
The peers that Cromwell created were nobodies in the view of the old nobility of England.

To be somebody, is to be a person of some importance:

He struts about with an air of importance as if he were somebody.

To be a party to a thing, is to be concerned in it, to consent to it, to be a participator in it.

I will be no party to this arrangement.
England was a party to the Treaty of Berlin.

To be a prey to doubt, to grief, means to be consumed with doubt, grief.

To be a slave to a thing, as a habit or a drug, is to be so addicted to it as to be unable to give it up.

102. To BE with other phrases

To be of age; to be under age. In England a person is said **to be of age** when he has attained to twenty-one years of age: he is said also then to have **attained his majority**, or to have **come of age**. **To be under age**, is to be under twenty-one years of age: such a person is called a **minor**. But we do not call one who is of age a **major**.

> In cases where either party [to a marriage] is under age and not a widower or widow, etc.—*Act of Parliament*
> He is of age; ask him; he shall speak for himself.—*Bible*

To be of a certain age, is an indefinite expression signifying the age of any person between forty and sixty.

To be off one's head, is colloquial for, to have lost balance of mind, to have lost control of reason, to be insane.

> The fellow talks as wildly as if he were off his head.

To be under a cloud. When a man rightly or wrongly falls under suspicion, he is said for the time to be under a cloud; the sunshine of success or favour no longer falls upon him; he is not in good repute.

To be under a person's thumb, is to be unduly under that person's rule or control.

To be with one in an affair, is to agree with him in it, to be in harmony with him in it, to be joined with him in it.

> He is thoroughly with us in our efforts at reform.

To be within hearing, is to be some distance off, but yet so near as to be able to hear. So, **to be within call**.

> Take care of what you say: there is a servant within hearing.
> Margaret slept in the biggest room upstairs, and her grand-daughter in a kind of closet adjoining where she could be within hearing, if her grandmother should call her in the night.—*Lamb*

To be within an ace of, is colloquial for, to be very nearly.

> He was within an ace of being shot, i.e. he narrowly escaped.

To be within an inch of, is another phrase of similar meaning.

To be down and out, to be beaten in boxing, and so, to be done for in other senses.

To be down in the mouth, is colloquial for, to feel depressed, to be mortified.

> He is down in the mouth because he has failed in the examination.

To be one's right hand man, is to be one's chief helper, to be a helper whose services could not well be dispensed with.

> This agent has been the Company's right-hand man for seven years.

To be the making of one, is colloquial for, to be the reason or cause of one's success.

> Accept this appointment: it may be the making of you.
> George Stephenson's perseverance was the making of him.

103. To Be At with phrases

To be at the beck and call of another, is for you to be so subserviently under his rule that he makes unreasonable demands on your service.

> You really must not expect me to be at your beck and call; I have my own business to attend to.

To be at one's best, is to be using one's powers to the utmost of one's ability and to the greatest advantage; to be in one's greatest prosperity.

> The days when Spain was at her best are long since gone.
> Is Macaulay at his best in his essay on Clive ?

To be at daggers drawn, is said of two parties between whom there is as much bitter enmity as if they stood face to face with daggers drawn, ready to stab each other.

> The quarrel between these two men has unhappily grown more bitter till now they are at daggers drawn.

To be at death's door, is to be so ill as to be about to die.

> This man seemed to be at death's door last night.

To be at ease, at one's ease, is to be in a condition of ease or tranquillity; to feel repose; to have facility or readiness.

> He is quite at ease in writing English.
> I felt I should be at my ease in the descriptive parts of a novel.—*George Eliot*

To be at home, is to be in one's own house. **To be from home**, is to be away from one's own house.

> He was at home when I called yesterday.
> Here, when my parents have been from home, I have stayed for hours together.—*Lamb*

To be at home in a subject, is to be fully acquainted with it.

> A discussion arose about the moral teachings of Socrates, but only one person in the company was at home in the subject.

To be at home with a person, is to be on friendly, familiar terms with him, as if one were an inmate of his home.

> He received me so cordially that I was at home with him at once.

Sometimes it is, **to feel at home** with a person.

To be at large, is to be unrestrained, free, at liberty.

> His dog is chained in the day time, but is at large at night.

To be at liberty; to be at fault; to be at any expense, at some expense, at no expense, are readily intelligible and should be committed to memory. (**At fault** originally meant ' puzzled '.)

> Who is at fault in this matter ?, i.e. who is to be blamed ?
> You are not at liberty to sign another man's name.
> It was at my expense that the child was educated.

To be at a loss, is to be puzzled, to be unable to decide; to be in uncertainty. The phrase often implies felt want or bewilderment arising suddenly. **To be at no loss,** is the opposite.

> I am at a loss to understand his motive.
> He is never at a loss for an appropriate word, i.e. in speaking he never needs to hesitate and wait for the appropriate word to come into his mind.

To be at one, is to be agreed, to be in harmony.

To be at sea. This phrase is used metaphorically and is applied to a person confused or in uncertainty of mind.

> This boy is quite at sea in history; he cannot answer a single question.

The phrase **at sea** is used with other verbs and means, away out from land; also, following a seafaring life.

> This man has a son at sea.
> Here is a piece of carved wood picked up at sea.

To be at sixes and sevens, is colloquially said of persons who cannot agree. The phrase implies, more or less, that the parties carry on strife and do not wish to agree. It is also used of **things** which are in a muddle or out of order.

> The servants have gone off, leaving everything at sixes and sevens.
> This political party, who are all at sixes and sevens among themselves, agree only upon one thing.

To be at the top of the ladder, or **at the top of the tree,** is to be as high as one can be in his profession or avocation, to be above all others in the same calling. And the phrases are used with a few other verbs.

> This professor was at the top of the tree in pure mathematics.
> This young clerk may yet mount to the top of the ladder in the Civil Service.

To be at one's wits' end, is to be greatly perplexed, not to know what to do in an emergency.

> I did not know what to do; I was therefore at my wits' end.
> This boy is at his wits' end for money to buy the books he needs.

To be at pains to do a thing, is to take trouble to accomplish it.

> I have been at pains to examine all these accounts.

104. To Be In with phrases

To be in the chair at a meeting, is to be chairman of the meeting.

To be in bad odour, to be not in good odour; also, **to get into bad odour.** These are equivalent and mean, to be or become unpopular by giving offence.

> A man who is known to be of bad habits cannot but be in bad odour with decent people.

To be in a bad way, is to be in a condition which is not prosperous or happy; or the phrase is used of a sick person who is not recovering. Sometimes it is, **to be not in a good way**.

> Affairs here have been in a bad way for some time past.
> These children have not been in a good way since their mother died.

To be in the doldrums, is colloquial for, to be in a state of listlessness or low spirits. A portion of the Atlantic Ocean north of the equator and near the coast of Africa is named by sailors, ' The Doldrums '. This region is often quite calm even when strong breezes blow in other parts of the ocean. Sailing vessels, when they got into this region, sometimes lay becalmed for a considerable time. The prepositional phrase is used with other verbs. **To be in the dumps,** has the same meaning.

> We had a day or two in the Doldrums, spending a week in crossing a belt three hundred miles in width; this was the most unpleasant part of the whole voyage.
> Pluck up courage and go about your work with spirit; you look as though you were in the doldrums.

To be in easy circumstances, is to be well off, to have a comfortable way of living.

To be in one's element, is to be in a position where everything around is congenial, to be in agreeable work or company. The opposite is, **to be out of one's element**.

> Would a craftsman be in his element in a counting house ?
> People raised suddenly from poverty to affluence are often quite out of their element in their new position.

To be in a fair way to do a thing, is to be likely to do it, to have the hope and means of accomplishing it.

> He is in a fair way to become a rich man.
> The doctor thinks his patient is in a fair way to recovery.

To be in high feather or **in fine feather,** is colloquial for, to be in high spirits, to be exultant.

To be in flower. Flowering shrubs or plants, when in the blossoming stage, are said to be in flower or in bloom.

> In England the rhododendron is in flower in early summer.

To be in a fix, is colloquial for, to be in perplexity; to be in a difficulty and unable to extricate oneself.

> His cart has stuck fast in the river, so that he is in a bad fix.

To be in keeping with, is to be suitable to, to harmonize with, to correspond to. The opposite is, **to be out of keeping with.**

> This simple kindly act is quite in keeping with his character.
> The bustle and stir of the town were out of keeping with the sadness of his spirit.

To be in one's line, is colloquial for, to pertain to one's business or calling.

> Mending nets is quite in the fisherman's line.
> You may make a speech or write a poem, but such things are not in my line.

To be in a person's good books, is to be in favour with him. **To be in one's bad books,** is to be out of favour with him.

To be in a pretty pass, means to be in a difficulty, with doubtful hope of escape. **To be in a mess,** has the same meaning. We also say, things have **come to a pretty pass.**

To be in sight, is said of a thing which can be seen. The opposite is, **to be out of sight.** To say, however, that a thing is out of sight, implies that it was recently visible.

> We watched them so long as they were in sight, i.e. we stood gazing after them as they went away and watched till they went out of sight.

To be in step. Two or more persons are said to be **in step** when, walking together, they all put down their right foot simultaneously and then the left foot simultaneously. **To be out of step,** is the opposite of this.

A person is said to **be in his teens** when he is between the age of twelve and twenty; all the numbers coming in between end in **-teen;** hence the phrase.

> In England, few girls are married while still in their teens.

To be in a temper, is to be in a bad temper. See next section.

To be in time, is to be as early as is necessary.

> ' Were you in time for the train ? ' ' Yes, just in time '—implying that there was no time to spare.
> He was not in time for the train, i.e. he was too late to catch the train.

To be in tune. A musical instrument is said to be in tune when it is in a fit condition for being played on. Metaphorically, a person is said to be in tune for a thing when he is in the humour to take to it readily; or generally, to be in a happy state of mind. The antithetic phrase is, **to be out of tune.**

> My harp is not in tune, or, is out of tune.
> Are you in good tune for study today ?
> I am out of tune with my surroundings.

To be in the van, is to be in the front rank, to take the lead.

> Shakespeare will always be in the van of English poets.

To be in the wind, is literally, to be in a position where the wind blows upon you, to be in a current of wind; also, metaphorically, the phrase is colloquially used of a rumour of news. ' What's in the wind today?' means, ' What news is there today?' The phrase would be used especially when an announcement was expected. The phrase in direct address would not be respectful to a superior and would be used only among equals. Also, **to be in the air**.

To be in the wrong box, is colloquial for, to be in uncongenial circumstances, not to be in a position to secure what one desires.

> He thinks to win this case in court; but when the trial is over, he will find that he is in the wrong box.

105. To Be On with phrases

To be on the alert, is to be watchful and ready for any emergency. The same meaning is expressed by, **to be on one's guard, to be on the watch, to be on the look-out**.

> The watchman was on the alert all night.

To be on edge, is to be excited (' keyed up '), or irritable.

To be on the wane. The moon is said to wax and wane; she is said to be on the wane when she has passed full moon and the bright disc is day by day diminishing. Hence the phrase means generally, to be gradually growing less, to be diminishing, to be decreasing.

> The power of the Turkish Empire had long been on the wane.

To be on the look out, or **to be on the watch**, is to be in the act of watching or looking for some particular object or for anything that may appear.

> He has been on the watch for you for three hours.
> On board ship there is always a man on the look out.
> This man is on the look out for a good investment for his money.

To be on one's high horse, is colloquial for, to stand on one's dignity, to assume a lofty tone or manner because one is offended.

To be out of temper, means to be out of good temper, to be in bad temper. Strangely enough, **to be in a temper**, also means, to be in bad temper.

> Do not go to such a serious business in a temper.
> I did not care to say much to him, as he was evidently out of temper.

To be on one's guard, is to be watchful, to be vigilant. The opposite is, **to be off one's guard**.

To be on the carpet, is to be under consideration, under discussion or debate. Also, and more usually, the phrase means, to be summoned to one's employer's room for reprimand.

What is on the carpet now ?, i.e. What topic is being considered ?
The unpunctual clerk was repeatedly on the carpet.

To be on velvet, is to be in a favourable position.

To be on good terms with oneself, is said of one who evidently has a high opinion of his own talents and attainments, one who is self-complacent.

Your schoolmaster is plainly on very good terms with himself.

To be on the eve of, or **verge of** doing a thing, is to be about to do it.

To be on one's last legs, is to be in a tottering or sinking condition, to be about to collapse.

' This poor man is on his last legs.' This, if said of a man's business, would mean that his business had failed and he was unable to hold out any longer. But if said of a man in respect of health, this phrase would mean that he is about to die.

In some sections of the Hindu community, the caste system is on its last legs.

To be on the right side of forty, is to be less than forty years old.

To be on the wrong side of fifty, or **on the shady side of fifty,** means, to be more than fifty years old.

106. To Be Out Of with phrases

To be out of the question, is said of a thing which is either quite impracticable, or not worth consideration.

His proposal for bringing water to the city is out of the question.

To be out of sorts, is colloquial for, to be slightly unwell.

I have been out of sorts today and not up to my work at all.

To be out of place, is to be inappropriate or inconsistent.

Advice about the training of children would be out of place in a book on chemistry.

To be out of one's mind, or **out of one's senses,** is to be insane.

This poor woman is quite out of her mind.
She cries and screams as if she were out of her senses.

A book is said **to be out of print,** or **not in print,** when the copies of it have all been sold and it is no longer to be had from the publishers.

The book you speak of is out of print; but if it should appear that there is a demand for it, no doubt a new edition will be issued.

107. To be neither here nor there, is used colloquially not of locality as the adverbs might suggest, but to mean, to be of no importance, to be inappropriate.

His opposition is neither here nor there; he has no influence.

At a meeting there are declared to be eighty-five votes for a motion and thirteen against. Someone calls out that the numbers are wrong; that there are fourteen against. But the chairman declares the motion carried, remarking that in the circumstances one vote more or less is neither here nor there.

To be full of oneself, is to be vain, to have an exaggerated estimate of one's own powers or position, to be puffed up, to be filled with vanity.

> He struts about so full of himself, that he is only a laughing-stock.
> He is as full of himself as if the whole town belonged to him.

To be lost on one. An effort made to help one is said **to be lost on one** when it is misused, or misunderstood.

To be under a wrong impression, is to have a misapprehension and to be influenced thereby. It is often implied that the wrong impression is unpleasant and burdensome. The verb **labour** is also used here.

> You are under a wrong impression in supposing that I wrote the anonymous letter which you saw in the newspaper.
> He is labouring under a wrong impression if he thinks that the doctor can cure him.

To be the order of the day. If the Government decide to curtail expenditure in its public works, for instance, then it could be said that retrenchment was the order of the day. Or if the authorities of a city go steadily forward making new streets, encouraging the citizens to build better houses, and generally improving their city, we may say in regard to it,

> Renovation and improvement are the order of the day.

The phrase does not necessarily imply the issuing of any particular ' order '; it rather refers to a course of action which is general and of continual or frequent occurrence.

He is his father's son, is said of one who in disposition or talents or looks is like his father. The colloquial phrase, **He is a chip of the old block**, expresses the same meaning.

Some of the phrases in this chapter joined with the verb *to be* may be attached in composition to other verbs; but the explanations given above will guide the student to their meaning in those cases.

CHAPTER XI

GROUPS OF IDIOMATIC EXPRESSIONS

108. There are certain sets of common idiomatic expressions belonging to particular subjects. We put together a few such sets of idioms.

Money; Debt; Business; Buying and Selling

Ready money or **cash** is money now available for use.

To **earn money**, is to work for it and receive it as wages.

To **make money**, is so to conduct business as to make profit.

To **save money**, is to spend less than one's income and so to lay up or reserve money.

To **raise money**, is to get together money for present use. To **raise the wind**, is a colloquial expression meaning, to obtain ready money by any sort of expedient.

To **throw away money**, is to spend it lavishly and foolishly.

He had his **money locked up** in bank shares, i.e. invested in bank shares and he could not readily sell them.

To be **in debt**; to be deep in debt; to be over head and ears in debt, are easily understood. To be **out of debt**, is said of one who has been in debt but is now free from it.

Bad debts, are debts regarded as irrecoverable, as not likely to be paid.

The man who **lends** money is the **creditor**. The man who **borrows** money is the **debtor**.

A creditor **lends** money **to** a debtor; a debtor **borrows** money **from a** creditor; one man **owes** money **to** another. Note the prepositions.

> ' I want a loan of thirty pounds.'
> ' What interest will you give?' ' Ten per cent. per annum.'
> ' Do you owe anything to anybody else?' ' Yes, I owe fifty pounds to a banker.'
> ' When will you pay me back the sum?' ' I hope to clear it off in six months,' i.e. to pay it all back in six months.

On 'Change, means, on the Exchange.

To be **in pocket** through a business transaction, is to have gained profit by it. To be **out of pocket**, is to have met with loss; also, to have spent all one's money.

Articles are said to be **dear** when they cost more than they are usually worth, and **cheap** when they cost less.

242

' A falling market ' is explained in Chapter IV (p. 59). ' A strong market ' means prices are rising.

When the price of articles gets lower, they are said to **come down**, or **fall** in price.

In England cloth is sold by the yard, butter by the pound, eggs by the dozen.

A trader **deals** in tea, tobacco, etc.

A man is said to **do business**, or to **transact business**, with another.

A man is said to **carry on business**, or carry on a trade; but to **follow a profession**.

When one's business is extraordinarily brisk, one is colloquially said to be doing **a roaring trade**.

' Does his writing **bring** him **in** anything? ' ' Yes, it brings him in (=produces as income) three hundred pounds a year.'

The sale of this field of grain should **bring in** (=yield) a large sum.

He gave ten pounds for a bullock, but I consider the animal well **worth the money**, i.e. good value for the price paid.

A man **of means**, a man **of wealth**, a man **of money**: these mean a rich man.

The **man** is **worth** two thousand pounds, means he has property worth two thousand pounds.

A man is **solvent** when he can pay all just monetary claims upon him. **Insolvent**, is the opposite.

A **bankrupt**, is a man declared by a court to be unable to pay his debts.

To **sell a person up**, is forcibly to sell his goods after legal process in order to pay his debts.

Of an article sold, you ask, What did it **sell for**? or What did it **fetch**? or What did it **bring in**?

Of an article bought you ask, What did it cost? or What did you pay for it? or What was the price of it?

An article is said to **sell well**, or to be well sold, when it fetches a good price.

What does he want for his cow? or, What is he asking for his cow?, i.e. What price has he put on the cow he is selling?

' What will you **take for** your saddle? ' ' I do not wish to part with it.' In these idiomatic expressions, the question means, ' What will you sell your saddle for? ' and the answer, ' I do not wish to sell it.'

The stationer's stock has all been disposed of, i.e. his stock of goods has all been sold.

You **buy** an article **in** the market, **in** a store, **at** a shop.

You **buy** things **from** a seller; he **sells** his articles **to** you.

You **buy up** goods which are **in short supply**.

A shopkeeper's goods are **on sale**, or for sale.

To **put up** articles **for sale**, or on sale, is to offer them for sale.

To **put up** a thing **for auction**, or **to auction**, is to offer it for sale by auction.

To **bring** a thing **to the hammer**, is to **sell** it **by auction**. The fall of the auctioneer's little hammer indicates that the article is sold.

> The creditors have a claim on everything; plate, books, and furniture will all go to (or *come under*) the hammer.

Men at an auction **bid for** the articles offered for sale. Two men often **bid against** each other and thus **put up** the price.

'What will this picture **go for** in the auction?', i.e. How much will it sell for in the auction?

'Did you buy anything at the auction?' 'No; I did not even **make a** single **bid**.'

The net proceeds of a sale, is what a sale brings in after all expenses of the sale are paid.

To **make a bargain**, or to **strike** a bargain, is to settle the terms of the bargain. Formerly an agreement or bargain was ratified by the parties 'striking' or shaking hands.

To **close a bargain**, is finally to agree to the terms of it.

To **drive a bargain**, is to settle with difficulty the terms of the bargain.

To drive a hard bargain, is to beat down the seller's price and induce him to accept what is offered.

A workman receives **wages**: a professional man gets a **salary** or **fees**.

A **salary** is a stipulated sum paid at periodic times, every month or every year, for services continuously rendered. In England salaries are commonly fixed by the year, though they may be paid quarterly or monthly.

To **buy for cash** or for **ready money**, is to pay down the price at the time of purchase.

To **buy on credit**, is to buy from a person, as for instance from a shopkeeper, intending to pay at a future time.

To **get** goods **on credit**, is to buy them on credit.

To **settle an account** *or* **pay a bill**, is to pay the amount of it in money.

Note the idiomatic expressions in the following.

I order goods from a shopkeeper, i.e. I let him know either orally or by letter or through someone else that I want such and such articles. He fills up the order and sends me the goods. He makes out his bill or invoice or account and sends it also to me. I send him back the bill and the amount of it in money, whereupon he receipts the bill and returns it to me. I file the receipted account, so that if, through the shopkeeper's mistake, a bill is ever presented for these goods again, I shall be able to produce the receipted account to show that they have been paid for.

To **pay one's way**, is to pay for things as one goes on, to live without getting into debt.

To **pay** a debt **by instalments**, is to pay a portion of it at one time and a further portion at another, and so on till the whole amount is paid. When all is paid, the amount is said to be paid **in full**, or the **debt** is said to be **discharged**.

' **Rice** is steadily **advancing**,' i.e. rice is advancing in price.

' **Sugar a shade firmer**, or just a **trifle easier**,' i.e. sugar is slightly higher or lower in price.

' **Consols firm** in the morning **at par**, but **left off easier** in the afternoon.' ' Consols ' is a contraction for the ' Consolidated Funds ', the British Government funds. The nominal or par value of these is £100 each. Consols are said to be at par when they sell at their nominal value of £100. The other part of the expression means, that when the market closed they were a little lower in price.

Railway **shares** are **looking up**, that is, they tend to become dearer, they tend to rise in money value.

To **dishonour a cheque**. If A pays B by giving him a cheque drawn on a banker, the banker may refuse to pay the amount if he has not enough of A's money in his hand. When he thus refuses to pay, he is said to dishonour A's cheque. Clearly it is a disgrace to have cheques dishonoured.

To **forge a cheque**, is deliberately to enter something wrong in the cheque, either altering the figures to enlarge the amount, or forging the name of the person who is represented as issuing it.

Buyer and seller are said to **come to terms**, when they mutually agree on the price to be paid.

You **deposit** money, **in a bank**; you **invest** money in shares or stocks; you **draw** money out of a bank; a miser **hoards** up money; a spendthrift **squanders** money.

Commission is a charge for doing business for another person. Also a small sum charged for a postal or money order sent by post.

Paper money, includes notes and cheques.

109. LETTERS: THE POST OFFICE

You **write** a letter **to** a person, not **upon** a person.

You **address** a letter, i.e. you put your letter into an envelope (pronounced on-velope) and write on the envelope the name and address of the person to whom you are sending the letter.

You **stamp** the letter, i.e. you affix the postage stamp.

You **post** the letter, that is, you put it into the post pillar box, or post office.

You **send** a letter **by post**, i.e. not by hand (or otherwise).

A letter **miscarries**, i.e. it somehow goes to the wrong address or is lost.

The postman **delivers letters**, i.e. he goes round the town and leaves the letters at the houses of the persons to whom they are addressed. He also **collects** letters from the **pillar boxes** or **post-boxes** in the district.

The **clerk** in the post office **sorts letters**, that is, he arranges and classifies them according to their destination.

After the letters are sorted, they are **put into** the **mail bag** and **dispatched**.

The man who is at the head of the post office in any town, is called **the Postmaster**.

The whole Postal Department is under the direction of the **Postmaster General**.

' Our **letters crossed**,' i.e. I wrote to you and you wrote to me, but my letter had not reached you when you wrote, nor had yours reached me when I wrote. The two letters, as it were, met and passed each other in the post.

The **Dead Letter Office** is explained in Chapter III (p. 36).

An **autograph** or **holograph letter**, is a letter written by the hand of the person whose name is at the foot of it. The term is applied only where persons commonly use a typewriter for their letters.

> The King sent an autograph letter of condolence to the widow of the deceased General.

Cipher writing, or **writing in cipher**, is writing in such an arrangement of letters or words previously agreed upon as only the writer and the receiver can understand.

110. Warfare

Many of the following expressions may be out of date so far as their application to actual warfare is concerned. But they continue to be widely used in a figurative way. Thus, ' he was up in arms at once ', means, ' he immediately took offence ', and ' to beat a retreat ', means, to give up any sort of undertaking.

A nation **declares war** against another. A nation, after trying negotiations with another, fails to obtain what it wants and **appeals to arms**, or appeals to the sword, i.e. **declares war**.

Two nations **go to war, wage war**.

A **war** is a contest carried on for some time between two states or nations. A **battle** is a combat, an encounter, an engagement between two opposing armies. In a war there may be many battles. A battle is **fought**; a war is **waged, carried on**.

A **civil war** is a war carried on between two opposing sections of the same nation.

An **offensive** or **aggressive** war is a war begun by attacking another nation. A **defensive war** is a war carried on by a nation to repel an invasion.

A **pitched battle** is one in which the hostile forces have taken up fixed positions. Figuratively, it means a determined contest of any kind in which there is bitter personal antagonism.

A **decisive battle** or engagement, is a battle which is so successful for one of the parties that it leads to peace being made because the worsted party has come to see how hopeless the struggle is.

Armies are said to be drawn up in **battle array**: to **join** battle; to **engage in** battle. One army **offers battle**, or **gives battle** to the other.

To **open a campaign**, is to begin the operations of a war.

Men **serve** in a campaign.

To **open fire**, is to begin the firing.

Which nation was the first to **draw the sword**, or to **take up arms**?, i.e. which first began war?

An army **takes the field**, i.e. begins a war.

The **battle field**, or the **field of battle**, is the place where the battle is fought. The **field is lost** or **won**, means, the battle is lost or won.

One army **gains**, or **wins**, or **obtains the victory**; the other **suffers** or **sustains defeat**. A victorious army **puts** the opposing force **to flight**.

The rebels are **up in arms**, that is, have taken the field.

Let the rebels **lay down** their arms, i.e. let them cease fighting.

A garrison **holds** a fortress.

A town **holds out** against a beleaguering army.

An army **lays siege** to a town.

To **raise a siege**. When an army, besieging a place, withdraws from the siege, it is said to raise the siege.

To **storm a fortress**, is to attack it fiercely and capture it.

To **strike one's flag**, or colours, is to surrender.

To **beat a retreat**, is to retire hastily before a superior force.

To **give quarter**, is to extend mercy to the conquered.

'Lambs at the mercy of wolves must expect no quarter.'

To **quarter soldiers** on the inhabitants of a town, is to make those inhabitants give them food and lodging.

The phrases, ' the **sinews of war** ' and ' **council of war** ', are explained in Chapter IV (pp. 82, 78).

To **engage the enemy**, is to bring the enemy into conflict.

A **capitulation**, is a surrender on conditions.

A **white flag**, is the sign of truce.

An object is said to be **within range**, when it is within the distance to which a bullet or shell will carry.

111. IDIOMATIC EXPRESSIONS ABOUT CLOCKS AND WATCHES

We speak of the **works** of a clock or watch, not the machinery, or the wheels. You **wind** or **wind up** a watch or clock. A clock or watch **runs down** and will not go again till it is wound up.

Your clock **loses** or **gains time**, i.e. it is slow or fast.

Clocks and watches **keep time** and **show time**.

Is your watch a good time-keeper?, i.e. does it go regularly without getting fast or slow?

His clock is ten minutes **fast**, i.e. before the proper time.

The clock has just struck eight. The clock is **on the stroke** of twelve, i.e. it is about to strike twelve.

> ' What's the time? ' ' It is five minutes to ten,' or ' five to ten ' or ' five past ten '.

112. IDIOMATIC EXPRESSIONS OF TIME

(1) Expressions of **Time** having no Preposition.

> He has ten pounds a month.
> He means to go home next week (or, next Saturday week).
> An hour after you left the rain came on.
> It rained all night.
> His brother was married yesterday morning.
> Aeneas left Troy the very night it was taken.
> She lived with them two years.
> I was sent for the other morning, i.e. one morning.

(2) Expressions of **Time** requiring a Preposition.

> The heat was intense at two o'clock.
> He went off on Friday.
> I expect an answer to my application by the end of June.
> We were in church a little before the clock struck eight.
> We shall arrive in less than half an hour.

For *in*, with expressions of time, and for the distinction between *in the same time* and *at the same time*, see p. 130.

(3) Expressions of **Time** with **since, before, ago**.

Never place *since* before an expression denoting duration or a period of time. But *since* is correctly put before an expression denoting a point of time.

> ' He has been ill since a week,' is therefore incorrect; it should be, ' He has been ill for a week.'
> ' He has been ill since Tuesday,' is correct.

Students often use *before* when they should use *ago*.

> ' He went to Calcutta before two months,' is wrong; it should be,
> ' He went to Calcutta two months ago.'

Before also has the meaning of ' formerly '

> The prince's health is no worse than before.

(4) Miscellaneous Expressions of **Time**.

A **little time ago**, or a little while ago, means a short time ago.

A **long time ago**, a **long while ago**, are also commonly used.

Long, long ago, is a very long time past.

In course of time, in process of time, i.e. as time wears on.

In an instant, in a **moment**, in a **second**, i.e. in a very brief space of time.

In an instant, means at once, without a moment's delay.

On **the spur of the moment**, means at once, without a moment's reflection, impulsively.

In **the nick of time**, means, just before it would have been too late.

> A ship . . . picked him up in the nick of time.

To be in time, or **to be in good time**, is to be early enough; **in time**, also means eventually.

> The farmer tries to get in his crops in good time.
> He came in time to see the fireworks.
> The cheat is in time found out, i.e. eventually found out.

In **times gone by**, i.e. in times indefinitely past, usually a long time ago.

He applied for a job **time after time**, i.e. repeatedly.

I have met him in the street **many a time**, i.e. frequently, often.

At times, means sometimes. **At all times** means always.

Government, **at stated times**, issues reports about education, i.e. at regular intervals, or at fixed periods.

Complaints have been made against this man **from time to time**, i.e. occasionally, often.

By and by another man appeared, i.e. after a little while the second man arrived.

Ever and anon the tolling of a bell was heard, i.e. time after time, repeatedly, though infrequently.

He gets into difficulties **every now and then**, i.e. occasionally.

The **dead of night**, is midnight.

At the eleventh hour, is at the latest available time. This phrase is derived from the parable of the labourers in the vineyard given in the Bible (see *Matthew* xx. 1-16).

The arrangements are **on the eve of** completion, i.e. are almost completed.

To **spend time**, to **pass the time**, is to use it up.

> This man has spent three hours in consulting a time-table.
> She has gone to pass the morning with her friend.

A man **loses time**, =lets time pass without turning it to account.

To **waste time**, to spend time uselessly.

To **kill time**, is to busy oneself in some useless thing, but so as to make the time pass without tediousness.

Spare time, is time to spare, leisure. **Spare** here is an adjective.

He has **plenty of time** on his hands, i.e. he has plenty of leisure.

I had **time enough** to do my work in, i.e. I had enough time to do it.

Time hangs heavy on his hands, i.e. he finds it difficult to use his time.

Such phrases as ' **For about a year** ', ' in about a year ', ' for about a month ', are intelligible, but the form of the idiom has to be observed.

> He has been in Ceylon for about two years, i.e. during two years, or perhaps a little more or less. The same meaning is tersely and correctly expressed thus: He has been in Ceylon two years or so.

Some ten days after the ceremony, i.e. about ten days.

To **beat time**, is to mark or note regular time in music by the motion of the hand or foot. The feet of the dancers **beat** or **keep time** to the music.

To **sing in time**, is to give each note in the music its proper duration of time.

He is working **against time**, i.e. he is working in the hope of finishing his work within a given limit of time: he and time are matched against each other and he means to see which will finish first.

This newspaper is **out of date**, i.e. the date of its publication is past, so that its news is now stale.

Time out of mind, or **time immemorial**, is time so long past that memory does not reach back to it.

> English youth have been so educated time out of mind.—*Thackeray*

He tries to **make the best of his time**, i.e. tries to use it to the best advantage. Also, to make the most of his time.

He will be here **in no time**, i.e. in a very short space of time. But the phrase ' in no time ' in this sense is colloquial.

To **have an easy time of it**, is to live in quiet and comfort, to lead a life of ease and to be without worry or hard work. ' It ' in this case is impersonal and redundant.

> So long as Mr Brown was the manager the clerks had an easy time of it, but there was a change when his successor came in.

To **take one's time**, is not to be in a hurry.

To **bide one's time**, is to wait patiently for a favourable opportunity.

> The deer are coming and the tiger is in the thicket biding his time.

To **serve one's time**, is to fulfil an engagement to serve an employer during a stipulated period. An apprentice serves his time.

' My **time is up** and I must go,' means, my time for waiting is ended and I must now go away.

Take your time, means, don't be in a hurry.

It is time we were there, =we ought to have been there by this time.

To **take time by the forelock**. The Greeks represented Time as an old bald-headed man with a single lock of hair on his head— a forelock.

> Time is painted with a lock before and bald behind, signifying thereby that we must take time by the forelock; for when it is once past there is no recalling it.—*Swift*

His time is come, means, the time of his death is come.

To **number one's days**, is to have regard to the shortness of human life; to consider one's latter end. The phrase is drawn from Moses's prayer to God: 'Teach us to number our days, that we may apply our hearts unto wisdom ' (*Psalm* xc. 12).

His days are numbered, means, he is soon to die, his end is near.

113. Expressions about Sight

An object is said to be *in sight* when you can see it. An object *not in sight*, is one not now visible. *Out of sight* is applied to a thing which lately was, but is not now, in sight.

The ship is gone out of sight; this implies that it lately was in sight.

You are said to **lose sight of** an object when it passes out of sight or beyond your field of vision. When a thing moves and you move too, watching it so as not to let it out of sight, you are said to **keep it in sight**. The hunter kept the deer in sight as long as he could. Therefore, to lose sight of, and keep in sight, are expressions of opposite meaning.

The proverbial phrase, ' **out of sight, out of mind** ', is applied when a thing is forgotten because not seen.

A frigate **hove in sight**, i.e. came into view.

I **caught sight** of boys who were trying to hide behind a hedge.

I **cannot bear the sight of it**, means, I cannot endure to look at it.

Your **field of view**, is the expanse over which your eye can sweep, usually limited to what can be seen through a window or a telescope.

The sights of a great city, are the objects in it worth seeing.

Sight-seeing, is going about to see noteworthy objects.

114. About the Sea Shore

To **go to the sea shore**, is to go down to the edge or shore of the sea. When one goes to live for a time for change of air by the shore of the sea, we say, he has gone to the **seaside**, and not **sea shore**.

To **go to sea**, is to take to a seafaring life.

To **be at sea**, is explained on p. 236.

The tide **ebbs** and **flows**.

Spring tides, are the high tides at full moon and new moon.   **Neap tides**, are the low tides midway between new moon and full moon.

An **able-bodied seaman**, an ' A.B.', is a skilled sailor.

An **ordinary seaman**, an ' O.S.', is an unskilled sailor.

115. EXPRESSIONS ABOUT **Ships**

To **live in a gale**, said of ships.

> No boat could live in such a storm, i.e. no boat could remain afloat through such a storm.   Live here means survive.

To **weather a storm**.   A ship is said to weather a storm or to **ride out** a storm, when it withstands successfully the brunt of the storm, when it comes safe out of the stress of weather which the storm occasioned.

To **ship a sea**, is to take in a quantity of water from a large wave breaking over the ship's side.

To **put to sea**, is to leave port and start on a voyage.

A ship is said to **founder**, when it goes down at sea and is lost.   It is said to **founder with all hands**, when in sinking it carries down all the people on board.   Those drowned at sea are sometimes said to sink into **a watery grave**, or sink down to a watery grave.

To **set sail**, is to spread out the sails.   And inasmuch as the result of spreading sails is the onward motion of the ship, to set sail has come to mean, to start on a voyage.

> The gallant navy set sail with Ulysses from Troy.

To **make sail**, is to increase the quantity of sail already spread.

To **strike sail**, is to lower sail or take in sail.

A ship is said to be **bound for** a place, when that place is the port to which she is sailing.

To **sail before the wind**, is to go in the direction towards which the wind is blowing.

To **sail close to the wind**, is to sail against the wind as much as possible.   It means metaphorically to come very near to breaking a law or principle.

A ship is said to be **water-logged** when her hold has got filled with water.   In this condition she does not **obey her helm** but is at the mercy of the waves.

To **take to the boats**, is to leave a sinking ship and get into the small boats which are carried on every large ship.

A **ship's log**, is the daily record kept on board recording the ship's progress in her voyage.

To **put the ship about**, is to change the course of the ship.

A ship **puts into** a port or **touches at** a port or place, i.e. she calls at that port or place for some reason and afterwards proceeds on her voyage. Note that we use either *she* or *it* of a ship.

Ships put into port **to fuel**, i.e. to get a fresh supply of fuel.

To **cast anchor**; to **weigh anchor**. To cast anchor, is to throw one or more anchors over the ship's side, and thereby moor the ship. To weigh anchor, is to raise or draw up the anchor so as to let the ship proceed.

To **drop anchor** and to **come to anchor** have the same meaning as to cast anchor. Ships **ride at anchor**.

A ship is said to **make the harbour** when she reaches the harbour. This is usually said when it has required great effort and skill to bring the ship to the harbour.

To **give a broadside**, is a naval phrase meaning, to discharge at once at an enemy all the guns along one side of a ship. Hence the phrase has come to mean, to make a vigorous attack upon an opponent, to assail with a volley of arguments.

I bore with his insolence as long as I could, and I then gave him such a broadside as made him hang down his head for shame.

To **be in the same boat with** a person, is to be equally exposed with him to risk or danger or misfortune.

To **sail under false colours**. Every ship at sea is expected to carry the flag or ' colours ' of the nationality to which it belongs. If a ship's captain, in order to deceive others, displays the flag of a nation other than his own, he is said to sail under false colours. Hence the phrase has come generally to mean, to pretend to be what one is not, to try to deceive.

The **flag half-mast high**, is the sign that someone on board is dead.

' **What flag is she flying ?** ' would be asked regarding a ship seen in the offing, of unknown nationality.

Trade follows the flag. The phrase means that wherever an army or navy gains conquests, commerce will soon follow into that region.

To **lose one's reckoning**, is to miscalculate. The master of a vessel at sea is said to lose his reckoning when from any cause—as, his nautical instruments getting out of order—he mistakes his latitude or longitude and therefore steers wrong. So when in ordinary affairs a man makes mistakes so that he cannot reach his aim, he is said to lose his reckoning.

A **man-o'-war** is a ship of war.

When a ship crosses the equator, it is said to **cross the line**.

When a ship sails round a cape, it is said to **double the cape**.

A **man before the mast**, is an ordinary sailor. The officers used to be behind the mainmast.

116. About Fire; Lights; Candles

You **light** or **kindle a fire**; you **light a lamp** or **a candle**. It is wrong to say, ' Fire a lamp ', or ' Fire a candle '. You **fire a gun** or a pistol or a cannon, i.e. you make it go off.

You **put out a fire, a light, a lamp,** or **a candle,** i.e. you extinguish it in any way. You **blow out** a candle, i.e. you put it out with a puff of your breath. The wind blows out a lamp or a candle.

When a lamp or fire or candle is put out in any way, or when of itself it ceases to burn, we say, it **goes out**, or it is gone out, or it has gone out.

The **lamp is out**: the fire is out: the candle is out, imply that the lamp, the fire, or the candle was burning, but has now ceased burning.

A fire, a lamp, a candle, a torch is lighted, burns, blazes, flickers, goes out, is put out, burns out, dies out.

Electric **lights** are switched **on** or **off**.

To **fan the flame**. To fan the flame, has the effect of increasing it. The phrase is commonly used of attempts to increase an evil influence, as sedition, agitation, passion, excitement, etc. To **add fuel to the flame**, is to add fresh provocation, to intensify strong feeling or passion.

> Openly he professed loyalty, but in secret he was fanning the flame of sedition.
> Abortive efforts to crush the rebellion only added fuel to the flame.

To **burn the candle at both ends**, is used when a person steadily over-taxes his energies so as to injure his health. It is implied that energy might have been husbanded and applied to better uses.

The **game is not worth the candle**, means, that the advantage or enjoyment to be gained is not worth the trouble spent in gaining it.

He is **not fit to hold a candle to you**. Before gas was invented, people were lighted through the streets of London by boys carrying torches or ' links ', hence called link-boys. Hence the phrase means, ' He is quite inferior to you.'

117. About Health

A man is said to be **well**, to be **ill**, to be **in good health**, in **rude** health, in **robust** health, in **poor** health, in **ill** health, in **delicate** health.

A man falls ill, gets ill, is taken ill, becomes ill, gets better, is well, is quite well, is convalescent, recovers, is himself again. (See p. 229.)

To be **on the sick list**, is to be laid aside by illness. The phrase would primarily be applied to soldiers unable from illness to do any duty.

He **shows a change for the better**, means, that his illness has taken a turn, and he is now improving.

He has had a bad **attack of fever** and is still very weak.

He has had sunstroke, or an attack of sunstroke.

He is **far gone in consumption**, and there is **no hope for him**, i.e. no one expects him to recover.

He is not **a strong man**. This may mean one or other of two things according to the connexion in which it stands.

(1) He is not a man of robust general health; he is rather a delicate man.
(2) He is not a strong-minded man who could be depended on to carry through vigorous measures in an emergency.

His spine is so injured that his **life is despaired of**.

He was **seized** with cholera and died in a few hours.

The doctor says that my sister's left **lung is affected**.

My brother **died of heart disease**.

118. EXPRESSIONS ABOUT Death

To **pass away**, means to die.

To **go the way of all flesh**, also means, to die, though the expression is old-fashioned.

To **breathe one's last**, is another euphemism for to die.

To be **gathered to one's fathers**. This is a Biblical phrase and means that the immortal spirit of the one who has died has gone to the world of spirits to be with the spirits of his departed fathers. Hence one who has died is **the departed**.

To **go to one's account**, is to die, suggesting the idea of accounting to God for the things done in this present life.

To **join the great majority**, is to die. The idea is, that far more persons of the human race have died and gone from this world than are living on the earth now. Hence, when one dies, it is sometimes rhetorically said that he has joined the great majority.

To **come into the world**, means to be born. To **depart this life**, is to die. Other phrases with like meaning are, **his hour has come, his course is run.**

To **die a natural death**; to **die a violent death**; to **come to an untimely end**. If one dies from ordinary natural causes, he is said to die **a natural death**. If one dies by violence, as by murder, he is said to die or meet **a violent death**. If one meets death early in life, as by drowning or starvation, he is said **to come to an untimely end**.

119. There is considerable variation in the forming of national names. Note the following.

Country	Individuals	
	Singular	Plural
Afghanistan	An Afghan	Afghans
Arabia	An Arab	Arabs
Austria	An Austrian	Austrians
Belgium	A Belgian	Belgians
Burma	A Burmese or Burman	Burmese
Canada	A Canadian	Canadians
Ceylon	A Sinhalese	Sinhalese
China	A Chinese or Chinaman	Chinese or Chinamen
Denmark	A Dane	Danes
Egypt	An Egyptian	Egyptians
England	An Englishman	Englishmen
Finland	A Finn	Finns
France	A Frenchman	Frenchmen
Germany	A German	Germans
Greece	A Greek	Greeks
Holland	A Dutchman	Dutchmen
Hungary	A Hungarian	Hungarians
India	An Indian	Indians
Ireland	An Irishman	Irishmen
Italy	An Italian	Italians
Japan	A Japanese	Japanese
Lapland	A Laplander or Lapp	Laplanders or Lapps
Malta	A Maltese	Maltese
Morocco	A Moor	Moors
Norway	A Norwegian	Norwegians
Pakistan	A Pakistani	Pakistanis
Persia	A Persian	Persians
Poland	A Pole	Poles
Portugal	A Portuguese	Portuguese
Russia	A Russian	Russians
Scotland	A Scotsman or Scot	Scotsmen
Siam	A Siamese	Siamese
Spain	A Spaniard	Spaniards
Sweden	A Swede	Swedes
Switzerland	A Swiss	Swiss
Tartary	A Tartar	Tartars
Turkey	A Turk	Turks
Wales	A Welshman	Welshmen

We have also a Christian, a Jew, a Mohammedan or Muslim, a Parsi, a Hindu, a Buddhist. Note that, as a *nation*, one speaks of *The English*; *The Scots*, *Scottish*, or *Scotch*; *The Welsh*. *A Briton* is a native of Great Britain. *The British* are the inhabitants of Great Britain. There is no single word to denote citizens of the United States, who are often, however, loosely described as *Americans*, and so differentiated from, e.g. *Canadians* or *Brazilians*.

CHAPTER XII

GROUPS OF IDIOMS WITH CERTAIN VERBS: *BREAK, CARRY, CAST, CATCH, COME, CUT, DO, FALL, GET, GIVE, GO, HAVE, HOLD, KEEP, LAY, MAKE, PLAY, PUT, SET STAND, TAKE, THROW, TURN*

120. BREAK

To **break cover**, is come forth from a lurking place as hunted game would do.

To **break a fall**, is to lessen the force of a fall either by active inter-ference or by happening to be in the way of the person or thing falling.

To **break ground**, is to plough or dig untilled ground; and meta-phorically, to commence an undertaking.

To **break the heart**, is to afflict grievously, to cause to die of grief.

To **break the ice**. In a company, conversation flags; there comes an awkward silence; the person who then introduces a topic which soon becomes matter of general conversation is said to break the ice. The phrase also means, to get over the feeling of restraint which one may have in the presence of a new acquain-tance.

To **break the news to a person**, is to communicate unexpected news to him in such a way as to diminish the shock.

> He did not care to break the matter personally to her husband.—*Thackeray*
> He broke the news to his wife as gently as he could that he had lost all his fortune through the failure of the bank.

To **break another person's spirit**, is to tame him into spiritless meekness.

To **break the back of a job**, is to have disposed of the main part of the task.

Broken health is impaired health.

A **broken constitution** is an impaired constitution.

Broken sleep is interrupted sleep.

We have also the expressions, **morning breaks**; **daybreak**—corresponding to **nightfall**; a **storm breaks**; a **break** (=rift, opening) in the clouds.

121. CARRY

To **carry one's point**, or to **gain one's point**, is to attain the goal aimed at; to overcome obstacles placed in one's way; to defeat opposition in argument or debate.　Both idioms imply strenuous opposition.

All reformers find it most difficult to get people to give up a long-standing custom.　But they carry their point in the end.

To **carry everything**, or **all, before one**; to **carry the day**.　These mean, to overcome all opposition, to win the victory, to succeed in the thing attempted.

How is it that of these two men engaged in the same business, one can scarcely get a living, while the other carries all before him ?

In the struggle with superstition, education if linked with true religion should carry the day.

To **carry away captive**; to **lead captive**, mean, to take away into captivity, as prisoners of war.

In ancient times, many prisoners of war were led captive and compelled to live as slaves in the land of their conquerors.

To **carry** a thing **too far**, is to continue it beyond what is prudent or safe.　How far will **this gun carry**?, means, how far will a bullet shot from this gun go?

To **carry matters with a high hand**, is to domineer, to take strong measures, to exercise authority with crushing force.

The Principal of the College carried matters with a high hand and expelled two students for what after all was but a trivial offence.

There were murmurs of disloyalty in Spain, but the Government carried matters with a high hand and very speedily crushed the incipient rebellion.

To **carry something** (e.g. an embarrassing situation) **off**, is to make a brave or passable show of it.

122.　CAST

To **cast an eye upon**, is to glance at.

To **cast**, or **throw, light upon**, is to illuminate.

At the inquest, after a long investigation, a woman came forward and stated some facts which cast fresh light on the way in which the man came to his death.

The hieroglyphic monuments of Egypt throw much light on the ancient history of that country.

To **cast into the shade**; **put into the shade**; **throw into the shade**. These are equivalent, and mean, to render less noticeable or less attractive or less remarkable.

A newspaper gives a thrilling account of outrage; next day's paper tells of more horrible things still; the latter account casts the other into the shade.

The two ladies threw my girls quite into the shade.—*Goldsmith*

To **cast a slur upon one**, is by word or act to cast a slight reproach upon him.　Many a man brings a slur on his own good name by stooping to some mean or disreputable act.

To **cast in one's teeth**, is to retort reproachfully, to make an insulting statement to one openly. There is implied a state of altercation between the parties. The statement made may be true or false; it is said in passion; and is intended to sting the person to whom it is spoken.

> He cast it in his friend's teeth that he had seen him drunk, whereas on inquiry it turned out that he had mistaken another man for his friend.

123. CATCH

To **catch fire**, is to become alight or ignited.

To **catch one's eye**, is to arrest one's notice by being seen, to fall under one's notice. Or, if I keep looking at a man till his look meets mine, I am said to catch his eye.

> I did not catch his eye, else I should have bowed to him.
> As I looked through the book, several printer's errors caught my eye.

To **catch a train**, is to arrive at the railway station in time to go by a train, and to go by it; so, to **miss a train**, is to arrive at the station too late to go by that train. So, to catch a steamer; to miss a steamer.

> I am sorry you have missed the train, for you cannot now catch this week's mail steamer.

This verb has a similar meaning in,

> The sail is so set as to catch the wind.

To **catch it**, is colloquial for, to get a scolding or a beating or some other unpleasant treatment. It is here indefinite.

To **catch at a straw.** The proverb is ' A drowning man will catch at a straw '. When a man in difficulties, finding nothing substantial to lay hold of, grasps at something trifling and unsubstantial, he is said to catch at a straw.

To **catch a Tartar**, is to seize or encounter an adversary who proves too strong for his assailant. A Tartar is a native of Tartary. The story goes that in battle with the Turks an Irish soldier shouted to his comrade, ' I've caught a Tartar.' ' Then bring him with you,' i.e. as a prisoner. ' But he won't come.' ' Then come along yourself.' ' But he won't let me.' The fact was that the Tartar had caught the Irishman. Hence the general meaning of the phrase as given above.

124. COME

To **come to close quarters**, is to tackle an antagonist closely. The phrase is used metaphorically also.

To **come to light**, is to become known.

To **come to pass**, is to happen, to occur.

To come to grief, is said of a person who meets with disaster, or of an article unexpectedly injured, or of a scheme that proves abortive.

To come to hand, is idiomatic for, to reach one.

> His letter came to hand yesterday=it reached me yesterday.

' Come, come ! ' has the sense of, ' do you really mean that? '

> ' Come, come ! that's not the whole truth; tell us all you know about the matter.'

To come to be, means, generally, to become.

> He has come to be highly thought of, i.e. he has so risen in people's esteem that they now think highly of him.
> His word has come to be considered of great weight.

To come amiss. This means, to come in an inconvenient or unsuitable time or way. When it is said of a man that **nothing comes amiss to him,** the meaning is, that he is a very capable man, able to do any work or meet any difficulty that presents itself to him.

> A legacy seldom comes amiss to anybody.

To come home to a person, is to appeal successfully to his reason or his self-interest; to touch his feelings closely.

To come of age, is to become adult, to have become 21 years of age.

To come to a head, is to mature, to be ready to burst forth—said, e.g. of a conspiracy.

> Get the boil lanced when it comes to a head.
> He allows his spiteful feelings to come to a head.

To come to a standstill; bring to a standstill; be at a standstill. A standstill is a stop or a standing at rest.

> When the steam is shut off, the machinery soon comes to a standstill.
> Trade in Turkey has been brought to a standstill owing to the uncertainty existing in regard to tariffs.

To bring a man to his (proper) level. This expression means, to bring a vain man down from his undue estimate of himself, and teach him to esteem himself at his true value.

> At first the stranger took on airs and pretended to be a man of great importance; but those who knew him years ago set themselves to take him down, so that in a short time he had come to his proper level.

To come to know; to come to one's knowledge. I come to know a thing, or a thing comes to my knowledge, i.e. the thing becomes known or is made known to me. It is the form of these idioms that needs to be noted. Neither expression implies anything as to the source of the knowledge. **I have been informed,** i.e. by some person. But I **have come to know,** i.e. through some person, or by letter, or through a newspaper, or by my own observation, or by any other means.

To **come to no good**; **come to a bad end.** It is said of an idle and thoughtless young fellow, ' That youth will come to no good.'

To **come out of a business with clean hands**, is sometimes said of a man who comes out perfectly innocent while others have done misdeeds. The phrase ' clean hands ' is in this phrase synonymous with uprightness, innocence.

To **come, or fall, under one's notice** or **observation.**

> A worse case of leprosy never fell under my notice.
> If such conduct as you describe comes under my notice, it shall receive a severe reprimand.

To **come short of**, or **fall short of**, is to be less than is requisite or expected. When great deficiency is meant, the word ' far ' is introduced into the phrase. And **short of,** which means ' less than ', is sometimes used with other expressions.

> Men have tried gold mining in India, but the results have come far short of, or fallen far short of, their expectations.

To **come off with flying colours**, is to emerge from a conflict with brilliant success. The idea involved is this: A regiment goes into battle with its banner or colours displayed; it engages in the fight and emerges with banner unscathed in the conflict, with colours fluttering in the breeze.

> At the recent examinations, Peter came off with flying colours.
> The claimant was beaten when his case was first tried, but he appealed to a higher court and now he has come off with flying colours.

To **come off second best**; to **get the worst of it.** These are similar in meaning. They mean, to be defeated in a contest, as in an argument, or in a legal action, or in public competition for a post to which only one person would be appointed. **It** in the second phrase is indefinite.

125. CUT

To **cut short**, is to shorten or abridge what is likely to lengthen out. A man is said to **cut short** his speech when he ceases speaking sooner than he might have been expected to. We say of a person that his life was **cut short**, meaning that he died prematurely. (Note the special meaning of **cut**, ignore.)

To **cut, or sting, to the quick.** The **quick** is the sensitive flesh, that which is susceptible of keen feeling. The phrase means, to cause acute pain.

> Your reproaches cut him to the quick.
> A good man is often stung to the quick by baseless imputations and slanders; the more upright he is the more keenly will he feel the pain.

To cut off in its prime, is to destroy a fair thing when in its prime.

> Cholera cut him off in his prime.

To cut the Gordian knot.

> ' *Gordian knot,* a knot tied by Gordius, a king of Phrygia, in the thong which connected the pole of his chariot to the yoke, and which was so very intricate that there was no finding where it began or ended. An oracle declared that he who should untie this knot should be master of Asia. Alexander the Great, fearing that his inability to untie it would prove an ill augury, cut it asunder with his sword. Hence a *Gordian knot* is an inextricable difficulty; and to *cut the Gordian knot* is to remove a difficulty by bold or unusual measures.' (Webster's Dictionary.)

And the phrase is sometimes used when an unexpected turn of affairs opens a way out of a serious difficulty.

> The eldest son maintained that all his father's property belonged to him; the other sons insisted that they should have equal shares with him. This led to strife, which was likely to prove endless till the eldest son's death cut the Gordian knot, for he died intestate and left neither wife nor children behind him.

To cut a figure; to cut a dash. To cut a figure, is to perform a conspicuous part, to attract attention either in wonder or admiration. **To cut a dash,** is colloquial for, to make a flourish, to make a vain show. Both these expressions, especially the latter, are slightly contemptuous and rather old-fashioned.

To cut and run, is to be off with all possible speed. The phrase was applied first to cutting a ship's cable and the ship sailing off immediately from her moorings.

126. Do

We have, in Chapter III, dealt with *Do* as an auxiliary verb, and as a substitutive verb, and now we take some idiomatic meanings of *Do* as a principal verb.

1. It means, to perform, to accomplish, to execute a work.

> Do your job.
> I cannot do more than indicate the line of thought which he pursued.
> Will you kindly show me how to do (=solve) this problem ?
> What shall be done to the man whom the king delights to honour ?—*Bible*
> Macaulay says of William III that no sovereign did so much to secure and extend the power of the House of Commons.

2. **Do** also means, to finish, to complete.

> Will the carpenters have done by twelve o'clock ?

The past participle **done** is often used in this sense of completeness; so that **to be done** is often equivalent to, to be used up, to be exhausted. For example, were a tailor to say that his thread was **done,** we should understand him to mean that his supply of thread was used up and was exhausted. So, **to have done,** is to have finished. **I have done writing.**

To **have done with**, is to have completed, to have no further concern with.

> I have now done with this disagreeable business.

3.   **Do** sometimes means, to cause, to bring about.

> Come with us and we will do you good.—*Bible*
> Have the heavy rains done your house any damage ?

4.   **Do** is sometimes intransitive and means, behave or act.

> Be careful not to do so again.   Do justly and love mercy.
> Moses did as the Lord commanded him.

5.   **Do** has, in some contexts, the peculiar meaning of, to cook, to make ready a thing for eating.   To **do a mutton chop**, is, to cook it and prepare it for eating.   When it is **done to a turn** it is perfectly cooked.

We have seen already that *done* sometimes means *used up*, and now we see that it sometimes means *cooked*; so that expressions like, *Are the cakes done ?   The rice is done*, would not of themselves enable one to determine whether the meaning was *Are the cakes exhausted ?* or *are the cakes cooked ? The rice is all used up*, or *the rice is cooked*.   But in such cases, all ambiguity is removed by the connexion in which *done* stands.

6.   **Do** is at times used in conversation for, to deceive, to play a trick upon, to humbug, to outwit.   The participle *done* is frequently employed in this way.

> He felt he had been done by designing men.
> Be careful as to the terms of your bargain, for that man will try to do you if he can.

7.   **Do**, again, sometimes means, to fare, to thrive, to profit —is the second **do** in the common phrase, **How do you do?**   The first **do** is the auxiliary.

The same verb, used in a comparable sense, is found with the meaning **to answer an end**, in such expressions as,

> ' That will do,' meaning, that will be enough to serve the purpose.
> ' It did very well,' i.e. it suited very well, it was quite sufficient.
> To look one way and move another, may do on water, but not on land.

To **do good, evil, well, ill**, are readily intelligible from the following.

> Do good in all the ways you can, to all the people you can, and just as long as you can.
> He is doing well (=succeeding) in his new line of business.
> The patient has been doing well (=progressing favourably) all day.
> He is doing good by his lecturing, i.e. he is accomplishing a good result.
> He is doing well by his lecturing, i.e. he is making a good deal of money by his lecturing.
> He is doing well in his lecturing, i.e. he is doing the work of a lecturer well.

To **do well out of** something, is to derive profit from it.

> The banker did well out of that investment.

To do one's best, is to exert one's power to the utmost, to put forth one's best and most diligent efforts.

To be well to do, is to be in prosperous circumstances, to be well off. **Well-to-do** is sometimes put before a noun as a compound adjective, and is also used as a noun.

> Two persons are early introduced in the book, both merchants, and both well-to-do men, who have risen in the world.
> Previous to 1840, correspondence in England was in many respects a luxury in which only the well-to-do could indulge.

To do one good, is to be of advantage or benefit to one.

> The medicine did me good.
> It does the mourner's heart good to tell the story of its grief.

To do one a favour or **a kindness.** A formally polite expression.

> Will you do me the favour of accepting a small present of fruit ?
> You will do me a kindness if you will append your name to this memorial.

To do a thing by fits and starts, is to do a thing impulsively and a small portion of it at a time.

> Can good character be built up by fits and starts of moral living ?
> To study by fits and starts is not the way to prepare oneself for the serious business of life.

To do a thing off-hand, is to do it at once without delay or hesitation; to do it with ease and without preparation.

> I gave him a difficult problem in Algebra and he did it off-hand.

To do a thing by hook or by crook, is to do it by any means, fair or unfair, direct or indirect; to certainly do it, no matter by what means.

> It is the part of the police to bring criminals to justice by hook or by crook.

It is said that a French admiral in a time of war once wanted to bring his warship into Waterford Bay, in the South of Ireland. At the entrance to the bay there are two headlands, one on each side, one called Hook Head, and the other Crook Head. The admiral declared that he would enter either 'by Hook or by Crook', meaning that he would pass in by keeping near to one or other of the headlands.

To do wrong, is sometimes used in the sense of, to make a blunder, to commit an error of judgement.

> So far as I can see, you have chosen the right course and you would do wrong to make a change.

To do honour to, or **do reverence to,** is to honour, to reverence.

To do the honours, is to act as host or hostess at an entertainment.

Do to death, is to put to death. Byron uses the words, ' Done to death by sudden blow '.

> The fairest shepherd on the hills,
> Having done himself to death for his lost love,
> Lay like a marble statue —*Morris*

To **do a city**, or **do the sights**, is to visit the city and see its outstanding features.

' **Done !** ' said in response to a proposal, means, I assent, I agree. ' **No sooner said than done !** ' means, that as soon as a thing is proposed to anyone, he immediately executes it, and utters this phrase as his response.

To **do a thing under the rose**, is to do it in a manner that forbids disclosure. Among the ancients the rose as a symbol of secrecy was hung up at entertainments, to indicate that nothing said there was to be divulged. Sometimes the Latin phrase *sub rosa*, meaning **under the rose**, is used.

To **have to do with**, is to have business with, to deal with.

> What have I to do any more with idols ?—*Bible*
> You may try to clear yourself of all blame, but you did have something to do with this disgraceful affair.

To **have nothing to do with**, is the contrary of to **have something to do with**.

> I will have nothing to do with him, i.e. I am resolved to have no dealings with him.

When one wants to get rid of another person who will not be shaken off, he may say to him, ' I will have nothing to do with you.'

127. FALL

To **fall foul of**, is to run against, to come into collision with.

> If this new clerk continues his criticisms, he will soon fall foul of the manager.

To **fall in**, is to form ranks, said of soldiers.

To **fall in love**, is idiomatic for, to fall into love.

> The young couple readily fell in love with each other.

To **fall out**, is to quarrel.

To **fall into abeyance**, is to cease to be exerted or used.

> This law has been allowed to fall into abeyance.

To **fall out of use**, is to cease to be used. We also say, **drop out of use**.

> As a language grows, new words are introduced and many words fall out of use.

To **fall to work**, or **set to work**, is to begin to do work. In these phrases **work** is a noun.

> He fell briskly to work and finished the job in two hours.
> Let the men set to work at once.

To **fall a prey to**, is to be the victim of. When people plot against a man to ruin him and succeed in their malicious attempts, he is said to fall a prey to their designs.

> A traveller in Russia sometimes falls a prey to wolves.
> The small island will surely fall a prey to the rapacity of another Power.

To **fall to the ground**, is to come to nothing, to be fruitless, to prove useless, to become ineffective.

> The meeting was large, yet his motion found no seconder, and therefore fell to the ground.

To **fall for** something, is to yield to its charms.

> Mary fell for a pretty dress.

To **fall flat**, is to collapse.

> The performance fell flat.

To **fall to one's lot**, to become one's fate.

> It fell to my lot to marry a princess.

128. GET

To **get clear of**, is to disengage oneself from, or become free from difficulty or annoyance.

To **get drunk**, is to become drunk; whereas to **get drink**, is to procure drink.

To **get one's back up** (colloquial), is to become irritated.

To **get on**, is to advance; also, to prosper.

> Let the men get on to the front.
> This man is industrious and is sure to get on in the world.

To **get hold of**, is often used to mean, to understand.

> I can't get hold of the meaning of this telegram.
> With great difficulty the drowning man got hold of the rope.

We also use expressions like the following.

> When I had got a mile on my journey, I found I had left an important letter behind me.

To **get rid of**; to **be deprived of**. To get rid or quit of a thing, is to get free from a thing you wish to be free from. To be deprived of a thing, is to have a thing taken from you which you wish to keep. Hence we do not say that people are deprived of a tax; they get rid of a tax, or are relieved of it, or are freed from it. A man may be deprived suddenly of his property.

> Get rid of me but get me another job.

To **get**, or **be given** the sack, is to be dismissed. *Sac* is an old French word for passport.

To **get the upper hand**; to **get the better of**. These mean, to get the ascendancy or the superiority, to prevail over.

> Of two rival spinning companies, one is richer and better managed than the other, and therefore soon gets the upper hand.
> Trickery in trade may for a time get the better of honesty, but is found out in the end.

To **get into hot water**; to **be in hot water**. **Hot water** is here metaphorical for perplexing, difficult, irritating circumstances. The phrases are colloquial.

> The schoolmaster got into hot water with the Inspector for taking part in political meetings.
> It often happens that a young wife is in hot water as long as her mother-in-law lives in the same house.

To **get into a mess**, is to drift into difficulties; to get into a muddle.

> His accounts seem to have got into a mess.
> If he follows his present extravagant course, his affairs will soon get into a pretty mess.

To **get into a scrape**, is to find oneself in an awkward predicament. The opposite is, to **get out of a scrape**.

> It is easier to get into a scrape than to get out of one.

To **get wind of**, is to hear a rumour of.

> I got wind of the plot through hearing the men's conversation.

129. GIVE

To **give a person to understand**, is to lead him to believe, to give him ground or reason for believing a thing. To **be given to understand**, is to be led to believe.

> The engineer gave me to understand that there would soon be a vacancy for a clerk in his office.

To **give oneself to**, is to devote oneself to it. The phrase is expressive of habit.

> Give yourself to study and you will almost certainly pass your examination.
> If a man give himself to bad habits, what good can be expected of him?

To **give oneself trouble about**, or **over a thing**, is to take pains about it.

> He gave himself endless trouble over my problem.

To **give someone a bit**, or **a piece, of your mind**, is colloquial for, to scold him, to find fault with him, to speak or write upbraidingly to him.

> He has treated me very badly and I mean to write a letter and give him a bit of my mind.

To **give** or **show a person the cold shoulder**, is to treat him coldly, to receive him without cordiality.

> How despicable it is for a man to give the cold shoulder to his former friends because he has now grown richer than they!
> If you have been rude to a person, you may expect him to show you the cold shoulder.

To **give chase**, is to pursue something that is running away from you.

> The thief heard my shout and ran off; I at once gave chase, but he escaped.

To **give way**, is to yield, to succumb, to fail.

> The embankment gave way and buried three of the workmen.
> Only once did his faithful wife give way to emotion.—*Thackeray*
> ' His reason has given way,' i.e. he has become insane.

To **give someone the slip**, is to avoid someone who is looking for you. To **let slip**, is to lose, or say, something by negligence.

> The thief saw the policeman and took care to give him the slip.
> We ought to give the more earnest heed to the things which we have heard, lest at any time we should let them slip.—*Bible*

To **give** a thing **a wide berth**, is to keep at a distance from it. A sailor gives a rocky headland a wide berth, i.e. he keeps his ship at a safe distance from it.

To **give good measure**, is to give rather more than full, correct measure. When a draper selling cloth, measures off the stipulated number of yards and then gives freely a little piece more, he is said to give good measure. So a man rebuking or scolding another is sarcastically said to give good measure when the rebuke or the scolding is more severe than the justice of the case requires.

To **give chapter and verse for a thing**, is to produce the proof of it.

> I can give you chapter and verse for every statement I am making.
> It is not easy to give chapter and verse for the opinion one has of Bacon's moral character.

To **give countenance** or **lend countenance**, to a project, is to favour it, to give one's support to it.

> Some of the greatest benefactors of mankind have had few friends at first to give countenance to their inventions or discoveries.

To **give currency to**, is to make current, make publicly known.

> It is wicked to give currency to lying scandal.

To **give place to**, is to yield up one's place to. You give place to another when you allow him to take your place. The phrase is also used of inanimate things, customs.

> Carriages have given place to motor cars, and sailing vessels to steamers.

A **give-and-take** policy, is a policy involving mutual concessions. Compare **come-and-go**.

To **give a false colouring to**, is to misrepresent.

> A man who is known to give a false colouring to a statement will not be believed even when he speaks the strict truth.

To **give loose rein to**, is to give licence to, to leave without restraint. The idea is derived from leaving a mettlesome horse unchecked by the reins.

> A libertine is one who gives loose rein to his lusts.
> The soldiers, having sacked the town, gave loose rein to their passion for plunder.

To give rise to, is to be the cause of, to originate. The phrase is often applied to rumours or suspicions.

> What gave rise to this evil rumour ?
> I don't know what gave rise to the idea that the seat of Government was to be changed.

To give vent to, is to allow to flow forth—usually said of one's own strong pent-up feeling, as anger, grief.

> I rushed out of the room to give vent to my feelings.—*Lamb*
> He gave vent to his indignation in language more vigorous than polite.

To give tone to, is to invigorate. In this phrase **tone** commonly means the healthy state of the organs of the body. The phrase is also used metaphorically of the character or faculties. The word **tonic** is derived from this use of tone.

> The chairman's opening speech gave fine tone to the meeting.
> The Swiss, living among mountains, are a hardy and thrifty people; the very nature of their country gives tone to their character.

To give, or **lend, dignity** to an occasion, is to bestow social importance.

> The attendance of the Governor gave dignity to the gathering.

130. Go

To go mad, is to become mad. **To go crazy,** is to become crazy. **To go blind,** is to become blind.

> My dog went mad and bit several other dogs.
> If you do not take care of your sight you will go blind.

To go hand in hand. When two or more persons cordially agree in pursuing the same course, they are said to go hand in hand— they are in union, they agree.

> In all political matters, these men went hand in hand.
> He will gladly go hand in hand with you in any matters calculated to promote temperance.

To go a long way, is to go far, to go to a great length; but is also used metaphorically to mean, to be nearly sufficient for; also, to take much trouble, to yield much or far, to go beyond the limits of prudence.

> This sum will go a long way in defraying the expenses of the dinner.
> The newspapers went a long way in criticizing the Government.
> This quantity of wheat will go a long way towards maintaining the family for a year.

To go to law, is to litigate, to seek redress by going into a court of law.

> People are much too fond of going to law.
> A man sometimes has to go to law to maintain his rights or to get offenders punished, and in such a case he may be thankful that he has a court to protect him.

To **go halves**; to **(go) share and share alike**. When two persons agree to divide a thing equally between them, they are said to go halves, or to (go) share and share alike. These phrases are commonly used of an enterprise, and the agreement to take equal shares—of say both risk and advantage—would be made beforehand.

> ' The dog and I always went halves.'
> A party of ten set out on a fortnight's tour and agreed to go share and share alike in the expenses.

To **go to great expense**, to **be at great expense**, both mean, to expend much.

> The city has gone to great expense to give a suitable welcome to the new Governor.

To **go out of one's way to do a thing**, is to deviate from one's ordinary course of conduct in order to do something.

> You should be willing to go out of your way to oblige a friend.

To **go hard with**, is to press heavily upon, to fare ill with.

> If cholera breaks out, it will go hard with our army.
> This man was very weak from illness and for some time it went hard with him to maintain his family.
> The doctor thinks it will go hard with this man whose spine is injured, i.e. he will not quickly recover.

To **go well with; go ill with**. When a man prospers, it is often said that things go well with him, or that the world goes well with him. In adversity, things go ill with him or the world goes ill with him. Strictly speaking, to **go well with** is to agree with, to match, to suit. A horse would not go well with a bullock in a plough, i.e. they would not pull well together.

> In harmonizing colours, yellow goes well with purple.
> It goes ill with the man who takes to drink.

To **go on (sick) leave**. When an official obtains leave of absence from ordinary duty, he is said to go on leave.

To **go on a fool's errand**, is to go on an expedition such as a fool might go on, to go on an expedition which leads to a foolish, bootless end.

> The many expeditions to Mount Everest: can we say that those who took part in them were sent on a fool's errand ?

To **go through fire and water for** a person, or purpose, is to encounter any difficulty and undergo any risk, however great, for his sake.

> This man would go through fire and water to serve his friend.
> He is so furious that he would go through fire and water to revenge himself on his foe.

To **go to the wall**, is to be hard pressed, to fail, to get the worst in a contest, or in the struggle of life.

> When the struggle comes, the weakest go to the wall.

To **go to the bad**, is colloquial for, to become of depraved character, to associate with evil companions. To **go to the dogs**, is colloquially used with the same meaning.

> If you make idle, dissipated people your companions, you are sure to go to the bad.

To **go to rack and ruin**. Here **rack** has the same meaning as **ruin**, the meaning being intensified by using both words. The phrase is used both with regard to one's outward circumstances and also with regard to character.

> Within the past few years the commerce of the country has gone to rack and ruin.

Certain slang expressions may here be noticed. **It is no go**, means, it is quite impracticable, an utter failure. A bustling person is said to be **always on the go**. An inert person has **no go**.

131. HAVE

To **have one's hands full**. When a man's hands are full of anything, he cannot use them to do anything else. Hence, when a man is so busily engaged that he cannot attempt anything more, we say, he has his hands full. The phrase, therefore, means, to have as much to do as one is able to do. Similarly, ' to have one's plate full ' or, ' to have a lot on one's plate '.

> Do not expect him to help you; he has his hands full already.

To **have clean hands**, is to be perfectly innocent, to be a person of honesty, probity, integrity. The phrase is commonly used in speaking of business transactions; one who cheats has not clean hands. Also, one who receives bribes or engages in any nefarious scheme has not clean hands.

To **have to do a thing**, is to be obliged to do it, either from necessity of circumstances or from the will of another person.

> He had to cut down the tree to save his house.
> I had to walk four miles before I could find any shelter.
> The builder has to take down the wall; the architect would not pass it.

To **have in hand**. To have cash in hand to pay an account is to have cash in possession to pay. To have a work **in hand**, is to have undertaken it, to be engaged upon it. To have horses well **in hand**, is to have them well under control.

> The rough business which Hamlet had in hand, the revenging of his father's death upon his murderer, etc.—*Lamb*

To **have a hand**, or **a voice**, **in a thing**, is to have some part in doing it, to be a participator in doing it. To **have a finger in the pie**, is colloquial for the same.

I am glad to say I had no hand in shutting up the College in this city.

The people of a country may well wish to have a voice in making the laws by which they are governed.

This man likes to have his finger in everyone's pie, i.e. he is a meddlesome fellow.

To **have a thing at one's finger ends**, is to be thoroughly familiar with a thing; also, to be able to apply one's knowledge readily.

He has the history of the Punic Wars at his finger ends.

To **have a mind** to do a thing, is to be willing to do it, to show willingness to do it.

He could tell you the whole story if he had a mind.

To **have a way of one's own.** The phrase is applied to some characteristic manner or skill.

He has a way of his own in dealing with his children.

To **have one's eye upon a thing; have an eye to a thing.** Either of these may be used when a man has set a thing before him as the goal he desires or towards which he works. But the latter phrase also means, to superintend, to watch so as to take care of.

The inspector of schools has his eye upon a professor's chair.

Please have an eye to the child and see that he does not go near the fire.

To **have the field before one**, is to have full opportunity of showing what one can do, to be unopposed. To **have the field to oneself**, is to be the sole worker in a particular direction.

To **have a short memory**, is to be unable to remember a thing even for a short time. But the phrase is often applied to a person who says he forgets a thing while at the same time you suspect that he cannot have forgotten it. Compare with this the proverb, ' Liars should have long memories.'

To **have the face to do a thing**, is to have the audacity to do it. Another slang expression is, to have the **cheek** to do it.

To **have a difference with a person**, is to have a mild quarrel with him. When the quarrel is adjusted and friendly relations are restored, the parties are said to have **made up their difference**.

To **have a bone to pick with one**, is colloquial for, to have a difference with him which has not yet been expressed.

To **have a brush with** an opponent, is to have a slight encounter, actually or metaphorically, with him.

Stanley in crossing the African continent had many a brush with hostile tribes.

The chairman had a slight brush with one of the speakers at the meeting.

To **have had its day; to have seen better days.** When an article which has been much used falls into disuse, we say of it that it has had its day. When an article, e.g. a car, has become worn and shabby, we say that it has seen better days. The phrase would be used also of a dilapidated house; or, of a *person* who, having been well off, had come down in the world.

> Horse-drawn mail vans have had their day in England.
> It is easy to tell from this man's bearing that he has seen better days.

To **have too many irons in the fire.** If a blacksmith puts so many irons into the fire that he cannot attend to them all as they grow red hot, some will be wasted. Metaphorically, the phrase means, to have so much work in hand that some part of it is left undone or is done very badly.

> That man's health is sure to break down under the strain of overwork: he has too many irons in the fire.

To **have no backbone.** In vertebrate animals, the backbone gives strength and unity of vigour to the frame. A creature without a backbone has no energy. The phrase is applied metaphorically to character or disposition, and also to popular movements. Thus we say of a vacillating person or one easily disheartened, that he has no backbone, i.e. he cannot be relied on to carry through a work requiring vigorous and sustained action.

> It takes good backbone to make strong character.
> At first there was a show of resistance to this new rule issued by the Prince, but the movement had no backbone and speedily collapsed.

To **have the true** or **right ring,** is to be genuine. A perfect coin has a clear, metallic ring when let fall on something hard.

> The statesman's speech on education had the right ring about it.

132. HOLD

To **hold one's tongue,** or **one's peace,** is to be silent, not to speak. The second phrase is formal; the first is more used in conversation.

> The fellow kept babbling away and would not hold his tongue.
> They were weeping bitterly, but when the good man spoke words of comfort, they held their peace.

To **hold oneself ready,** or **in readiness,** is to be ready, to be in a state of preparedness.

> Hold yourself in readiness to ring the bell when I give the signal.

To **hold in check,** is to curb or restrain within due bounds. You hold a spirited horse in check, i.e. by means of bit and bridle. To **hold in play,** is to keep a person's attention occupied while you are accomplishing something which you do not wish him to know.

> A trusted man of influence may be able to hold a mob in check.
> I, with two more to help me, will hold the foe in play.—*Macaulay*

To **hold one's own**, is to keep secure what is one's own, or to maintain one's own position against opponents; to keep what advantage one already has. Pretty much the same meaning is expressed by, to **hold one's ground**, or **keep one's ground**, or **maintain one's ground**. To **hold one's own**, is often used in regard to bargaining or argument, as well as in regard to advantage generally.

To **hold up one's head**, is to be able to look every man in the face. One who has no reason to be ashamed can, as a man of rectitude, hold up his head. The phrase implies pride of one's character or position. Moreover, a deceiver may hold up his head and bear himself like an honest man.

To **hold one's head high**, is to bear oneself proudly, to have the appearance or demeanour of a proud man.

> A mark of true nobility is, not to hold one's head high, but to bear oneself humbly in a high station of life.

To **hold true**, is to regard as true, to continue to be true.

> I hold it true with one who sings
>> To one sweet harp in divers tones,
>> That men may rise on stepping stones
> Of their dead selves to higher things.—*Tennyson*

133. KEEP

To **keep within bounds**, is to restrain oneself or another so as to be within due limits.

> When his passion is roused, it is hard to keep him within bounds.

To **keep out of the way**, is to absent oneself intentionally, to avoid being in the way.

> Collins, having cheated the clerk, will keep carefully out of his way for some time to come.

To **keep a thing to oneself**; **keep one's own counsel.** These are alike and mean, to be silent about one's own purposes; not to announce the thing that one knows.

To **keep a thing dark**, is to keep it hidden or concealed, not to disclose it or make it known.

> There is an air of mystery about that man; he never consults anybody about his plans but keeps everything dark, no matter how trifling it may be.

To **keep** a person **in the dark** about a thing, is to keep that thing hidden from him, not to divulge it to him.

> If you have any important private matter on hand, you had better keep your young brother in the dark about it, else he will soon publish it all over the town.

To **keep oneself to oneself**, is to live apart, to shun society.

To **keep company with** a person, is to associate with him as a companion, to be often in his society.

> If you keep company with bad men you will soon learn their ways.

To **keep the house,** or **the room,** or **one's room,** is said of a person who is ill or who is convalescent, or of one who is obliged from any cause to remain indoors. Sometimes it is, **keep to the house, keep to one's room.** The correlative expression is, to **leave the house,** to **leave one's room.** We also say, keeps his bed, leaves his bed.

> He has had a severe illness, and still keeps to the house.
> A warrant is out for his arrest, and so he keeps his rooms.
> The doctor does not yet allow my father to leave his room.

To **keep house,** is to manage the business of a household. This phrase is used of a woman who acts as housekeeper or household manager.

To **keep open house,** is to be ready to entertain all comers, to be at all times hospitably inclined.

To **keep a good table**, means, habitually to provide food of excellent quality for one's own eating and drinking and for one's guests; to entertain one's guests sumptuously.

> No one ever sees poor dinners at my friend's house; I can tell you from long experience that he keeps a good table.
> He kept the table of a gentleman.—*Lamb*

To **keep watch; keep watch and ward**. To keep watch, is to be on the watch, to maintain a watchful attitude.

> Tom had better keep watch tonight against thieves.

To **keep a sharp look-out,** is to maintain a keen watch.

> They keep a sharp look-out on board ship.

To **keep pace with,** is to keep up with, to keep abreast of, to advance or progress equally fast with—said of walking and running, or of mental movements.

> Can a child keep pace with a full-grown man ?
> I cannot keep pace with John in mathematics.

To **keep the peace; to break the peace**. These are contrary expressions; the definite article cannot be omitted.

> Two men quarrel and fight; they are said to break the peace.
> They are brought before a magistrate and are bound over to keep the peace, i.e. to refrain thenceforward from quarrelling.

To **keep one's eyes on another person,** is to watch him, to observe his movements and actions.

> The policeman tries to keep his eye on the thief that he may catch him stealing. The thief keeps his eye on the policeman lest he should be caught.

To **keep someone at arm's length**, is to keep him off and not allow him an opportunity of close contact.   This phrase may also be used of men who oppose each other in arguments.

To **keep one's head above water**.   A swimmer does this.   Figuratively the phrase means, to avoid so getting into debt or trouble as to be overwhelmed by it; to be able to pay one's way.   To **get one's head above water**, is to tide over difficulties.

> If the peasant can only keep his head above water in this year of scarcity, he may hope to do well next year.

To **keep good hours**, is to be habitually early in returning home at night, or in retiring to bed.   The opposite is, **keep bad hours** or **late hours**.

> A rake does not keep good hours.

To **keep body and soul together**, is to keep alive, to keep from starving.

> She hardly eats as much as would keep body and soul together.

To **keep the wolf from the door**, is to keep away extreme poverty, starvation, or death by hunger.

> Thousands have a daily fight to keep the wolf from the door.

134. LAY

To **lay waste**, is to make desolate.

> Some of the finest cities of Europe have been laid waste by bombing.

To **lay bare**, **lay open**, is to disclose or reveal what was intended to be kept secret.

> Cicero did not rest till he laid bare the whole conspiracy of Catiline.

To **lay someone under an obligation**, is to do him a favour so that he feels indebted to you.

> You have laid me under a great obligation by taking so much trouble to get me an appointment.

To **lay oneself open to**, is to expose oneself to.

> Fault-finders lay themselves open to attack if a fault is found in them.
> When a merchant seems to grow suddenly rich while other men engaged in the same business can scarcely by honest trading make average profits, he lays himself open to the suspicion of fraud.

To **lie in wait for**, is to await in concealment, to be waiting as if in ambush; to waylay.

> The murderer lies in wait for his victim; the tiger, for its prey.

To **lay**, or **set**, **a trap**, is to prepare a trap and place it in position for catching prey; to prepare a scheme to deceive another and draw him in.

> A poacher lays (or sets) a trap to catch rabbits.
> A general in warfare often lays a trap for his enemies.

To **lay on the shelf**, is to lay aside as no longer fit for use, just as books not in use are put on the shelves of the bookcase. A retired person is sometimes spoken of as (laid) on the shelf. Also a question or scheme started and set aside, is said to be on the shelf, or shelved.

To **lay down the law**, is to speak in tones of authority.

To **lay up for a rainy day**, is to make provision for a time of trouble and difficulty.

For people to **lay their heads together**, is for them to consult together, to take common counsel.

135. MAKE

To **make peace**, is to reconcile, to bring about a state of peace between parties at variance.

> There had been feuds for ages between the rival states; it was an alien power that finally made peace between them.

To **make room**, is to open a space or passage for a person or thing; to remove obstruction.

> In packing a box, one fills it till he can make room for nothing more.
> By sitting together more closely, the passengers in the bus made room for more.

Room here means open space, while **a room** is an apartment.

> Is there room on this road for two cars to pass each other ?
> He means to make a room at the back of his house.

To **make way, make headway**, or to **make one's way**, is to progress slowly and steadily in the face of difficulty. To **make way for**, is to allow space or room for.

> I've talents enough to make my own way.—*Thackeray*
> Our ship had made but little way since the storm.—*Defoe*
> These students are studying Persian, but they do not seem to be making much headway.
> The crowd made way for the governor as he advanced.

To **make a hash** of anything, is to spoil it.

> The secretary made a hash of the club accounts.

To **make haste**, is to hasten, to hurry.

> Make haste and shake down the apples.

To **make friends**, is to win or secure the friendship of others.

> This man is so genial, he will make friends wherever he goes.

To **make a will**, is to make a testamentary disposal of property. The document containing this is called **a will**.

> The old man was anxious to make his will, and therefore sent for a lawyer to draw up the document in proper form.

To **make use of**, is to use, to turn to account.

> There are more books in the library than I can make use of.
> You make a poor use of your learning if you turn it to evil purposes.

To **make love to**. A man is said to make love to a woman when he shows affection for her and seeks to win her love.

> It was in vain that the young Marquis made love to Lady Mary.

He makes a good soldier, means, He has the qualities of a good soldier and exercises them.

She will make you a good wife, means, She has the qualities in her for becoming a good wife for you.

To **make answer**, is to reply.

To **make sure**, is to ascertain positively; also to make secure.

To **make sure of**, is to consider as certain; also, to secure for oneself.

To **make terms**, is to come to an agreement.

To **make short work of**, is to bring to a sudden end, to dispose of speedily.

> The locusts made short work of the ripe standing corn.
> This lawyer will make short work of his adversary's arguments.

To **make amends for**, is to compensate for damage, injury, or insult. The phrase often implies that personal feeling has been offended.

> By his kindness today, he had made amends for past insolence.

To **make an example of** a person, is to treat him so that the result will be a warning to others.

> So many boys come late to school that I must make an example of those who come late tomorrow.

To **make a point of** doing a thing, is to set it before you as a thing to be certainly done.

> John makes a point of reading a fresh book every month.

To **make a clean breast of something**, is to disclose fully and without reserve.

> When a man has to give evidence, he must make a clean breast of the whole matter.

To **make a living**, is to earn a livelihood for oneself.

To **make (both) ends meet**, is to be able to supply the necessaries of life while keeping expenditure within income.   The phrase implies that the pinch of poverty is felt.

> It is far better to struggle and make ends meet than to get into the clutches of a money-lender.

To **make common cause with**, is to co-operate with; to unite with and share the common risk, work, and reward.

To **make one's escape**, is to escape by one's own efforts.   The phrase implies that difficulties lay in the way.

> Donalbain made his escape to Ireland.—*Lamb*

To **make one's mark**, is to do some noteworthy thing, which brings honour or distinction. To **leave one's mark**, is to leave behind the effect of one's work.

> He was not long at college before he made his mark.
> Men like Pitt, Beaconsfield, and Gladstone leave their mark on the history of their country.

To **make a mountain of a molehill**, means, to give great importance to trifles.

> A man through great timidity or sloth often exaggerates a small obstacle and makes a mountain out of a molehill.

To **make a virtue of necessity**, is to do a very disagreeable thing as though from duty but really because you must do it.

> Knowing that the landlord would forcibly eject him from the house, he came and delivered up the key, making a virtue of necessity.

To **make much ado about nothing**, is to make a great fuss about a trifle.

To **make no bones about** a thing, is colloquial for, to make no scruple about doing it. The phrase implies that the thing is disagreeable.

> You need not raise imaginary difficulties, but just go and do the work and make no bones about it.

To **make bold to do a thing**, is to venture to do a thing even though it may seem bold to do it.

> Dobbin made so bold as to bring her refreshments.—*Thackeray*
> I make bold to say that Government should spend less on higher education and more on primary schools.

To **make neither head nor tail** of a thing, is colloquial for, not to understand it or any part of it; not to be able to see anything distinct or definite in it.

> He spoke so rapidly and in such a confused way that I could make neither head nor tail of his meaning.

To **take no account of** a thing, is to disregard it through oversight or because it is not worth regarding.

> Government need take no account of this senseless agitation.

To **make oneself scarce**, is a colloquial phrase meaning to go off.

> May I trouble you to make yourself scarce.—*Trollope*

To **make a fool of oneself**, is to act stupidly. To **make a fool of someone**, is to dupe him.

To **make little of, light of, nothing of**, is to disparage, to treat as of small or no account. To **make nothing of**, has a second meaning. If a pupil is too stupid to learn, we say the teacher can **make nothing of him**, i.e. cannot succeed with him. Or, of a passage in a book, if I say I can **make nothing of it**, it means, I cannot understand it.

> When I spoke of his health, he made light of his illness.
> I can make nothing of what he says, i.e. I cannot understand him.

To **make much of**, is to value highly, to treat as of great importance, to regard with partiality. To **make too much of**, is to overestimate. We have also, **to make enough of**, which is commonly used with a negative expression.

> Can one make too much of humility and purity and faith and truth ?
> My father patted me on the cheek and stroked my head and seemed as if he could never make enough of me.—*Lamb*

To **make the best** or **the most of** a thing, is to reap the greatest advantage one can from it; to reduce to the least possible inconvenience.

> The accident was a bad one, but the surgeon made the best he could of the few appliances within reach.

To **make the best of a bad bargain**. When a man buys a thing which does not turn out as well as he expected, that thing is often called **a bad bargain**. Hence the phrase means, to turn a disappointment to the best possible account.

To **make hay while the sun shines**. Sunshiny weather is the most suitable for making hay. Hence the phrase metaphorically means, to take advantage of a favourable opportunity while it lasts, to turn opportunity to advantage.

> When trade was brisk, he worked hard, and made his fortune: he believes in making hay while the sun shines.

To **make a tool**, or **catspaw of** someone, is to use him as a means of attaining or accomplishing your object. The story goes that a monkey, seeing nuts roasting at a strong fire and wishing to have them, but not liking to burn his own paw, laid hold of the paw of the cat and by means of it pulled the nuts to himself.

To **make a man of** someone, is to elevate him, to raise him from an inferior position into an independent and prosperous condition, so that he can act in a manly way.

> A friend took up this poor lad and kept him at school for seven years, and his education has made a man of him.

To **make believe**, is to pretend, to act under pretence.

> He made believe he was going off for a month, and then unexpectedly returned in a week and found his sons up to all sorts of mischief.

To **make as if** one would do something, is to pretend to be going to do that thing.

To **make a shift**, is to get along by some means, though with difficulty. Hence the noun ' makeshift '.

> A miser will always make a shift to save money,

To **make faces**, is to make grimaces.

To **make merry**, is to be jovial, to indulge in hilarity; also, to feast merrily. Hence the word **merry-making**.

> They spent their holidays in eating and drinking and merry-making.
> Thou never gavest me a kid, that I might make merry with my friends.—
> *Bible*

To **make free**, is to take a liberty to which one has no right.

> No one should make free to open a letter addressed to another person.
> I make free to say in this gentleman's presence, that his conduct has not been straightforward.

The phrase implies boldness or impertinence, whereas the phrase, **take the liberty of**, does not indicate anything disrespectful.

To **make free with**, is to treat freely or without ceremony.

To **make oneself at home**, is to act with as much freedom and with as little ceremony as if you were at home. The phrase is used of a person who is in another person's house. To **make one feel at home**, is to set another person so much at his ease in your house that he will speak and act as freely as though he were in his own house.

To **make one's mouth water**. If a hungry man smells food, the saliva gathers in his mouth, and he longs to taste the food. So the phrase means, to excite a longing for. It is especially used when the thing desired cannot be obtained and enjoyed. In this phrase, **water** is a verb.

> The hungry children stood gazing into the baker's shop and it made their mouths water to see the rows of fresh loaves.

136. PLAY

To **play**, in certain phrases means, to act like, to act in the character of. To play the fool, is to act like a fool. To play the spy, is to do the work of a spy. To play the woman, is to act a womanish part.

> Here is a little fellow who has been trying to play the man for the last hour and it is very amusing to hear his pompous talk.

To **play**, is often used in the sense of, to act, to operate on, e.g. The fire engine played (=poured water) on the burning house. In such phrases as, **call into play**, **bring into play**, the word **play** means active operation.

> The guns of the fortress were called into play and the attack of the Bulgarians was checked.

To **play truant**, is to stay away, to loiter, to idle. The phrase is commonly used of a schoolboy who when sent to school goes off to play. It also sometimes means, to absent oneself from duty when one is supposed to be at his post.

> Schoolboys playing truant should be punished.

To **play into the hands of another**, is so to act as to be of advantage to another.

> Two contractors come to me with estimates for a work; they seem to be perfectly independent. One estimate is much higher than the other, and even the lower one seems high; so I accept neither. Afterwards I find that the contractors are friends, and that he who gave the higher estimate was only playing into the hands of the other; he meant by bringing his higher estimate to induce me to close at once with the other contractor.

To **play**, or (more usually) **be, at cross purposes**, is said of two parties who oppose each other, unconsciously, or who have opposing plans but with the same end in view.

> You two men have been at cross purposes for six months; yet in fact you are both working for the same object.

To **play fast and loose with**, is to disregard one's promises or engagements.

To **play second fiddle**, is a colloquial phrase meaning to take a subordinate part, like one who plays ' second ' to a leading performer on the violin (cf. ' to play the lead '). The phrase sometimes implies that he who occupies the subordinate position is expected to further the designs of his superior. Sometimes the phrase is **to be second fiddle**, the instrument being taken for the performer.

> Mr Gladstone was the chief speaker at the meeting and Lord Rosebery was content to be second fiddle.

To **play with edged tools**. There is a common saying, ' Children and fools should not handle edged tools.' Hence the phrase is applied to a man who has to do with a matter which requires delicate handling.

> To interfere in a quarrel between a man and his wife is like playing with edged tools; you are pretty sure to get the worst of it.

To **play one false**, is to be deceitful to him, to cheat him.

> I relied on his help and he played me false.

To **play a double game**, or **act a double part**. These mean to do one thing openly and a different thing in secret. The thing done openly is done to deceive, or to draw off attention from the thing done secretly; whereas the thing done in secret is the real object aimed at.

> An honest man will scorn to act a double part.
> Generals often play a double game in war, but this is regarded as part of the tactics of war.

To **play the game**, is to observe the rules, to act honourably.

137. PUT

Put enters into several idiomatic expressions.

To **put in mind**, is to remind.

To **put to the sword**, is to slay with the sword.

To **put to trial**, or to **put on trial**, is to try, to bring to a test.

To **put** a thing **to the test** or **proof**, is to try it, to examine it carefully.

To **put to shame**, is to make ashamed, to disgrace.

To **put** a thing **to the vote**, is to take a vote upon it.

To **put** (or **get**) things **ship-shape**, is to settle them in proper order.

To **put to sea**, is to start on a voyage.

A ship **puts into port**.

To **put one's oar in**, is colloquial for, to interfere, to meddle.

To **put to use**, is to utilize.

To **put** one **to silence**, is to silence him.

To **put in order**, is to array in orderly fashion.

A mother **puts** her children **to bed**; the children **go to bed**.

A commander **puts** his enemies **to flight**; the enemies **take to flight**.

A magistrate **puts** the law **in force** against a criminal.

To **put** or **set** one **at his ease**, is to free him from trouble or restraint.

To **put one to it**, is to press one hard, to press him to the utmost of his powers. **It** in this phrase is impersonal.

> I felt so exhausted that I was put to it not to fall over.

To **put it to one**, is to lay a matter before one for his consideration that he may form an opinion upon it. This phrase would be used by one who was trying to persuade others.

> I put it to you, Is it wise to remain indifferent while the Government is making great efforts to extend education?

To **put a case**, is to set it forward for consideration.

To **put down one's foot**, is to make a decided stand, to resist further encroachments.

To **put one on his guard**, is to warn him.

To **put one on his mettle**, is to rouse him to do his best in trying circumstances.

> The cry of wolves behind put my horse on his mettle and he brought me in safety to the village.

To **put one's hand to a thing**, is to undertake it, to begin it.

To **put** a thing **well**, is to express one's meaning clearly and forcibly in speech or writing.

To **put the screw on one**. This means to coerce him; particularly, to restrain another in regard to expenditure, or idling.

> He could put the screw upon his son George.—*Thackeray*

To **put the cart before the horse**, is to begin at the wrong end to do a thing, to attempt a thing while neglecting to do first what ought to be done first.

> You certainly do put the cart before the horse. You have actually brought the masons to build a house but have not yet got the bricks.

To **put one's shoulder to the wheel**, is to make a great effort oneself instead of looking to others for help.

To **put a thing down in black and white**, is to put it in writing, so that a record is available.

> You tell me a long story; but put down what you want in black and white; and I will weigh its merits.

To **put**, or **set**, **right**, or to **put to rights**. These mean to adjust, regulate, correct, put in good order.

> The carpenter will soon put the broken table to rights.

To **put a good face**, or **the best construction, on a thing**, is to regard it in the most favourable way. The phrases are applicable to conduct, and commonly to unseemly conduct.

> A lawyer tries to put the best face on the delinquencies of his client.

To **put one out of countenance**, is to make him appear ashamed.

To **put this and that together**, is to infer from a conjunction of circumstances.

To **put forth**, or **throw out, a feeler**. When a man brings forward a proposal or makes an observation to elicit the opinions of others, he is said to put forth or throw out a feeler. The phrase is derived from the habit which certain insects have of feeling before them with feelers or antennae in order to discover by touch anything in front of them.

> In his statement about Egypt in the House of Commons, the Prime Minister threw out a feeler to test the opinion of Parliament.

To **put a spoke in one's wheel**. A spoke or pin is used to lock machinery when it stops. Formerly, English carters put a spoke into the wheel of a cart when going down hill, to act like a brake. The phrase therefore metaphorically means, to obstruct progress, to prove a serious barrier or hindrance.

> Brown was getting on well in business till Robinson opened a rival establishment, and that put a spoke in Brown's wheel.

To **put something by for a rainy day**, is to save.

To **put someone through it**, is to wear him out, e.g. by long interrogation.

To **put one's foot in it**, is to blunder. So, facetiously, it is said:

> As soon as he opened his mouth he put his foot in it.

138. Set

To **set a scheme on foot**, is to start it, to set it going.

To set a thing **on fire**, is to apply fire to it and make it burn; also, to inflame—said of the passions. To set or **put** a thing **on the fire**, is to place it upon the burning fuel, to heat or cook it. You may set a metal pot **on the fire**, but you cannot set it **on fire**.

The girl set the pot on the fire. He set the withered leaves on fire.
In some parts of America, a great stretch of prairie may be set on fire by sparks from a passing train.

To **set store by**, is to value highly.

That he might say farewell to her by whose love he had set such little store.—*Thackeray*

To **set the Thames on fire**, is to do something extraordinary or brilliant.

He's a steady worker, but never likely to set the Thames on fire.

To **set one's face against**, is resolutely to resist.

Attempts were made to draw the prince into rebellion, but he set his face against such intrigues.

To **set one's house in order**, is to arrange one's affairs.

He found the affairs of his brother's widow in desperate confusion; it was years before he could get her to set her house in order.

To **set people by the ears**, is to stir up ill-will among them, to provoke them to quarrel or wrangle.

When civil dudgeon first grew high,
And men fell out they knew not why;
When hard words, jealousies, and fears
Set folks together by the ears.—*Butler's ' Hudibras '.*

To **be well set up**, is to have a good physique, to have a strong and well-built bodily frame.

To **set one's teeth**, is to determine to endure hardship; but to **set one's teeth on edge**, is to jar his nerves, repel him.

139. STAND

To **stand in another man's shoes**, is to occupy his place.

To **stand in need of**, is to be in need of.

These doors stand in need of painting.
He stood in sore need of a loan of two hundred rupees.

To **stand in terror of**, is to be in terror of, to be afraid of.

Old Osborne stood in secret terror of his son.—*Thackeray*

To **stand in good stead**, is to be of great advantage to one in a time of difficulty.

The wolves were after the traveller, but his horse stood him in good stead and he escaped.

To **stand one's ground**, is to maintain one's position.

Peasants and burghers, however brave, are unable to stand their ground against veteran soldiers.—*Macaulay*

To **stand to one's guns**, is to persevere when hardships press. The phrase is derived from the practice of artillerymen standing to their guns and working them against an attacking foe.

To **stand in one's own light**, is to act in a way disadvantageous to oneself.

> He stood in his own light when he refused this appointment.

To **stand to reason**, is to be consistent with reason.

To **stand one's trial**, is to be tried in a court of law.

He **cannot stand it**, means, He is not able to endure it.

> The peasants have been so sorely down-trodden, that they are resolved to stand it no longer.

To **stand on ceremony with**, is to treat with cold rigid civility; to be overpunctilious in etiquette.

To **stand on one's dignity**, is to maintain a dignified and unbending attitude; in a dignified way to make one's authority felt. A person offended or insulted stands on his dignity and insists that an apology be made to him.

To **stand someone** a drink, or a meal, is to pay for it oneself.

140. TAKE

Many idioms using **take** are given in Chapter III, Section 38.

To **take into account**, is to regard, to consider.

> Before dismissing you, he might have taken your long and faithful services into account.

To **take to task, call to account**, is to reprove and require explanation.

> Take him to task for his idleness.

To **take advantage of**, is to use any benefit offered by; also, to seize by cunning or surprise

To **take** a thing **in hand**, is to undertake to do it, to attempt to accomplish it.

> Several have taken in hand to write the history of this country, but few have been successful.

To **take the law into one's own hands**, is to punish a person supposed to be guilty without his being legally tried.

To **take notice of** a thing, is to observe it; also, to remark upon a thing, as in a speech.

> He listened to my objections, but took no notice of them in his reply.

To **take** a city **by storm**, is to capture it by a fierce attack.

To **take** people **by storm**, is to captivate them unexpectedly.

> His singing took the audience by storm.

To **take** one **by surprise**, is to come upon him unexpectedly.

To **take upon oneself**, is to assume or undertake.

> He takes all the responsibility upon himself.
> He takes it upon himself to say that the doctor does not understand this man's ailment, i.e. presumes to say.

To **be taken aback**, is to be taken by surprise and flurried; to be startled.

To **take part with**, is to unite or join with—said of persons.

> Who took part with Guy Fawkes in the Gunpowder Plot ?

To **take part in**, is to unite or join in—said of things.

> Several good speakers took part in the debate.

To **take another person's part**, is to side with him, to defend him.

To **take (or pay, or give) heed to**, is to attend to carefully.

> I will take heed to what you say.

To **take in good part**, is to receive without resentment—said of a disagreeable thing, as a rebuke, or admonition.

> I tried to give James some wholesome advice; but instead of taking it in good part, he grew angry.

To **take to one's heels**, is to run away, to scamper off—said of men or animals.

> At the report of my gun, the thief took to his heels.

To **take to one's bed**, is to be obliged to lie down in bed through illness.

To **take in tow**, is to drag along in water by means of a cable or chain. The phrase is also used colloquially for, to help one forward by managing his affairs for him.

To **take a statement on trust**, is to accept it as true without inquiry, to accept it as true believing that he who makes it is trustworthy.

> Beware of taking on trust any statement which reflects upon the character of another.

To **take it into one's head**; to **come into one's head**, are colloquial for, to occur to one, to suggest itself to one. The expressions sometimes imply whimsicality.

> John took it into his head to wake up all the servants at midnight.

To **take pride in**, is to delight in, to be proud of.

> She takes pride in doing her embroidery very neatly.

To **take a leaf out of another's book**, is to take a hint from another's mode of action, to imitate him, to adopt another person's plan in the hope of reaching a result like this.

> I thought I was taking a leaf out of your book, being careful to make the best bargain I could.—*Trollope*

To **take the bull by the horns**, is to grapple courageously with a difficulty that lies in your way.

> If you have factious opposition to deal with, do not dally with it, but take the bull by the horns.

To **take a leap in the dark**, is to do a hazardous thing without any idea of what it may result in.

> You took a leap in the dark in going into partnership with this man.

To **take for better for worse**. When a man marries a woman, he takes her for better for worse, i.e. he promises to maintain her as his wife whether their means of living improve or get worse.

To **take things easy**, or **take it easy**, is to pass through life without allowing oneself to be worried by work or anxieties. The phrase to **have an easy time of it** means, to be without worry or hard work. To **have an easy time of it**, is because of outward circumstances; to **take it easy**, is because of inward disposition.

To **take a fancy**, or **liking, to** a thing, is to conceive an admiration for it or a desire to have it. And the phrase would also be used of a person

> He has taken quite a fancy to my house.
> From the first she took a fancy to your mother.
> My dog has taken a liking to lying among the hay.

To **take**, or **let, one into a secret**, is to make known the secret to him, he also being expected to regard it as a secret.

> Two men plan a burglary but are not able to accomplish their object without a third person; so they take a third into the secret and carry the nefarious business through.

To **take the lead**; to **get the start**. When of several competitors, one at starting gets ahead of the others, he is said to **get a start**. In a competition when one gets ahead and takes the leading place, he is said to **take the lead**. The phrase **have the start** is also used.

> All the boats started together, but my brother's soon took the lead.
> If you will only let me get the start of you by five minutes, I will swim to the opposite shore as soon as you.

To **take one home**, is to accompany one to his home and take care of him on the way.

To **take care of**, or **look after, number one**, means, to look carefully and selfishly after one's own personal interest or safety. The phrase is colloquial.

To **take the measure of a man**, is to form after careful observation a due estimate of a man. The phrase is commonly used when a man whose measure is taken, is one who is puffed up with self-esteem. And sometimes the expression to **teach a man his measure** is used.

To **take the cake** (or **the biscuit**). This is a slang expression meaning ' to take first prize '—usually in some absurdity.

To **take the bread out of another's mouth**, is to deprive him of his means of living. Sometimes by a plausible story, a man to gratify personal revenge persuades an employer that his servant is dishonest and so procures his dismissal. He is said to take the bread out of that servant's mouth.

141. THROW

To **throw cold water upon** a project, is to discourage it, to disparage the project and so discourage the projector.

To **throw dust in one's eyes.** If such were literally done, the result would be that the man would be unable to see. So metaphorically the phrase means to deceive one.

> He talked glibly to me about his plans and tried to show me that if I would lend him two hundred pounds he would soon be able to repay me with large interest; but all the time I felt that he was only trying to throw dust in my eyes.

To **throw off the mask**, is said of one who, having acted a deceitful part for a time, suddenly declares his real intentions. His deceit was as a mask to conceal his intentions.

> Bolingbroke at first paid homage to King Richard, but when his cause grew stronger, he threw off the mask and claimed the crown.

To **throw up the sponge**, is to give up a contest, to surrender.

A magic lantern, or projector, **throws** a picture **on the screen**.

142. TURN

To **turn adrift**, is to expel from some position or office; to throw a person on his own resources.

To **turn one's back upon**, is to abandon, to reject or refuse unceremoniously, to change to a directly opposite course.

> I am glad to say he had turned his back upon his former vices.
> He turns his back on his former friends, i.e. he slights them and no longer goes with them.

To **turn one's coat**, is to change sides, to change to the opposite party. One who does this is called a **turncoat**.

To **turn over a new leaf.** This means to change completely one's course of action. The expression is always used in the sense of changing from bad conduct to better. The idea is that every man's life is a blank book, which he by his actions is filling up as his life goes on; one page is blurred and blotted with many misdeeds, and as he turns over a new leaf he resolves that the next page shall have a fairer record.

> After a long career of crime, the convict suddenly turned over a new leaf and became a model citizen.

To **turn** a matter **over in one's mind**, is to consider it carefully and look at it from all sides.

> You have made a very important proposal to me; I will turn the thing over in my mind and give you an answer tomorrow

To **turn the scale**. When an article is being weighed with beam and scales, a little thing will finally make one scale or the other go down. And when a man's judgement is divided between two opinions, and something arises which makes him decide to choose one rather than the other, that something is said to **turn the scale**.

> The Spaniard was urged to visit England; and he would have liked to go, but the claims of his family seemed to require him to remain at home. While in this uncertainty, his young son fell ill, and that turned the scale. So he will not see England for the present.

To **turn one's hand to**, is to engage oneself in.

> This handy fellow seems to be able to turn his hand to anything.

To **turn tail**, is to retreat ignominiously. It is said primarily of a dog running away like a coward.

To **turn the day against one**; to **turn the fortunes of the day**. These mean, to reverse superiority or success.

> The coming of Blucher at Waterloo turned the day against Napoleon.
> In ancient times the fall of a king from his horse in a field of battle often turned the fortunes of the day.

To **turn the tables** on someone, is to reverse his success or superiority.

To **turn a thing to account**, is to utilize it.

> She had kept the trinket . . . in the hope of turning it to better account.— *Dickens*

To **turn up one's nose at a thing**, is colloquial for, to treat it with contemptuous dislike or disgust.

> He has been reduced almost to beggary, and yet he turns up his nose at any suggestion that he should work.

To **turn one's head**, or **one's brain**, is so to confuse him that he seems to have lost his judgement; to make giddy or conceited, or wild or insane.

> Flattery seems to have turned his head.
> Some men's heads are turned by sudden good fortune.

To **have a turn for**, is to have capacity or fitness for.

> This boy has a turn for drawing; send him to a school of art

CHAPTER XIII

MISCELLANEOUS IDIOMATIC EXPRESSIONS

143. We now take a collection of miscellaneous idiomatic expressions, following generally the alphabetical order of the verbs.

144. **To affect ignorance** of a thing, is to pretend or seem to be ignorant of it. **To be blind to** a thing, is to omit noticing it and to do this either by intention or otherwise.

He affected ignorance of the law.

145. The noun **account** enters into various expressions.

To run up an account. When I buy things at a shop time after time and do not pay for them when purchasing, but allow them to be charged against me in the shopkeeper's book, I am said to run up an account.

To cook, or **doctor, an account,** is to tamper with or falsify an account in order to deceive.

From the balance sheet presented to the shareholders, the Company appeared to be flourishing, but it afterwards turned out that the Secretary had cooked the accounts.

146. **To bait a trap.** **Bait** is some tempting morsel put on or in a trap to lure the victim into the trap. **To bait a trap,** is to put bait on or in a trap when you are setting it for your victim. An angler is said to **bait his hook.** The phrase is also used metaphorically.

A new company started, promising large business and guaranteeing eight per cent profit. Many were induced to invest in it, but it eventually turned out that the guarantee was worthless, and that the promise of such high interest was only baiting the trap for the unwary.

147. **To bandy words.** When two men contend with each other and fling words back and forward at each other recklessly, they are said to **bandy words.** The phrase implies a slight degree of contemptuous censure.

Why waste your time bandying words with that impudent person ?

148. To **bear the brunt of,** is to endure the main force or shock of.

The centre of the army has to bear the brunt of the battle.
The ship could not make for any harbour but had to bear the brunt of the storm, i.e. had to endure its fury.

To **bear hard upon,** is to press heavily upon, to oppress, to be felt as severe.

This new law will bear hard upon fishermen.

149. To **bear sway**, is to exercise authority, to rule.

> This country will never be settled till a strong government bears sway over the whole region.

150. To **beard a man,** is literally to catch him by the beard. The phrase now means, to oppose a man openly to his face, to defy him.

> I bearded the scoundrel in his own home.

151. To **beat the air.** Literally, this is plainly a profitless expenditure of energy. Hence the phrase means generally, to make efforts that are vain, useless, fruitless.

> His speech merely beat the air; there was no cogency in his argument.

152. To **beggar description.** A scene in nature or in human life is said to beggar description when it is of such a kind as to be beyond one's power to describe adequately. Shakespeare wrote of Cleopatra:

> For her own person,
> It beggared all description.

153. Certain **Words of Salute** are noteworthy.
Bid (or **say**) **good-bye; bid farewell,** mean, to take leave.

> I bade him adieu on board the steamer.
> He may bid good-bye to all his dreams of getting rich by speculation in mines, i.e. he may abandon such dreams.

The words, **good-bye, farewell,** are compound words. **Good-bye** is a contraction for ' God be with you ', **farewell** is two words joined together, meaning, ' May you fare well '. These are *parting salutes*. ' Good morning ', ' Good afternoon ', ' Good evening ', ' Good night ', are alternative forms of both greeting and farewell; ' hello ' (hallo)—greeting, and ' good-bye ' are slightly more familiar and colloquial.

154. To **bid** (or **make**) **one welcome,** means to welcome or receive one cordially. To **wear out** or **outstay one's welcome,** is to stay so long that the host wearies and wishes his guest gone.

> I am happy to bid you welcome to our house.
> Since you invite us again so soon, it is plain that we did not outstay our welcome last time.

155. To **bid fair to,** means to be likely to, to give fair prospect of. The idea involved is one of excelling.

> His health is so good that he bids fair to live till he is sixty.
> These trees bid fair to outgrow those planted five years ago.

156. To **blow one's own trumpet,** is to trumpet forth one's own praises, to parade one's own good deeds.

> Some men are good at blowing their own trumpet.

157. To **blunt the edge of** a knife or sword, makes it less effective for doing its work. To blunt the edge of an objection or an argument, is to weaken its force as an objection or argument. Time blunts the edge (=dulls the keenness) of grief.

158. To **book to a place**, is a phrase which has come into use chiefly in connexion with travelling, and means, to purchase a ticket which entitles you to travel to the place. To be **booked for**, is explained below.

> This passenger, *or* this luggage, is booked to Madras.
> He inquired about steamers, and booked for London by the P. and O. line.
> You are booked for two songs in the concert = It has been arranged that you sing two songs in the concert

159. **Bolt** is a word which enters into some phrases.

' His horse bolted,' means his horse ran off, having become uncontrollable. We can also say,

> The thief bolted as soon as he caught sight of the policeman.

To sit bolt upright, is to sit with the upper part of the body perfectly erect. It is commonly used of a person who, having been in a reclining posture, suddenly sits straight up.

To bolt a door or window, is to fasten it securely with a bolt or bar.

To bolt food, is to swallow it in mouthfuls without taking time to masticate it.

> It is better to take half the quantity well chewed, than to bolt the whole in a hurry.

160. To **breathe freely**, is to be relieved from such suspense or anxiety as caused one to hold his breath.

> I was in the tunnel when the train came up before I was aware, but I squeezed myself close to the wall and escaped. Not till the last coach passed did I breathe freely.

161. To **bring a charge home to one**, is to prove the truth of the charge against him, to convict him of the charge. A moral truth is **brought home** to a man when he is made to feel the force of it.

To **bring** (or, to be brought) **to want** or **to beggary**, is to reduce to utter poverty.

To **bring to light**, is to disclose, to discover.

> A skilful detective would bring all their schemes to light.

To **bring to mind**, is to recall.

162. To **buckle to**, is to apply oneself diligently to a work or business.

> We must waste no more time, but buckle to at once.

163. To **build castles in the air**, is to indulge in reveries or visionary schemes.

164. To **burn a hole in the pocket**, is said of money that seems to ask to be spent, and disappears quickly.

Money given to a schoolboy only burns a hole in his pocket.

165. To **bury the hatchet**, is to make peace. The **hatchet** referred to in the phrase, was a weapon used by North American Indians. When tribes of these people who had been at war, made peace, it was a custom among them that their leaders should sit down together and all smoke in turn from the same pipe, called the ' pipe of peace '. They then used to bury their hatchets and other weapons of war.

> Buried was the bloody hatchet;
> Buried was the dreadful war-club,
> Buried were all warlike weapons.
> And the war-cry was forgotten:
> There was peace among the nations.—*Longfellow's 'Hiawatha '*

166. To **buy a house over one's head**. A landlord lets a house to a tenant; I go to the landlord and purchase the house while the tenant is in occupancy: I am said to buy the house over the tenant's head. Similarly one can say: ' I appealed to the General Manager over the local manager's head.'

167. To **buy a pig in a poke**, is colloquial for, to purchase a thing without previously examining it to see what its real value is. A ' poke ' is an old word for ' sack '.

You need not press me to buy shares in this new company. I have no means of knowing whether the statements in the prospectus are true, and I will not buy a pig in a poke.

168. To **call in question**, is to express doubt about the correctness of a statement.

I am not disposed to call in question anything that John says.

169. To **call a spade a spade**, is idiomatic for, to speak in plain terms; to speak without mincing matters.

I have learned to call wickedness by its own terms: a fig, a fig, and a spade a spade.—*John Knox*

He is not reckless or vulgar in his language, but still he can call a spade a spade.

170. To **canvass** a subject, or question, or situation, is to examine its accuracy, or validity, or stability; to examine it critically. To ' canvass votes ' is to solicit them.

171. To **change colour**, is to turn pale through sudden or strong emotion, as with fear, anger, shame, or a consciousness of wrong-doing detected.

172. To **change hands**. Property is said to change hands when it passes from one owner to another either by sale, or gift, or heirship, or in any other way.

This house has changed hands twice in the last ten years.

There were pickpockets in the crowd and several watches changed hands.

173. To **change one's quarters**, is to change one's place of residence: usually it means to change one's lodgings.

174. To **clip one's wings**. To clip a little from the tip of one wing of a bird deprives it for a time of the power of flying. So figuratively, to clip one's wings, is to deprive him of power, to render him weak or ineffective.

> The minister is ambitious, but the Prince will clip his wings.

175. To **collect oneself** or, **one's wits**, an idiom rarely used in speech today, is to recover from a surprise or a state of flurry, to regain self-control. To **recollect oneself**, is the more general usage.

> The traveller was suddenly struck down by a blow on the back of the head. He lay stunned and bleeding for a time and before he was able to collect his wits, he was robbed by two ruffians.

176. To **command respect** or **esteem**, is to have such excellent qualities of disposition and character as to win esteem.

> Probity and purity will command respect anywhere.
> This man commands the esteem of his whole village.

177. To **commit to memory**, is to learn by heart. Note that it is not, commit to *my* memory; or *commit to the memory*.

To **commit oneself**, is to bind oneself by word or act.

> I should like to do as you ask, but I have already committed myself to another.

178. The noun **credit**, meaning **honour**, enters into phrases.

To **bring credit to**; **do credit to**; **reflect credit on**.

> This boy will yet bring credit to his teachers.
> Such a crop as this reflects credit on your good farming.
> This pupil does credit to your teaching.

Take credit for; **get credit for**; **give one credit for**. The examples following show the usage of these.

> The captain takes credit for saving the ship by his skill, i.e. he considers that to him is due the merit of saving the ship.
> The captain gets credit for saving the ship, i.e. people generally consider that he saved it.
> I give the captain credit for saving the ship, i.e. I consider that the honour or merit of saving it is due to him.

When the definite article is put before ' credit ', **of** is used instead of **for**.

> He gives this dog the credit of saving his child's life.

179. To **cross**, or **pass**, **the Rubicon**. The Rubicon was a small river separating ancient Italy from Cisalpine Gaul, the province assigned to Julius Caesar. When Caesar crossed this stream, he passed beyond the limits of his own province and became an invader of Italy. Hence, the phrase means generally, to take a decisive step forward, to adopt some measure from which it is impossible to recede.

180. To **cry over spilt milk**, is to cherish useless regrets.

181. To **curry favour**, is to seek to win favour by gifts or flattery.

It is obvious that by your presents of fruit you are only trying to curry favour with him.

182. To **dance attendance on one**, is to pay great court to him and humour his whims.

183. To **dig the grave of one's reputation**. When a man of repute makes a mistake which proves fatal to his reputation, it is sometimes said of him that by that fatal mistake he dug the grave of his reputation.

184. To **disabuse one's mind**, is to remove a misapprehension, to do away with a false impression. Also, To **disabuse a person**. To **undeceive a person** has a similar meaning.

I would like to disabuse your mind of the idea that your colleague has a feeling of hostility to you. On the contrary he spoke in the most friendly terms of you.

I reasoned with him for an hour, but could not disabuse him of the notion that the lawyer who had his case in hand was incompetent.

185. To **dismiss from one's mind** or **from one's thoughts**. The meaning of this is, to cease to think about a thing. We could also say, **banish from one's mind** or **from one's thoughts**. If there is any difference of meaning in the two verbs in the phrase, **dismiss** would mean **for a time**, and **banish** would mean **altogether**.

Dismiss all care from your mind and go to sleep.

This evil rumour has been preying on his mind for some time and he finds it impossible to banish it from his thoughts.

186. To **drop a hint**, is to let fall a remark meant to be taken as a hint or indication of something more important which is kept in the background. The remark in this case is made with apparent carelessness, but yet with the intention that it shall be carefully noted. The person attending to the hint and understanding it is said to **take the hint**.

As I talked about your neighbour, I dropped you a hint that he is not very honest; but you did not seem to take it.

187. To **drop a subject**, is to cease discussing it, or cease conversing about it. When two men have disputed and cannot come to an agreement, they sometimes wisely let the matter drop.

188. To **err on the safe side**, or **on the right side**, is to choose a course which may in fact be inaccurate, but which will keep you safe from risk or harm. For instance, a man binds himself to deliver to a builder by a certain date ten thousand well-shaped and well-burnt bricks. He delivers eleven thousand lest some should prove crooked or not well burnt. He is said to err on the safe side.

189. To **escape one's lips**. It is the collocation that is noteworthy here. We do not say, escape one's *mouth*, or escape one's *tongue*, but escape one's **lips**. Sometimes we use **pass one's lips**. For instance, if one were cautioning another not to reveal some secret, he might say, ' Do not let this matter pass your lips.' Also, if a child says some word which its father dislikes and never wishes his child to utter, the father might say, ' Never let that word escape your lips.'

190. To **fall on one's feet.** When a man is successful rather by luck than his own good management, he is said to have fallen on his feet

> George, who had a post at £300 a year, has been appointed as tutor to a young millionaire at a salary of £1,000, so that he has fallen on his feet.

191. To **feather one's nest,** is to provide for oneself especially from property not one's own passing through one's hands; so that the phrase implies dishonesty. Certain birds gather feathers to line their nests; hence the form of the phrase.

> In some countries the tax collectors make a point of feathering their own nests well while they have opportunity.

192. To **feel the pulse,** is used metaphorically for, to find out one's secret opinions, to sound a person or a people

> I did not know whether he would receive back his runaway son and I went to feel the old man's pulse on the subject.
>
> The Prime Minister sometimes makes an important statement in Parliament in order that through the comments made on it in the public press he may feel the pulse of the nation.

193. To **feel one's way,** is to proceed cautiously so as to avoid risks and dangers—as one would do in a dark room; he puts out his hand before him and moves cautiously forward lest he should come against or stumble over something.

> A man starting a new business should feel his way carefully for a time.

194. To **fight shy of** You are said to fight shy of a person or thing when you make attempts to avoid him or it.

> He tried to draw me into partnership with him in business, but I fought shy of him.
>
> I fight shy of air travel because the movement makes me sick.

To **go on,** or **fight, to the bitter end,** is to carry on a contest reckless of the consequences, to continue the fight as long as possible and without the shadow of relenting.

> The two sides were determined to fight it out to the bitter end.

To **fight to the death,** is to fight on and die rather than give in.

195. To **suit a person down to the ground,** is to suit him completely or admirably. It is said, for instance, of an offer which falls in precisely with a man's tastes or likings.

196. To **eat one's heart out**, is to brood over one's sorrows or disappointments, the result being depressed spirits and a broken heart.

To **eat humble pie**, is to have to humiliate oneself, to have to apologize. The phrase is said to be derived from a pie made from the ' umbles ', or heart, liver, and kidneys of a deer (cf. ' offal '). These inner parts were considered very mean fare, and were formerly given to the huntsmen and servants.

> ' He did give us the meanest dinner of beef, shoulder, and umbles of venison which he takes away from the keeper of the forest, and a few pigeons, and all in the meanest manner that ever I did see.'—Pepys's *Diary*

To **eat one's words**, is to retract one's assertions under compulsion. A man may also be brow-beaten and coerced into eating his words where, nevertheless, what he said was right.

> It is hard for a haughty man to have to eat his words.

197. To **end in smoke**, is colloquially said of efforts that come to nothing, or are useless.

> He made a great fuss about having an investigation, but it all ended in smoke.

198. To **enjoy oneself**; to **avail oneself of**. The reflexive pronoun must follow these verbs. You should not say, ' On my last visit to London I enjoyed very much ', but ' I enjoyed myself ', etc. So you must not say, ' He availed of the opportunity of ', but ' He availed himself ', etc. But it is correct to say, ' I enjoyed my last visit to London very much '.

199. Contests of the days of chivalry supply some phrases.

To **enter the lists**. **The lists** was the name given to the open space in which the knights encountered one another in the tournament, and to enter the lists was to ride into this space in order to do so. The phrase has come to mean, to enter on an encounter with an opponent or with competitors. To enter on the lists against a person, is to accept his challenge. To **enter the field**, has a similar meaning.

> Only one gold medal is offered for competition and three young men have entered the lists, each hoping to win it.
>
> Two members are to be elected to the Town Council, and five candidates have entered the field, *or*, are already in the field.

To **throw down the gauntlet**; to **take up the gauntlet**, mean respectively, to offer or give a challenge, and to accept a challenge. A gauntlet is a glove of mail. In the days of chivalry when one knight challenged another to contend with him, he threw down his gauntlet, and the knight who picked it up was the one who accepted the challenge.

> It is not for a small country to throw down the gauntlet to right and left.

To **run the gauntlet**, is to undergo severe criticism or ill treatment. The punishment here referred to was common among sailors. If one of their crew had offended, the others stood in two rows facing one another, each one having a rope's end in his hand; the offender was made to run between the two rows, and each sailor hit him as he passed.

> Most books have to run the gauntlet of the literary critics of the London press.

200. To find a clue to. The word **clue** here means, thread nwound from a ball to guide one in a labyrinth. And so the phrase means, to find something that will guide you in a perplexing difficulty.

> The whole circumstances of the murder are wrapped in mystery, and the police can find no clue by which to trace the murderers.
> I haven't a clue to his whereabouts.

201. To find fault with a person, is to blame him. To find fault with a thing, is to find it deficient in some particular. The phrase implies that you point out the fault. Sometimes a censorious person is stigmatized as a **fault-finder**, the meaning being, that he loves to find out faults in others.

> I cannot find fault with Miss Sharpe's conduct.—*Thackeray*
> Fault-finders should be fault-menders.—*Proverb*
> People sometimes find fault with others when they should blame themselves.

202. To burn one's fingers; to get one's fingers burned. These mean, to get oneself into unexpected trouble. When a man engages in speculation and suffers losses, or meddles with something which promises well and turns out a failure, we say, he burns his fingers or gets his fingers burned.

To **snap one's fingers at**, is to despise, to treat with contempt, to show that you do not care a snap of the fingers.

> The Prime Minister thinks he may snap his fingers at the demands of the people, but he will find out his mistake

203. To open fire, is to begin to fire with musketry or artillery.

> The warships opened fire on the forts.
> The opposition opened fire with a caustic speech by their leader.

To **hang fire**, used of a firearm, is to be slow in going off. So, metaphorically, of men or actions.

> If the affair hangs fire now, it will never come off.

204. To fly in the face of, is directly to oppose or defy when it is foolhardy to do so.

> Why should you recklessly fly in the face of danger ?
> It is foolhardy to fly in the face of the King's prohibition.

205. To **fool** (or **fritter**) **away** money, or time, is to spend it foolishly and on trifling things.

206. To **follow the crowd**, is to believe or act as most people do, without taking the trouble to consider whether the thing believed or done is right or wrong.

> It requires force of character not to follow the crowd.

To **follow a speech**, or a piece of music, is to keep one's attention fixed on it as it proceeds.

To **follow a trade**, is to practise it.

To **follow in the wake of another**, is to follow another person's course. The wake is the track left by a ship in the water.

To **follow suit**, is literally to play a card of the same suit or sort as that first played; hence, to follow the line of conduct adopted by a predecessor.

> In the infant school, one little urchin began to cry and all the other children soon followed suit, so that in a short time we had fine music.

207. To **force one's hand**, is to compel him to disclose what he is aiming at.

208. To **gain ground**; to **lose ground**. A man is said to **gain ground** when he slowly and steadily succeeds; and to **lose ground** when he gradually falls back and is not successful. These phrases imply slow but continuous transition. They are used also of health. A belief **gains ground**, i.e. it grows, it spreads.

209. To **gild the pill**, is to cover over a disagreeable thing with something pleasant.

> They demanded a large war indemnity from us and gilded the pill by offering us two warships.

210. A man is said to **save the situation** when in an emergency he provides what is needed to prevent a catastrophe. Or, an event occurring unexpectedly may save the situation.

211. To **go off**, or **fly off**, **at a tangent**. A tangent is a line which touches a circle. To go off at a tangent, is literally to leave the circle and go off in a line which would never lead back to the circle again. The phrase is used of a person who instead of following up a train of thought or a line of action, strikes off into something else.

> A lawyer should be skilled in the art of reasoning; it will not do in arguing a case to fly off at a tangent into outside matters.

212. As the evening twilight fades, it is said to **grow dark**.

> As it grew dark, I became anxious for their safety, for the wind rose and the boat had not come to land.

To **grow grey**. When a man is so long in one appointment

or service that he has grown old in it, we say he has grown grey in the service.

> Brown began work at the age of eighteen, and has grown grey in the same office.

213. To hang by a thread. The idea is that the thread may snap at any moment and the thing suspended fall.

> He has been growing weaker and his life now hangs by a thread.

214. To haul over the coals, is to censure a man, reprove him severely.   The phrase is colloquial and probably derived from the barbarous ordeal of dragging a man through the fire in order to find out whether he is guilty or not.

> If your bad habits become known, you will get hauled over the coals, and richly deserve it.

215. To hide one's light under a bushel, is literally to put a box over a light and thus conceal it.   ' Neither do men light a candle and put it under a bushel, but on a candlestick; and it giveth light unto all that are in the house.' (*Bible*).   From this the phrase is derived.   It means generally, to conceal or obscure one's talents.

> To keep such a learned man in his present obscure position, is to hide his light under a bushel.

216. To hit the public taste, is to agree with it, to match it.

A **good hit,** or a **lucky hit,** means a successful attempt, or a peculiarly happy remark.

To **hit the nail on the head.** When one wants to drive a nail into wood, the proper part of the nail to strike is the head.   The phrase has come figuratively to mean, to do or say the right thing.

217. To drive a nail home, is to hammer the nail till the head of it will not allow it to be driven farther into the wood; to drive a nail as far as it will go.   The phrase has come metaphorically to mean, to bring a thing to full achievement, to convict a person thoroughly by argument or rebuke.

> The carpenter will drive every nail home before he pronounces the work finished.
> I spoke to him plainly of his duty, and I think I drove the nail home.

218. To strike home, is to strike close and with telling effect.

> Your opponent is floundering in his arguments; when your turn to reply comes, strike home.

219. To husband one's resources, is to manage one's means with frugality, to so use one's resources as to reserve something for an emergency.

> A careful general will husband his resources, if there is any fear of his supplies being cut off.

220. To **jog another person's memory**, is colloquial for, to put one in mind of a thing apparently forgotten.

> He has forgotten his promise, I fear; you had better jog his memory.

221. To **kill two birds with one stone**, is a colloquial phrase which is quite intelligible literally. Metaphorically it means, to accomplish two things at one stroke.

> I had to go to Bristol to meet a friend and while there I had my photograph taken; so that I killed two birds with one stone.

222. To **know full well**, is to know perfectly, to be fully convinced. The phrase is used only when there is ample opportunity of getting full knowledge and when this full knowledge has not been properly turned to account.

> You knew full well that the flood would carry the bridge away.

223. To **lead**, or **have**, or **bear**, **a charmed life**, is said of one who passes through great dangers without receiving injury. The phrase is derived from the old notion that charms or spells or incantations could render one invulnerable in danger. This superstition is exploded; but the phrase remains.

> King Arthur seemed to his followers to lead a charmed life.
>
> Here is a nurse who has attended all kinds of infectious cases and yet has never caught any infection; she has a charmed life.
>
> In his numerous adventures and hairbreadth escapes hitherto, he has seemed to bear a charmed life.

To **lead a person a dance**, is deliberately to cause him more exertion or trouble than necessary.

To **lead a person a dog's life**, is by fussy, irritating meddlesomeness to give him a miserable existence.

> What with his bad habits and his constant fault-finding and blundering, he led his family a dog's life.

To be **in leading strings**, is to be a mere puppet in the hands of others– originally said of a child learning to walk.

224. To **learn by heart**, is to commit to memory. To **learn by rote**, is also to commit to memory, but unintelligently.

225. To **leave the beaten track**, is to travel by a route not commonly used. The phrase is also used metaphorically, chiefly of speakers and writers who discuss questions in ways not trite and common.

> He left the beaten track of travellers, and visited a great many out-of-the-way places.
>
> Previous writers have all discussed the question of sanitation in one way; this author leaves the beaten track and has given us a fresh and interesting book.

226. To **leave one in the lurch**, is to desert a person in a difficulty when he expects you to stand by him. **Lurch** is a technical term

from an old card game, meaning something like ' low score '.
See Shakespeare, *Coriolanus* II, 2, 106.

> He stood by me so long as all went well, but at the first approach of
> trouble he went off and left me in the lurch.

227. **To leave much to be desired**, is to be unsatisfactory.

228. **To let the grass grow under your feet.** The idea is that
of a person lingering in one spot. For instance, if I want any
work done with the least delay, I say, ' Now, don't let the grass
grow under your feet ! '—meaning, ' Do the thing assigned you
with the utmost dispatch.'

229. **To let by-gones be by-gones**, means, to let things that are
past and gone remain untouched and forgotten, to let them lie as
things of the past which need not now be brought up again.

To let the cat out of the bag, is colloquial for, to make known
a thing intended to be kept secret.

230. **To (levy) blackmail.** **Blackmail** was money extorted by
freebooters, and given to them as a bribe to exempt property from
their depredations. The freebooters were able to defy the officers
of the law and carry on their schemes in spite of them. Hence,
to blackmail, is generally, to extort by intimidation.

231. **To lick into shape**, is colloquial for, to give form or method
to. The old notion was that the young bear was born shapeless
and its mother licked it into shape. There is also the contemptuous
phrase, **an unlicked cub**, applied to an ill-disciplined youth.

232. **To lie, or put, in a nutshell.** This is said of a thing which is
capable of, or presented in, brief expression.

> The explanation of his strange conduct lies in a nutshell—the man is
> insane.
> He put the whole matter in a nutshell, i.e. he summarized it.

233. **To live fast**, is to live luxuriously, to indulge every appetite
and taste and whim, to lead a life of dissipation. Hence a **fast liver**
is a spendthrift, a libertine.

> He who lives fast dies soon.

234. **To live from hand to mouth**, is to use up one's income as
fast as it comes in. This is commonly said of poor people who
spend all their money as soon as it is earned, and therefore implies
improvidence, want of prudent saving for a time of difficulty.

235. **To let loose**, is to set free what was bound. You let
loose a chained dog, a muzzled hound, etc. The phrase is also
sometimes used of passions.

> He keeps his dog chained during the day, but lets him loose at night.
> The angry passions of the mob were let loose against the miscreant and
> they wrecked his house.

To **let loose the dogs of war**, is to set in motion the destructive forces of war.

236. To **break loose**, is to gain liberty by forcible means; to escape from restraint or control.

> No man should allow his passions to break loose.
>
> If the lion breaks loose from his keepers, he will do a great deal of mischief.

237. To **lord it over** someone, is to domineer over him, to act as a lord. It in the phrase is impersonal.

> The love of power is so strong in human nature, that when a man becomes popular he seeks to lord it·over his fellows.

238. To **lose one's head**, is to lose calmness of mind, or cool balance of judgement; hence, to become excited and act rashly.

> The colonel seemed to lose his head as we went into action, and as a consequence the regiment suffered many casualties.

To **lose oneself**, is to lose one's way, to get into a place where you do not know the way out.

> I nearly lost myself in the jungle.
>
> The lawyer lost himself in the middle of his case, i.e. he got so confused that he did not know how to proceed.

239. To **meet one's engagements,** is to pay one's debts as they become due, to meet or discharge one's obligations.

> Being unable to meet his engagements, the merchant became bankrupt.

To **meet half-way**. This is said of two persons who hold two different opinions, but who by mutual concessions come to terms; they are said to meet each other half-way, or one is said to meet the other half-way.

> My view of what should be done differed widely from his, but I was willing to yield and meet him half-way.

240. To **mind one's own business**, is to attend to one's own affairs without meddling with the concerns of others.

To **mind one's p's and q's**, is to be punctiliously careful as to one's own behaviour. The phrase is used particularly when one is in danger of being caught in a fault.

> The manager suspects his chief clerk of dishonesty, and if the clerk does not mind his p's and q's, he will soon find himself without a job.

241. To **mount guard**, is to take the position of a sentinel.

> Fearing that an attempt would be made to break into the jail and rescue the prisoners, the officer ordered ten soldiers to mount guard with fixed bayonets.

242. To **move heaven and earth** to accomplish a purpose, is to use all and every means to accomplish a purpose.

> He will move heaven and earth to get evidence to convict his cousin of this theft.

243. To **muster in force**, is to assemble in large numbers.

> The citizens mustered in force to welcome the Prime Minister.

244. To **nip in the bud**. The phrase means generally to destroy in the early stages of growth, to kill in infancy.

> Diphtheria is a disease which nips many a life in the bud.
> He seized the ringleaders and nipped the insurrection in the bud.

245. To **occur to one**; to **strike one**; to **suggest itself to one**, are equivalent.

> It strikes me you should send for a doctor without delay.
> Did the idea never suggest itself to you that this might be your long-lost cousin?
> It did not occur to me that the man was only playing a part.

246. To **owe to oneself**, has two meanings: (1) When a man accomplishes a result through his own unaided exertions, we say he owes it to himself that he had done this. (2) If a man is being reproached or blamed unjustly, he owes it to himself to mention any extenuating circumstances.

> It was altogether owing to himself that James won the prize; he got little help in study from anyone else.
> You complain that all your friends deserted you. I owe it to myself to say that I tried hard to befriend you behind your back.

247. To **pay one back in the same coin**, or **in his own coin**, is to return like for like, to give tit for tat, to retaliate. The phrase is used of injuries, real or supposed.

> He is revengeful and wants to pay others back in their own coin.

248. To **pat on the back**; to **give a pat on the back**. These are colloquial and mean to give a word of encouragement or praise.

> A child is often encouraged by a pat on the back.

249. To **pay respect**, is to do honour. The phrase implies considerable deference. To **pay one's respects** is, to offer polite attentions.

250. To **pick holes in**, is to seek out faults. But the phrase is colloquial.

> An envious or discontented man finds wonderful delight in picking holes in one who is more successful than himself.

To **pick someone's pocket**, is to steal articles from his pocket. One who does this is called a **pickpocket**.

To **pick a lock**, is to open a closed lock by means of any other instrument but the key.

251. To **pick a quarrel with** a person, is to provoke him to quarrel, to find an excuse for drawing him into a quarrel.

> The soldier seems determined to pick a quarrel with the sailor.
> Live in peace with your neighbour instead of trying to pick a quarrel with him.

252. To **plead guilty**, is to confess oneself guilty. To **plead poverty** or **ignorance**, is to assign these things as reasons for one's appearance or one's action

This man was convicted of stealing a quantity of rice. He pleaded guilty, but he also pleaded poverty, saying that hunger drove him to the theft. He could not plead ignorance of the law.

253. To **plough the sands.** As no crop would grow on the sands of the seashore, to plough the sands is a phrase meaning to busy oneself in a way which cannot lead to any profitable result.

254. To **plume** (or **pride**) **oneself on** a thing, is to be proud of that thing as pertaining to oneself.

This student plumes himself on his attainments in logic.

255. To **pocket**, or **swallow, an affront** or **insult**, is to receive it without showing resentment or seeking redress. Such a show of weakness may arise through fear of further insult or attack.

A debtor, unable to pay, has often to pocket insults from his creditor.
When a person finds himself surrounded by foes, he has to pocket many an affront.

256. To **poison the ears**, or **mind of another**, is to prejudice another, to present a particular view of a case to another and thereby to so bias his judgement that he will not give due weight to the other side.

A judge must not allow anyone to poison his mind against either plaintiff or defendant.

257. To **promise well.** This phrase is commonly used, not of persons, but in a neuter, intransitive sense, meaning, to afford hope or ground for expecting a good result.

The rain has been plentiful and the crops promise well.
That you cannot write a decent letter does not promise well for your passing the examination.

258. To **provide against a rainy day,** is to lay up in store against a time of difficulty or calamity, to save money for any emergency that may arise. Also, to **lay up for a rainy day.**

In prosperity one should lay up for a rainy day.
The Post Office Savings Bank gives opportunity to a poor man to provide against a rainy day.

259. To **pull in,** or **draw in, one's horns,** is to withdraw from a position one has taken up. A snail draws in its horns when apprehensive of danger. The phrase is used of a man who has boasted great things and is obliged to withdraw his words and assume a more humble demeanour.

A stubborn man who has slandered another and will not apologize, will draw in his horns if threatened with legal proceedings.

260. To **pull well with,** is to act together in harmony, to unite efforts. A yoke of oxen pull well together, or one ox is said to pull well with the other one. The phrase is also used of a number of people acting in concert.

The directors of this company do not pull well together.

261. To **push**, or **seek**, **one's fortune**, is to make one's way in the world, to advance one's position in life.

Four Scots came to England to seek their fortune.

262. To **quarrel with one's bread and butter.** **Bread and butter** stands here for, one's means of living. If a clerk is quarrelsome, or instead of bearing patiently with deserved reproof, gets angry and provokes the manager to dismiss him, he is said to quarrel with his bread and butter.

If you get a reproof, even though you should feel it to be scarcely deserved, grit your teeth and bear it; your superior is hasty and might dismiss you if you show resentment. Why should you quarrel with your bread and butter ?

263. To **rack one's brains**, is to strain or exercise one's thoughts to the utmost.

264. To **rate soundly**, is to censure strongly.

I rated my steward soundly for his slackness.
The engineer rated his clerk soundly for the stupid blunder he had made in his calculations.

265. To **rest on one's laurels**, is to rest satisfied with honours already won, and to make no attempt to gain further distinction.

Henry has gained a valuable prize, but he is too ambitious to rest on his laurels.

To **rest on one's oars**, is to suspend effort after something has been attained. The phrase is drawn from rowing a boat; after the crew have rowed for a certain distance or for a certain time, they rest on their oars, i.e. they suspend rowing and rest for a time.

The agitators have been vigorously at work during the winter, but at present they seem to be resting on their oars.
Many a student who had worked hard to enter college thinks he may rest on his oars after entrance: he should rather regard the larger opportunity for study opened before him as an incentive to more diligent work.

266. To **rip up**, or **open**, **old sores.** When a sore is almost healed, to rip it open is to take the most effective means for preventing it being healed. Metaphorically, the phrases mean, to revive or reopen a quarrel which was almost forgotten.

267. To **ride a hobby.** A **hobby** here means a favourite subject which one dwells on unduly or to the weariness of others, and **to ride a hobby** is to constantly refer to this favourite subject particularly in conversation. Formerly a ' hobby ' meant a horse or cycle: hence the verb in the expression.

Cultivate the listener's art. Talk just enough to develop your companion's powers. If he has a hobby let him ride it.—*Miss Braddon*

268. The town **rings** with his praises, means, the town is filled with the report of his good deeds.

269. To **harp on the same string**. If a harp were always touched on the same string, the sound by its monotony would produce weariness. When a speaker keeps repeating the same sentiment, or the same topic, though perhaps in different words, he is said to harp on the same string.

270. To **restore to health**; to **be restored to health**. No pronoun should be inserted in these. Do not say, he is restored to his health; nor good food and exercise will soon restore you to your health.

271. To **rise to one's feet**. When a person who has been sitting rises into a standing posture, he is said to rise to his feet.

To **rise to the occasion**, is to put forth unusual and sometimes surprising efforts so as to cope with an emergency.

> A flood threatened to burst the reservoir, but the villagers rose to the occasion and did not desist till they had made all secure.

To **rise like a phoenix from its ashes**. The phoenix was a fabulous Arabian bird. It had no mate, but when about to die made a funeral pile of wood and aromatic gums which it fanned into a flame, and burned itself to ashes. From the ashes a young phoenix was alleged to rise.

> William the Conqueror went through the kingdom stamping out revolt, but as he moved forward, rebellion rose behind him like a phoenix from its ashes.

272. To **rule the roast**, or **roost**, is to lord it over others, to domineer over those with whom one is associated. So the carver rules the roasted meat; or the cock the perch in the hen-house.

> The new-made duke that rules the roast.—*Shakespeare*
> In almost every party there is some self-confident person who tries to rule the roost.

273. To **run in the same groove**, is to move forward on the same path, to advance in harmony.

> It is clear that the ideas of both reformers ran in the same groove.
> Loyalty is an easy and convenient sentiment when self-interest runs in the same groove.

To **run in the blood**, is said of a peculiarity, mental or physical, which clings to certain families.

> Effeminacy of form runs in the blood of this family.
> A propensity for thieving seems to run in the blood of these villagers.

To **run a risk**, is to expose oneself to risk, hazard, or danger.
To **undertake a risk**, is to take on oneself a risk.

> ' You run the risk of losing money if you engage in this business.' ' I know it, but am prepared to undertake the risk.'
> He plunged into the river to save his brother, but in doing so he ran the risk of losing his own life.

To **run short**. A thing is said to **run short** when it is exhausted too soon or before the need for it is over. Persons are said to **run short of** a thing, i.e. to use it up when more of it is needed.

> Our stock of provisions is likely to run short *or* run out.
> There is no fear of our running short of cocoa-nut fibre.

274. To **save one's bacon**, is a colloquial phrase, meaning, to preserve oneself from harm, to escape.

> If you join in this plot, you are sure to get punished; so you had better stand aloof and save your bacon.

To **save another person trouble**, is so to act as to keep him clear of trouble.

To **save appearances**, is to present a fair outside, to do something to avoid exposure.

275. To **say grace**, is to ask God's blessing before beginning a meal.

> The Bishop said grace, and the company began a sumptuous dinner.

276. To **scatter to the winds**, is a vigorous way of saying, to scatter abroad. The phrase implies such effectual scattering that the parts cannot be gathered together again. To **throw to the winds**, is to fling aside as useless.

> The miser's wealth at his death fell into the hands of his nephews and was soon scattered to the winds.

277. The scent. Certain verbal expressions are used with this word and are worth noting. A dog follows the scent of an animal and pursues it till he overtakes it. Metaphorically **the scent** of a thing is an idea, inkling, or suspicion that such a thing is intended. Commonly the word is used when there is a secret plot of evil design.

To **be on the right scent**, is to have a clue to the end sought, to be on the right track.

To **get the right scent**, is to get a clue to some mystery, to get an inkling of something aimed at.

To **put one on the right scent**, is to put one on the track which will lead to the thing intended.

After these the student will readily understand the meaning of, to **get the wrong scent**, to **give one a false scent**, to **throw one off the scent**.

> When conspirators suppose they are suspected, they adopt many devices to throw people off the scent.
> Some remarks casually dropped by a woman put the police on the right scent and they soon discovered the whole gang of brigands.

278. To **see the light**, is to be brought to light, to be revealed or disclosed.

> Some years ago it was supposed that a celebrated doctor had discovered a quack cure for leprosy. If there was any such discovery, it never saw the light.

To **see how the land lies,** is a nautical expression. It literally means, for a sailor to observe how the land is situated with respect to his ship so that he may know how to shape his course; metaphorically, to consider the circumstances in an emergency so as to judge how to proceed.

To **see how the wind blows,** is a nautical phrase applied metaphorically. It means, to observe what influence, favourable or adverse, is likely to affect the existing state of things.

> I sent in a written application to the magistrate yesterday, and today I called on his chief clerk to find out if possible which way the wind is blowing, i.e. to discover if possible whether the magistrate is disposed to favour my application.

To **see the world**; to **see life.** When a man is determined to leave home and roam about, we say that he wishes to see the world, or to see life, i.e. to see and know the different modes of life which people follow.

> My thoughts were bent on seeing the world.—*Defoe*

To **see a thing through coloured spectacles,** is to regard it favourably because of one's prejudices.

279. To **seek God**; to **seek His face.** These mean, to desire and pray for God's guidance and favour.

> Seek ye the Lord while he may be found.—*Bible*

280. To **send one about his business.** When a man is pestering you, and you dismiss him contemptuously and hastily, you are said to send him about his business.

> The fellow came bothering me for an appointment, but I sent him about his business.

To **send word,** is to send a message; to **get word,** is to receive a message.

> He sent me word that he would come in a week.
> I have got word that my brother has been taken seriously ill.

281. To **serve one's turn,** is to serve or suit one's purpose.

> I have enough to serve my own turn.—*Shakespeare*

To **serve one right,** is to treat him as he deserves, usually applied to an act of retaliation or of petty revenge.

> After his rude behaviour toward your father, you served him right not to speak to him.
> His punishment served him right.

282. To **set at defiance,** to **hurl defiance at,** mean, to defy vigorously. The last of these implies more impassioned and angry hostility than the other two.

> No man can afford to set the laws of his country at defiance.
> The raving lunatic thought the sun an envious god and hurled defiance at him.

To **set at liberty**, or **set free**, is to release, to emancipate.

The prisoners were set at liberty when the three-fourths of their term of imprisonment was over.

Remember that though **freedom** is a synonym of liberty, we cannot say **set at freedom**.

283. To **show fight**, is to adopt the attitude of one ready to fight.

The crocodile showed fight the moment he was attacked.

The thief, when the police got near him, turned and showed fight.

284. To **show a bold front**, is to adopt an attitude of determined resistance.

If you only show a bold front, he will yield to your demand.

Our general showed a bold front, and the enemy withdrew without striking a blow.

285. To **show the white feather**, means, to show signs of cowardice. It is said that no good gamecock has a white feather, this being a mark of bad breeding.

286. To **shut one's mouth**, is to put him to silence, to put him to shame, to confound him.

You can easily shut his mouth if you remind him of his former bad conduct.

287. To **slip through one's fingers**, is to escape or be lost through carelessness and before one is aware. A man fails to seize a good opportunity and the chance slips through his fingers. A man comes easily into a large fortune and through bad management lets it slip through his fingers, i.e. he allows it to be frittered away.

To **let a thing slide**, is to allow it to pass unnoticed or unimproved, through negligence or indifference.

288. To **sound a person**, is to find out or ascertain his intentions or secret wishes. To **take soundings** at sea is to let down a lead into the water to find out the depth. This no doubt is the origin of the phrase.

I've sounded my Numidians man by man.—*Addison*

I'll break my staff, bury it certain fathoms in the earth, and, deeper than did ever plummet sound, I'll drown my book.—*Shakespeare*

289. To **sow broadcast**, is to take seed handful by handful and scatter each handful widely by a single jerk of the hand. Figuratively, it means to scatter widely or without stint.

The emissaries of the banished king were sowing sedition broadcast.

290. To **speak extempore**, is to make a speech without premeditation; or more commonly, to make a speech without having notes before you. Remember that **extempore** is a word of four syllables.

A large crowd gathered in a few minutes, and though the missionary spoke extempore, he gave a fine address.

To **speak for itself**—said of a work. When a work bears evidence on the face of it of how it has been performed, it is said to speak for itself.

> You come to test whether the bridge has been strongly built. You see how it sways with the force of the current. The work speaks for itself.
> The Bible carries its own evidence with it; it speaks for itself to the open mind.

To **speak well for,** is to give good testimony regarding, to bear favourable testimony to. But when this phrase is used, it is most commonly a *fact* and not a *person* that is said to speak well for one.

> The neatness of his writing and the accuracy of his English spoke well for him.
> It spoke well for him that in the midst of great temptation he had never been known to succumb.

To **speak one's mind,** is to tell candidly. The phrase implies that you feel that something is going wrong and that you must say what you think about it.

To **speak a ship.** When two ships approach at sea, the captain of one sometimes conveys a message to the other by radio or other means. This is ' speaking a ship '.

> We spoke the mail steamer about sixty miles from Aden.

To **speak of one in high terms,** is to praise him whether the praise is deserved or not.

To **speak volumes,** is to bear abundant evidence for or against. Here also the agent of the verb would be a fact, not a person.

> The coincidence of these two artful dodges occurring on the same day speaks volumes for the character of the rogues who are to be found in New York.
> It speaks volumes for England's love of liberty that she freely gave millions of money to buy out all the slaves in her possessions and set them free.

291. To **split hairs,** is to make subtle and useless distinctions. To **split the difference,** is to divide the difference equally. For instance, a seller asks fifty pounds for his car; a buyer offers forty; they finally agree to split the difference, and so the car is sold for forty-five.

292. To **stare one in the face,** is to stare into his face; also, to be before the eyes, to be undeniably evident. To **stare one out of countenance,** is to keep staring at him till he turns his face away. To **look one full in the face,** is to take a full, steady look into his face; also, to face or confront steadily. When this last phrase is used, it is often implied that you suspect some deception in the person, and you look him full in the face suspecting that he will betray the deception by wincing under your gaze.

Degradation and ruin stare the drunkard in the face.
I looked him full in the face, but no trace of deceit was there.
The law stares them in the face while they are breaking it.—*Locke*
The difficulties of your position are not small, and you must look them fairly in the face and devise means of grappling with them.

293. To **start a question**; to **raise a question.** These mean, to propose or suggest a topic for consideration. **Start** implies more abruptness; **raise** implies previous arrangement.

We were considering the best way of doing away with the existing land laws, when he suddenly started the question of popular education.
It will be useless to raise the question of protective duties at this meeting, for there are more subjects than we shall be able to discuss.

294. To **steal a march**, is to march in a secret way, to gain an advantage over another stealthily. For instance, two appointments are vacant; two persons resolve to go together at noon tomorrow to the gentleman who has them in his gift; but one of them without telling the other goes early in the morning and secures the better appointment of the two: he is said to steal a march on the other person.

295. To **steer clear of**, is to avoid. The helmsman of a ship tries to steer clear of rocks and shoals and every obstacle. The phrase is not confined to navigation, but has come to be used generally in the sense of, to avoid.

A man should, if possible, steer clear of money lenders.

296. To **stick at nothing.** When a man will do anything, however bad, in order to accomplish his purpose, he is said to be one who will stick at nothing. The phrase implies readiness to stoop to baseness or deception to reach one's end.

Beware of that ambitious man; he is one who will stick at nothing if he can only serve himself.

297. To **stop short**, is to stop suddenly when you are expected to go on, to stop without reaching the goal.

The sailor stopped short in the middle of his story.
Why did you stop short when so near the end of your journey ?

To **stop teeth**, is to fill holes in decayed teeth as dentists do.

298. To **strain every nerve**, an overworked idiom to be generally avoided, is to use one's utmost efforts.

He strained every nerve to get the post, but was unsuccessful.

To **strain** or **stretch a point**, is to make a special and often inconvenient effort; to go beyond what is usual, to transcend a general rule.

299. To **strike**; to **strike work**; to **go on strike.** These are equivalent and mean, to cease work in order to compel improvement in their conditions of work. Men who have struck work, are often said to be **out on strike.**

The mill owner would neither shorten the hours of labour nor give an increase of wages, and so the factory hands struck work.

Rather than go on strike, workmen should submit to arbitration, if their employers are willing to settle disputes peaceably.

To **strike while**, or **when, the iron is hot**, is a phrase which figuratively means, to take advantage of an opportunity when it arises.

To **strike oil**, is to have lucky success in some enterprise. It was first used of finding oil wells in America.

300. To **swallow the bait**. The bait of the angler hides the barbs of his hook; the fish in swallowing the bait swallows the hook and is caught. So men sometimes catch others by guile, by offering them large promises.

Candidates for parliamentary honours often make large promises of what they will do for the people if chosen. These promises are bait thrown out to catch votes. Many people swallow the bait and elect the candidate who makes the largest promises.

301. To **take** a thing **to heart**, or to **lay** a thing **to heart**, is to be sensibly affected by it, to feel it deeply; also, to ponder over a thing seriously so as to be moved by it.

I wish this boy would lay to heart the wise counsels his master has given him.

She has taken her father's death so much to heart that she will not be persuaded to eat anything.

To **take to pieces, pull to pieces, rend to pieces, tear to pieces, tear to tatters, tear to shreds,** are phrases to be committed to memory. To **take to pieces,** implies careful separation of parts; to **pull to pieces,** implies rough handling in the separation. Both these expressions are used metaphorically of the way in which a man deals with the arguments of an opponent. To **tear,** implies violent action.

She gave the child a newspaper, but he soon tore it to shreds.

By skilfully dovetailing parts of the evidence, he built up a fine theory which his adversary soon pulled to pieces.

302. To **talk against time**, is either (1) to talk so quickly as to finish within a given time what one has to say; or (2) to keep on talking till a certain time expires.

To **talk shop**, is to use the phrases peculiar to one's employment. A student incessantly talking about his books and his examinations, or a lawyer about his cases and his clients, would be regarded as talking shop.

303. To **tell to one's face**. This means, to say or tell in direct open opposition; to tell in one's presence and directly to him. The phrase is used only of unpleasant statements.

The judge told the witness to his face that after what he had stated he could not believe him.

It requires more moral courage to tell a man of a fault to his face than to speak of it behind his back.

304. To **tempt Providence**, is to take unnecessary or reckless risks.

It was surely a tempting of Providence when Captain Webb tried to swim the river below the Falls of Niagara; he lost his life in his daring attempt.

305. To **tie one's hands**, is to restrain him from action.

His own conduct is so bad that he cannot reprove another; he has tied his own hands.

I would help you if I could, but I have spent all my spare money, so my hands are tied.

306. To **tread** or **trample under foot**, is a strong way of saying, to tread upon, to stamp upon. Note the preposition, and note also that the phrase takes no article before the noun. Even when the nominative is plural, it is still **under foot** and not **under feet**.

Trampling treaties under foot, the Marshal invaded Spain with a large army.

Why should the leaders of society trample their convictions under foot and refuse to condemn this wretched custom?

307. To **think good**, is to approve of or consider proper or expedient. To **think right, proper, fit**; here **think** means deem, consider, judge. To **think well of**, or **think highly of**, is to hold in high esteem, to appreciate highly; to **think more of**, implies comparison. To **think little of**, and **think less of**, are the opposites of the preceding pair of phrases. To **think better of**, is to regard with more favour; also, to think more carefully about a thing and come to a wiser judgement.

I must say I think well of your suggestion.

Do you really think it proper to write me such a letter as this?

The North American Indians think more of a few glass ornaments than of a fine sealskin.

The autocrat was thought much of by those who knew how unselfishly he ruled.

He thought fit to address me in insulting language, i.e. he actually did so address me. *Think fit*, in such expressions implies blame for the action as unworthy and unbecoming.

308. To **travel incognito**, is to travel under an assumed name. This is sometimes done by celebrities, so that thus they may escape intrusive attention.

One of the kings of Scotland used often to travel about incognito through his kingdom that he might find out the real feelings and modes of life of his subjects.

309. To **tread in the footsteps of**; to **follow in the footsteps of.**
These mean, to follow the example of.

> It is utter folly to tread in the footsteps of those who have gone before
> us simply because they have gone before us; if a better way opens up
> to us, let us in God's name take it.

310. To **tread on the heels of,** is to follow close behind.

> So swift trod sorrow on the heels of joy.

To **tread on the toes**, or **corns, of another**, is to refer pointedly
in a disagreeable way to something in the conduct of another.

> I reminded him of one of his escapades as a schoolboy, and evidently
> trod on his corns.

311. To **treat with contempt**; to **hold in contempt.** These mean
to despise. Note the verbs and the preposition used with each.
The latter phrase refers to the feeling in the mind; the former,
to that feeling shown in conduct. To **hold in honour**, is the opposite
of, to hold in contempt. There is also the phrase, **to treat with
silent contempt.**

> I treated both him and his offer with utter contempt.
> His conduct to me has been so perfidious that I hold him in contempt.

312. To **tremble in the balance.** When a matter is in a state of
so great uncertainty, that a trifle would turn the scale either way,
that matter is said to tremble in the balance. We have also, **hang
in the balance**, with the same meaning.

> For some years his reason was trembling in the balance before it finally
> gave way.
> A single false step, a single hasty act, may involve the whole world in
> war. When such momentous issues hang in the balance, let us be sure of
> our facts and sober in our judgement before taking any action that will
> render war inevitable.

313. To **trouble one's head**, or **one's self, about** a thing, is to
consider it, to think it over, to give attention to it. But the phrase
is commonly used in a negative form. When it is said of a man
that he will not trouble his head about some matter, the meaning
is that he might fairly be expected to give attention to it, but he is
too indifferent to do so, or regards it as too troublesome. To
bother oneself, or **one's head, about a thing**, has much the same
meaning. Both the phrases are conversational.

> Here are two army officers: one is anxious to discourage and stamp out
> all petty quarrelling among the men under him, but the other does
> not trouble his head about such matters.

314. To **fish in troubled waters**, is to make personal profit out
of a disturbance.

315. To **pour oil on troubled waters.** It has been found by
actual experiment that oil poured on angry waves produces a more

or less smooth surface. The phrase is commonly used metaphorically, and signifies, to say or do anything which soothes and calms angry passion.

> On going to his house I found everything in a state of angry commotion. I sat down and reasoned with him and his sons and showed them that they were far too ready to put a wrong construction on one another's acts and words. They seemed to calm down as I spoke, and I am thankful I was able to pour oil on the troubled waters.

316. To **walk with God,** is to have habitual communion of soul with Him.

> Do justly, and love mercy, and walk humbly with thy God.—*Bible*

317. To **wash one's hands of a business**. This phrase, now in common use, is derived from a striking scene in Bible history. At the trial of Jesus Christ, Pilate, the Roman Governor, called for a vessel of water, washed his hands before the people and said, ' I am innocent of the blood of this just person: see ye to it.'

So when a man gets involved in a matter, and when he sees that it will not end as he had hoped, he, fearing disaster or blame or dishonour, withdraws from all connexion with it, and says, ' I wash my hands of this whole business.'

318. To **whistle for the wind**. Formerly when sailors got into a calm region, they whistled, making believe that the wind would come if thus called for. Of course, the effort was utterly useless and even ridiculous. The phrase is also applied by comparison to foolish projects.

> You surely did not expect to reach any good end in this way. You might as well whistle for the wind.

319. To **win** or **gain laurels**, is to achieve success in a contest, to win the victory. In the ancient Grecian games, the winner was crowned with a laurel wreath. To **bear away the palm**, has a similar meaning.

> This young man has gained laurels as a poet.
> He has had his first competitive examination and has won his laurels.

320. To **do a thing with a good grace**, is to do an unpleasant thing with a pleasant manner. For instance, a man, knowing that he must do some menial task, does it without at all showing that it is unpleasant to him. In such a case he is said to do it **with a good grace**. The opposite of this is, to do it **with a bad grace**. To **be in one's good graces**, is to have his favour.

321. To **work on another person's fears**, is to appeal to his fears and thereby get him to do something which serves a purpose of my own. For instance, a prince is haunted by the fear that he will be poisoned; a man knowing this pretends to reveal to the prince a plot to poison him and obtains a reward, while in reality there may have been no plot. The pretended informer is said to work on the fears of the prince.

To **work well**. A thing is said to work well when it answers or suits its purpose.

> The Atlantic cable has worked well for many years.
> The new rules issued by the Educational Department are working well.

322. To **worship the rising sun**, is used figuratively for, to honour the man who is coming into office, to pay respect to the man who is rising in power and influence.

> The newly-appointed manager has taken over and his clerks worship the rising sun.

323. Proverbial Sayings

As a rule we have not given Proverbial Sayings, terse and expressive though many of these are. Clearly, such sayings are not likely to be commonly used in the conversation or writing of well educated Englishmen. We append, however, a very few which are sometimes met with.

What can't be cured must be endured. The word **cured** here means ' remedied '. Try to find a remedy for every mishap you can, but if you meet with some things for which you can find no remedy, then bear them meekly and patiently. This expresses the spirit of the maxim.

Prevention is better than cure. It is better to prevent a misfortune if you can, than to find a remedy for it after it has taken place.

A rolling stone gathers no moss. The literal meaning of this is obvious. Metaphorically, the maxim is applied to a man who does not settle long enough in one place to gain anything in it. Such a man is often spoken of as **a rolling stone**, and the reference is to this proverb.

Rome was not built in a day. This saying is applied to a work which requires long time for its accomplishment. It is sometimes quoted to remind impatient persons that great things require time and trouble, and must not be done hastily.

Better late than never. If a thing ought to be done, better do it even after long delay than not do it at all.

Easy come, easy go. This saying is applied when what is acquired without effort is spent without thought. For instance, a man inherits great wealth and spends it foolishly. Men say of this, ' It is a case of easy come, easy go.'

As you make your bed, so you must lie. This proverbial saying means, that you must accept and bear the consequences of your own doings. It is applied only when those consequences are unpleasant.

This young man would not follow his father's occupation of wood-carving, but would insist on preparing himself for a clerkship. He now regrets his decision, but as he had made his bed, so he must lie on it.

Other such sayings are: **Too many cooks spoil the broth. A stitch in time saves nine.**

324. OTHER IDIOMATIC SAYINGS

There are friends and friends, is an expression used to denote that all professed friends are not equally deserving of the name, that there are different kinds of friends. Similarly, a man who has found that all shopkeepers are not alike, but that some do their business honestly while others do not, or that some execute orders neatly and promptly while others do not, may indicate his sense of the difference by saying, **There are shopkeepers and shopkeepers.** So we have,

There are dinners and dinners.—*Bacon*

There is no love lost between them, is a euphemism for, there is hatred between them. It is said of two parties.

These two neighbours do not quarrel openly, but certainly there is no love lost between them.

All his geese are swans. The swan is like the goose but larger and finer-looking. The phrase is applied to a man who always represents his own possessions as better than similar things belonging to another. For instance, when a farmer boasts of his land, his cattle, his children, and so on, as the best in the neighbourhood, even though they are just like other people's, we say of him, ' All his geese are swans.' The phrase is, of course, ironical.

There are wheels within wheels. When it is found that a difficult business is more complicated than we had supposed, we say, ' There are wheels within wheels '—just as in very complicated machinery, wheels sometimes work within other wheels. The saying is used metaphorically when there are hidden complications in a scheme.

An Englishman's house is his castle. This is a common saying, meaning that every Englishman is, or would like to be, as secure in the privacy of his own house as if he were a lord in his castle: e.g. officials will have no right to enter his home but he will remain undisputed master there.

' **It's too bad !** ' is an exclamation of indignation or disapproval. The phrase is colloquial.

325. A further set of miscellaneous phrases.

Let sleeping dogs lie. This, meaning, ' avoid stirring up trouble ', phrase is used, e.g. when men who have quarrelled have allowed their quarrel to go to sleep—a quarrel which an irritating word would readily revive.

We have in earlier chapters given several phrases of **Time**. A few may be added here, for example.

> The time of Cromwell, is the age or period in which Cromwell lived.
> I have not time today to attend to this matter, means, I have not leisure to attend to it,
> The word time is often used for the present life as contrasted with eternity.
> Men of the time. Unless there is a reference in the context to past time, this phrase means, men of the present day. So we have the phrase, men of the day, with the same meaning.
> Who are accounted the best novelists of the day ?

' He is always busy **in his waking hours**,' i.e. in the hours when he is not asleep.

People are said to be **at close grips with poverty**, when they are so poor that they have a great struggle to maintain themselves; they find it very hard to get work to do, or, if they can get any work it is such as they cannot perform.

Some people have savings **which they can fall back upon** in case of need, i.e. they can turn to their savings or other resources and use them when necessity arises.

' He filled his house with **second-hand furniture**,' i.e. the furniture was not new but had been previously in use in some other person's house, or perhaps in several houses successively.

' He filled his house with **second-rate furniture**,' i.e. the furniture was not of good quality.

A man is said to **give the lie** to another when he accuses him of falsehood.

' **What is the matter?** ' is a question often asked and having different meanings in different circumstances. It may mean, what has happened to put you in a flurry? Or, it may mean, what is it that is perplexing you or vexing you? Or, it may mean, what difficulty has arisen in your circumstances? what is it that prevents you doing something you had intended doing? Or, again, it may mean, what ails you? what is the ailment from which you are suffering?—said to one who is ill.

' **That's nothing to me**,' is an expression signifying that the matter does not concern me; I take no interest in it.

> Hundreds might be carried off by the plague in Calcutta; thousands might perish through an earthquake in Java; tens of thousands might be slaughtered on the battlefields of Macedonia; but these catastrophes were nothing to the jolly vagabond who jogged on from village to village, living on the fat of the land, as though life were meant to be only a happy holiday.

' **His blood is up**,' means he is angry, he is in a passion. The contrary phrase is, to be in cool blood, or cold blood.

> Men will say things when their blood is up which they regret after they have cooled down.

Be good enough to; have the goodness to; be so good as to; please.
The first are polite, rather formal, forms of request commonly
put into friendly letters, or used in polite speech. The common
and less formal word is simply, ' please '.

> Be so good as to come and join us at tea tomorrow at four o'clock.
> Have the goodness to call at the watchmaker's for my watch.
> Be good enough to let me know when you will return from your holiday.

At a meeting, **a vote is often taken by a show of hands.** That is,
the chairman puts a proposal or motion to the members and asks
those in favour of it to hold up their right hand, and when those
votes are counted, he calls on those who are against the motion
to hold up their right hand. The question is decided according
to the majority of votes for or against.

I had rather, or **I would rather.** It seems doubtful which of these
is the correct form. Commonly the phrase is shortened into
I'd rather. The meaning is, **I would prefer to.** The phrase is one
of comparison and is followed by an infinitive without **to** being
expressed.

> I'd rather be a dog and bay the moon than such a Roman.—*Shakespeare*
> I had rather lose all I have than become rich by ruining another man.—
> *W. M. Taylor*

It cannot (can't) be helped. To **help** commonly means to give
assistance, to aid, to succour; also, to remedy. When there is
no remedy for a thing, we say there is no help for it, or it cannot be
helped, or there is no helping it.

> ' Run for a doctor as fast as you can.' ' But the rain is coming down in
> torrents ! ' ' It can't be helped, you must go at once.'

It remains to be seen, i.e. what the issue will be no one can certainly
tell, but it will yet appear.

> What the issue of his action at law will be, remains to be seen.
> If the city falls a prey to the enemy, it remains to be seen what flag will
> fly over the citadel.

You had better, means, it is better that you should. Other
personal pronouns may take the place of **you** in the phrase. The
word **better** in the phrase scarcely conveys the idea of comparison;
it is rather similar in meaning to **well.** But if any comparison is
implied, it would be equivalent to ' better than anything else '.

> You had better take the short road.
> The boys had better stop shouting.

To choose **which you please.** It is the phrase **you please** which
has a particular idiomatic meaning here. The whole phrase means,
to choose that thing which pleases you. You want to buy a ring;
a jeweller comes and places a number of beautiful rings before you,

and says, ' Now, sir, choose which you please.' A subject is proposed for debate in a debating society, and one member says, ' I shall take either side of the question; let my opponent choose which side he pleases.'

Wear and tear, is the deterioration caused to an article by constant use.

A wolf in sheep's clothing, is a dangerous person who pretends to be harmless.

APPENDIX—THE ENGLISH BIBLE

1. THE BIBLE ITSELF

THE Bible, the sacred book of all Christians, has in many respects a unique character and position among the books of the world. As an old authority writes: ' Apart altogether from its sacred character, the Bible is the grandest book that the world has ever produced for feeding the intelligence, the conscience, the taste, the imagination of the young. It is all that Homer ever was to the Greek or the Roman, and much more. There is history in it, there is poetry, there is romance, there is philosophy; it is a fountain of wisdom, great, simple, and universal; it is a storehouse of instruction and illustration for every form of human emotion, for every phase of human character, for every incident of private life, for every kind of social and political institution. There was never a richer or nobler granary out of which to feed the heart and mind of a nation. It is a model of style, or rather of many styles; it speaks in a language at once pure, rich, and strong, at once popular and classical, and presents for the formation of our vocabulary an inexhaustible well of English undefiled. May the day never come when the simple facts of the Bible shall cease to be studied in our schools as the foundation of all human knowledge, or its ideas and its literary form to shape the conscience, to develop the taste, and to fire the imagination of our youths.'

The influence of the Authorized Version of 1611 on the English language has also been profound. A modern historian of literature writes: ' It gave, to all classes alike, an idiom in which the deeper emotions of life could be recalled. It gave grace to the speech of the unlettered, and it entered into the style of the most ambitious writers. Its phrasing coloured the work of poets, and its language has so embedded itself in our national tradition that if the Bible is forgotten, a precious possession will be lost.'[1]

2. BIBLE NAMES COMMONLY REFERRED TO IN ENGLISH LITERATURE

ABIGAIL. A wife of King David. The name occurs in English literature with the meaning of ' waiting-woman '.

ABRAHAM. The father and founder of the Jewish nation; Milton, e.g. calls the Jews ' Abraham's race '.

ABSALOM. Son of King David (2 *Samuel* xviii.).

ADAM. The first of the human race. See *Genesis* ii.-iv. The ' Old Adam ' means the unregenerate spirit in man. ' Adam's ale ' is water.

---

[1] B. Ifor Evans: *A Short History of English Literature*, 1940.

ADULLAM. The cave of A. (1 *Samuel* xxii.). The ' Adullamites ' was the name given to a political group who seceded from their party in 1866. Now applied to any seceding political body.

AGAG. ' And Agag came unto him delicately ' (1 *Samuel* xv. 32). Hence ' to walk delicately, like Agag ', means, to behave circumspectly.

ANANIAS. There are two of this name mentioned in *The Acts of the Apostles*: (1) the high priest (*Acts* xxiii.), and (2) the lying husband of Sapphira (*Acts* v.). Reference to the latter is generally understood.

BAAL. Or Bel, one of the chief gods of the Canaanites—hence, a false god.

BABEL. The story of the building of the city and tower of Babel, and of the confusion of tongues, is given in *Genesis* xi. 1-9.

BALAAM. To whom God spoke through the mouth of the ass on which he was riding (*Numbers* xxii.-xxiv.).

BARABBAS. The robber, released instead of Jesus (*Matthew* xxvii.).

BEELZEBUB. ' Prince of the Devils ' (*Matthew* xii. 24).

BEHEMOTH. Possibly the hippopotamus (*Job* xl. 10).

BELIAL. The spirit of evil. A man or son of B. is a reprobate. See *Deuteronomy* xiii. 13.

BENJAMIN. Brother of Joseph, type of the youngest and favourite son (*Genesis* xxxv., xliii., etc.).

BEULAH. Land of B., the happy land, or heaven (*Isaiah* lxii. 4).

CHERITH. The brook beside which Elijah was fed by ravens (1 *Kings* xvii.).

CLOUD. A c. no bigger than a man's hand—a small omen of great things to follow. See the story of Elijah in 1 *Kings* xviii.

DAN. From D. to Beersheba, i.e. from one end of the land (originally Canaan) to the other.

DANIEL. The story of D. in the lions' den, protected by God, is found in *Daniel* vi.

DAVID. King of Israel, who as a lad slew the giant Goliath (1 *Samuel* xvii.). The friendship of David and Jonathan is proverbial (ibid. xviii.).

DELILAH. The Philistine woman who betrayed Samson by cutting off his hair (*Judges* xvi.).

DIVES. Latin for the ' rich man ' in the parable of Lazarus (*Luke* xvi.).

DORCAS. A ' Dorcas Society ' is a group of Church ladies who meet and make clothes for the poor. D. is mentioned in *Acts* ix.

EDEN. The Garden of E., where dwelt Adam and Eve, supposed to have been in Mesopotamia (*Genesis* ii.).

ELIJAH. The prophet, who was fed by ravens, and was finally translated to heaven (1 *Kings* xvii., etc.).

ELISHA. He succeeded Elijah as prophet, and whose ' mantle ' he inherited. He cured Naaman the Syrian of leprosy (2 *Kings* ii., etc.).

ENDOR. The witch of E., consulted by Saul (1 *Samuel* xxviii.).

ESAU. See JACOB.

EVE. The name given by Adam to his wife (*Genesis* iii. 20).

EXODUS. The ' way out ' of the Israelites from Egypt, and the name of the second book of the Bible.

GADARENE SWINE. The miracle is told in *Mark* v.

GALLIO. He ' cared for none of these things '—see *Acts* xviii.

GAMALIEL. The apostle Paul sat at the feet of G. (*Acts* v. 34, xxii. 3).

GENESIS. Meaning ' beginning ' or ' origin ', the name of the first book of the Bible.

GOLIATH. See DAVID.

HEROD. H., the Great, king of Judaea, 40-4 B.C., ordered the ' slaughter of the innocents '—see *Matthew* ii.

HEWERS OF WOOD AND DRAWERS OF WATER. The story of Joshua's dealings with the wily Gibeonites; who were spared death to become slaves to the Israelites, is told in *Joshua* ix.

HOLOFERNES. H. was Nebuchadnezzar's general, killed by Judith. See the Apocryphal book of *Judith* iv.

ICHABOD. The word means ' the glory has departed ' (1 *Samuel* iv. 21).

ISHMAEL. I. was a son of Abraham, but the word has come to mean ' an outcast ' (*Genesis* xvi.).

JACOB AND ESAU. These were twin sons of Isaac and Rebecca. Esau, a hunter, sold his birthright to his brother for a mess of pottage. The story is told in *Genesis* xxvii.

JACOB'S LADDER. Set up on earth but reaching to heaven, seen by Jacob in a dream (*Genesis* xxviii.).

JEHU. A furious driver (2 *Kings* ix. 20).

JEREMIAD. A complaining, alluding to the book called *The Lamentations of Jeremiah*.

JEZEBEL. Type of a wicked woman—see 1 *Kings* xvi., xix.; 2 *Kings* ix.

JOB. The book of *Job* describes his downfall, which brings to him ' Job's comforters '. These tell him in effect that his ruin has been caused by his own sin. Job himself is a type of patience.

JONAH. The man of misfortune. See the story in the book so named.

JONATHAN. See DAVID.

JOSEPH. The story of Joseph is given in *Genesis* xxxvii.-xxxix.: it is that of the unknown shepherd of Palestine, carried to Egypt as a slave, but who ultimately became chief minister to Pharaoh. After his death, however, arose another king of Egypt ' who knew not Joseph '.

LAODICEANS. The people of the church of L. were ' lukewarm ', neither ' cold nor hot ' (*Revelations* iii. 14-22). Hence a ' Laodicean policy ' is a feeble and unenthusiastic one.

LUCIFER. The morning star. ' The application of the name to Satan (the rebel archangel) arises from a mistaken interpretation of *Isaiah* xiv. 12—" How art thou fallen from heaven, O Lucifer, son of the morning ".'

MAMMON. Stands for ' riches ' or ' covetousness ' (*Matthew* vi. 24; *Luke* xvi. 9-13).

MEDES AND PERSIANS. The laws of the Medes and Persians have become proverbially unchangeable (*Daniel* vi.).

NIMROD. ' The mighty hunter before the Lord ' (*Genesis* x. 9).

PASSOVER. This is the Jewish feast which celebrates the ' passing over ' of the houses of the Israelites when the Egyptians lost all their first-born (*Exodus* xii.).

PHARISEES. An old Jewish sect, now applied to sanctimonious and hypo-critical people.

PILATE. P. was Roman Governor in Judaea when Jesus Christ was crucified (*Matthew* xxvii.; *Mark* xv.; *Luke* xxiii.; *John* xviii.-xix.). 'What is truth?' said jesting Pilate, and would not stay for an answer.'—Bacon's *Essays*.

RECHABITE. An abstainer from intoxicants; for R. see *Jeremiah* xxxv.

RIMMON. 'I bow myself in the house of Rimmon' (2 *Kings* v. 18), i.e. 'I am prepared occasionally to accommodate my principles to my material convenience.'

SAMARITAN. The parable of the Good Samaritan is given in *Luke* x. 30-7. 'The Jews have no dealings with the Samaritans.'

SAUL. 'Is Saul also among the prophets?' (1 *Samuel* x. 11). Frequently quoted to express astonishment at finding a man most unexpectedly occupying some distinguished position.

SENNACHERIB. The story on which Byron's poem 'The Destruction of Sennacherib' is based is found in 2 *Chronicles* xxxii.

SOLOMON. King of Israel after David, and renowned for wealth and wisdom (1 *Kings*).

TALENT. The parable of the talents is told in *Matthew* xxv. 14-30. Here the word means 'money'; only the familiarity of the story has given rise to its ordinary meaning of 'ability of mind'.

TUBAL CAIN. 'Instructor of every artifice in brass and iron' (*Genesis* iv. 22).

VALLEY OF THE SHADOW OF DEATH. This is described in Bunyan's *Pilgrim's Progress*. It is mentioned in *Psalm* xxiii. 4.

VIRGINS. The parable of the virgins, the wise, who came to meet the bridegroom with their lamps prepared, and the foolish, whose lamps had no oil, is found in *Matthew* xxv. 1-13.

WEIGHED IN THE BALANCE AND FOUND WANTING. See the account of Daniel's interpretation of the king's dream (*Daniel* v.).

WISDOM OF SOLOMON. This is one of the books of the Apocrypha.

3. BIBLE PHRASES COMMONLY USED IN THE ENGLISH LANGUAGE

ALL THINGS. All things to all men. 1 *Corinthians* ix. 22.

ALONE. It is not good that the man should be alone. *Genesis* ii. 18.

BALM IN GILEAD. Is there no balm in Gilead? *Jeremiah* viii. 22.

BONES. Can these bones live? *Ezekiel* xxxvii. 3.

BREAD. Cast thy bread upon the water: for thou shalt find it after many days. *Ecclesiastes* xi. 1.

BURDEN AND HEAT. The burden and heat of the day. *Matthew* xx. 12.

CHAPTER AND VERSE. Chapter and verse, now means 'exact authority for statement', but derives from the habit of quoting 'chapter and verse' of a Bible text.

CHEERFUL GIVER. God loveth a cheerful giver. 2 *Corinthians* ix. 7.

CLOTHED. Clothed, and in his right mind. *Mark* v. 15.

COALS OF FIRE. Heap coals of fire upon his head. *Proverbs* xxv. 22.

CORN. There was corn in Egypt. *Genesis* xlii. 1.

CRUMBS. The crumbs which fell from the rich man's table. *Luke* xvi. 21.

DARKNESS. Darkness which may be felt. *Exodus* x. 21.

DECENTLY AND IN ORDER. Let all things be done decently and in order. 1 *Corinthians* xiv. 40.

DISCHARGE. There is no discharge in that war. *Ecclesiastes* viii. 8.

DREAMER. A dreamer of dreams. *Deuteronomy* xiii. 1.

ENEMY. An enemy hath done this. *Matthew* xiii. 28.

ETHIOPIAN. Can the Ethiopian change his skin, or the leopard his spots ? *Jeremiah* xiii. 23.

EWE LAMB. The poor man had nothing, save one little ewe lamb. 2 *Samuel* xii. 3.

FAINT, YET PURSUING. Faint, yet pursuing. *Judges* viii. 4.

FALL. And great was the fall of it. *Matthew* vii. 27.

FALLEN FROM GRACE. Fallen from grace. *Galatians* v. 4.

FATTED CALF. Bring hither the fatted calf, and kill it (*Luke* xv. 23)—to celebrate the return of the PRODIGAL SON. See below.

FLESH IS WEAK. The spirit indeed is willing, but the flesh is weak. *Matthew* xxvi. 41.

FOOL. Answer a fool according to his folly. *Proverbs* xxvi. 5.

FRIEND, GO UP HIGHER. Friend, go up higher. *Luke* xiii. 10.

GASP. At the last gasp. 2 *Maccabees* vii. 9.

GIANTS. There were giants in the earth in those days. *Genesis* vi. 4.

GOD AND MAMMON. Ye cannot serve God and mammon. *Matthew* vi. 24. See MAMMON in Appendix 2 above.

GOOD WORKS. Full of good works. *Acts* ix. 36.

GREY HAIRS. Bring down my grey hairs with sorrow to the **grave**. *Genesis* xlii. 38.

GRIND. Grind the faces of the poor. *Isaiah* iii. 15.

HEART. A man after his own heart. 1 *Samuel* xiii. 14.

HIP AND THIGH. He smote them hip and thigh. *Judges* xv. 8.

HOSPITALITY. Given to hospitality. *Romans* xii. 13.

HOUSE IN ORDER. Set thine house in order. *Isaiah* xxxviii. 1.

KEEPER. Am I my brother's keeper ? *Genesis* iv. 9.

LABOUR OF LOVE. Labour of love. 1 *Thessalonians* i. 3.

LEOPARD. See ETHIOPIAN above.

LOCUST. That which the palmerworm hath left hath the locust eaten. *Joel* i. 4.

LOINS. Gird up now thy loins like a man. *Job* xxxviii. 3.

LORD, HOW LONG ? Then said I, Lord, how long ? *Isaiah* vi. 11.

LORDLY DISH. She brought forth butter in a lordly dish. *Judges* v. 25.

MILK AND HONEY. A land flowing with milk and honey. *Exodus* iii. 8.

MULTITUDE OF SINS. Charity shall cover the multitude of sins. 1 *Peter* iv. 8.

PEACE. Saying, Peace, peace; when there is no peace. *Jeremiah* vi. 14.

PEARL OF GREAT PRICE. A pearl of great price. *Matthew* xiii. 46.

PEARLS BEFORE SWINE. Neither cast ye your pearls before swine. *Matthew* vii. 6.

PLAYED THE FOOL. I have played the fool. 1 *Samuel* xxvi. 21.

PRODIGAL SON. Type of the repentant sinner or returned wanderer. See *Luke* xv. 11-32, and FATTED CALF above.

QUIETNESS AND CONFIDENCE. In quietness and confidence shall be your strength. *Isaiah* xxx. 15.

REAP THE WHIRLWIND. They have sown the wind, and they shall reap the whirlwind. *Hosea* viii. 7.

ROOT OF THE MATTER. Seeing the root of the matter is found in me. *Job* xix. 28.

SALT OF THE EARTH. Ye are the salt of the earth. *Matthew* v. 13.

SALVATION. Work out your own salvation. *Philippians* ii. 12.

SCAPEGOAT. Let him go for a scapegoat into the wilderness. *Leviticus* xvi. 10.

SERVANT A DOG. Is thy servant a dog ? 2 *Kings* viii. 13.

SIGNS OF THE TIMES. The signs of the times. *Matthew* xvi. 3.

SIN. Be sure your sin will find you out. *Numbers* xxxii. 23.

SKIN OF ONE'S TEETH. See above, p. 82.

SMALL THINGS. For who hath despised the day of small things? *Zechariah* iv. 10.

SOLOMON. Solomon in all his glory. *Matthew* vi. 28.

SOWN THE WIND. See REAP THE WHIRLWIND above.

SPOILED THE EGYPTIANS. They spoiled the Egyptians. *Exodus* xii. 36.

STARS IN THEIR COURSES. The stars in their courses fought against Sisera. *Judges* v. 20.

STOLEN. Stolen waters are sweet. *Proverbs* ix. 17.

THIEVES. Fell among thieves. *Mark* x. 30.

THRONE OF GRACE. See above, p. 83.

TROUBLE. Man is born unto trouble, as the sparks fly upward. *Job* v. 7.

WARS. Wars and rumours of wars. *Matthew* xxiv. 6.

WASTED HIS SUBSTANCE. Wasted his substance with riotous living. *Luke* xv. 13.

WIFE OF THY BOSOM. The wife of thy bosom. *Deuteronomy* xiii. 6.

WINE. Wine is a mocker. *Proverbs* xx. 1.

WORDS. He multiplieth words without knowledge. *Job* xxxv. 16.

YEARS. I will restore to you the years that the locust hath eaten. *Joel* ii. 25.

INDEX

(The references are to page numbers. Numbers in bold type indicate more detailed treatment. Entries in capitals represent headings of subjects.)